FRAMEWORK FOR EFFECTIVE TEACHING®

Teacher's Guide, Grade 1 Book 1

FRAMEWORK FOR EFFECTIVE TEACHING®

Teacher's Guide, Grade 1 Book 1

PROGRAM AUTHORS
Marilyn Jager Adams
Carl Bereiter
Jan Hirshberg
Valerie Anderson
S. A. Bernier

CONSULTING AUTHORS
Michael Pressley
Marsha Roit
Iva Carruthers
Bill Pinkney

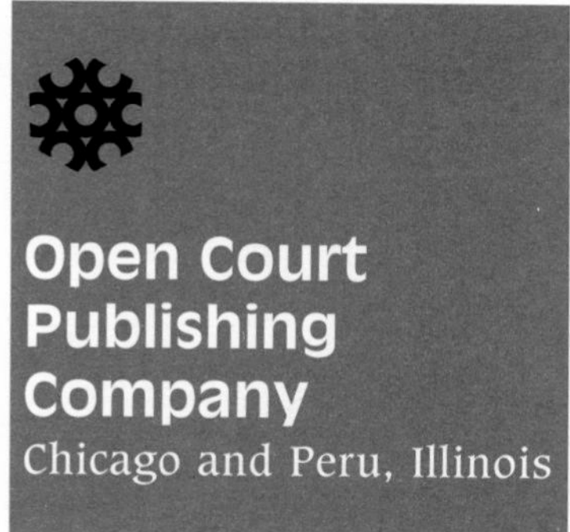

Acknowledgments can be found on page 331 of this book and are hereby incorporated as part of this copyright page.

Printed in the United States of America

ISBN 0-8126-1100-4

4 5 6 7 8 9 10

Contents

▲ Full-length trade books

▲ Full-length trade books
■ Dramatized on audiocassette

▲ Full-length trade books
■ Dramatized on audiocassette

Using Open Court's *Collections for Young Scholars*®

A Program for the 21st Century

Open Court's *Collections for Young Scholars®* represents a profound departure from mainstream reading programs. Its completely new approach to the teaching of reading demands more of students. Yet if a reading program is to prepare students to lead productive lives in twenty-first century society, it must be demanding. Basic literacy skills are not enough. Traditional approaches are not adequate.

Students who experience *Collections for Young Scholars*

- learn how to read and respond to a variety of texts
- acquire strategies for accessing information and for exploring concepts from many areas of knowledge—including some that do not even exist today
- learn how to communicate effectively using both oral and written language
- learn how to work both independently and collaboratively
- give sustained effort to thinking and problem solving

THE PRINCIPLES

Collections for Young Scholars is built upon principles that reflect the consensus of leading literacy researchers and practitioners on what is essential for reading success.

No Assumptions

In *Collections for Young Scholars,* initial reading instruction relies on the explicit teaching of sounds, on the blending of sounds into words, and on the leverage of using this knowledge for reading and writing.

For phonics instruction to work, it has to be systematic. It cannot start somewhere in the middle. It cannot assume that children will "pick it up somehow." *Collections for Young Scholars* does not assume that children already know the letters or can distinguish individual sounds. It systematically teaches letter knowledge and phonemic awareness before and during the introduction of sound/spelling associations. The introduction of sound/spellings is also systematic. And, because young children find it difficult to analyze the phonemic structure of words, the program offers direct instruction in blending. The teaching of writing begins with interactive dictation. All of these techniques are used together in predictable and recurring activities that teach children how to think about the sound/spelling associations and about their connections with word meanings.

Authentic Literacy Experiences

Young students need to be reminded every day that literacy is a powerful tool. They need to see that attaining literacy is the goal of their hard work in learning the written code. Along with systematic instruction in the sound/spellings, students participate daily in reading-aloud activities with authentic, high-quality literature in Big Books and student anthologies. From the beginning, the students experience a range of text genres, including nonfiction. There are also plenty of opportunities for writing, allowing the students to understand the uses of writing even as they are learning to write. These experiences help to reinforce students' print awareness and their understanding of the structure and conventions of written language.

Throughout the program, students are encouraged to construct meaning by interacting with and responding to outstanding literature. They read widely, write frequently, and listen and speak effectively. The focus is always on building knowledge rather than routinized performance.

Integrated Instruction

The use of learning frameworks ensures substantive integration of instruction. Lessons in which learning is presented as isolated, unrelated bits and pieces are replaced with learning units tied to important concepts that call on students to make connections across all areas of the curriculum and to acquire knowledge that can be used beyond a single lesson. Activities within a unit are integrated through reading, writing, discussion, and exploration activities that become increasingly complex and demanding.

Intentional Learning

Learning to read empowers students. Learning to *learn* enables them to use that power intelligently and to take charge of their own lives and their own learning process as soon as possible. In *Collections for Young Scholars,* learning is the goal of instruction, rather than an incidental outcome. Students explore critical areas for depth and understanding rather than march through large amounts of material for superficial learning. The intent of instruction is to engage the students in the kinds of activities that will prepare them for the reading, thinking, and problem-solving typical of real-world situations. Students also learn how to monitor themselves rather than always relying on the teacher.

Support and Challenge for *All* Students

As society becomes more and more diverse and classrooms become accessible to more and more children with special needs, instruction must be designed to ensure that *all* students have access to the best instruction and the highest quality materials and are subject to the same high expectations. Nothing is more discouraging and frustrating to children who are learning English or who have special needs than having to complete low-level skill sheets while their classmates participate in exciting discussions, read challenging and interesting materials, and pursue individual interests.

Collections for Young Scholars is designed so that every student is able to participate fully in class. No student gets bogged down in repetitive practice. Grouping is flexible and based on interest, not ability. The top priority of the program is to give all children important insights into the vast amount of knowledge available so that they can set learning goals for themselves.

Diverse and individual needs are met by varying the time and intensity of instruction, not by using watered down content or by having the students read simplified and pointless texts or complete boring, repetitive skill sheets. In addition, students have access to a variety of activities that provide for differing language proficiencies and abilities. Multicultural activities are a natural part of the curriculum, not an add-on. Students for whom English is the primary language work with and learn from their classmates who are learning English as a second language. Conversely, English Language Learners have opportunities to practice their new language in an environment in which their ideas and contributions are sought and valued by their classmates and teacher.

Plentiful and Relevant Practice Opportunities

It is important to give students time during the day in which to practice what they are learning. Time for practice, called Workshop, is an integral part of *Collections for Young Scholars.* In Workshop, students work independently, collaboratively, or with you to practice and review material taught in their lessons. Practice materials are also important, and the program contains a number of such materials that can be used as needed by individual students or small groups.

The goals are to use all class time as efficiently and productively as possible. No time is wasted on mindless repetition and seat work.

Teacher Leadership, Collaborative Learning,

In *Collections for Young Scholars* classrooms, the learning environment is established by the teacher. The powerful learning frameworks in the program help you to focus students' attention on real learning and away from busywork. The program encourages you to model how to pursue both personal and collaborative learning and how to communicate that learning to others.

Equally important, the program provides students with ample opportunities to learn from and work with classmates in collaborative learning groups. These groups allow students to work on topics of mutual interest, to share ideas, and to help each other gain understanding of complex concepts. Learning groups composed of both English-speaking students and English Language Learners encourage the students to learn more about each other's languages and backgrounds and make it possible for those students learning English to ask questions they might be reluctant to raise in a whole-class setting. Carefully structured activities involve special-needs students in learning groups in ways that make their ideas and efforts crucial to the group's success.

Home/School Connections

Families are kept informed of their children's classroom activities and consulted on matters of importance to their children. Homework assignments are extended in ways that invite family members to become closely involved in their children's learning. In turn, families are expected to participate actively in helping their children attain full literacy.

High Expectations, Positive Assessment

Students perform to the level of expectations set by their surroundings. It is unfair to them not to expect their best. Open Court has a long tradition of respecting the intelligence of children and teachers. *Collections for Young Scholars* carries on that tradition by providing high-quality literature and meaning-based, relevant activities that honor the abilities of the program's users.

Although expectations are high, assessment is positive. It focuses on what the children do right, not on what they do wrong. Above all, it helps them to move continuously up the learning ladder.

THE LEARNING FRAMEWORKS

In *Collections for Young Scholars,* principles are translated into instruction by means of learning frameworks. Learning frameworks are basic techniques that recur frequently and provide predictable approaches to instruction. The use of learning frameworks frees the children to focus on the content of a lesson without the distraction of learning a new format for its presentation. The result is coherent instruction that incorporates and develops all key areas of the literacy curriculum. Within and across grade levels, key skills and concepts are introduced at a level appropriate to the children's maturity, then presented in increasingly complex or expanded versions.

In each teacher's guide, the learning frameworks are noted by an asterisk (✱). The learning frameworks for each grade level are shown on the following chart, with the grade 1 frameworks shaded. The grade 1 frameworks are discussed in detail on pages 32F–39F.

The Learning Frameworks

- Reading Skills and Fluency
- Writing Skills and Fluency
- Knowledge Building
- Authentic Literacy Experiences
- Monitoring, Assessment, and Individualization

	Kindergarten	Grade 1
*	Phonemic Awareness	
*	How the Alphabet Works: Part 1	
*	How the Alphabet Works: Part 2	
*	Introducing the Sounds and Using the Alphabet Cards	
*		Introducing the Soun
*		Blending
*	Using the First-Step Stories	
*		Reading Phonics Mini
*		Dictation and Spelling
*	Writing	
*		Sentence Lifting
*		
*		
*		
*		
*		Research
*		Reading the Student A
*		
*	Exploring Through Discussion	
*		
*	Reading Aloud	
*		Reading Big Books
*	Using the Big Book and Print Awareness	
*	Assessment and Monitoring	
*	Workshop	
*	English Language Learners	

	Grade 2	Grades 3–6
ne Sound/Spelling Cards		
p-by-Step Practice Stories		
	Writing Process	
	Writing Seminar	
	Exploring Through Reflective Activities	
	Exploring Through Research	
	Cognitive and Responsive Reading	
	Reading Roundtable	
	Formative Assessment (Separate Teacher's Guide)	

Senior Author Team

The goal is to let children in on the excitement of literacy—not just doing things they couldn't do before, but knowing things they never knew before, thinking about things they never thought about before, and understanding things they never understood before.

—Marilyn Jager Adams

Marilyn Jager Adams is a Senior Scientist in the Psychology Department at Bolt Beranek and Newman, Inc., a research and development laboratory in Cambridge, Massachusetts. She is also a Senior Research Scientist at Brown University and has been affiliated with the Center for the Study of Reading at the University of Illinois since 1975. She is the author of *Beginning to Read: Thinking and Learning About Print* (MIT Press, 1990), written on behalf of the U.S. Secretary of Education as mandated by Congress. The book, the most comprehensive study of beginning reading undertaken to date, examines instructional practices from a historical perspective and critiques them in terms of theoretical and empirical research in education, psychology, and linguistics.

Carl Bereiter is Professor at the Centre for Applied Cognitive Science at the Ontario Institute for Studies in Education in Toronto and a member of the National Academy of Education. He has coauthored many curriculum projects, including Open Court's reading and mathematics programs. He is coauthor with Marlene Scardamalia of *The Psychology of Written Composition* (1987) and *Surpassing Ourselves: The Nature and Implications of Expertise* (1993); and he has published extensively on the nature of teaching and learning. Computer-supported intentional learning environments and collaborative knowledge building have been the subjects of his most recent classroom investigations and publications.

Beginning readers have a lot to learn about how written language works. But at the same time, they are fully-formed human beings who wonder, think, get absorbed by a good story, enjoy and make jokes. A good reading program will honor all these facts. This program, when taught in the right spirit, will do that.

—Carl Bereiter

In order for children to learn how to read, they have got to break the code. And by teaching them about how the sound structure of their language works, you're only making it that much easier for them to break the code.
—Jan Hirshberg

Jan Hirshberg holds an Ed.D. in reading, language, and learning disabilities from Harvard University. She has taught in elementary school classrooms and has also served as a school district reading consultant. At Harvard she was a teaching fellow, research assistant, instructor, and lecturer at the Graduate School of Education. Her reading specialities are in linguistics and early literacy. Her work has focused on how children learn to read and write and on the logistics of teaching reading and writing in the early elementary grades. She is an author of the kindergarten and grade-1 levels of Open Court's 1989 reading and writing program as well as *Collections for Young Scholars.*

Valerie Anderson is Research Associate at the Centre for Applied Cognitive Science at the Ontario Institute for Studies in Education and is on the editorial advisory boards of *The Reading Teacher* and *The Journal of Reading Behavior.* Anderson has extensive experience both in designing curriculums and in training teachers. She has been coauthor of a number of curriculum projects, including *Thinking Games* (with Carl Bereiter), *The Reading Connection,* and *Catching On.* Her main professional focus is on training teachers how to apply the latest educational theories in their classrooms. Her most recent work with children has centered on helping them learn to use thinking strategies to become independent readers.

Young children need to learn to do more than simply go through the motions of reading and writing. They need to learn to take an active role in the wondering, problem solving, and responsiveness that literate people engage in as they read and write.
—Valerie Anderson

Consulting Authors

You've got to have a dream. And when you have a dream, you've got to find out what it takes to make that dream come true. Everything takes something. There's no free lunch. It's not just going to happen. You're going to have to do something. And, if you're willing to pay that price, you can make the dream a reality. —Bill Pinkney

Michael Pressley is Professor of Educational Psychology and Statistics at the State University of New York at Albany, as well as Principal Investigator for the National Reading Research Center, centralized at the Universities of Maryland and Georgia. He does both basic laboratory research on cognition and learning and applied work in educational settings. Memory development and reading comprehension strategies have received much of his attention.

Marsha Roit spends considerable time in classrooms working with children to develop and demonstrate reading and writing activities and training teachers and administrators. Her work has been published in a variety of education journals, including *Exceptional Children, Journal of Learning Disabilities, Educational Leadership,* and *The Elementary School Journal.* She has presented her work at national and international conferences.

Iva E. Carruthers is Professor and former Chairperson of the Sociology Department of Northeastern Illinois University. She is also President of Nexus Unlimited, Inc., a human resources development and computer services consulting firm, and of Ed Tech, a computer software development company. In addition to developing educational software aids for teaching history and interdisciplinary subjects, she has produced fourteen study guides on African-American and African history.

Bill Pinkney is the first African American to sail solo around the world, traveling around the five great capes in his sailboat named *Commitment.* Only forty-one individuals have accomplished this feat. More than 30,000 students across the United States were able to share in his legendary voyage, thanks to advanced satellite and computer technologies. Not only did he give these students lessons in math, science, geography, and social studies, but Captain Pinkney also modeled for them the courage, perseverance, skill, and commitment required to realize one's dreams.

Instructional Consultants

Charles Abate, Ed.D.
Elementary Principal
Orchard Elementary School
Ridgewood, New Jersey

Doris B. Ash, M.S.
Assistant Director
Fostering a Community of Learners Research Project
University of California, Berkeley

Mary Lamon, Ph.D.
Project Director
Middle School Curriculum Development Project
St. Louis Science Center
St. Louis, Missouri

Martha E. Rutherford, M.A.
Assistant Director
Fostering a Community of Learners Research Project
University of California, Berkeley

Teacher Reviewers

Barbara Appleberry, *Grade 1*
Mollison Elementary School
Chicago, Illinois

Marie Beacham, *Grade 1*
Ephraim Elementary School
Ephraim, Utah

Joyce Bell, *Grade 1*
Brown School
Newburyport, Massachusetts

Kim Carey, *Grade 6*
Crestmont Elementary School
Northport, Alabama

Peggy Clelland, *Grade 1*
Washington Terrace Elementary School
Ogden, Utah

Emmy Daniel, *Grade 1*
South Shores School
Decatur, Illinois

Tony Dillon, *Grade 1*
John Foster Dulles School
Chicago, Illinois

Dorothy Dorsey, *Grade 4*
Glenmount Elementary School
Baltimore, Maryland

Kay Ericksen, *Grade 5*
Ephraim Elementary School
Ephraim, Utah

Debra Evans, *Grade 3*
Goldblatt Elementary School
Chicago, Illinois

Margaret Ewing, *Grade 3*
Abraham Lincoln Elementary School
Palm Desert, California

Sr. Susan Faist, *Grade 2*
Christ the King School
Toledo, Ohio

Mary Fatsi, *Grade 1*
Brooklyn Elementary School
Brooklyn, Connecticut

Susan Fowler, *Grade 2*
Yaquina View Elementary
Newport, Oregon

Bonnie French, *Grade 6*
Carl Sundahl Elementary School
Folsom, California

Lena Gates, *Grade 1*
Crispus Attucks School, P. S. 21
Brooklyn, New York

Lila Gilchrist, *Grade 3*
The Orchard School
Ridgewood, New Jersey

Leticia Gonzalez, *Grade 4*
Saenz Elementary School
Alice, Texas

Lora Gordy, *Grade 5*
Buckingham Elementary School
Berlin, Maryland

Janice Green, *Grade 1*
Francis T. Bresnahan School
Newburyport, Massachusetts

Joyce Haffey, *Grade 4*
St. Therese School
Kansas City, Missouri

Jackie Herath, *Grade 3*
Sunderland Elementary School
Sunderland, Maryland

Karen Horace, *Grade 6*
Goldblatt Elementary School
Chicago, Illinois

Patricia Horst, *Grade 5*
Harding Elementary School
Clinton, Ohio

Hurtice Howard, *Grade 1*
Julia L. Armstrong Elementary School
Greenville, Mississippi

Nancy Hughes, *Grade 2*
Eleanor Roosevelt School
Vancouver, Washington

Celeste James, *Grade 1*
John Foster Dulles School
Chicago, Illinois

Christine Johnson, *Grade 1*
Kelley School
Newburyport, Massachusetts

Patricia Johnson, *Grade 3*
Crispus Attucks School, P. S. 21
Brooklyn, New York

Laurie Jones, *Grade 4*
Grantswood Community School
Birmingham, Alabama

Lisa Kane, *Grade 5*
Disney Magnet Elementary School
Chicago, Illinois

Charlotte Lewis, *Grade 1*
L. B. Weemes Elementary School
Los Angeles, California

Rhet Lickliter, *Grade 6*
Park Tudor School
Indianapolis, Indiana

Sandra Loose, *Grade 1*
Indian Lane Elementary School
Media, Pennsylvania

Frank Lopez, *Grade 5*
Parker Elementary School
Panama City, Florida

Kathryn Lopez, *Grade 1*
Millville Elementary School
Panama City, Florida

Mary Ann Luebbert, *Grade 6*
Russell Elementary School
Hazelwood, Missouri

Ruth MacGregor, *Grade 3*
Mildred M. Fox School
South Paris, Maine

Lynne Malone, *Grade 3*
Carver Elementary School
Dawson, Georgia

Pam Martin, *Grade 1*
L. B. Weemes Elementary School
Los Angeles, California

Melony Maughan, *Grade 1*
Grantswood Community School
Birmingham, Alabama

Ursula McClendon, *Grade 3*
George West Primary School
George West, Texas

Phyllis Miles, *Grade 4*
Our Lady of Mount Carmel
Carmel, Indiana

Sue Miller, *Grade 1*
The Valwood School
Valdosta, Georgia

Nancy Mitchell, *Grade 2*
Pleasant Ridge School
Grass Valley, California

Trudy Mockert, *Grade 1*
Nicolaus Copernicus School, P. S. 25
Jersey City, New Jersey

Anna Molina, *Grade 1*
Ezra Nolan School, P. S. 40
Jersey City, New Jersey

Roberta Montoya, *Grade 3*
Alamosa Elementary School
Albuquerque, New Mexico

Carol Neyman, *Grade 5*
Cotton Boll Elementary School
Peoria, Arizona

Margaret Nichols, *Grade 1*
Brown School
Newburyport, Massachusetts

Cindy Noland, *Grade 2*
Jefferson Elementary School
Parkersburg, West Virginia

Bettye Nunnery, *Grade 2*
Otken Primary School
McComb, Mississippi

Jane Offineer, *Grade 5*
Belden Elementary School
Canton, Ohio

Sara Oliveira, *Grade 5*
Portsmouth Elementary School
Portsmouth, Rhode Island

Kathleen Pabst, *Grade 3*
Charles Drew Elementary School
San Francisco, California

Judith Palermo, *Grade 1*
St. Helen's School
Chicago, Illinois

Terri Patterson, *Grade 4*
Paradise Elementary School
Las Vegas, Nevada

Becky Philips, *Grade 2*
Sunderland Elementary School
Sunderland, Maryland

Donna Powell, *Grade 2*
Melville School
Portsmouth, Rhode Island

Barbara Purcell, *Grade 3*
Education Service Center
Corpus Christi, Texas

Caron Reasor, *Grade 6*
La Quinta Middle School
La Quinta, California

Sharon Robinson, *Grade 2*
Flournoy Elementary School
Los Angeles, California

Judith Roy, *Grade 1*
Grantswood Community School
Birmingham, Alabama

Maxine Rushing, *Grade 4*
Plymouth Day School
Detroit, Michigan

Kathy Rodger-Sachs, *Grade 4*
The Orchard School
Ridgewood, New Jersey

Agnes Schutz, *Grade 1*
Alamosa Elementary School
Albuquerque, New Mexico

Donna Sedlacek, *Grade 3*
Bear Creek Elementary School
Lakewood, Colorado

Ruth Seiger, *Grade 1*
Francis T. Bresnahan School
Newburyport, Massachusetts

Cheryl Sheehan, *Grade 1*
Nicolaus Copernicus School, P. S. 25
Jersey City, New Jersey

Margaret Simmons, *Grade 6*
Corpus Christi Elementary School
San Francisco, California

Renee Singer, *Grade 1*
Grantswood Community School
Birmingham, Alabama

Jacqueline Smith, *Grade 1*
John Foster Dulles School
Chicago, Illinois

Patricia Terrell, *Grade 4*
Gatewood Elementary School
Oklahoma City, Oklahoma

Barbara Uhrin, *Grade 2*
Amos Hutchinson Elementary School
Greensburg, Pennsylvania

Celia Waddell, *Grade 5*
Grantswood Elementary School
Birmingham, Alabama

Laurie Walters, *Grade 1*
L. B. Weemes Elementary School
Los Angeles, California

Robin Wexler, *Grade 5*
Roosevelt Elementary School
River Edge, New Jersey

The Grade 1 Program of *Collections for Young Scholars*®

A child's success in first-grade reading looks like the single best predictor—and in fact an awesomely powerful predictor—of her or his ultimate educational outcome, however you measure it.

—Marilyn Jager Adams

The grade 1 program is a very special part of *Collections for Young Scholars*®. In this part of the program, students gain access to the most important technology ever developed—written language. It is no exaggeration to say that how well children learn to read in first grade profoundly affects how well they do throughout their school years—and their lives. Children who quickly develop the skills necessary to read with fluency and comprehension gain access to all the world's knowledge. They acquire the power to educate themselves and to expand their range of thought and reflection. Children who do not develop these skills become caught in a downward spiral of frustration and failure.

A task so fundamentally important to children as helping them learn to read demands serious attention. It demands that we bring to bear all the knowledge that the sciences of the human mind and of language development have struggled for over the past decades. These sciences have taught us a great deal—and yet, reassuringly, they have also taught us that what great teachers have always done has been absolutely right:

- Teach the sounds and letters early, intensely, and quickly
- Never let students lose sight of the purpose and goal of learning the skills
- Get students into real reading as quickly as possible
- Allow them to gain fluency in writing, enabling them to use it as a tool of inquiry as well as communication
- Give them responsibility for their own work, their own mental development, and their own paths of inquiry as soon as possible

Open Court's approach to beginning reading instruction has been successful in many thousands of classrooms for more than three decades. Since the first publication of the program in the early 1960s, the approach has recognized that if children are to learn to read with fluency and comprehension, they need both explicit, systematic skill instruction and rich experiences with authentic literature.

Collections for Young Scholars, while retaining the basic core of the approach that has worked so well for long, incorporates the experiences of a new generation of teachers and the wisdom of highly respected reading

researchers, including Marilyn Jager Adams, the author of *Beginning to Read* and a leading proponent of balanced reading instruction.

THE MATERIALS

It is not just the presence of a variety of activities that makes a program of reading instruction effective or ineffective. It is the way in which its pieces are fitted together to complement and support one another, always with the full consideration of the needs and progress of the children with whom it will be used.

In *Collections for Young Scholars,* explicit skills instruction is balanced with extensive reading of both predictable, patterned texts and quality literature. From the very beginning, children experience a wide variety of literary forms and genres.

Core Resources

The teacher's guide for grade 1, *Framework for Effective Teaching®*, is contained in four separate volumes:

- *Thinking and Learning About Print,* Part A
- *Thinking and Learning About Print,* Part B
- *Framework for Effective Teaching,* Grade 1, Book 1
- *Framework for Effective Teaching,* Grade 1, Book 2

Thinking and Learning About Print, Parts A and B

Thinking and Learning About Print, Parts A and B are intended for use in the first half of grade 1. The thirty lessons in Part A provide the children with a solid foundation in phonemic awareness and introduce them to sound/spelling associations, at the rate of about one per lesson. Part A accompanies the Big Books *Look Who's Reading!* and *Animals.*

The forty lessons in Part B continue the introduction of sound/spellings. Part B accompanies the Big Books *Captain Bill Pinkney's Journey* and *Machines in Our Garden.*

Together, the lessons in *Thinking and Learning About Print,* Parts A and B are designed to ensure that by December/January of the grade 1 year, all students will be reading, with fluency and comprehension, the text in the student anthologies in the second half of the program.

Big Books

The companion Big Books for *Thinking and Learning About Print,* Parts A and B support the children's developing phonemic and print awareness and invite them into the world of good literature, even before they are reading on their own. Multicultural selections familiarize the children with many cultures and traditions. At the same time, they focus on topics that every child can relate to and expand upon. The small versions of the Big Books allow the children the pleasure of having their own books to read, reread, and share with others.

Fine Art selections in the Big Books reinforce the themes the children are reading about and show them that pictures are another form of communication.

Look Who's Reading! contains engaging traditional and contemporary rhymes, poems, and songs.

Animals introduces the children to nonfiction through articles, photo essays, and picture essays about many different aspects of animal life.

Captain Bill Pinkney's Journey encourages the children to share in the excitement of Captain Pinkney's solo trip around the world on the sailboat *Commitment* while they learn important science and social studies concepts.

Machines in Our Garden uses the familiar backdrop of a garden to introduce the children to the concept of simple machines and how they work.

Framework for Effective Teaching, Grade 1, Books 1 and 2

Framework for Effective Teaching, Grade 1, Book 1 is for use, in general, at the start of the second half of the grade 1 year. Its thirty lessons complete the introduction of sound/spelling associations and relate instruction to the Volume 1, Book 1 *Collections for Young Scholars* student anthology.

Framework for Effective Teaching, Grade 1, Book 2 is for use, in general, at the end of the grade 1 year. Its twenty-three phonics lessons serve as a review of everything the children have learned about sound/spelling associations and tie instruction to the Volume 1, Book 2 *Collections for Young Scholars* student anthology.

Collections for Young Scholars, Volume 1, Books 1 and 2

The student anthologies that accompany *Framework for Effective Teaching*, Grade 1, Books 1 and 2 are filled with beautifully illustrated selections by award-winning authors and artists. Realistic fiction, historical fiction, poetry, nonfiction selections, and full-length trade books captivate the children and make them eager to read more on their own. Literature from around the world offers the children differing perspectives on many topics. Fine Art selections are included with each unit. These works show the children how the topics they are reading about can be represented visually.

Each book is organized into learning units that focus on important concepts. The units build valuable background knowledge and encourage the children to question, wonder, and think.

Step-by-Step Practice Stories and Phonics Minibooks

The Step-by-Step Practice Stories work with the Phonics Minibooks to consolidate the children's growing knowledge of the sound/spelling associations. These materials help the children experience success with reading from virtually the beginning of the year.

The forty Step-by-Step Practice Stories focus on one new element at a time. They are bound in workbook form and found in the Phonemic Awareness and Phonics Kit. Each story is assembled before reading begins. The children may color or decorate the stories as they wish. After reading the stories in class, the children may take them home to share with their families

Twelve Step-by-Step Practice Stories accompany *Thinking and Learning About Print,* Part A; the rest accompany Part B.

Each of the eighteen Phonics Minibooks is cumulative, reviewing and reinforcing the elements that have been taught since the last minibook. They are simple, full-color stories with bright covers. The Phonics Minibooks are also available as reproducible masters (found in the Phonemic Awareness and Phonics Kit) that may be copied for the children to take home.

Phonics Minibooks 1–5 are introduced in *Thinking and Learning About Print,* Part A; 6–12 in Part B; and 13–18 in *Framework for Effective Teaching,* Grade 1, Book 1.

Reading/Writing Connection Workbooks

The Reading/Writing Connection workbooks make the children aware of and comfortable with the connection between reading and writing. For the children, the workbooks provide a place to practice what they are learning about reading and writing across the year. For you, they provide a continuous record of the children's growing abilities.

There are four Reading/Writing Connection workbooks in the grade 1 program:

- Reading/Writing Connection: Phonics, to accompany the Phonemic Awareness and Phonics Kit
- Reading/Writing Connection: Thinking and Learning About Print, Parts A and B, used with lessons in the first two volumes of the teacher's guide
- Reading/Writing Connection: Volume 1, Book 1, used with *Framework for Effective Teaching,* Grade 1, Book 1
- Reading/Writing Connection, Volume 1, Book 2, used with *Framework for Effective Teaching,* Grade 1, Book 2

In the lessons in the teacher's guides, references to the Reading/Writing Connection are indicated by a chevron (➤).

Teacher Toolbox

The lessons in the teacher's guide are supported by the following resources contained in the Teacher Toolbox:

- **Learning Framework Cards**—reference tools in convenient card format that contain descriptions and discussions of the key learning frameworks used throughout the grade 1 program (see pages 32F–39F). The cards also contain suggestions for applying the learning framework to other areas of the curriculum and for working with English Language Learners.
- **Teacher Tool Cards**—cards that provide basic lessons on Writer's Craft/Reading, Grammar and Mechanics, and Spelling and Vocabulary that can be used to meet individual needs at any time, not just during reading. Each Tool Card contains tips for dealing with common problems related to the subject of a lesson and suggestions for working with English Language Learners.
- **Home/School Connection materials**—a variety of resources, including convenient masters of letters, written in English and in Spanish, that explain to families what the children are learning in class; activity sheets that the children and their families can complete together; and bibliographies that list children's literature for families to share at home.
- **Assessment materials**—a variety of resources, including a guide to assessment techniques and materials used in the program and masters of observation logs, performance assessment rubrics, cumulative class folders, and individual student profiles.
- **Instructional Posters**—wall posters that illustrate reading strategies and the phases of the writing process.
- **Listening Collections Audiocassette**—tape that contains selections from the Big Books and student anthologies.

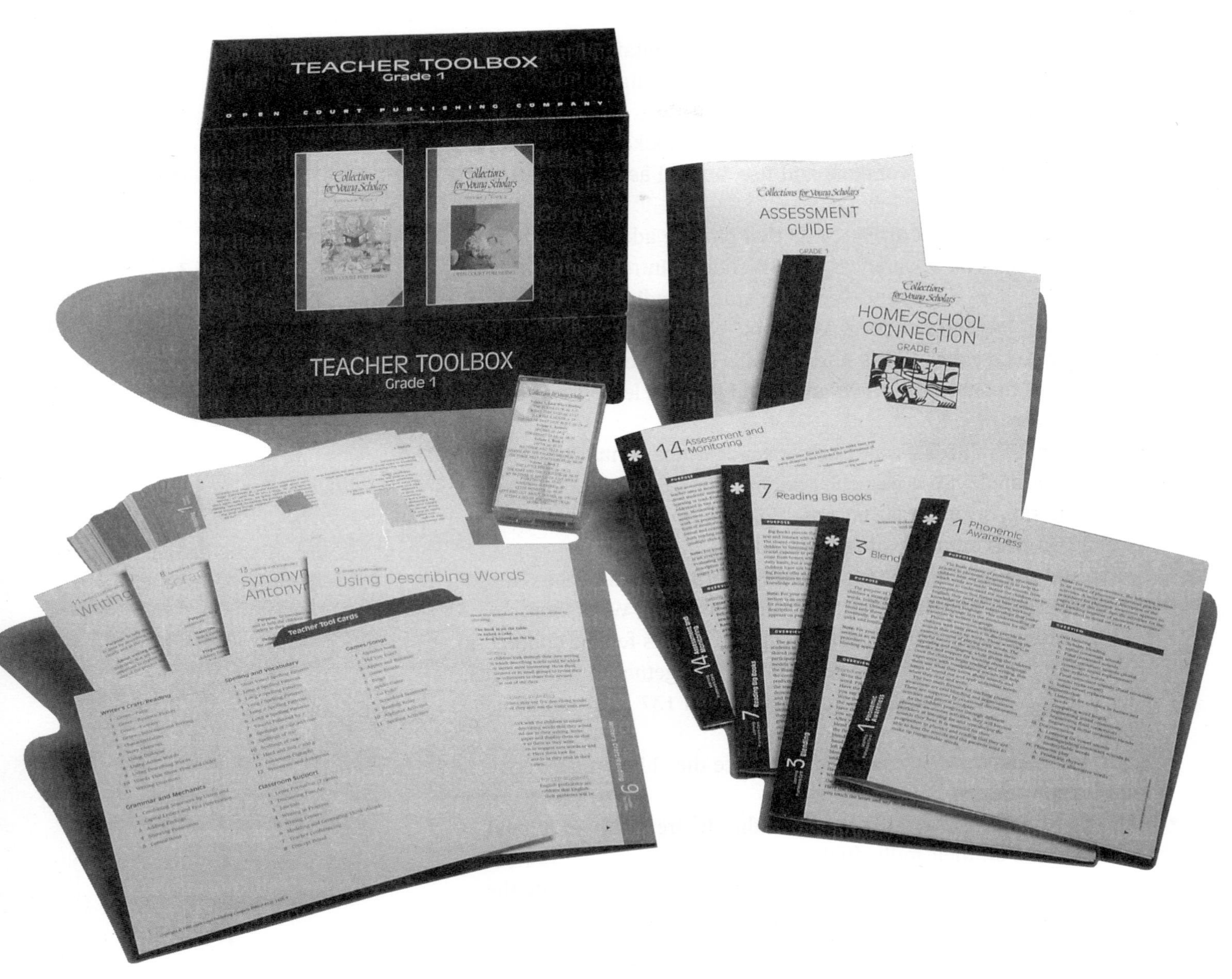
TEACHER TOOLBOX
Grade 1
OPEN COURT PUBLISHING COMPANY
Collections for Young Scholars
TEACHER TOOLBOX
Grade 1
Collections for Young Scholars
ASSESSMENT GUIDE
GRADE 1
Collections for Young Scholars
HOME/SCHOOL CONNECTION
GRADE 1
14 Assessment and Monitoring
7 Reading Big Books
3 Blend
1 Phonemic Awareness
Synonyms
Antonyms
Using Describing Words
Teacher Tool Cards

Phonemic Awareness and Phonics Kit

The Phonemic Awareness and Phonics Kit also contains resources to support the lessons in the teacher's guide. The kit contains the following materials:

- **Phonemic Awareness and Phonics Guide**—a booklet that contains an overview of the kit's contents and use, as well as a wealth of activities for Workshop.
- **Learning Framework Cards**—cards that provide additional information about Phonemic Awareness, Oral Blending, Introducing the Sounds and Using the Sound/Spelling Cards, Blending, Dictation and Spelling, and English Language Learners.
- **Phonemic Awareness Cards and Phonics Cards**—easy-to-use duplicates of the phonemic awareness and phonics lessons in the teacher's guide.
- **Sound/Spelling Cards**—wall cards, each of which contains a picture that is associated with a particular sound. The cards provide powerful mnemonic support and reinforce multiple spellings for a given sound for children who are beginning to decode.
- **Individual Sound Card sets**—miniature reproductions of the Sound/Spelling Cards for use by the children during Workshop.
- **Letter Card sets**—individual sets of alphabet cards for the children to use as they learn the alphabet and put letters together to form words.
- **Outlaw Word Flash Cards**—cards that contain 137 high-frequency words.
- **Alphabet Flash Cards**—cards that reinforce the children's letter-knowledge.
- **Activity Sheets**—masters that provide the children with additional practice based on their individual needs.
- **Step-by-Step Practice Stories**—masters of stories that provide the children with an engaging way to apply the phonic principles they are learning.
- **Phonics Minibook Take-Home Stories**—masters of the Phonics Minibooks that allow the children to take the stories home to share with family and friends.
- **Phonics Audiocassette**—tape that contains Sound/Spelling Card stories.

Assessment Materials

The *Collections for Young Scholars* grade 1 program provides a multidimensional, continuous assessment system designed to measure change in students' performance, to check their progress, and to detect their strengths and weaknesses in each area of the literacy curriculum.

The booklet Assessment Guide, Grade 1, found in the Teacher Toolbox, provides an overview of the types of assessment used in the program and explains how to use each. The booklet Assessment Masters, Grade 1, also in the Teacher Toolbox, contains convenient observation logs and monitoring logs for recording observations of individual students' progress in phonemic awareness, sound/spelling associations, print awareness, and so forth. Reading assessment sheets provide a place to record individual students' reading performance as they read aloud in Workshop or other available time. Writing performance assessment rubrics help organize evaluations of different aspects of students' writing. Masters are also provided of multiple-choice tests, free-response tests, and other written tests.

In addition to being assessed by monitoring, performance assessments, and written tests, each child also develops a portfolio of samples of his or her work.

Getting Started

THE GRADE 1 LEARNING FRAMEWORKS

Instruction in the grade 1 program of *Collections for Young Scholars* is organized by way of key techniques, or learning frameworks that recur frequently. These frameworks, which are indicated in the teacher's guide by an asterisk (✱), consist of:

1. Phonemic Awareness
   1A. Oral Blending
2. Introducing the Sounds and Using the Sound/Spelling Cards
3. Blending
4. Dictation and Spelling
5. Reading Aloud
6. Reading Phonics Minibooks and Step-by-Step Practice Stories
7. Reading Big Books
8. Reading the Student Anthologies
9. Exploring Through Discussion
10. Writing
11. Workshop
12. Research
13. Sentence Lifting
14. Assessment and Monitoring
15. English Language Learners

Organizing instruction by learning frameworks means that by varying the time and intensity of instruction, individual and special needs can be addressed without ability grouping. All children in the classroom receive the same high-quality learning experiences. However, because children learning English occasionally require extra help, the teacher's guide provides **Tips for English Language Learners** whenever the tips are appropriate for a specific lesson.

The Learning Framework Cards found in the Teacher Toolbox contain detailed discussions of each learning framework.

HOW THE LEARNING FRAMEWORKS ORGANIZE INSTRUCTION

The learning frameworks form the basis of instruction that incorporates and develops all key areas of the literacy curriculum. Although the learning frameworks are each clearly identifiable, as the chart on pages 14F–15F shows, they often overlap to reinforce learning of key skills and concepts:

Reading Skills and Fluency

Reading skills are taught explicitly and systematically. Instruction is sequenced, attentive to individual needs, and includes a great deal of relevant practice with engaging yet predictable reading materials. The goal is to ensure that by December or January of the first-grade year, the children have acquired the skills necessary to read—with fluency and comprehension—the many different kinds of literature they encounter in their student anthologies and in trade books. Skill instruction is not abandoned after that point, rather it takes the form of steady review and reinforcement.

There are four key reading skills and fluency learning frameworks: Phonemic Awareness, Introducing the Sounds and Using the Sound/Spelling Cards, Blending, and Reading Phonics Minibooks and Step-by-Step Practice Stories.

* Phonemic Awareness

Phonemic awareness is taught by means of two techniques: oral blending and segmentation. These two techniques complement each other. Oral blending puts sounds together to make words, while segmentation separates words into sounds. The activities are brief and gamelike, making them appealing and engaging. Sometimes the activities involve a puppet, who repeats word parts that you say. The children then imitate or correct the puppet. The activities are carefully sequenced, and each series begins with a great deal of teacher support for every child. As the children advance, this support is gradually removed and the activities become more difficult.

The Phonemic Awareness learning framework provides the children with easy practice in discriminating the sounds that make up words. The ability to hear the sounds and the patterns used to make up words is essential to the children's progression to phonics and reading. The phonemic awareness activities are purely oral and do not involve the teaching of any sound/spelling associations.

Because the phonemic awareness activities require the children simply to listen to and reproduce sounds, the activities work equally well with all children. The easy-to-harder sequence of the activities provides ample support for both English Language Learners and special-needs children, and the gamelike nature of the activities encourages all children to participate readily.

* Introducing the Sounds and Using the Sound/Spelling Cards

The Sound/Spelling Cards are used to introduce sound/spellings one by one by means of a see/hear/say/write sequence.

1. See—The children see the spelling(s) on the Sound/Spelling Card.

2. Hear—The children hear the sound(s) used in words and in isolation in a brief, alliterative story that is related to the picture and the associated sound.
3. Say—The children say the sound, both during the story and in isolation.
4. Write—The children write the spelling(s) of the sound.

This learning framework provides a systematic introduction that helps to reinforce the association of sound and spelling in the children's minds.

Each of the Sound/Spelling Cards contains the common spelling or spellings of a sound. With the exception of the long vowel Sound/Spelling Cards, each card depicts both an action-sound association and a picture of an object whose name includes the sound. The double association of the picture on the card fixes a reference point that the children will use constantly when they refer to the sound in future blending, dictation, and writing contexts.

The see/hear/say/write sequence is especially beneficial for English Language Learners, even for sounds that are not found in their primary languages. Because the Sound/Spelling Cards are language independent, it is unnecessary for the children to know the English name for the picture on the card in order to associate the action with a sound.

* Blending

Blending is the heart and soul of phonics instruction and the key strategy children must learn to open the world of written language. In the grade 1 program of *Collections for Young Scholars,* blending is a daily activity. As you write the spelling for each sound in a word, the children say the sound, relying on the associations fixed by the Sound/Spelling Cards. Next, they blend the sounds together into a word, then they use the word in a sentence. The connection with word meaning is reinforced constantly so that the children recognize that what they've blended is indeed the word they know from spoken language.

Many English Language Learners understand more spoken English words than they can read. Therefore, blending can provide valuable support to these children by allowing them to figure out words that they cannot read.

* Reading Phonics Minibooks and Step-by-Step Practice Stories

Because reading, rereading, and reading some more are crucial elements in building fluency and in setting the children on the path leading to reading independence, this learning framework has them read and reread Step-by-Step Practice Stories and Phonics Minibooks several times—individually and with partners. Both Step-by-Step Practice Stories and Phonics Minibooks feature stories that the children can read on their own by using their increasing knowledge of written language. Each Step-by-Step Practice Story focuses on a single sound/spelling combination, while each Phonics Minibook is cumulative, reviewing and reinforcing the elements that have been taught since the last minibook.

Partner reading of Step-by-Step Practice Stories and Phonics Minibooks allows children who are more advanced in their reading to work with those needing extra help. Reading alternate pages with a supportive partner, for example, provides English Language Learners with a less-intimidating atmosphere in which to attempt to pronounce new words and sounds.

Writing Skills and Fluency

Early explorations with writing help children to construct valuable insights about how written language works. For this reason, writing is developed alongside reading. The writing skills and fluency learning frameworks stimulate the children to think about writing and how it is used and stress the importance of communicating in print.

The writing skills and fluency learning frameworks are Dictation and Spelling and Sentence Lifting.

* Dictation and Spelling

Through dictation the children become aware that reading and writing are interrelated. Just as blending gives them a strategy for figuring out unfamiliar words, dictation gives them a strategy for spelling words. As they learn that sounds and spellings are connected to form words and that words form sentences, the children begin to learn the standard spellings that will enable others to read their writing. As they learn to encode correctly, the children develop their visual memory for words—spelling ability—and thus increase their writing fluency. Proofreading is an integral part of dictation, encouraging the children to look critically at their writing and giving them an early introduction to an essential part of the writing process.or English Language Learners, interactive dictation reinforces the sound/spelling associations, thus providing valuable support. Proofreading teaches the children to evaluate and correct their spelling and gives them an immediate second chance for success.

* Sentence Lifting

Sentence lifting, or using sentences from the children's own writing to illustrate what is wrong or what is right or what could be better helps the children learn to revise and to proofread their own work. The Sentence Lifting learning framework shows the children that the first thing they write down is not always the best and that it is all right to "mess up" their papers by marking things they want to change.

Because children with the same first language often have similar problems with the conventions of written English, English Language Learners profit from small-group sentence lifting sessions. These sessions serve both to show children what they have done right as well as to help them correct mistakes.

Authentic Literacy Experiences

Reading and writing skills and fluency are not developed in isolation. So that the children can see a purpose for learning sounds and spellings, there are daily opportunities for them to hear and read authentic literature from all genres. Frequent opportunities to write allow the children to build writing proficiency alongside reading.

There are three learning frameworks for literacy experiences: Reading Aloud, Reading Big Books, and Writing.

* Reading Aloud

The following procedures are most effective in conducting daily reading-aloud sessions:

- Introduce the story by telling its title and by commenting briefly on the topic. You should not summarize the story.
- Activate the children's prior knowledge quickly and simply.
- Remind the children to interrupt your reading to clear up anything they do not understand.
- Read the story expressively, modeling reactions and questions.
- Point out illustrations and invite the children to comment on them.
- After reading, call on volunteers to retell the story.
- Discuss the story with the children, encouraging their own responses and questions.

Reading aloud serves multiple purposes: It provokes the children's curiosity about text, conveys to them an awareness that text has meaning, and demonstrates to them the joys and pleasures that reading brings to life. For maximum effectiveness, reading-aloud sessions involve the children's active attention, prompting them to wonder and to ask questions about the meaning of the text and to think about how the ideas in the text fit into their own prior knowledge.

For English Language Learners in particular, reading-aloud sessions provide needed opportunities to observe and practice the strategies they need for reading in English. In addition, hearing their classmates discuss problems they may have had with a reading selection allows English Language Learners and special-needs children to see that even skilled English readers sometimes need help.

* Reading Big Books

The reading-aloud procedure is especially effective for reading Big Books. The shared reading of Big Books engages the children in listening to a reader and provides exposure to written language, which is especially crucial for children who have not been read to frequently in the home. Shared-reading experiences invite the children to participate in reading behaviors and to use the strategies of expert readers: responding to the illustrations, wondering about the content and predicting what might happen, and commenting on events and characters. Sharing Big Books with children also helps them develop an awareness of the nature of print—how words look on a page, the spaces between words, the connection between pictures and words, the left-to-right and top-to-bottom progression of reading and writing, the clues that announce the beginnings and ends of sentences, and so forth—and the conventions of books—title pages, tables of contents, page numbers, and much, much more.

The nature of reading the Big Books—sharing and experiencing written language—lends itself well to learning English. Repetitive passages and illustrated text help English Language Learners with vocabulary development. Big Book reading is doubly valuable as an introduction to the print conventions of English.

* Writing

Writing includes a wide range of activities: class books, journal writing, individual writing. Support is provided to help the children plan and develop their writing. For first grade children, the writing process includes modified forms of prewriting, drafting, revising, proofreading, and publishing.

The Writing learning framework directs the children's attention to the kinds of print they encounter daily and stresses the importance of communicating in print. This learning framework also helps the children develop a sense of audience and learn the importance of sharing ideas, providing feedback, and engaging in revision.

The conventions of spelling, punctuation, and grammar are taught in natural contexts and as aids in written communication. Children are encouraged to use invented spelling as a transition to standard spelling.

Conferences with you along with small-group and individual work give English Language Learners many opportunities to practice and develop their English language writing.

Knowledge Building

Although young children are fascinated with the world around them, most have little awareness of how much there is to know about the world. They have limited experiences with the cognitive strategies they must apply if they are to become full participants in the literate world. The goal of knowledge building is to help the children enter that world by increasing their ability to think about, appreciate, and contribute to the vast richness of human knowledge.

The key knowledge-building learning framework is Research.

* Research

Children build knowledge through reading, writing, and problem-solving activities that encourage them to activate prior knowledge, ask questions, confirm understandings, predict outcomes, interpret, wonder, think, and compare their ideas with those of others. These activities introduce children to the world of scholarship, with its tradition of intellectual inquiry, its specialized forms of symbolization and language (print, numbers, icons), its rich conceptual systems, and its unique joys.

The Research learning framework introduces the children to the research process, which provides an organized way of thinking about and exploring questions that arise in all areas of content learning.

Research activities are especially important to English Language Learners because they allow the children to display their already-learned competencies and to show their classmates that they, too, have complex and sophisticated ideas.

Authentic Literacy Experiences/Knowledge Building

There is a natural overlap of authentic literacy experiences and knowledge building. Indeed, authentic literacy experiences provide the basis for knowledge building.

Two powerful learning frameworks extend and interweave the instruction found in each of these areas: Reading the Student Anthologies and Exploring

Through Discussion. These two learning frameworks give children access to a wide range of important knowledge-building concepts through an array of reading, writing, speaking, and listening activities.

* Reading the Student Anthologies

This learning framework is related to Volume 1, Books 1 and 2 of *Collections for Young Scholars.* It gives the children opportunities to use their new-found reading skills with a variety of text types. Biographies and autobiographies; history, geography, and science selections; photo essays; and discussions of art and music introduce the children to the vastness and variety of human knowledge and experience. Stories, poems, and songs about both familiar and unfamiliar characters, cultures, and events stretch their minds and encourage them to think and reflect about how they interpret the world.

The selections in the anthologies are tied to thematic learning units, each of which is arranged around an important concept. The units build sequentially, allowing the children to see that knowledge is cumulative and helping them to tie together ideas and information in a coherent fashion.

Opportunities to explore how written language works in the context of authentic and motivating literature are crucial for special-needs children and for English Language Learners. For this reason, the *Collections for Young Scholars* student anthologies include many poems and rhyming games that have short, manageable text. By reading these several times, the children quickly catch on to English language print conventions.

* Exploring Through Discussion

Discussing with the children what they are learning and how they are learning it allows them to express their doubts and concerns as well as their excitement about ideas and language. Whole-class discussions of a reading selection encourage the children to express their opinions and ideas clearly and to listen attentively and to respond appropriately to the opinions expressed by others. These discussions are opportunities for the children to think, predict, and draw connections between the selection they are reading and other selections or with their own experiences.

The Exploring Through Discussion learning framework is a principal means of helping children tie together all of the things they are learning about language and literacy and to examine the edges of their knowledge and understanding. Discussion activities are also opportunities to elaborate on content-specific vocabulary, to emphasize the proper vocabulary, and to provide the children with more information about a selection, all of which are important to English Language Learners and special-needs children.

Monitoring, Assessment, and Individualization

Collections for Young Scholars provides for multidimensional, continuous monitoring and assessment to ensure that all children are progressing toward clearly established goals and benchmarks. Individualization is accomplished through Workshop. When necessary, instruction is individualized for those English Language Learners who need additional help.

The learning frameworks for monitoring, assessment, and individualization are Assessment and Monitoring, Workshop, and English Language Learners.

* Assessment and Monitoring

The Assessment and Monitoring learning framework aligns the goals of the curriculum with what students are expected to learn. It is a tool that measures change in students' performance, checks their progress, and detects their strengths and weaknesses in each area of the literacy curriculum. The Assessment and Monitoring learning framework applies equally well to all students, regardless of their specific individual needs.

* Workshop

Workshop gives the children an early experience of managing their own learning process. In Workshop, the children work independently or collaboratively to practice and review material taught in the lessons or to complete projects of their own choosing. As the children gradually take more and more responsibility during Workshop, they learn to set learning goals, to make decisions about the use of time and materials, and to collaborate with their classmates. Of equal importance, Workshop gives you a designated time to work with individuals or with groups to reinforce learning, to provide extra help to those who need it, and to assess and monitor the progress of individuals or of the whole class.

With your guidance, Workshop can be a supportive but open forum in which special-needs and gifted children express themselves freely and experiment with different approaches to learning. It is also a good way for children to help each other over hard spots. Placing English Language Learners in pairs and in small groups takes away an emphasis on individually producing English, something that can interfere with learning a second language in the initial stages.

* English Language Learners

In *Collections for Young Scholars,* English Language Learners receive the same high-quality instruction as do all other students. Instruction respects and builds on English Language Learners' existing knowledge and competencies. A wide range of oral language activities gives them opportunities to hear and to use English for valid communicative purposes—to learn new things from and with their classmates. Frequent reading and writing experiences help the children acquire English vocabulary, learn English spellings, and become familiar with the mechanics of writing and the writing process.

Preparing to Use *Framework for Effective Teaching,* Grade 1 Book 1

Before you begin *Framework for Effective Teaching,* Grade 1, Book 1, you should do the following:

GET ACQUAINTED WITH THE INSTRUCTIONAL GOALS

A discussion of the goals of each of the key techniques or learning frameworks used in this guide can be found on the Learning Framework Cards in the Teacher Toolbox.

CHECK YOUR MATERIALS

Check to see that you have the following materials for each student:

- *Collections for Young Scholars®*, Volume 1, Book 1
- Phonics Minibooks 13–18
- Reading/Writing Connection: Volume 1, Book 1

In addition to this teacher's guide, you should also have the following teacher resources:

- Teacher Toolbox
- Phonemic Awareness and Phonics Kit

ORGANIZE YOUR MATERIALS AND SET UP YOUR CLASSROOM

- The **Teacher Toolbox** serves as easily accessible storage for your instructional materials. Unpack the materials (see page 28F) and use the dividers to organize the box.
- Display the **Sound/Spelling Cards** from the Phonemic Awareness and Phonics Kit. Place the first twenty-six cards above the chalkboard or along a wall, with only the back of each card visible. These cards form a model alphabet for the children to use during the first lessons.

  In lessons in which sound/spellings are introduced, you will be told to turn a particular card to display the picture side. Several cards have more than one spelling for a single sound. It is recommended that you cover all but the sound being introduced. You can do this with self-sticking notes.

  The remaining Sound/Spelling Cards will be introduced one at a time. You should display each card as it is introduced.

- Set up the **Phonics Minibook** display case. The books should be readily available so that the children can reread a particular title or titles as many times as they please.
- Check your **Workshop** materials and update and change them as necessary.
- Display the instructional posters. These posters remind the children of the reading strategies and stages of the writing process and serve as a constant aid to them as they read and write and engage in research.
- Provide space for a **Concept Board** (a bulletin board or chart paper attached to the wall) where you and the children can share your ideas, questions, and wonderings as you read and respond to selections.

GET ACQUAINTED WITH THE LESSON FORMAT

The thirty lessons in *Framework for Effective Teaching,* Grade 1, Book 1 are arranged into two units: Games and Folk Tales. Each lesson within a unit corresponds to about one day's teaching of approximately two to three hours.

Each unit opens with an introduction that provides background information about the unit concept. It also lists and annotates professional reference books to help you find additional information and read-alouds and audiovisual materials to share with the children. A list is also included of community/school resources, including people, agencies, and instruction that might be helpful to you. Following the introduction, there is an overview of the unit, charting the selections, new learning, link to the unit concept, and writing involved in each lesson.

Each lesson opens with an overview that lists any new learning that appears in the lesson, the materials needed, and any special preparation to be done in advance of a class. A Getting Started section contains brief, engaging activities that you can use to bring the children together and focus their attention for the learning that follows. As a rule, these activities quickly review and reinforce what the children have learned in previous lessons.

Activities in a lesson are arranged under three heads: Reading, Writing, and Guided and Independent Exploration. Under these headings, the lessons each contain the following:

Reading

- **Introduction of the final sound/spellings.** The Sound/Spelling Cards are used to introduce sound/spellings at the rate of about one per lesson. The introduction continues through all of *Thinking and Learning About Print,*

Part B and concludes in *Framework for Effective Teaching,* Grade 1, Book 1. A complete review of all the sound/spellings occurs in *Framework for Effective Teaching,* Grade 1, Book 2.

- **Direct instruction in blending of sound/spellings.** Blending activities continue through the *Framework for Effective Teaching,* Grade 1, Book 2.
- **Suggestions for reading the student anthology and the Phonics Minibooks.** Reading of selections from *Collections for Young Scholars,* Volume 1, Book 1 is tied to activities that familiarize the children with reading strategies and increase their book awareness. Reading of Phonics Minibooks is teacher-guided but also involves partner or individual reading. The reading of Phonics Minibooks reinforces the sound/spelling lesson being taught and leads the children to think about how the various sound/spellings, language and word structure systems work. Phonics Minibooks 13–18 are used with *Framework for Effective Teaching,* Grade 1, Book 1.

  The lesson also provides information about the author/illustrator of the anthology selection being read.

Writing

- **Dictation.** Interactive dictation provides important practice in fixing the sound/spelling associations and is a starting point for fluency in writing. Dictation occurs in a Word-Building game that the children play with Letter Cards. In odd-numbered lessons, whole words and sentences are dictated.
- **Suggestions for independent and collaborative writing.** Individual and collaborative writing activities familiarize the children with the formal writing process, including modified versions of prewriting, drafting, revising, proofreading, and publishing. Suggestions for possible writing projects are also included. **(See Learning Framework Card 10.)**

Guided and Independent Exploration

- **Suggestions for Workshop.** In Workshop, the children have opportunities to work independently, with partners, or in small groups. In addition, you are able to give extra attention to children who need it during this time. **(See Learning Framework Card 11.)**

PLANNING YOUR INSTRUCTION

In *Framework for Effective Teaching,* Grade 1, Book 1, the basics are always taught through direct, whole-class instruction. After that, instruction can be individualized to meet your needs and those of your students.

By this time, the children will be familiar with the procedures for presenting instruction. After initial whole-class presentations, they should now move readily into Workshop for small-group, work with partners, or independent work.

Work with the Teacher activities Every child will be in a small group with you at one time or another, and most children will need different kinds of instruction at different times. English Language Learners benefit especially from small-group activities.

Preteaching allows you to prepare children for a lesson to come. It also provides a way for you to give instruction in advance to children who might otherwise have difficulty during the regular whole-class presentation. **Reteaching** allows you to review a whole-class lesson with children who had difficulty with it. **Enrichment** sessions allow you to extend the content of a whole-class lesson for those who require additional challenges. These types of activities should be available at times to every child so that each can develop special interests and individual talents.

Collaborative/Independent activities At this point in the year, the children should have many options to choose from for both collaborative and independent work. Options for collaborative work should include partner reading or rereading of Phonics Minibooks and Step-by-Step Stories, listening to audiocassettes, and playing games. The children should be allowed to select their own independent activities. They should be able to choose from reading, writing in journals, and completing Activity Sheets.

You should also spend some time during each Workshop period listening to individual children read. They may read Step-by-Step Practice Stories, Phonics Minibooks (for which assessment checklists are available), the student anthology, trade books, or children's magazines.

Framework for Effective Teaching® Book 1

Games

UNIT INTRODUCTION

BACKGROUND INFORMATION FOR THE TEACHER

Play is an important aspect of childhood that is common to children of all societies. Everywhere in the world, children play certain traditional games unique to their own area or culture. It is often through play that young children "try on" the various roles of adulthood and learn important social skills. In addition, many games are passed down from parent to child, creating a link between past and present that brings the generations closer together.

There are an enormous variety of games in the world; indoor games, outdoor games, board games, word games, traditional children's pastimes such as Hide-and-Go-Seek and Kick the Can, games requiring complicated equipment, and games requiring only the player's imagination. There are games that develop physical skills and games that develop strategy and mental acumen. It is important for children to participate in many kinds of play activities. Through imaginative play, young children can experiment with different roles and learn to interact with their peers. Through word play they experiment with language, and through structured games they may learn about cooperation and the importance of following rules.

UNIT 1

In this unit, the children will read stories about a variety of characters who are engaged in everything from a relay race to a sidewalk game to a game of imagination. These selections are sure to get the children thinking about the many games they play. They will see that others play the same kinds of games and have the same kinds of feelings—the desire to participate, the wish to win or do well, and the joy of playing with a friend.

Encourage the children to tell about their own favorite games, what makes them fun, and what they may have learned while playing them. Have them compare their own experiences with games with those that they read about during this unit.

As you proceed through the unit, you may find it useful to think about such questions as the following:

- What are your own favorite games? What makes them fun?
- What kinds of things make it less fun to play a game?
- Are rules important?
- How important is winning? How important is losing?
- Who should be able to play?
- What does it mean to be a part of a team?
- What does it mean to be a good sport if you are losing? If you are winning?

Resources

Among the following resources are professional reference books, audiovisual materials, and community/school resources. The reference books are intended to help you develop the concepts and organize information to share with the children in whatever way you choose. The community/school resources include people, agencies, and institutions that may be helpful in your exploration.

In addition to the resources listed here, a bibliography appears in the student anthology. The children may want to use the bibliography to find other stories about games.

Professional Reference Books

Bernarde, Anita, *Games from Many Lands.* Lion, 1970. This guide includes instructions for twenty-three games played by children from China, the Congo, Russia, and other countries around the world.

Kaye, Peggy. *Games for Math.* Pantheon Books, 1987. Interesting, active games engage children in mathematical thinking and discovery.

Lankford, Mary D. *Hopscotch Around the World.* Morrow, 1992. This is a collection of hopscotch games from around the world, complete with rules and patterns.

Lappe, Frances Moore, and Family. *What to Do After You Turn Off the TV.* Ballantine Books, 1985. A guide to easy games and activities for parents and other adults to share with children.

Nelson, Esther. *Dancing Games for Children of All Ages.* Sterling Publishing Company, 1973. This book contains more than forty musical games and dances, including simple musical scores.

Rogers, Fred, and Head, Barry. *Mister Rogers' Playbook: Insights and Activities for Parents and Children.* Berkeley Books, 1986. Fred Rogers offers over 335 games and projects that children and adults can do together.

Zatopa, Patricia. *Simply Fun! A Book of Hand-Me-Down Games.* Explorer's Guide Publishing, 1991. An adult's guide to the rules and regulations for fifty-one games that have been handed down from generation to generation.

Read-Alouds

Ball, Duncan. *Jeremy's Tail.* Orchard Books, 1991. When Jeremy plays pin the tail on the donkey he travels out the door and around the world in his blindfold.

Brinkloe, Julie. *Playing Marbles.* Morrow, 1968. Three children play the ever-popular game of marbles.

Hutchins, Pat. *What Game Shall We Play?* Greenwillow, 1990. Seven animals search for their friends while wondering what they should play. Finally, a wise owl suggests a game they've been playing all along.

Russo, Marisabina. *Where Is Ben?* Greenwillow, 1990. A boy plays hide and seek with his mother while she tries to bake an apple pie.

Wisniewski, David. *Rain Player.* Clarion, 1991. After a drought is predicted, a young Mayan man challenges the god of rain to a game of pock-a-tok, a cross between soccer and basketball.

Audiovisual Materials

Dr. Seuss Beginner Book Videocassette: The Cat in the Hat Comes Back; Fox in Socks; There's a Wocket in my Pocket! Random House Home Video. The narrator encourages the viewer to "play the story game" using these popular Dr. Seuss stories. 30 minutes; videocassette.

A Rainbow of My Own. Don Freeman. Live Oak Media, 1991.
After a rainy afternoon spent playing games with an imaginary rainbow, a young boy returns home to find a real rainbow waiting for him. 5 minutes; videocassette.

Rainy Day Games. Macmillan Video Almanac for Kids, Volume 1. Caravatt Communications, 1985. A visual guide to fun rainy-day activities. Videocassette.

Community/School

- Physical education teacher
- Music teacher
- Representative from a park or recreation department

Concept Board

Provide a space in your classroom where you and the children can share your ideas, questions, and wonderings as you read and respond to the selections in the unit. This area will be called the Concept Board. It might be a bulletin board or a large sheet of chart paper attached to a wall. The Concept Board will be a place where you and the children can post any information about games that children gather and wish to share with classmates. This information might include written notes or stories, drawings, magazine or newspaper pictures and articles, or whatever they wish to add to illustrate their growing knowledge about games. From time to time you should direct the children's attention to the Concept Board and discuss the materials that are on it. After reading each selection, you should discuss what the children have learned that might be new or that they might not have thought of before. In addition, encourage them to express anything that they might be wondering about based on what they have read. Have them write, or dictate, their ideas and post them on the board. Review earlier information, particularly questions that the children may have had, to determine if they have new information they can add.

Learning Unit: Games

SELECTION	LINK TO THE UNIT CONCEPT	LESSON	NEW LEARNING	WRITING
Introduction, pages 9–16		1	/ō/ spelled ***oe***	Independent and Collaborative Writing
A Game Called Piggle, pages 17–41 humorous fiction written and illustrated by Crosby Bonsall	Word play can be a lot of fun.	2	/ō/ spelled ***ow***	Independent and Collaborative Writing
		3	/ō/ spelled ***oa***	Independent and Collaborative Writing
A Shared Reading Story ▲ **Jafta,** pages 42–61 realistic fiction by Hugh Lewin, illustrated by Lisa Kopper	Our imaginations can provide us with endless games.	4	/ū/ spelled _***ue*** and ***ew***	Minilesson: Revising
		5		Minilesson: Proofreading
The Big Team Relay Race, pages 62–94 humorous fiction by Leonard Kessler, illustrated by Linda Kelen	Group effort and team spirit are very important in playing certain games successfully.	6		Independent and Collaborative Writing
		7	/ow/ spelled ***ow***	Exploring the Writer's Craft
		8	/ow/ spelled ***ou***	Minilesson: Dialogue
Mary Mack, pages 95–109 a clapping rhyme illustrated by Bob Barner	**Mary Mack** is an easy-to-understand clapping rhyme that the children should learn quickly and enjoy.	9		Independent and Collaborative Writing
		10		Independent and Collaborative Writing
FINE ART pages 110–118 ***Untitled (Soapbox Racing)***, William H. Johnson; **Children playing games; Game board;** ***Ballplay of the Sioux on the St. Peters River in Winter***, Seth Eastman	People around the world and throughout time have played games, as recorded in the visual arts of those cultures.	11		Exploring the Writer's Craft
▲ ■ **Matthew and Tilly,** pages 119–148 realistic fiction by Rebecca C. Jones, illustrated by Beth Peck	Sometimes it is more fun playing games with others than alone. In sharing games, children may become good friends.	12	endings ***-er, -est***	Exploring the Writer's Craft
		13	/aw/ spelled ***aw*** and ***au***	Independent and Collaborative Writing
Unit Review, pages 149–155		14		Independent and Collaborative Writing

▲ **Full-length trade books** ■ **Dramatized on audiocassette**

LESSON 1

Lesson Overview

New Learning

- /ō/ spelled *oe*

Outlaw Word

bear

Materials

- Student Anthology, ***Collections for Young Scholars***™ Book 1, pages 10–11
- Sound/Spelling Card 35, Long O
- Learning Framework Cards 3, 4, 8
- Reading/Writing Connection, pages 1–2
- Activity Sheet 71

Prepare Ahead

- Large sheet of chart paper (see page 14)
- Scrambled Sentences game cards and answer keys (see page 15)

GETTING STARTED

Choose one or more of the following activities to focus the children's attention and to review some of the concepts they have been learning.

Sound Review Name a Sound/Spelling Card and call on a child to say the sound the card represents. The child should then give a word that contains the sound and identify where the sound is heard in the word. That child then names a new card and calls on another child to say the new sound and a new word. Continue in the same manner.

Identifying Rhymes Write three words on the chalkboard—one in the middle and the other two at the ends. Have the children say the words quietly to themselves and then point to the word that does not rhyme with the others. Ask the children to read the word aloud in unison at your signal. Use these words:

bug hug dog
hand hot sand
packer banker tanker
drag fox snag
fat mist fist
pickle tickle tackle
bubble button mutton
buggy mouse house

1 READING

PHONICS

Introduce /ō/ Spelled *oe* Review the spellings, *o* and *o_e* on Sound/Spelling Card 35, Long O. Point to the *oe* spelling and tell the children that this is another spelling for the long *o* sound.

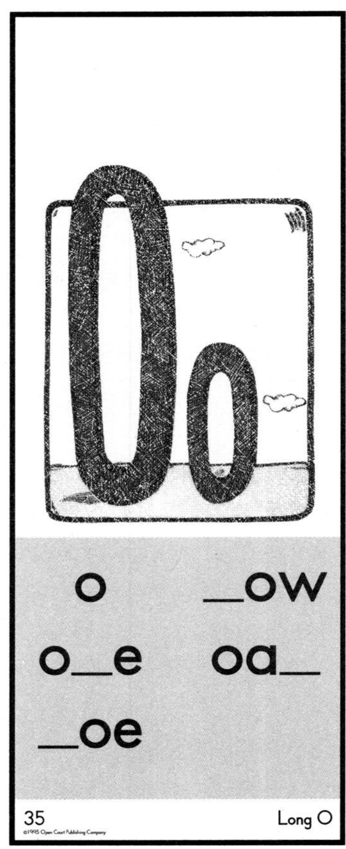

* **Blending** Have the children practice reading words with the *oe* spelling. You should write the words spelling by spelling and have the children say the sounds and blend them together as you build the word. When there is a sound whose spelling is represented by more than one letter, for example *o_e* and *oe*, write the entire spelling as a unit. In this way the children see the whole spelling that cues them to the sound before they make the sound. Talk about any words that may be unfamiliar to the children, and have the children use them in oral sentences.

Help the children blend the following words. A complete discussion of the blending procedure can be found on **Learning Framework Card 3.**

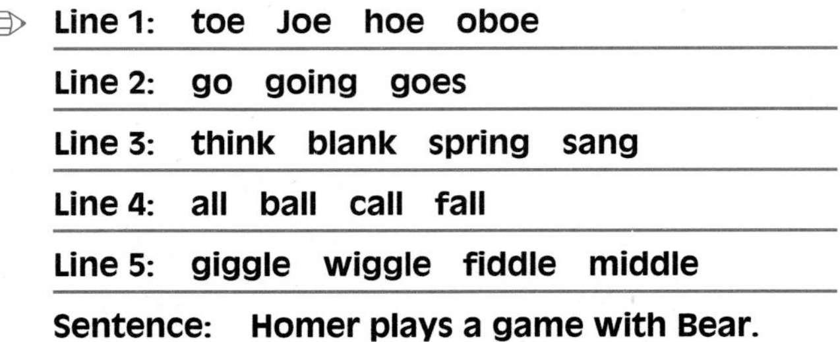

Line 1:	**toe Joe hoe oboe**
Line 2:	**go going goes**
Line 3:	**think blank spring sang**
Line 4:	**all ball call fall**
Line 5:	**giggle wiggle fiddle middle**
Sentence:	**Homer plays a game with Bear.**

MONITORING BLENDING In the next five lessons, observe six or seven children a day by calling on them individually to determine if they are able to blend words. In this lesson, check the blending of the words with /ō/ spelled *oe*. Record your observations in Teacher's Observation Log 3.

Words In line 2, have children underline the word *go* in *going* and *goes* and ask them to name the ending that has been added to make each word. Have children use each word in a sentence.

Have the children repeat the words in line 4 and name the spelling pattern they see *(all)*. Form other words with the *all* pattern by saying, "How can I make ______?" As the children give the spelling, write the new word on the chalkboard. Example words include *hall, tall, wall, small,* and *stall.*

Line 5 introduces words from the story "A Game Called Piggle." Focus first on *giggle* and *wiggle* and then on *fiddle* and *middle.*

Give a clue about one of the words; for example, "This word has the /g/ sound at the beginning and in the middle." Ask the child who correctly identifies the word to erase it; then that child will choose another word and give a clue for it. Continue with different children selecting the word and giving the clue each time.

Sentence Introduce the outlaw word *bear* by writing the word on the chalkboard. Touch the word and tell the children that this is the word *bear.* Have several children use the word in sentences. Then write one of these sentences on the chalkboard and underline *bear.* Have several children read the sentence.

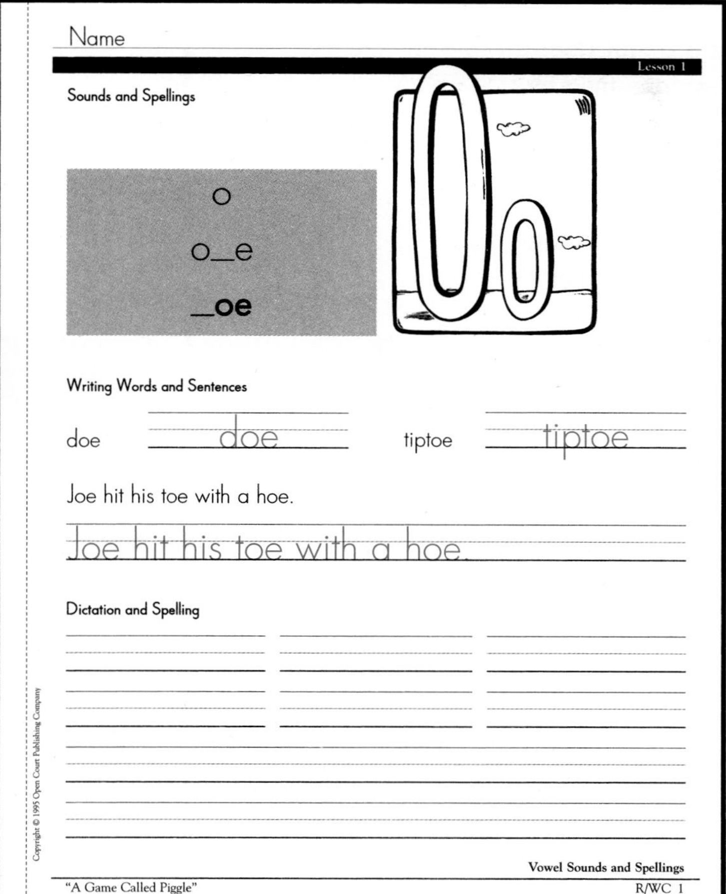

Name

Lesson 1

Sounds and Spellings

o
o_e
_oe

Writing Words and Sentences

doe — doe

tiptoe — tiptoe

Joe hit his toe with a hoe.

Joe hit his toe with a hoe.

Dictation and Spelling

Copyright © 1995 Open Court Publishing Company

Vowel Sounds and Spellings

"A Game Called Piggle" R/WC 1

Reading/Writing Connection, page 1

➤ Have the children open their Reading/Writing Connection book to page 1. Have them complete the top half of this page by reading and copying the words and the sentence.

✱ READING THE STUDENT ANTHOLOGY

UNIT PREVIEW BY THE CHILDREN
pages 10–11

Activating Prior Knowledge

Ask the children to think about the different kinds of games they play at home, outdoors, and in the classroom; and about games they play with their families, with other children, and by themselves. Ask the children to discuss their experiences with playing games. If necessary, remind them that some games involve words and that they have played games in class involving sounds and rhyming.

Setting Reading Goals and Expectations

With this unit, the children begin using the hardcover student anthology, *Collections for Young Scholars*®, Volume 1, Book 1. Take a few minutes to let them share the experience of beginning a "real book." Call their attention to the title page, the table of contents, and the page numbers. Then spend a little more time helping them to browse the first unit, Games.

Procedures for Browsing the Unit

- Turn to the unit opener on pages 10–11. Look first at the unit title and think about what it means and what kinds of selections may be in the unit.
- Look at the illustration on the unit opener pages. It may answer questions about the title or it may bring up more questions.
- Turn to the selections in the unit. Read the titles and quickly browse the selections, looking briefly at the illustrations and the print. Let the children report on and discuss things that they notice in their browsing and feel are important. Let them raise questions.

For a review of the procedures for browsing a unit, see **Learning Framework Card 8, Reading the Student Anthologies.**

When the children have had time to browse the unit and have shared their comments, ask them to return to pages 10–11, the unit opener. Use the illustration to initiate a discussion of the games the children recognize. Ask the children if they have played any of the games shown or if they have watched others play them. Identify any games that the children do not know.

Indicate the Concept Board and tell the children that this space will be used to keep track of what they know and what they learn about games as they read the selections. Mention that the children probably already know something about games. Ask them to name some games that they like to play or some games that they know about. Record any information the children share about games, such as games have rules, games have winners, or some games are played by teams.

Tell the children that they may draw, cut from magazines, or bring from home any pictures of people playing games that they would like to share with the class.

If the children have any questions or express wonder about some games, list these on the Concept Board.

➤ When the children have discussed the subject of games and browsed the unit selections, invite them to draw or write their thoughts about games on page 2 of their Reading/Writing Connection book.

When the children have completed this page, explain that throughout this unit they will be participating in activities that will extend their experiences and deepen and expand their knowledge of games. These exploratory activities may include writing, drama, art, and discussions.

TIP FOR ENGLISH LANGUAGE LEARNERS

Invite English Language Learners to share their experiences and provide new knowledge to other children. Encourage English Language Learners to talk about any game that is popular in their native country. Have them *say* the name of the game and tell how it is played. The children may wish to compare the game to one that is shown in the unit opener.

TEACHING TIP

It may be helpful to organize your Concept Board into two parts: first, new ideas; second, questions.

TEACHING TIP

Have the children do some partner reading daily. Using previously read Phonics Minibooks and Step-by-Step Practice Stories for this purpose will help the children review and solidify their knowledge of the sounds and spellings they have learned. This is a good opportunity to read with children individually and to record their progress.

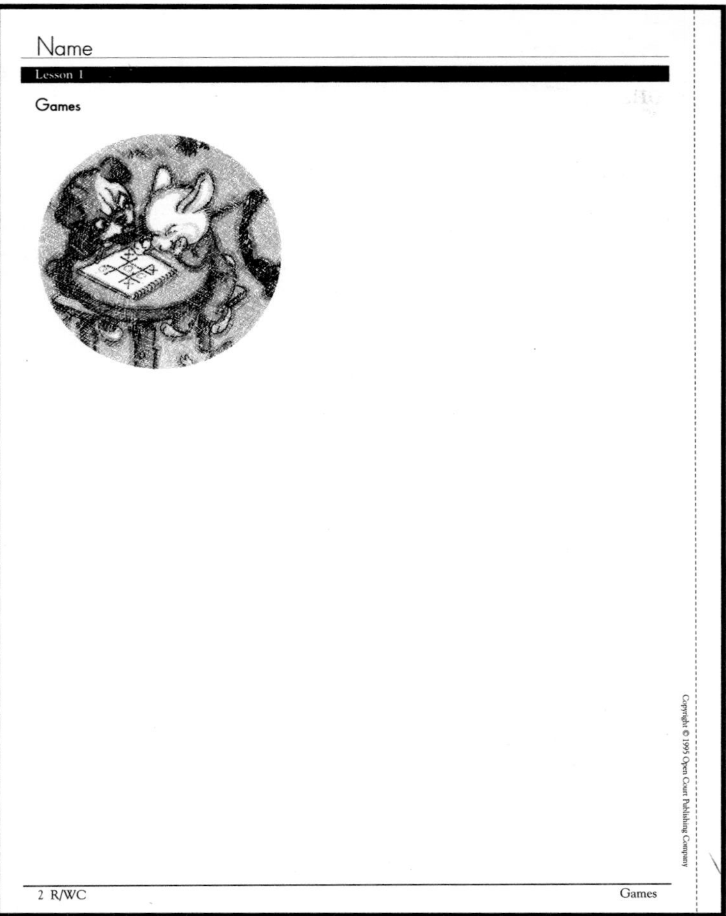
Name

Lesson 1

Games

Copyright © 1995 Open Court Publishing Company

2 R/WC Games

Reading/Writing Connection, page 2

2 WRITING

✱ DICTATION AND SPELLING

Have the children use the bottom of page 1 of their Reading/Writing Connection book to write the words and sentence you dictate. As you dictate each word, have the children repeat the word, think about the sounds that they hear in the word, check the Sound/Spelling Cards to be sure of the spelling, and write the word. When there are multiple spellings for a sound—as with long *o*—encourage the children to ask for help. If children are unsure, tell them which spelling to use.

Dictate the following words and sentence. Suggestions for dictation appear on **Learning Framework Card 4.**

Line 1: open over poet

Line 2: stone woke hope

Sentence: Steve told a joke.

Help the children proofread the words after completing each line. Remind them to circle any words or parts of words that could be better and to write them correctly above or beside the original word.

* INDEPENDENT AND COLLABORATIVE WRITING

The writing process involves a variety of activities: developing a topic, planning, drafting, revising, proofreading, and publishing. Emergent writers who use *Collections for Young Scholars*™ have been working on topic development, planning, writing, and publishing through a variety of independent and whole-class writing experiences. Discuss what the children have been doing so far in writing, and what the important writing activities are: developing topics, planning, and so on.

Writing in this unit will begin with a subject all children are familiar with—games. Games is a broad topic that gives a wide range of writing options. In order to help children better define their topics, the class will begin working on developing a game chart. Talk with the children about the value of charts and posters as a means of communicating information. Remind them of the charts that they use during reading to help them remember the strategies that good readers use.

Make a Games Chart To further illustrate that charts and posters can communicate information quickly and effectively, begin a class Games Chart. Start by having the children name their favorite games and list them on the board or on chart paper. If children seem to be at a loss, refer them to the Concept Board. Talk about some of the ideas noted there. Some children may even notice that the Concept Board is also a type of chart or poster.

In order to make this chart more useful, talk about categorizing the games in some way, for example, as indoor games, outdoor games, board games, card games, team games, or by any other groupings that the children suggest. You can do this as a simple set of lists, or create a web with the word *Games* in the center and categories and examples extending from the center.

Some children may want to copy ideas from the chart into their journals and some may want to add information not included on the chart.

By this point in the year, the children should be accustomed to working on their own. They should feel comfortable in choosing an activity or project to complete and in deciding whether to work on it independently or with a partner or group. Beginning with this lesson, the Workshop section of the lessons will no longer include separate suggestions for Student Collaboration and Independent Activities. Instead, these suggestions will appear together beneath the heading Collaborative/Independent Activities. The children should have a choice of working alone or with others, and many of the individual activities suggested here can actually be completed either alone or in pairs or groups. In addition to the activities we suggest, the children always have the option of reading or writing during Workshop. An Activity Sheet will be provided with each lesson; however, as many children as possible should be engaged in real reading or writing activities during this time. Feel free to choose from among these suggestions based upon the needs of your children.

3 GUIDED AND INDEPENDENT EXPLORATION

WORKSHOP

Remind the children that they may use this time to work on projects on their own or in small groups. Be sure that each child knows what projects he or she may choose and how to complete any independent work. Suggestions for teacher-guided, collaborative, and independent activities follow.

Learning Framework Card 11, Workshop, contains a complete discussion of establishing and conducting Workshop and suggestions for helping English Language Learners during Workshop.

Work with the Teacher

- Repeat today's Blending exercise with a small group of children. Encourage them to read each word as a whole word. Ask volunteers to underline the letter or letters that make the long *o* sound in each long *o* word.
- Preteach the *ow* spelling of the /ō/ sound to children who need extra help with learning new sounds and spellings. Point to Sound/Spelling Card 35, Long O, and review the three spellings the children already know for the /ō/ sound: *o* as in *go; o_e* as in *tone,* and *_oe* as in *hoe.* Call on volunteers to give additional words that contain these spellings of the /ō/ sound. Then introduce the *_ow* spelling. Write on the chalkboard several words in which /ō/ is spelled *_ow;* underline the spelling in each word and then with the children, blend the words.
- Read tomorrow's anthology selection, "A Game Called Piggle," pages 12–19, with those children who may have difficulty with this first experience in reading from the student anthology.

Collaborative/Independent Activities

- Pairs of children can reread Phonics Minibook 11, "Dog Dreams." Remind them to follow the usual procedure for reading in pairs. Encourage them to help each other blend difficult words.
- Working alone or with others, children can list all the words they can think of that contain the /ō/ sound spelled *o, o_e,* or *_oe.* They may look through books for these words. They should then use some of these words in sentences and illustrate the sentences. Challenge them to include words with all three spellings in one sentence. Allow time for them to share their sentences and illustrations with their classmates.
- Before Workshop begins, prepare new Scrambled Sentences games, using some of the words from recent Blending and Dictation lessons. Distribute the new games to groups or individuals who are interested in playing today. Remind them that their goal is to form meaningful sentences by arranging word cards in the correct order. Tell the children to copy the completed sentences on scratch paper and check their work against the answer keys located inside the game envelopes. As an option, two or more children or groups can race to complete the first sentence.
- Distribute Activity Sheet 71 and tell the children that they can complete this page by reading the words and writing them in the correct column: inside the bottle if the word is something relating to a baby, inside the footprint if the word is a body part, or inside the sailboat if the word has to do with water.
- As always, encourage the children to read or browse books independently. Invite them to revisit their favorite Big Book selections in their small versions of the Big Books. They may be surprised at the number of words they can now read on their own!

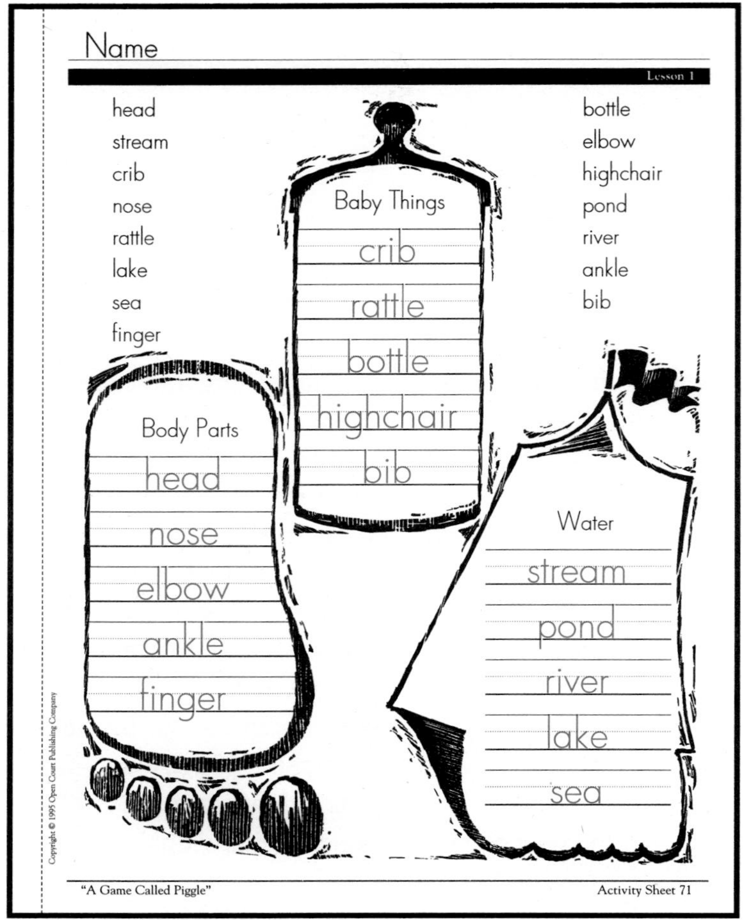

Name
Lesson 1
head
stream
crib
nose
rattle
lake
sea
finger
bottle
elbow
highchair
pond
river
ankle
bib
Baby Things
crib
rattle
bottle
highchair
bib
Body Parts
head
nose
elbow
ankle
finger
Water
stream
pond
river
lake
sea
"A Game Called Piggle"
Activity Sheet 71

Activity Sheet 71

LESSON 2

Lesson Overview

New Learning

- /ō/ spelled *ow*

Outlaw Words

give, some

Materials

- "A Game Called Piggle," pages 12–19
- Sound/Spelling Card 35, Long O
- Learning Framework Cards 3, 8
- Reading/Writing Connection, pages 3–4
- Activity Sheet 72
- Home/School Connection 14

GETTING STARTED

Choose one or more of the following activities to focus the children's attention and to review some of the concepts they have been learning.

Long Sound/Short Sound Spellings Use this activity to review the /ō/ spellings the children have learned so far. Write one word on the chalkboard at a time. Have the children read the word quietly to themselves. Tell them that if the word contains a long *o* sound, they should hold their arms out to their sides. If the word contains a short *o* sound, they should hold their hands close together in front of them. After the children have done this, ask them to read the word aloud in unison. You might want to use some of the following words:

rope	over	note
pop	soft	lock
hoe	close	

Long Vowel Spelling Review This activity will review some of the spellings of long vowel sounds the children have learned so far. Divide the class into two teams. On both ends of the chalkboard, write the following words:

tray	speed	open
slide	go	heap
cry	tape	
clue	rude	

TEACHING TIP

After you write the word on the board, count quietly, 1, 2, 3, so all children will have time to read the words.

(If you have more than twenty students, you should include additional words with long vowel sound/spellings.) Tell the children that you will say a sound and that one child from each team should go to the board, circle a word with that sound, and underline the letter or letters that spell that sound. For each sound that the children identify correctly, their team receives a point. At the end of the activity, point to each of the words one by one and have the children read them aloud in unison.

1 READING

PHONICS

Introduce /ō/ Spelled *ow* Point to Sound/Spelling Card 35, Long O, and ask what sound this card represents. Have the children tell about the spellings they have learned for the sound /ō/. Point to the *ow* spelling and tell the children that this is another way to spell the long sound of *o*.

* **Blending** Have the children blend the following words. A complete discussion of the blending procedure can be found on **Learning Framework Card 3.**

Line 1:	snow blow flow grow
Line 2:	grown shown stone cone
Line 3:	tow toe rowed rode
Line 4:	owner elbow shadow window
Line 5:	pillow yellow follow shallow
Sentence 1:	Give me more time to think.
Sentence 2:	Homer wants to piggle some more.

Words In line 2 have the children compare the two spellings for the sound /ō/. Have children underline the spelling for /ō/ in each word.

In line 3, draw attention to the homophones *tow* and *toe*. Discuss the meaning of each and have children use each in a sentence. As a child gives a sentence, point to the word and show the spelling that matches the meaning. Repeat with the homophones *rowed* and *rode*. Ask the children if they know another kind of /r/ /ō/ /d/. When they suggest the word *road*, write it on the chalkboard and have a child use it in a sentence.

In line 4, blend the words in syllables—*own—er, el—bow*. As the children blend the words in line 5, help them notice that the spelling /ow/ is in the last syllable of each of these words.

To review the words, have the children point to the words that complete some sentences. Example sentences are

The flowers in the garden have______ tall.
The guide ______ the boat down the river.
The ______ truck took the car to the garage.
At the lake, I swam in the ______ water.
I bend my arm at the ______.

Sentences Introduce the outlaw words *give* and *some* before writing the sentences on the board. Write the word *give* on the board and read it to the children. Call on children to use it in a sentence. Then write the first sentence on the board, underlining the new word *give.* Repeat the procedure with the word *some.*

➤ Have the children turn to page 3 of their Reading/Writing Connection books. Help them complete this page.

Reading/Writing Connection, page 3

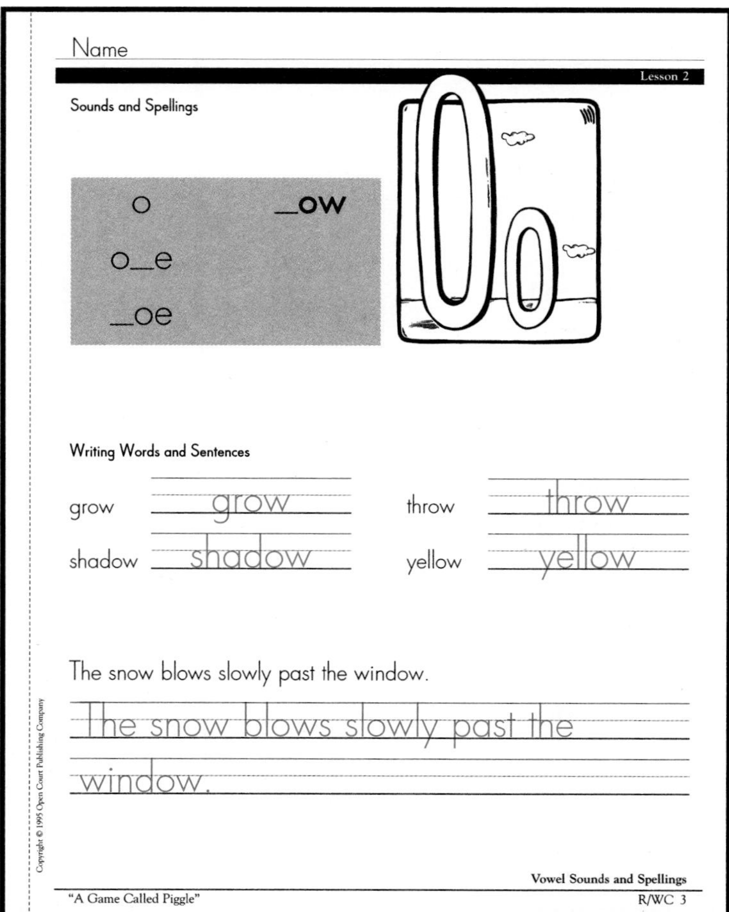

Name

Lesson 2

Sounds and Spellings

o
o_e
_oe
_ow

Writing Words and Sentences

grow grow
throw throw
shadow shadow
yellow yellow

The snow blows slowly past the window.

The snow blows slowly past the window.

Vowel Sounds and Spellings

"A Game Called Piggle" R/WC 3

✱ READING THE STUDENT ANTHOLOGY

"A Game Called Piggle"
pages 12–19

About the Selection

What child wouldn't want to have Bear as a friend? Not only does Bear agree to play a game called Piggle with Homer, he also shows Homer just how to play this rhyming game. Homer catches on, and so will the children as they read this charming excerpt from *Piggle.* The warm friendship shared by Bear and Homer is communicated not only by the text but also by the delightful illustrations.

Link to the Unit Concept

In "A Game Called Piggle," the children learn about one type of game that can be played with words. As Bear and Homer play Piggle, it becomes obvious that word play can be a lot of fun.

About the Author/Illustrator

Crosby Bonsall has distinguished herself as both an author and illustrator of children's books. Besides *Piggle,* the book from which this selection is taken, Bonsall's many books for beginning readers include *And I Mean It, Stanley; Mine's the Best;* and *The Case of the Scaredy Cats.* In "A Game Called Piggle," as in many of her other works, the world of childhood is depicted as a place filled with wonder, humor, imagination, and joy. Bonsall's heartwarming illustrations are a perfect complement to this sweet and simple story.

Activating Prior Knowledge

Begin by asking the children if they have ever played any word games. Have them open their readers to page 12. Read the selection title aloud. Explain that this story comes from a book called *Piggle*; ask whether anyone has read this book. If some children have already read *Piggle,* ask them not to tell what the game of Piggle is just yet, so that their classmates can figure it out on their own as they read the story.

Setting Reading Goals and Expectations

In this program, the children use reading strategies that help them to become better readers. Browsing a text before reading it is an important strategy. Explain to the children that good readers look over the text and pictures of a book or story before reading it in order to get ideas of what the book or story is about and to think about what problems they might have in reading the book or story. You might want to point out the poster Setting Reading Goals and Expectations and read it with the children at this time.

Model the browsing procedure by talking about what you notice in the text and pictures as you look through the story. Invite the children to contribute their own observations about the story while browsing. At the end of this discussion, think aloud about your purpose for reading by saying something like the following: *I wonder how this game called Piggle is played. Maybe I can find out by reading the story.* For a review of information about browsing a selection, see **Learning Framework Card 8, Reading the Student Anthologies.**

Recommendations for Reading

Have the story read aloud. Begin by calling on volunteers to each read several sentences as other children read along silently. Then call on volunteers to read longer passages and invite the children to chime in on rhymes or to comment on anything in the story that puzzles or surprises them.

If children are having difficulty blending any of the words, remind them to check the Sound/Spelling Cards. If any words cannot be easily blended, pronounce the words for the children.

Note: Partner reading of the story is a good option for Workshop.

TEACHING TIP

If necessary, tell the children the following words: *now, sounds,* and *know.* The children have not yet learned all the sounds and spellings contained in these words.

About the Reading Strategies

In reading this selection, children can use the reading strategy for wondering, something young children do all the time in daily life. Explain that you will model this strategy as you read this selection together.

Think-Aloud Prompts for Use in Oral Reading Notice the think-aloud prompts with the page miniatures. As with the prompts that appeared with the Big Book selections, these are merely suggestions. Continue to model using appropriate strategies while reading and to encourage children to use the strategies on their own. For a review of information about modeling and generating think-alouds, see **Learning Framework Card 8, Reading the Student Anthologies.**

STRATEGIC
R·E·A·D·I·N·G
PROMPTS
These prompts may be used as guides when working with reading strategies.

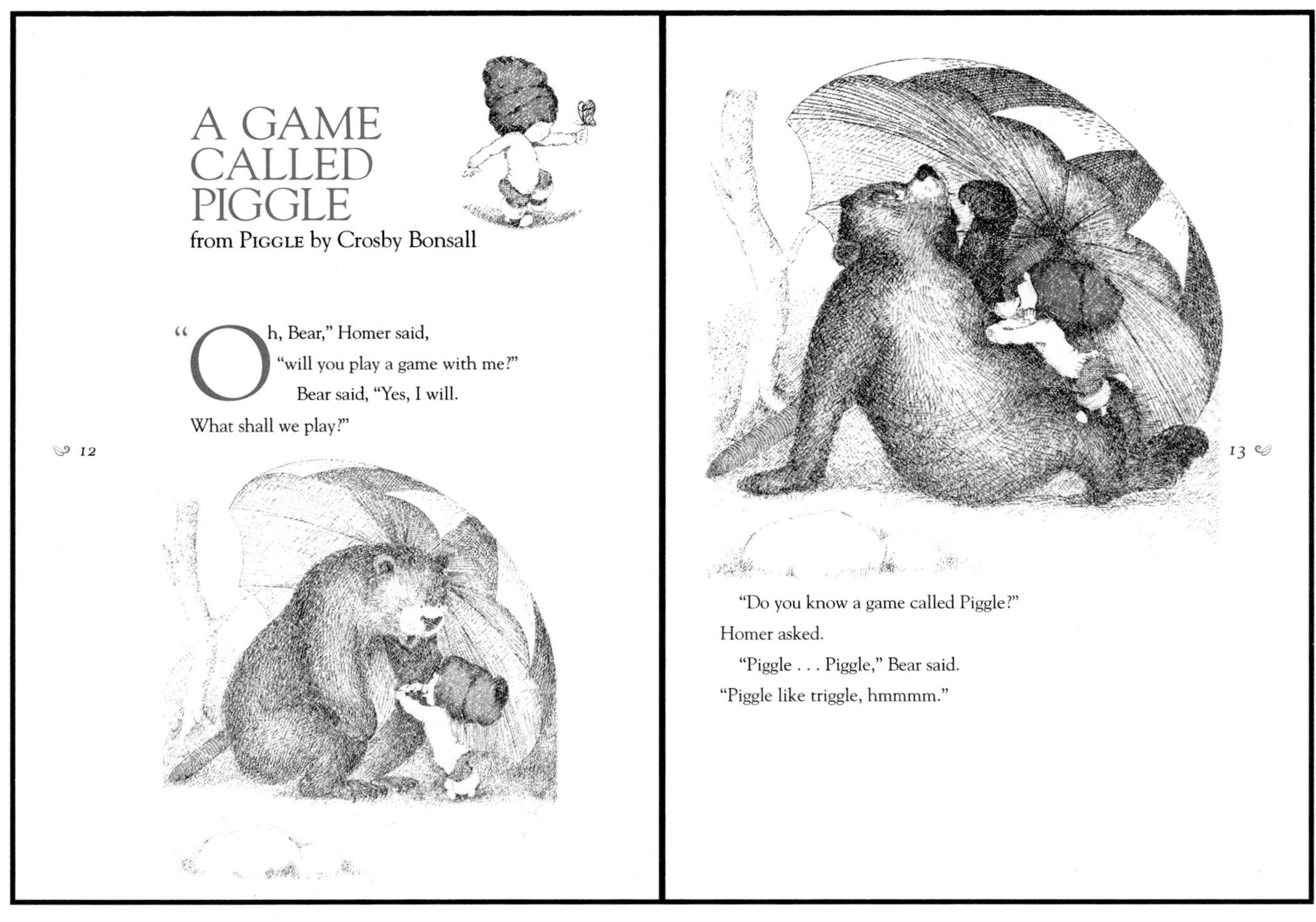
A GAME CALLED PIGGLE
from PIGGLE by Crosby Bonsall
"Oh, Bear," Homer said, "will you play a game with me?" Bear said, "Yes, I will. What shall we play?"
12
13
"Do you know a game called Piggle?" Homer asked.
"Piggle . . . Piggle," Bear said. "Piggle like triggle, hmmmm."

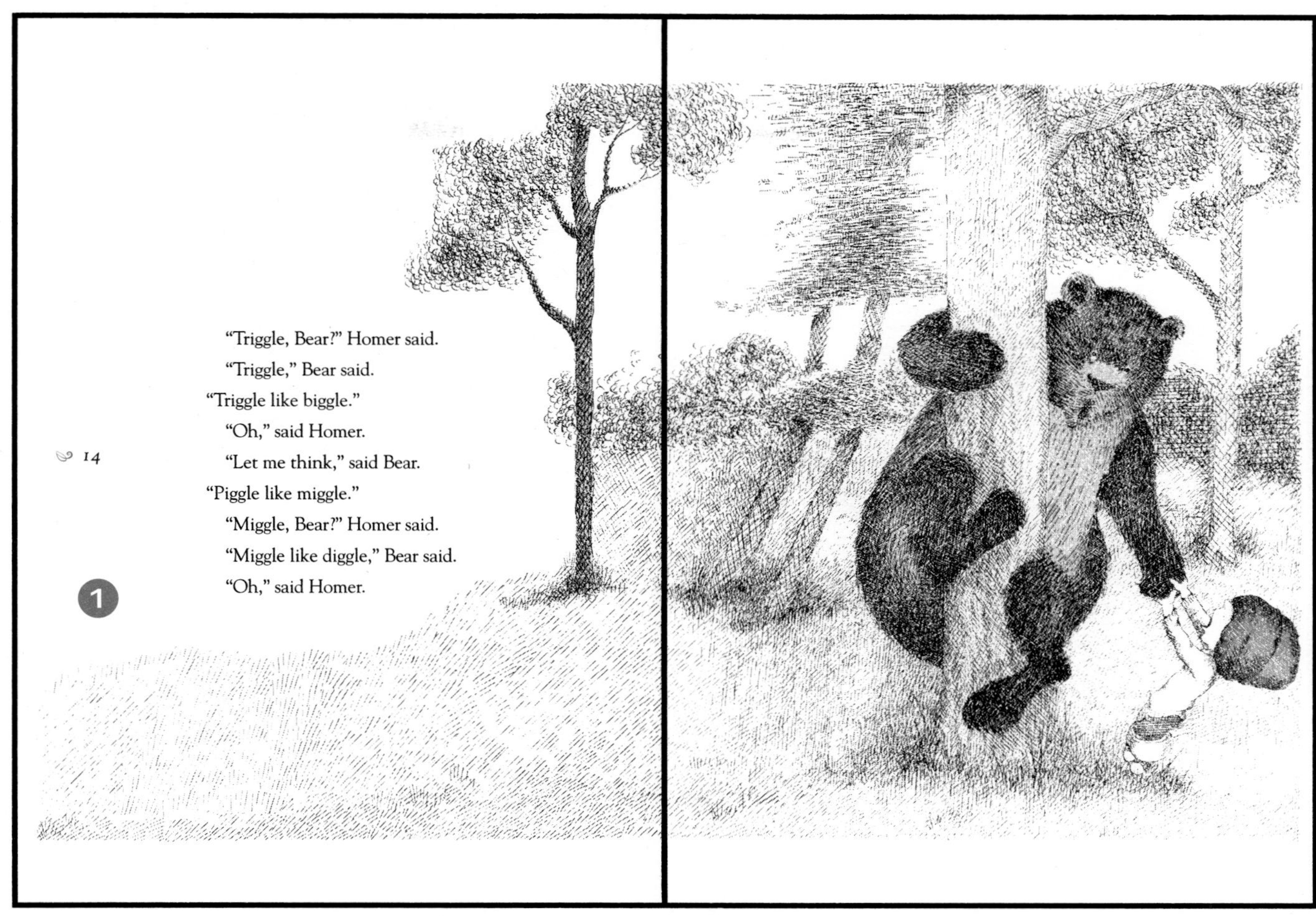

"Triggle, Bear?" Homer said.
"Triggle," Bear said.
"Triggle like biggle."
"Oh," said Homer.
"Let me think," said Bear.
"Piggle like miggle."
"Miggle, Bear?" Homer said.
"Miggle like diggle," Bear said.
"Oh," said Homer.

14

1 If necessary, model **wondering** by saying: *I wonder what kind of game they're playing here.*

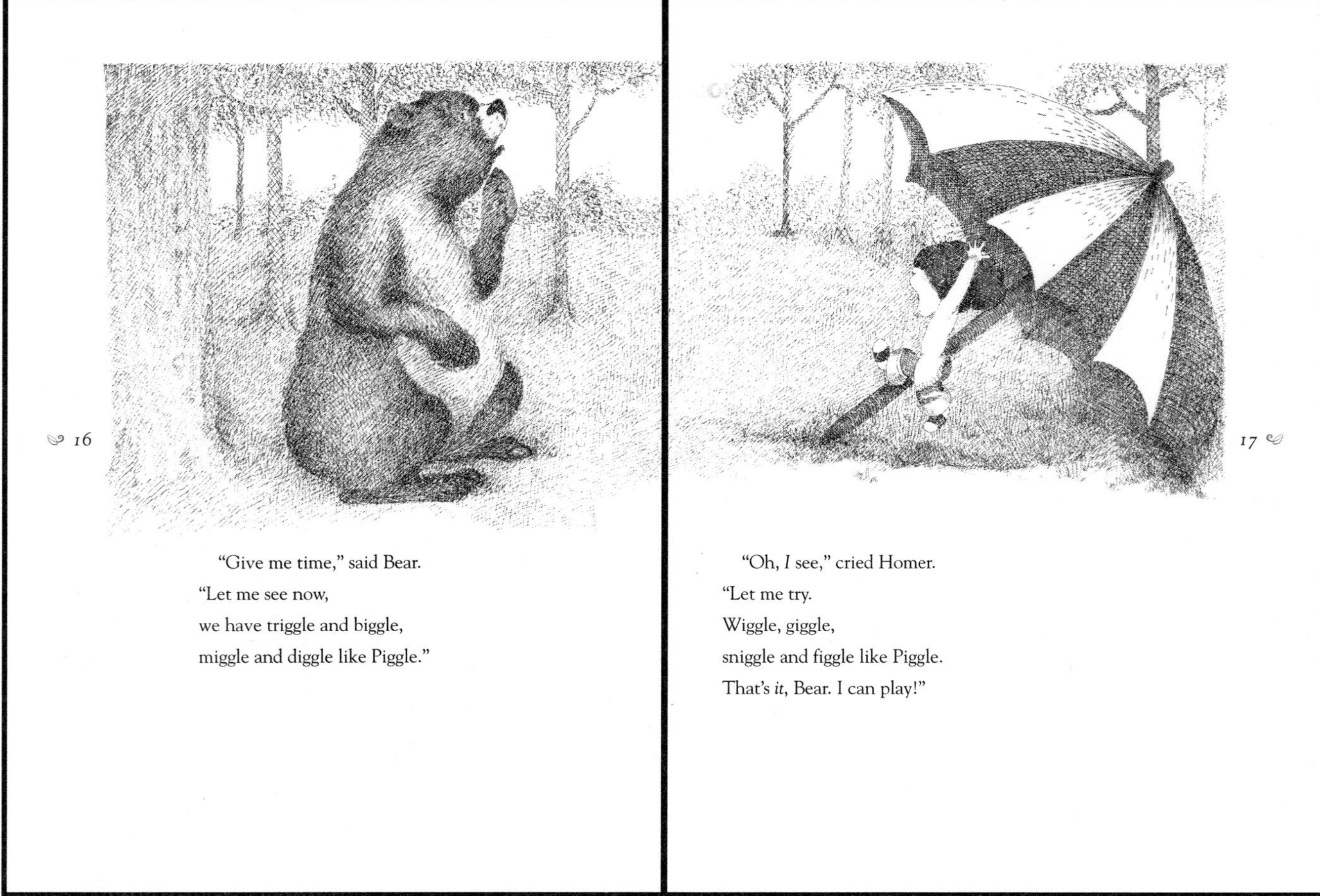

16

"Give me time," said Bear.
"Let me see now,
we have triggle and biggle,
miggle and diggle like Piggle."

17

"Oh, *I* see," cried Homer.
"Let me try.
Wiggle, giggle,
sniggle and figgle like Piggle.
That's *it*, Bear. I can play!"

"Yes, you can," cried Bear.
"Maybe I know the game of Piggle
after all. It sounds nice."
"Yes, it does," Homer said.
"Let's piggle some more.
Ishy, wishy, fishy, dishy."
Bear sang, "Diddley, widdley,
fiddley, riddley."
And together they sang,
18 "Mumpity, wumpity,
dumpity, lumpity."

Responding to the Selection

- Ask the children what they noticed about the words in the story. The children may mention the dialogue, the punctuation marks, the song that Bear and Homer sing, or other aspects of the text. If no one mentions the rhyming words, have the children look at the words *triggle, biggle, miggle, diggle,* and *Piggle* on page 16. Ask: *How are the ends of these words alike?*
- Invite a volunteer to explain how to play Piggle. Children may be able to list one or two rules for playing this game. You may wish to write these rules on the chalkboard.
- Encourage the children to talk about what new things they have learned about games in this story and things they might not have thought of before. You might add this information to the Concept Board.

➤ Help the children complete page 4 of their Reading/Writing Connection books. They should choose the word that completes each sentence and write it in the blank.

Reading/Writing Connection, page 4

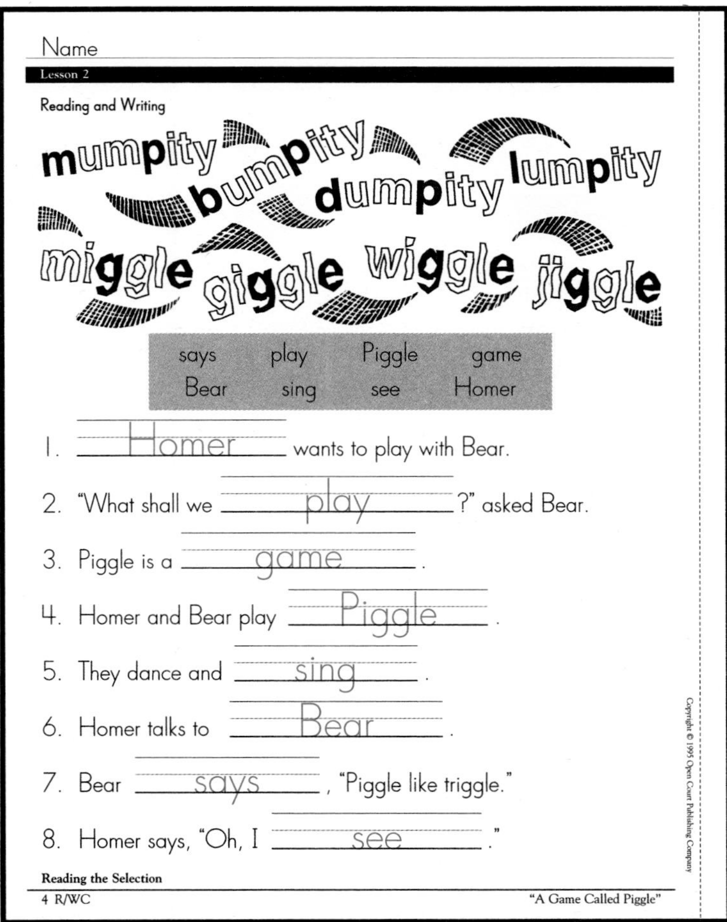

Name

Lesson 2

Reading and Writing

mumpity bumpity dumpity lumpity

miggle giggle wiggle jiggle

says	play	Piggle	game
Bear	sing	see	Homer

1. Homer wants to play with Bear.
2. "What shall we play?" asked Bear.
3. Piggle is a game.
4. Homer and Bear play Piggle.
5. They dance and sing.
6. Homer talks to Bear.
7. Bear says, "Piggle like triggle."
8. Homer says, "Oh, I see."

Reading the Selection

4 R/WC "A Game Called Piggle"

✱ READING ALOUD

Be sure to set aside time later in the day for reading aloud. If the children enjoyed this excerpt from *Piggle,* you may wish to read the entire book to them. *The Day I Had to Play with My Sister* is another book by Crosby Bonsall that deals with a game, Hide-and-Seek.

2 WRITING

✱ DICTATION AND SPELLING

Word-Building Game The children should use pencil and paper to build the following words. Remind them to write the words in a column. The column format allows children to make maximum use of what they have already done to help them write the next word.

Pronounce the first word and have the children write it as you write at the board. The children should check and correct their word. Then pronounce the next word in the list and have the children write it below the first, reminding them that the first word will help them write the new one. You should write the new word on the board. Continue on through the list.

bow
bowl
bold
hold
hole
hope
hoe

INDEPENDENT AND COLLABORATIVE WRITING

Revisit the chart or web begun yesterday. Read with the children the information they included and see if there is any additional information they would like to add. To help children get ready for writing their own piece about a game, have the class select a familiar game from the chart, for example, Statues. Talk about what important information they would need to tell someone who has never played this game before. This may include the type of game (indoor/outdoor), the number of players, the purpose of the game, and how to play it. Set up a planning web with the game in the center and then have the children talk about what important things they should include when writing about this game. Alternatively, you may want to set this up as a chart rather than a web. It may look something like this:

Outdoor Games

Name	Number of Players	Purpose	How to Play

Once this planning has been done, refer children back to the chart and have them choose a game they would like to write about. In order to plan their writing, they may want to make a web for their game, use the headings on the chart, or draw a picture.

As the children are working on their plan, confer with them. Conferencing provides an opportunity to support children throughout the various aspects of the writing process, to help them solve problems, and to receive feedback. Ask questions that will help children elaborate on their ideas. Are there any special rules for this game? I've never heard of this game. Can you tell me more about it? What is special about this game that I need to know? Why do you like this game so much? Conferencing is also a perfect opportunity for observing children and their understanding of the writing process.

3 GUIDED AND INDEPENDENT EXPLORATION

WORKSHOP

Remind the children that they may use this time to work on projects on their own or in small groups. Be sure that each child knows what projects he or she may choose and how to complete any independent work. Suggestions for teacher-guided, collaborative, and independent activities follow.

Work with the Teacher

- Preteach Phonics Minibook 13, *The Snow Game,* to children who may have difficulty reading the story on their own.
- Invite individual children to read aloud to you from books or magazines that they are reading for pleasure.
- Review long vowel spellings for children who need additional support. You may want to use words that will be used in the Reading Relay game in Getting Started, Lesson 3.

Collaborative/Independent Activities

- A small group of children may enjoy making a Piggle Dictionary. This project will probably take two to four days to complete, depending on how many children work on it. Have each child select a nonsense word from "A Game Called Piggle," pages 12–19 in the student anthology, and copy that word on a sheet of paper. (If there are more children than nonsense words, the children can make up some "Piggle-esque" words of their own to use.)
- Suggest that children reread "A Game Called Piggle" with a partner. Tell them that one partner should read everything that Bear says and the other should read everything that Homer says. When they finish reading, they can trade parts and read the story one more time.
- Groups of three or more children might enjoy trying the game called Piggle. To structure the game, tell the children to play as follows. Two children start the game. One calls out the first word, the second calls out a rhyming word, and they play back and forth until one player gets stumped or calls out a rhyme that has already been used. (The rest of the group can act as "referees.") The other player then gets to start a new round by picking a new partner and calling out a new word. Play continues in this fashion until everyone has had a turn, at which point the children may start over if they wish.
- Challenge individuals or pairs of children to draw a picture of a person and label each body part that contains the /ō/ sound.
- Distribute Activity Sheet 72 and invite the children to play their own game of Piggle. Tell them to read the series of words on each line at the top of the page and to write a fourth word that fits the Piggle scheme. They should then check the appropriate box to see whether the word they wrote was a real or a nonsense word. At the bottom of the page, the children can continue to play by writing three words that rhyme with each word provided. The last line gives the children an opportunity to use their own name in the game.

Home School Connection

Distribute Home/School Connection 14. This letter introduces the Games unit to the children's families and gives suggestions for activities and reading children can do with their families.

Name

Lesson 2

Play Piggle

		real	not real
(Student answers will vary.) hop, top, mop			
lunch, bunch, crunch			
lumpy, bumpy, dumpy			

hoppity

wiggly

(your name)

Activity Sheet 72

LESSON 3

Lesson Overview

New Learning

- /ō/ spelled ***oa***

Materials

- "A Game Called Piggle," pages 12–19
- Phonics Minibook 13, ***The Snow Game***
- Sound/Spelling Card 35, Long O
- Learning Framework Cards 3, 4, 6
- Reading/Writing Connection, pages 5–6
- Activity Sheet 73

Prepare Ahead

- Flip a Sound lid (see page 30)
- Reading Relay Flash Cards—/ō/ spellings (see page 30)

GETTING STARTED

Choose one or more of the following activities to focus the children's attention and to review some of the concepts they have been learning.

Flip a Sound Game Place Letter Cards *a, e, i, o, u* in a container. Using a marker, write *long* and *short* on opposite sides of a plastic lid. Children flip the lid and choose a card. They must say a word with the chosen vowel's long or short sound as indicated by the lid.

Reading Relay Game Form two teams of children in which the players on each team sit one behind the other. Make sufficient flash card words so that there is one card for each child. Words that review the /ō/ spellings include:

toe	jolt	pole	tone	Joe	cope
bowl	poem	nose	fold	row	most
so	doe	roll	hoe	bow	old
sore	below	cold			

To play the game, the first child on the team picks up a word card, reads the word, then takes the card and goes to the end of the line. If a child reads the word incorrectly, the opposite team has an opportunity to say the word. The teams take turns choosing a card and blending and saying the word. The game ends when all the members on one team have successfully read a word.

1 READING

PHONICS

Some of your students may not have mastered all the long vowel spellings. Some may have difficulty blending with these. This is normal. It is important that you not wait for mastery of each spelling before going on to the next. Students will have many opportunities to practice using these sounds and multiple spellings.

* **Introduce /ō/ Spelled *oa*** Point to Sound/Spelling Card 35, Long O, and ask the children what they know about the card. Point to the spelling *oa* and tell the children that this is another way to spell the long *o* sound. Quickly review all the spellings.

* **Blending** Help the children blend the following words. A complete discussion of the blending procedure can be found on **Learning Framework Card 3.**

MONITORING BLENDING Continue the observations started in Lesson 1 by observing six or seven children as they blend /ō/ words. Record your observations in Teacher's Observation Log 3.

Line 1:	**goat boat coat float**
Line 2:	**soap toad coast road**
Line 3:	**toe cold hole snow coal**
Line 4:	**cocoa blows oars soak**
Line 5:	**nuzzle grumble cuddly actually**

After the children sound and blend the words in line 3, call individual children to the chalkboard to underline the different spellings for /ō/. Encourage the children to refer to Sound/Spelling Card 35, Long O.

Line 5 introduces words from *Jafta,* which will be read in the next lesson. Point out the double consonant spellings in the words and the *-le* and *-ly* endings. The children may have some difficulty blending *actually*. They should adjust their pronunciation once they recognize the word.

Review the words using a sponge die labeled with the numbers 1–5 and one star. Tell a child to choose a word line and then roll the die. He or she should read the word in the line that matches the number rolled. If a star is rolled, the child can read any word in the line. Continue passing the die to other children.

➤ Reading/Writing Connection, page 5, provides additional practice with the long *o* sound spelled *oa*. Work with the children to complete the top part of the page.

Name

Lesson 3

Sounds and Spellings

o _ow
o_e **oa_**
_oe

Oo

Writing Words and Sentences

soap soap toast toast

A toad sat on the boat.

A toad sat on the boat.

Dictation and Spelling

Vowel Sounds and Spellings

"A Game Called Piggle" R/WC 5

Reading/Writing Connection, page 5

✻ READING THE STUDENT ANTHOLOGY

"A Game Called Piggle"
pages 12–19

Activating Prior Knowledge

Have the children turn to page 12 in their anthologies. Then ask the children what they remember about this story from the reading they did yesterday.

Recommendations for Reading

- Have the children look over the story silently. Then invite volunteers to each read aloud several sentences or a page from "A Game Called Piggle." Encourage the children to chime in on the rhyming words during the oral reading.
- After each page has been read aloud, invite volunteers to identify all the rhyming words on that page. Also, have the children point out anything else they noticed about the words in the story.

Responding

- Invite several volunteers to explain or demonstrate how they would teach the game to someone else. Have the children compare their

TEACHING TIP

Partner reading of the story is a good option for Workshop. You, too, should choose a child to read with. As you read with each child, note his or her progress.

methods with the one Bear uses to teach the game to Homer. You might add this information to the Concept Board.

- Encourage the children to play Piggle with their own names or with words from the story. Remind them that when piggling, they may use any rhyming words, either real or invented.
- Discuss whether this is a real story or a make-believe story and why.

Vocabulary Discuss with the children any words or phrases used in interesting or unusual ways in the selection. Ask children to use these words and phrases in oral sentences. These words or phrases may be posted on a bulletin board or chart for the children to use in their own writing. Suggest that the children might keep their own list of words in their journals. Words from "A Game Called Piggle" might include *game, hmmmm,* and *think.*

➤ Reading/Writing Connection, page 6, focuses on sequence words. Read the rhymes with the children, then explain that the sentences below each rhyme retell the story in the rhyme, but in a mixed up way. The children should decide what order the sentences should follow, then write in the word from the box that will help explain the order in which things happened.

Reading/Writing Connection, page 6

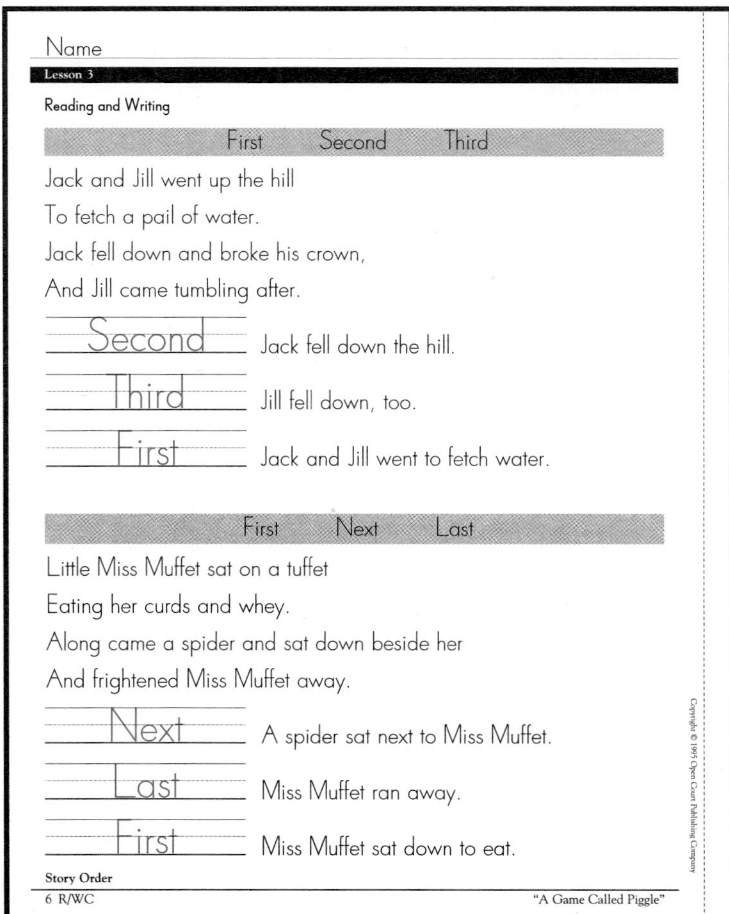

Name

Lesson 3

Reading and Writing

First Second Third

Jack and Jill went up the hill
To fetch a pail of water.
Jack fell down and broke his crown,
And Jill came tumbling after.

Second Jack fell down the hill.

Third Jill fell down, too.

First Jack and Jill went to fetch water.

First Next Last

Little Miss Muffet sat on a tuffet
Eating her curds and whey.
Along came a spider and sat down beside her
And frightened Miss Muffet away.

Next A spider sat next to Miss Muffet.

Last Miss Muffet ran away.

First Miss Muffet sat down to eat.

Story Order

6 R/WC "A Game Called Piggle"

Copyright © 1995 Open Court Publishing Company

✻ READING ALOUD

Be sure to set aside time later in the day for reading aloud. You may wish to share one or more of the following books with the children.

The Snowy Day by Ezra Jack Keats
Summer Snowman by Gene Zion
The Winter Picnic by Robert Welber

After reading one or more of these books, ask the children to talk about games they have played or fun things they have done—or would like to do—in the snow. After discussing these, children may want to add new ideas or questions on to the Concept Board.

✻ READING A PHONICS MINIBOOK

The Snow Game
Phonics Minibook 13

Getting Ready to Read

Allow the children to look through the book, commenting on what they see in the pictures and what they think the story will be about.

Recommendations

Have the children read a page of the story to themselves, then call on a different child to read each page of the story aloud. If a child has difficulty with a word, follow the procedures shown on **Learning Framework Card 6, Reading the Step-by-Step Practice Stories and the Phonics Minibooks.** Reread the story at least twice, calling on different children to read.

Printed in the United States of America

ISBN 0-8126-1283-3

10 9 8 7 6 5 4 3 2 1

2

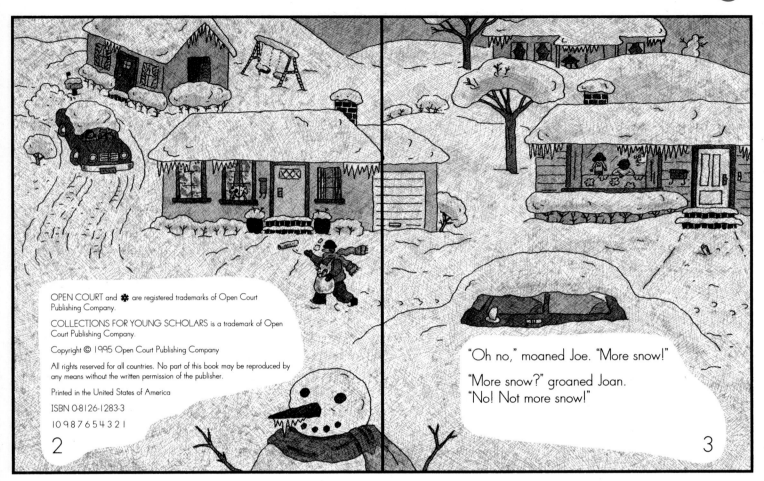

"Oh no," moaned Joe. "More snow!"

"More snow?" groaned Joan.
"No! Not more snow!"

3

"Come to the window," said Joe.
"Snow is on the sidewalks.
Snow is on the roads.
Snow is everywhere!"

4

"I'm tired of winter.
I'm tired of the cold.
And I'm tired of the snow!"
moaned Joan.

5

"We could make a snowman or go sledding," said Joe.

"I'm tired of snowmen, and I'm tired of sledding," said Joan. "I just want summer to come."

6

"Okay," said Joe. "Then we will make summer come. We will go to the beach. Get your coat. Here we go."

7

"Here we are at the coast," said Joe. "Do you like it?"

"This is the coast?" asked Joan. "It's a yard full of snow!"

8

"The grass has grown too high. We can't see the water. Help me mow a path," said Joe.

"We are mowing?" asked Joan.

9

"The sand is so hot.
Wiggle your toes in it.
We'll make a sand castle," said Joe.

"A sand castle?" asked Joan.

10

"Here, I'll show you," said Joe.
"Take this pail and some coal."

"It still looks like a snowman,"
said Joan.

11

"Okay, then follow me.
We will go on a boat!
Here are some oars," said Joe.

"Joe, you can't row in snow!" said Joan.

12

"Okay, then we'll just float.
We'll let the wind blow us.
I'll just push us off," said Joe.

"Blow us? Without a sail?" asked Joan.

13

"Whoa!"

14

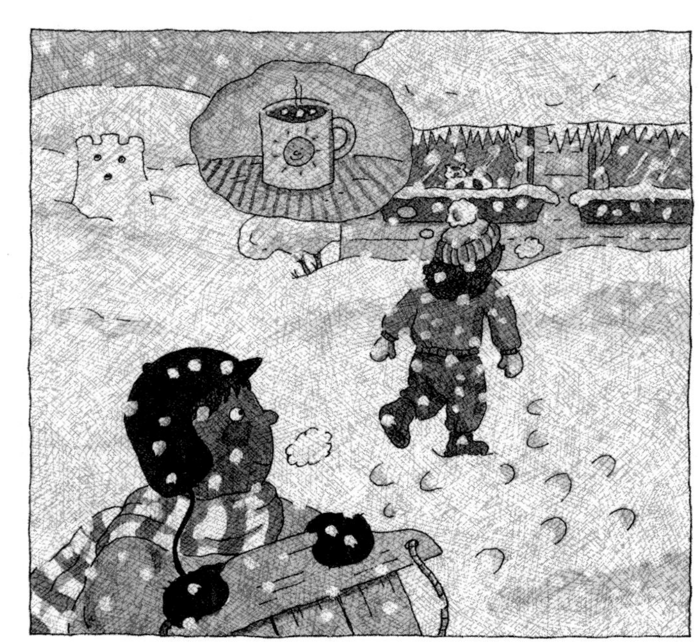

"I am soaked," said Joan.
"It's time to go back to winter.
I need a cup of hot cocoa!"

16

Responding

After reading, have the children tell in their own words what happened in the story and discuss any difficulties they had. To determine that the children are focusing on the words in the story, ask the following questions, having children point to the word in the story that answers each question.

- Where does Joan go to look at the snow?
- What is Joan tired of?
- Where does Joe pretend to go?
- What does Joe pretend to make?
- What does Joe pretend that the sled is?
- What do Joe and Joan say as the sled rushes down the hill?
- What does Joan need?

Allow time for the children to pair up and reread the story with partners.

ASSESSMENT TIP Listen to eight to ten children individually read one of the stories in Phonics Minibook 13, *The Snow Game*. Record your observations and keep them in the students' folders.

TIP FOR ENGLISH LANGUAGE LEARNERS

Provide an opportunity for the children to respond to their own and to each other's reading. Pair English Language Learners with native English-speaking children who are a little above their reading level. If possible, have the children tape record themselves rereading the story. Encourage them to work together on any problems they are having with the text. After they have finished reading, have the children listen to their tape recording and comment on their own and their partner's reading of the story.

2 WRITING

* DICTATION AND SPELLING

Have the children turn to page 5 of their Reading/Writing Connection book. Dictate the following words and sentence, using the suggestions for dictation that appear on **Learning Framework Card 4.**

During Dictation and Spelling, some of your students may still show some confusion using the different spellings for the long vowels. This is natural. It is important that you not wait for mastery of each spelling. Students will have many opportunities to work with the various long vowel spelling patterns in reading and writing.

Remind children to check the cards for the long vowel spellings. If they are unsure, tell them the correct spelling.

Line 1: **toe gold grow**

Line 2: **snowing saying meeting**

Sentence: **Joe rows a boat.**

Proofread as usual.

INDEPENDENT AND COLLABORATIVE WRITING

Begin writing today with Seminar. Seminar provides yet another opportunity for children to share their work but this time with their peers. Seminar also provides support for children who may be having problems coming up with ideas to write about. Select several children to be Seminar leaders. Have them come to the author's chair and share their plans. Encourage children to give feedback about what they liked, why they liked the plan or what was special about it. Children should also feel free to ask questions of the author. You may have to model some of these comments: "Oh, yes, that's a good point. You need special equipment to play that game;" or "That's interesting. I've never thought about playing that game that way. How did you come up with that idea?"

After Seminar, have children begin working on their piece about games. Remind them that this is just a draft and that there will be opportunities for them to make changes during the next few days. For those children who may not be comfortable writing about their game, suggest that they make a poster or chart.

As you conference with students, see if there are one or two children who are willing to have you share their work tomorrow when you talk about revision.

Activity Sheet 73

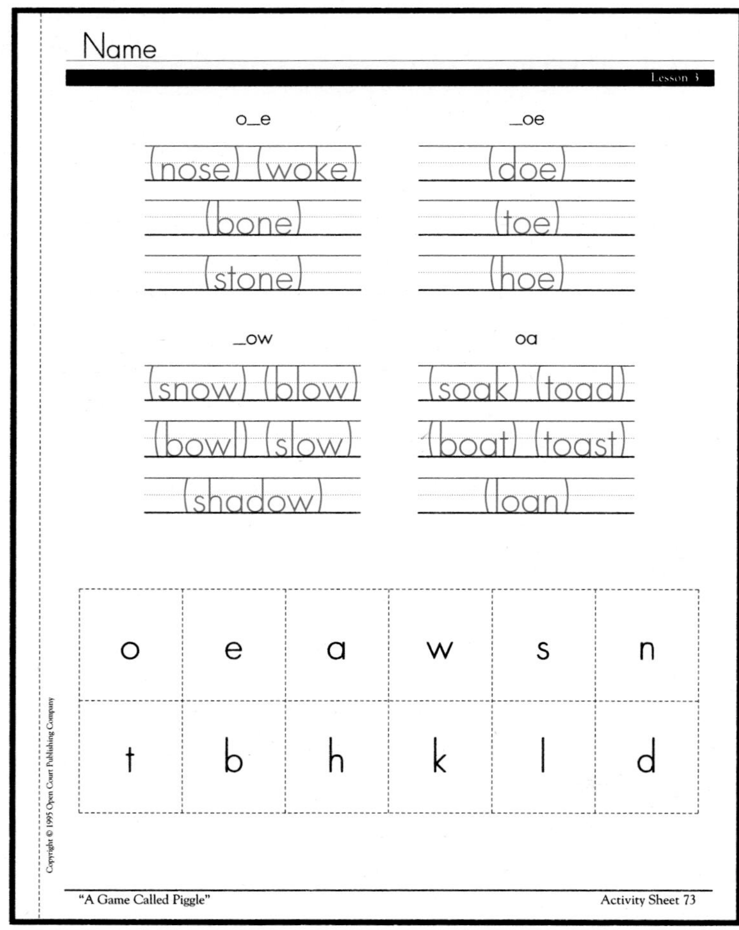
Name

Lesson 3

o_e

(nose) (woke)
(bone)
(stone)

_oe

(doe)
(toe)
(hoe)

_ow

(snow) (blow)
(bowl) (slow)
(shadow)

oa

(soak) (toad)
(boat) (toast)
(loan)

o	e	a	w	s	n
t	b	h	k	l	d

"A Game Called Piggle" Activity Sheet 73

3 GUIDED AND INDEPENDENT EXPLORATION

WORKSHOP

Remind the children that they may use this time to work on projects on their own or in small groups. Be sure that each child knows what projects he or she may choose and how to complete any independent work. Suggestions for teacher-guided, collaborative, and independent activities follow.

Learning Framework Card 11, Workshop, contains a complete discussion of establishing and conducting Workshop and suggestions for helping English Language Learners during Workshop.

Work with the Teacher

- Review the long *o* spellings, *oa, oe,* and *_ow* with children who could use additional practice. Just before Workshop begins, write *oa, oe,* and *_ow* on the board. Beneath them, write the following sentences:

  J__ hurt his big t__.
  The tree has gr__n three feet.
  Do t__ds eat t__st?
  Dad needs a truck to t__ his b__t.
  Last spring, we planted tomat__s in the garden.
  A g__t ate my winter c__t .
  You can't m__ the grass with a sn__ bl__er
  The farmer h__d a r__ of potat__s.

- Ask a child to blend the first sentence, telling her or him to fill in the blanks with the long *o* sound. Then have another child come to the board and fill in the blanks with the appropriate spellings. Follow this procedure to complete each of the remaining sentences.
- Repeat today's Blending lesson with individual children in order to assess their progress. Encourage the children to blend the words as whole units, rather than sound by sound. Then have the children take out Phonics Minibook 13 and locate some of the Blending words. Ask each child who locates a word to read aloud the sentence that contains that word.

Collaborative/Independent Activities

- Have children reread Phonics Minibook 13, *The Snow Game,* with their partners. Tell the pairs that as they read they should copy down all of the words in the story that contain the long *o* sound. While one child reads, the other can write, trading places at the end of each page. When they have finished the story, they should go over the list of words they have copied and underline the letters in each word that spell the long *o* sound.
- Throughout the Games unit, it will be suggested from time to time that interested children use their Workshop time to create their own versions of familiar games. Today, pairs or small groups of children might enjoy making up their own Riddle Me This riddles. Remind the children of how the Riddle Me This game is played. Tell them that they should take turns making up riddles for their partners or group members to solve.
- The children may continue to work on the pieces they are writing about games.
- Activity Sheet 73 reviews /ō/ spellings. Distribute the page and tell the children to cut out the letter boxes at the bottom of the activity sheet and use them to make words that have the various /ō/ spellings. You might suggest to the children that they work in pairs, or invite them to refer to pages they have completed in their Reading/Writing Connection books that focus on /ō/ spellings.

LESSON 4

Lesson Overview

New Learning

- /ū/ spelled ***ew*** and _***ue***
- Revising

Outlaw Word

laugh

Materials

- ***Jafta***, pages 20–27
- Sound/Spelling Card 36, Long U
- Learning Framework Cards 3, 8
- Reading/Writing Connection, pages 7–8
- Outlaw Word Flash Cards
- Activity Sheet 74

Prepare Ahead

- Basket with /ū/ words printed on index cards (see pages 42–43)
- Bingo materials

GETTING STARTED

Choose one or more of the following activities to focus the children's attention and to review some of the concepts they have been learning.

A Tisket, a Tasket Game This version of A Tisket, a Tasket will give the children practice reading words with the /ū/ vowel sound. Have the children sit in a circle, and invite a volunteer to pretend to be a traveler. Give the traveler a basket that contains cards with words containing various /ū/ spellings printed on them. The traveler should move around the circle and say

A tisket, a tasket
a green and yellow basket,
I took a word to my friend
and on the way I dropped it.

On the last line, the traveler should stop in front of another child and drop one of the cards. That other child should pick up the card, read the word, and identify the /ū/ spelling. That child then becomes the new traveler.

Here are some words to use:

cube funeral cucumber uniform cure mule
use confuse pupil bugle amuse human music

Flip a Sound Game Play the Flip a Sound game as introduced in the previous lesson.

1 READING

PHONICS

Introduce /ū/ Spelled *ew* and *_ue* Direct attention to Sound/Spelling Card 36, Long U, and review the spellings the children know for the sound /ū/. Write the words *mule* and *music* on the chalkboard, blend the words with the children, and identify the *u_e* spelling in *mule* and the *u* spelling in *music.* Then write the words *few* and *cue* and read them. Point out the new spellings *ew* and *_ue,* and underline them.

* **Blending** Help the children blend the following words. A complete discussion of the blending procedure can be found on **Learning Framework Card 3.**

Line 1:	**few pew cue hue**
Line 2:	**value argue rescue**
Line 3:	**barbecue fewer continue**
Line 4:	**cure fumes museum porcupine**
Line 5:	**flamingo lizard zebra hyena**
Sentence:	**Jafta likes to laugh.**

Words Help the children blend the words in lines 1–3 with the new spelling. Some of these words may be unfamiliar to the children. Discuss the meanings of the words and have them used in oral sentences.

Line 4 reviews long *u* spellings that the children already know.

Line 5 introduces animal words from the upcoming selection, *Jafta.*

Review the words in lines 1–5 by having the children touch and read the word that completes sentences you give, such as

The ______ has sharp quills.
A word that means "less" is ______.
Another word for a shade of a color is a ______.
______ from cars pollute the air.
A ______ is an animal with black and white stripes.
A word meaning "disagree strongly" is ______.
When you keep doing something, you ______.

TEACHING TIP

If the children are having trouble recognizing that some vowel spellings comprise more than one letter, write the vowel spelling in colored chalk to highlight this distinction.

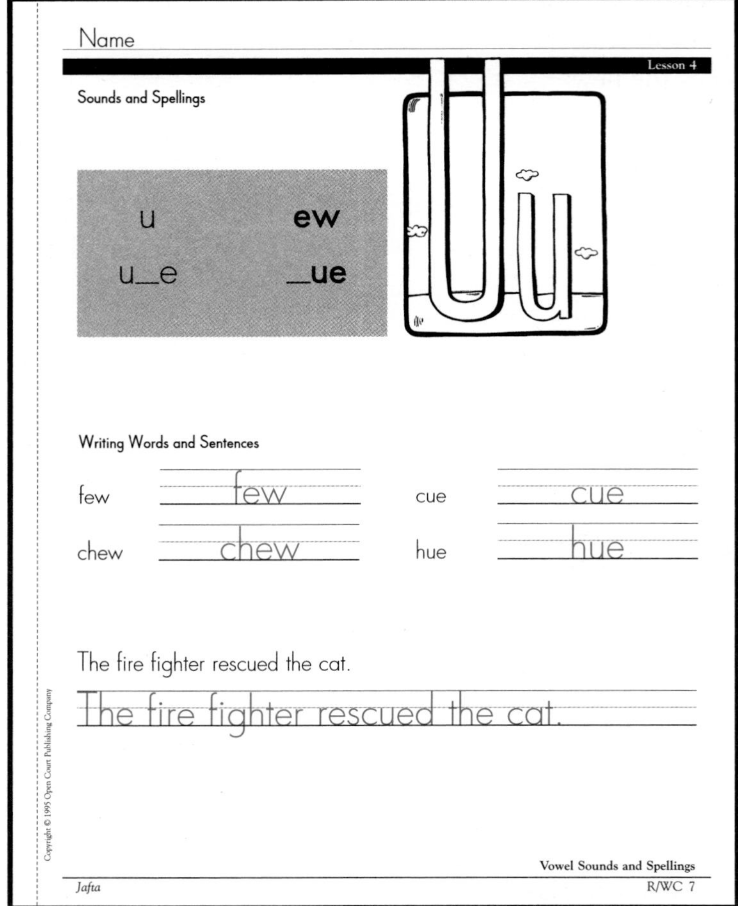

Name

Lesson 4

Sounds and Spellings

u ew

u_e _ue

Writing Words and Sentences

few few cue cue

chew chew hue hue

The fire fighter rescued the cat.

The fire fighter rescued the cat.

Vowel Sounds and Spellings

Jafta R/WC 7

Reading/Writing Connection, page 7

Sentence Introduce the outlaw word *laugh* before writing the sentence on the chalkboard. Write the word *laugh* on the chalkboard and read it to the children. Call on children to use the word in sentences. Then write the sentence on the board, underlining the new word *laugh.* Have children read the sentence.

➤ Help the children complete page 7 of their Reading/Writing Connection book at this time.

* READING THE STUDENT ANTHOLOGY

Jafta
pages 20–27

About the Selection

In *Jafta,* a young African boy uses a series of comparisons to describe the moods and feelings he experiences, ranging from happiness through exuberance to fatigue and crossness. The children will easily identify with the emotions Jafta expresses, for they are common to children the world over. Although the feelings described by Jafta are universal, his observations are firmly rooted in his African village as he compares himself to a lion cub, a zebra, an elephant, and other native animals.

The pictures are as important as the text in evoking the grace, beauty, and strength of the animals whose actions and characteristics mirror Jafta's moods and feelings.

Link to the Unit Concept

In this selection, Jafta describes the different kinds of play evoked by his various feelings and moods. For example, when he is happy, he jumps like an impala and dances like a zebra; when he is cross, he stamps like an elephant.

About the Author

As a white person growing up under the apartheid system in South Africa, Hugh Lewin felt a sense of moral outrage at the deplorable conditions under which black South Africans were forced to live. "I have always believed, and still do believe, that all men are equals in the eyes of God," he wrote in his autobiography. Lewin's beliefs translated into political activism, which in turn resulted in his being incarcerated for seven years in a South African prison. After his release from prison, Lewin left his native land for England, where his two daughters were born. There he began writing his series of *Jafta* books as a way of helping his daughters learn about South Africa.

Activating Prior Knowledge

Have the children open their readers to page 20. Call on a volunteer to blend and read the selection title aloud. Tell the children that this story is about a child in South Africa. Remind the children that Captain Bill Pinkney visited South Africa. Discuss what children may know about animals that live in Africa.

Setting Reading Goals and Expectations

- Have the children browse the selection, commenting in any way they choose on the text or pictures. Model the browsing procedure by talking about what you notice in the text and pictures as you glance through the story. For more information about browsing, see **Learning Framework Card 8, Reading the Student Anthologies.**

Recommendations for Reading

- Read the story to the children as they follow along in their book. Say, "As I read the story aloud, ask about any words or ideas you don't understand."
- Use the suggestions under the page miniatures to model responding to the text and pictures and asking questions about information in the selection. Encourage the children to discuss possible meanings of unfamiliar words and to tell how they figured out those meanings.
- After the reading, have the children page through the story again. Let them comment on or wonder about anything they notice about the words or the pictures. Invite volunteers to read words or sentences they think they know.

About the Reading Strategies

In reading this selection, the children will need strategies for decoding unfamiliar words. Refer them to the poster Clarifying Unfamiliar Words and Passages and read the questions that accompany the first three strategies on this chart with them. Explain that you will model using these strategies as you read the selection together.

Think-Aloud Prompts for Use in Oral Reading Notice the think-aloud prompts with the page miniatures. These are merely suggestions. Continue to model using appropriate strategies while reading and to encourage children to use the strategies on their own. For a review of information about modeling and generating think-alouds, see **Learning Framework Card 8, Reading the Student Anthologies.**

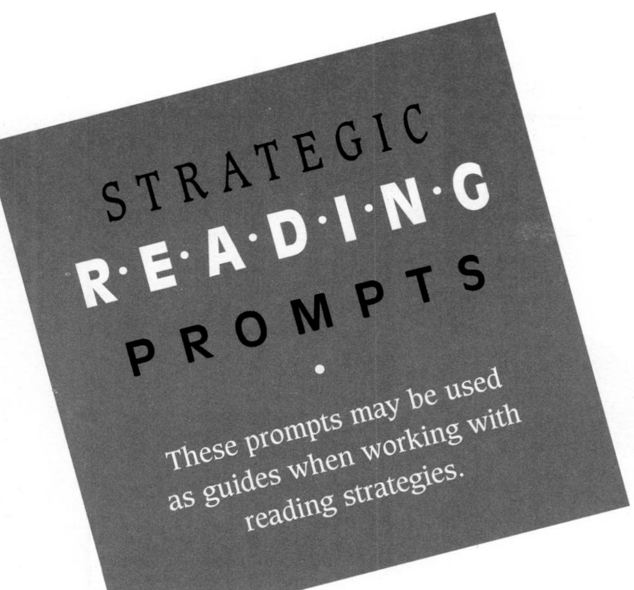
STRATEGIC
R·E·A·D·I·N·G
PROMPTS
These prompts may be used as guides when working with reading strategies.

1 You might model reacting to information in the text be saying something like the following: *I didn't know that lion cubs could purr. I thought only house cats did that—I didn't know big wild cats do that too.*

2 If the word *hyena* was not discussed during the browsing of the story, you might say: *That's a funny word. The animal in the picture must be a hyena—it looks something like a dog.*

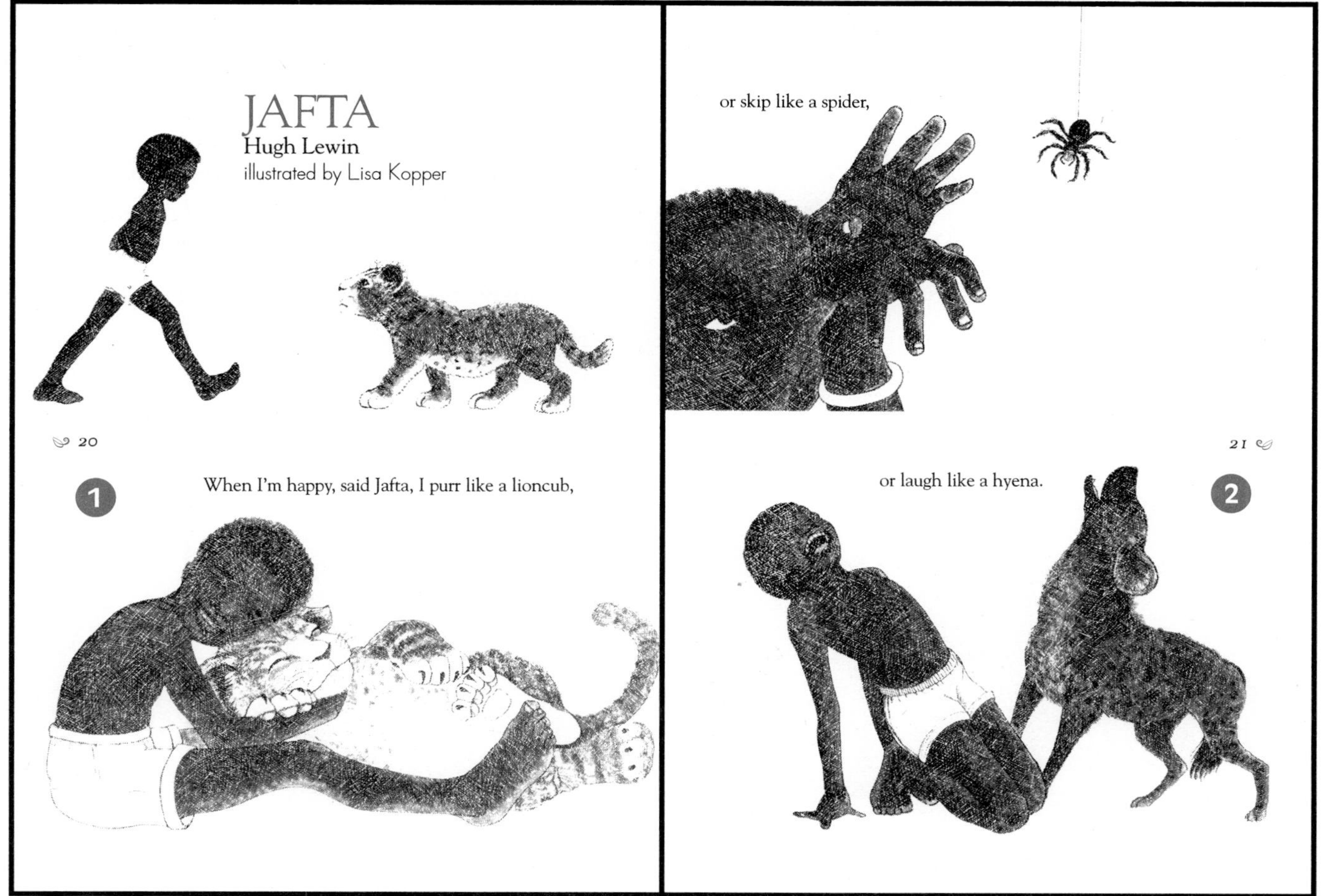
JAFTA
Hugh Lewin
illustrated by Lisa Kopper

20

1 When I'm happy, said Jafta, I purr like a lioncub,

or skip like a spider,

21

or laugh like a hyena. 2

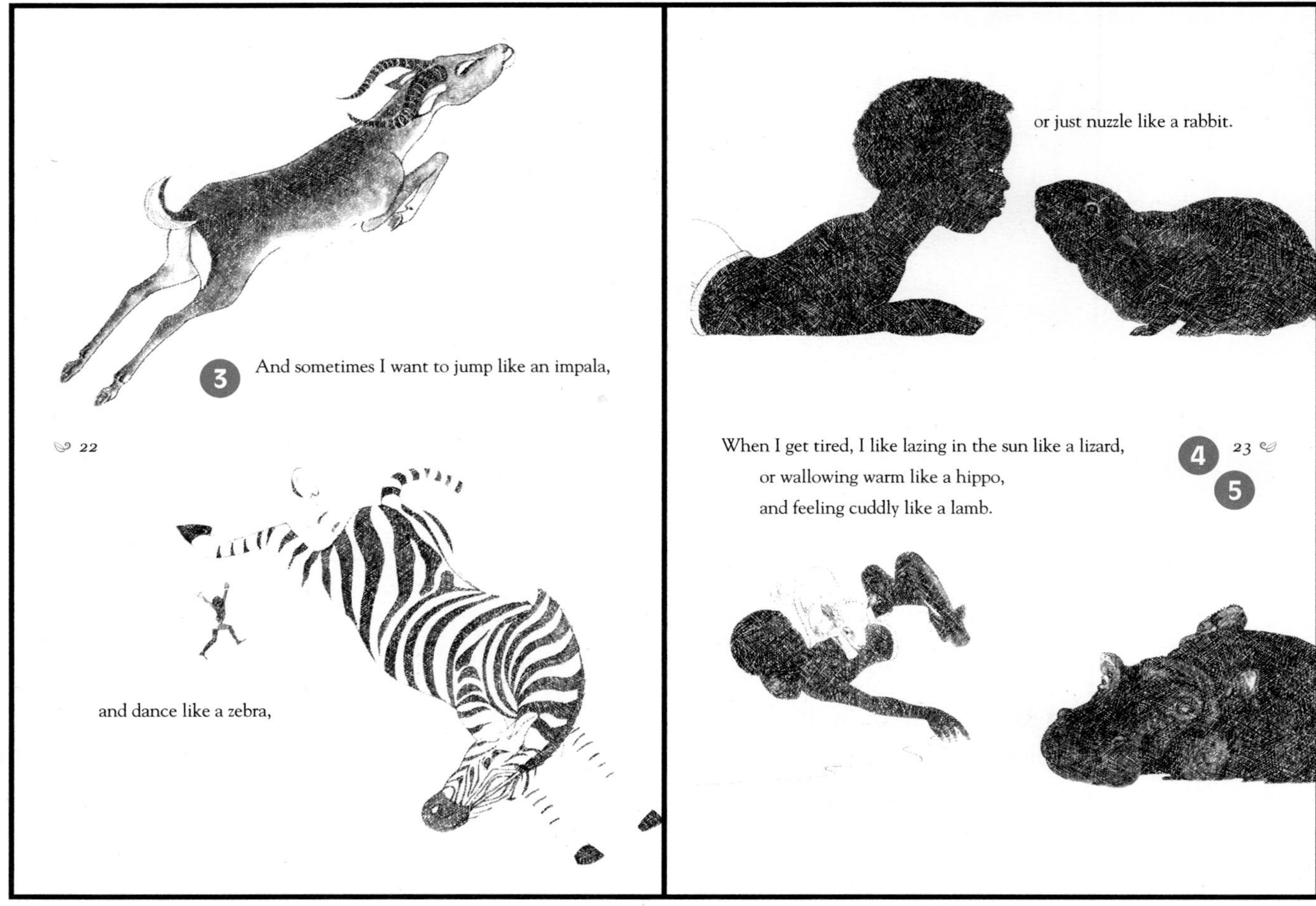

3 And sometimes I want to jump like an impala,
22
and dance like a zebra,
or just nuzzle like a rabbit.
When I get tired, I like lazing in the sun like a lizard, 4
or wallowing warm like a hippo, 5
and feeling cuddly like a lamb.
23

3 If the word *impala* was not discussed during the browsing of the story you might say: *I've never seen this word before. How can we tell what an impala might be?*

4 Say: Lazing *is a new word to me. It sounds like* lazy, *but how can we tell from the picture what the word might mean?*

5 Say: Wallowing warm—*I'm not sure, but I know that* wallowing *means to roll around in something messy like mud, so* wallowing warm *might mean rolling around in mud that is warm from the sun.*

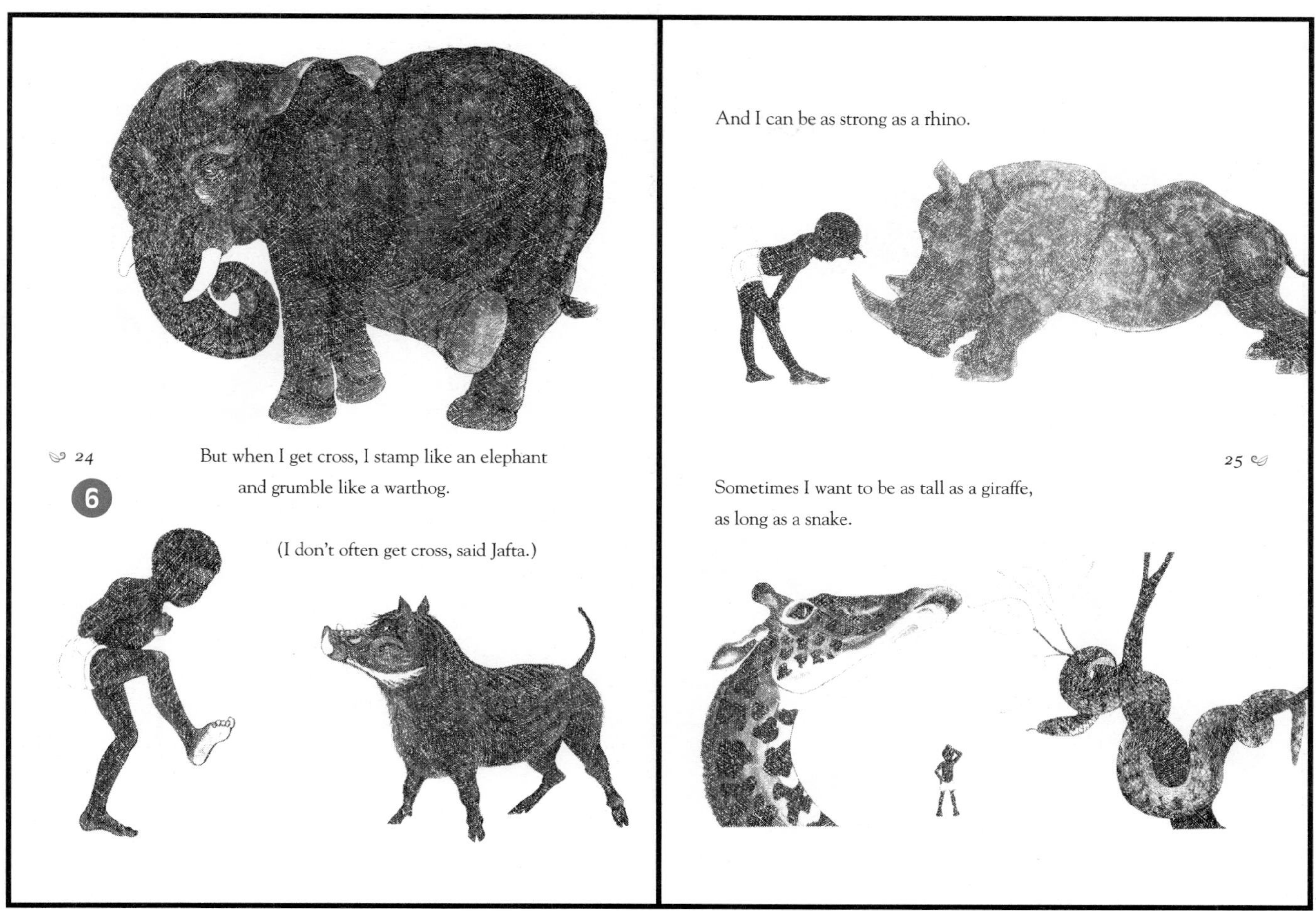

24
But when I get cross, I stamp like an elephant
and grumble like a warthog.
6
(I don't often get cross, said Jafta.)
And I can be as strong as a rhino.
25
Sometimes I want to be as tall as a giraffe,
as long as a snake.

6 If the word *warthog* was not discussed during the browsing of the story you might say: Warthog—*how can we tell what that means?*

And I want to run as fast as a cheetah,
as quick as an ostrich,
or swing through the trees like a monkey,
and fly high high high like an eagle,
26
7 or just stand very still, like a crane on one leg.
But actually, said Jafta,
I don't think there's anything quite so nice
27
as being a flamingo flying off into the sunset . . .

7 The words *cheetah, ostrich, crane,* and *flamingo* can all be clarified by looking at the pictures.

Responding to the Selection

- Invite volunteers to point to and say new words that they have learned in the story.
- Children might want to discuss whether Jafta is actually playing with each of the animals shown in the illustrations, whether he is watching these animals, or whether he is imagining how these animals behave. Remind children to tell why they think the way they do about these questions.
- The writer describes games that Jafta plays when he is on his own or has no one else to play with. Ask the children what kinds of games they play when they have no one else to play with.
- As new words, ideas, and games are mentioned, have the children add them to the Concept Board.

➤ Help the children complete page 8 of their Reading/Writing Connection book. They should choose the word that completes each phrase and write it in the blank.

TEACHING TIP

Have the children do some partner reading daily. Using previously read Phonics Minibooks and Step-by-Step Practice Stories for this purpose will help the children review and solidify their knowledge of the sounds and spellings they have learned. This is a good opportunity to read with children individually and to record their progress.

Reading/Writing Connection, page 8

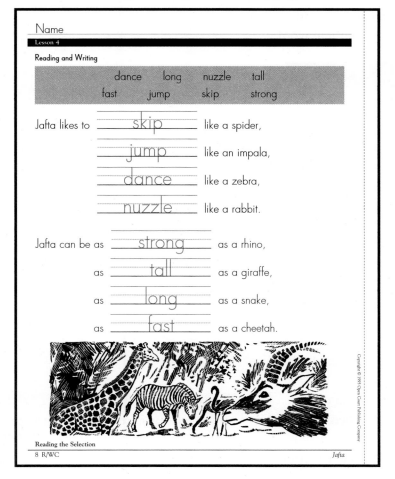

Name

Lesson 4

Reading and Writing

dance long nuzzle tall
fast jump skip strong

Jafta likes to skip like a spider,
jump like an impala,
dance like a zebra,
nuzzle like a rabbit.

Jafta can be as strong as a rhino,
as tall as a giraffe,
as long as a snake,
as fast as a cheetah.

Reading the Selection

8 R/WC Jafta

✱ READING ALOUD

Be sure to set aside time later in the day for reading aloud. *Jafta* is the first in a series of books that Hugh Lewin has written about this young South African boy. Other books in the series that you may wish to share with the children are listed below:

Jafta's Mother
Jafta's Father
Jafta and the Wedding

2 WRITING

✱ DICTATION AND SPELLING

Word-Building Game Have the children use pencil and paper for building the following words:

oat
boat
boast
coast
coat
cone
bone

You may want to challenge children by having them come up with a new word at the end by changing one of the spellings in the final word.

Minilesson

Revising

Discuss with the children that every author rereads his or her work to see whether it needs revising. Explain that writers do this to see whether their writing makes sense, to see whether any new information needs to be added, or whether anything needs to be taken out.

Use a piece about games to help clarify the revising process. Explain to the children that you are going to be sharing one child's piece and that the whole class will be helping that student revise his or her work. Using a piece of work selected yesterday as you conferred with children, read the selection. You may want to write the piece on chart paper or on the board. Talk about the following ideas:

- whether the piece makes sense
- what needs to be added
- what might need to be taken out—what isn't important to the topic

You may want to refer to the chart developed in the previous lessons to check whether the important information is included in the piece. If you have written the piece on the board, use a caret and add the new information. Draw a line through anything being deleted.

TEACHING TIP

Make a transparency of the piece that is going to be revised and show it to the class as you read it.

Have children take out their own pieces about games and have them reread their work to see whether it makes sense, whether anything needs to be added, or whether anything needs to be taken out. Children should be encouraged to work with a peer. If children work in pairs, have them read their pieces aloud to each other. Often oral reading makes it easier to hear where to make changes.

TEACHING TIP

You may want to make a poster of the three revising points; or if you have children who are having problems getting started, you could let them be responsible for making the poster.

As you conference with children today, look for writing pieces that you can use in proofreading tomorrow. Be sure to ask children for permission to use their work.

3 GUIDED AND INDEPENDENT EXPLORATION

WORKSHOP

Remind the children that they may use this time to work on projects on their own or in small groups. Be sure that each child knows what projects he or she may choose and how to complete any independent work. Suggestions for teacher-guided, collaborative, and independent activities follow.

Work with the Teacher

- Play Bingo with the children, using cards that contain, along with other familiar spellings, some of the spellings that the children have recently learned for /ō/ and /ū/. Among the words that you call out should be some of the /ō/ and /ū/ words that the children have learned during recent Blending exercises.
- Play the Word-Building game with a small group of children who need extra practice in dictation and spelling. Have the children use their own pencil and paper. You may repeat today's word list or dictate any list of words you choose, depending on the needs of the children. When they have finished writing, help the children proofread and correct their work.
- Reread *Jafta*, having children follow along in their anthologies. Have them identify and read sentences of their choice.

ASSESSMENT Listen to several students individually read one of the stories in a Phonics Minibook. Record your observations and keep them in the students' folders.

Collaborative/Independent Activities

- Some children may not have finished revising their piece on games. Suggest that they continue working with their partners as they discuss ways to make their writing clearer or more interesting.
- Use peer tutoring to help children learn the outlaw words that have been introduced so far. Pair up children who read the words confidently with those who have been having some difficulty remembering the words. Have the confident readers drill their partners with Outlaw Flash Cards. When they have gone through all of the cards, the partners can work together to write a sentence containing one or more outlaw words.
- Before Workshop begins, write the following sentences on the board:
  "When I'm happy, I ______ like a ______."
  "When I'm angry, I ______ like a ______."
  "When I'm tired, I like to ______ like a ______."

  Remind the children that Jafta described his feelings by comparing himself to different animals. Tell interested children that they can describe their own moods and feelings in this way by copying, completing, and illustrating the above sentences.
- Activity Sheet 74 reviews spellings for /ō/. Explain to the children that they should use the information in the story to complete the picture on this page.

Name

Lesson 4

What an Eagle Sees

An eagle flies high in the sky. He sees three deer by the lake. Some roses grow by the road. A boat floats on the lake.

Activity Sheet 74 "Jafta"

Activity Sheet 74

LESSON 5

Lesson Overview

New Learning

- Changing ***y*** to ***i*** before adding endings
- Doubling final consonant before adding endings
- Proofreading

Materials

- ***Jafta***, pages 20–27
- Learning Framework Cards 3, 4
- Reading/Writing Connection, pages 9–10
- Activity Sheet 75

Prepare Ahead

- Long Vowel Cards (see page 60)

GETTING STARTED

Choose one or more of the following activities to focus the children's attention and to review some of the concepts they have been learning.

Dictate to the Teacher Write the word *boat* on the chalkboard and call on a child to read it. Then have the children tell you how to change the word to make the following words:

coat
cot
cut
cute
cup
cub
cube

Discriminate Sounds Say the following words. If the children hear a long vowel they should hold their arms out wide. If they hear a short vowel they should hug their arms in close. The words are

hug	coat	page
bug	cap	few
huge	soap	pan
cute	sand	

1 READING

* **Blending** Help the children blend the following words. A complete discussion of the blending procedure can be found on **Learning Framework Card 3.**

MONITORING BLENDING Finish your observations of students' blending. Record your observations in Teacher's Observation Log 3.

Line 1:	**happy happier happiest happily**
Line 2:	**win winning winner**
Line 3:	**smile smiling sneeze sneezed**
Line 4:	**cheering cleaned spraying waited**
Line 5:	**clocks cloaks setting seating**

After the children have blended line 1, point out that the *y* was changed to *i* before the endings were added. Give sentences with *happy, happier, happiest,* to point out the comparative forms.

For line 2, ask what small word is inside each of the larger words. Help the children notice that the final consonant was doubled before the endings *-ing* and *-er* were added. Discuss why this was done, pointing out that this is done when the base word has a short vowel sound.

After blending line 4, have the children find and underline the base word in each word. The words in line 5 contrast long and short vowel spellings.

Review the words by giving clues and asking children to touch and read words that answer the clue. Example clues are

- a word that ends in *-ing*
- a word that has the base word *clean* in it
- the word that has one letter changed from *clocks (cloaks)*
- the word with the *-ly* ending

➤ Reading/Writing Connection, page 9, may be completed at this time. Have the children read each question and write an answer. Call on them to read their answers to the class.

Name

Lesson 5

Writing Sentences

1. What can you do like a deer?

(Answers will vary.)

2. What can you do like a snake?

3. What can you do like a tiger?

4. What can you do like a toad?

Dictation and Spelling

Vowel Sounds and Spellings

Jafta R/WC 9

Reading/Writing Connection, page 9

✻ READING THE STUDENT ANTHOLOGY

Jafta
pages 20–27

Activating Prior Knowledge

Ask the children to turn to page 20 in their readers. Then ask what they remember about this story from their previous reading. Allow the children to talk about anything related to the text or the pictures.

Recommendations for Reading

- Allow time for the children to look over the story silently. Then have them read the story aloud, with you participating as a member of the group. Have the children blend unfamiliar words. If a word cannot be blended or is unfamiliar to children, for example, *impala*, read the word for the children.

  Note: Paired reading of a selection is a good option for Workshop.

Responding to the Selection

- Invite volunteers to tell what they liked best about the story.
- You might ask the children what animals in the story they would like

to be like, and why. Since some of these animals may be unfamiliar to children, ask them what animals that they know would they like to be like and why.

- Ask the children if they have ever felt like Jafta does and what they like to do when they feel like him.

Vocabulary Discuss any interesting words or phrases from the selection that the children might want to use in their writing. Have several children use these words in oral sentences. Add these to the vocabulary chart begun in Lesson 3. Words may include the following:
cuddly, grumble, nuzzle

* READING ALOUD

Be sure to set aside time later in the day for reading aloud. As noted in the previous lesson, *Jafta* is the first in a series of books that Hugh Lewin has written about this young South African boy. Additional titles in this series are listed below.

Jafta—The Journey
Jafta—The Town
Jafta—The Homecoming

TIP FOR ENGLISH LANGUAGE LEARNERS

Provide an opportunity for English Language Learners to add meaning to the vocabulary associated with the selection. Encourage the children to illustrate a word that Jafta uses to describe an action or a feeling. The children may choose any action or feeling word they like. Have them write the word at the top of the illustrated page. Illustrating favorite words helps to make the words personally meaningful for the children.

Reading/Writing Connection, page 10

Name

Lesson 5

Writing Sentences

i like cheetahs. A cheetah has lots of spotes like my cat. cheetahs are fast runrs. Cheetahs can cach animals

I like cheetahs. A cheetah has lots of spots like my cat. Cheetahs are fast runners. Cheetahs can catch animals.

Proofreading and Revising

10 R/WC Jafta

2 WRITING

✱ DICTATION AND SPELLING

Have the children open their Reading/Writing Connection books to page 9. Dictate the following words and sentence, using the procedure for dictation described on **Learning Framework Card 4.**

Line 1: few huge argue

Line 2: big bigger biggest

Sentence: The cub is digging a hole.

Remind the children to check the Sound/Spelling Cards and ask for help with long vowel spellings they are unsure of.

Have the children proofread as usual.

INDEPENDENT AND COLLABORATIVE WRITING

Have several children share their revised pieces during seminar. After the children have shared their work have them talk about how they have revised or changed their piece.

Minilesson

Proofreading

Now that the children have revised their work, explain to them that the next thing writers do is proofread. Have the children talk about what it means to proofread: look for spelling mistakes, check for capitalization (particularly at the beginning of a sentence), and check for final punctuation.

Write the sample piece for proofreading on the board or chart paper or make a transparency. Read through the piece once and then decide what to check first. For example, read through the piece looking for ending punctuation. Then go back and look for capitals and then spelling. As children proofread for spelling they should look for words that don't look right and then use the Sound/Spelling Cards to make them better. Just as in Dictation and Spelling, circle the incorrectly spelled word and write the correct spelling above or next to it. Repeat this procedure with another child's piece.

TEACHING TIP

Make a poster or chart with the proofreading points on it as a reminder for children.

➤ Reading/Writing Connection, page 10, provides practice with revising. Have the children complete the page as a whole-class activity or in small groups. If they do it in small groups, you should hold conferences with the groups.

Once children have finished this page, have them check their own stories for punctuation, capitalization, and spelling mistakes. Again, children should be encouraged to work with a partner or in a small group.

3 GUIDED AND INDEPENDENT EXPLORATION

WORKSHOP

Remind the children that they may use this time to work on projects on their own or in small groups. Be sure that each child knows what projects he or she may choose and how to complete any independent work. Suggestions for teacher-guided, collaborative, and independent activities follow.

Work with the Teacher

- To reinforce word endings, play a game of Tic-Tac-Toe with two teams of children. Make two Tic-Tac-Toe grids on the chalkboard, each with three rows and three columns. Place the endings *-s, -ed,* and *-ing* on the grids. You might use the following patterns:

-s -ing -ed	*-ing -s -ed*
-ed -ing -s	*-ed -s -ing*
-ing -ed -s	*-s -ing -ed*

Call out a word from the list below and use it in a sentence. Have one person from each team go to the chalkboard and cross out the ending they hear in the word you called out. Repeat this step until a team completes a horizontal line.

Use the following word list:

waves	waving	keeping
drives	riding	tapped
rides	tapping	hopped
wipes	hopping	played
smile	stopping	enjoyed
wades	sleeping	

- Preteach the first part of "The Big Team Relay Race," pages 28–31 in the student anthology, to those children who may have difficulty reading it on their own tomorrow.
- Take time to listen to different children read Phonics Minibook 13, *The Snow Game*. This can be done individually or in small groups.

ASSESSMENT Listen to the final eight to ten students individually read one of the stories from Phonics Minibook 13, *The Snow Game*. Record your observations to be kept in the students' folders.

Collaborative/Independent Activities

- Working in pairs, the children may write and illustrate sentences containing words with the long *u* sound spelled *u, u_e, _ew,* or *_ue.* Allow time for them to share their sentences and illustrations with their classmates.
- At this time, children who are not yet finished proofreading their games-related writing pieces may rejoin their partners or groups and continue their work. If you have put up a proofreading poster, remind the children to refer to it.
- Some children might like to play the Fish for a Spelling game. Place long vowel cards (each index card has a long vowel spelling) in a container. Have the children take out scratch paper and pencils and sit in a circle around the container. Review with them the rules of play: Take a card, then name a word with that spelling. Write the word. Encourage them to help one another spell and to look at the Sound/Spelling Cards for help.
- Activity Sheet 75 requires the children to sound out some of the less familiar animal names mentioned in *Jafta.* Have the children read the words in the box at the top of the page, and determine how many syllables each word has. Explain to the children that to complete this activity sheet they need to figure out how many syllables each of the words in the box has, then write the words with two syllables inside the outline of the zebra, and the words with three syllables inside the elephant. The children can then draw a picture of one or more of the words they have listed in the box at the bottom of the page.

Home/School Connection

Remind the children to read Phonics Minibook 12, *Mail Train*, to their families at home.

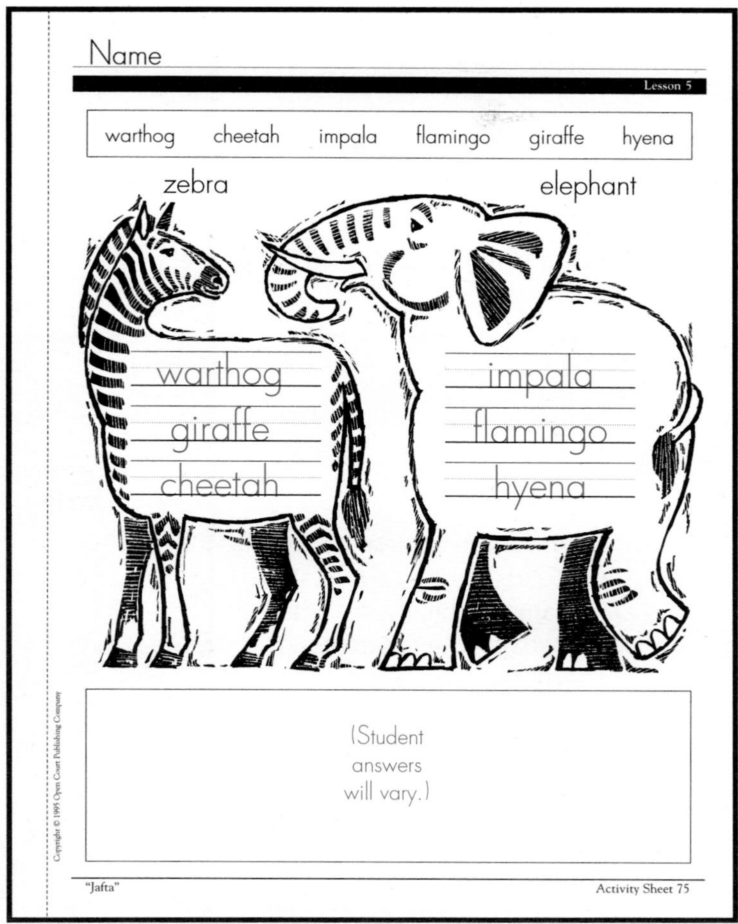

Activity Sheet 75

LESSON 6

Lesson Overview

New Learning

- /ow/ spelled ***ow***

Outlaw Word

who

Materials

- "The Big Team Relay Race," pages 28–31
- Sound/Spelling Card 39, Cow
- Learning Framework Cards 3, 8
- Reading/Writing Connection, pages 11–12
- Activity Sheet 76

Prepare Ahead

- Construction paper in two colors for nine cards (see page 64)
- Long ***u*** Flash Cards (see page 71)
- Go Fish! Cards (see page 71)

GETTING STARTED

Choose one or more of the following activities to focus the children's attention and to review some of the concepts they have been learning.

Long Sound/Short Sound Spellings Use this activity to review the /ō/ spellings the children have learned so far. Write one word on the chalkboard at a time. Have the children read the word quietly to themselves. Tell them that if the word has the /ō/ sound, they should hold their arms out from their sides. If it has the /o/ sound, they should hold their hands close together. Then have the children say the word. Use words such as:

toes	hat	lock	snow
hello	open	soft	boat

Sound/Spelling Card Review Say a long vowel sound and have the children give the various spellings.

1 READING

PHONICS

Introduce /ow/ spelled *ow* Display Sound/Spelling Card 39, Cow. You may want to cover the spelling *ou* until it is introduced in the next lesson. Point out the spelling *ow* and ask what the children already know about a sound made by these letters. Tell them that today they will learn a new sound made by these letters, the /ow/ sound. Then read the Cow story.

Wow! Can you see poor Brownie the Cow?
She got stung by a bee and look at her now!
She jumps up and down with an /ow/ /ow/ /ow/ /ow/.

Poor Brownie found that a big buzzing sound
Meant bees all around—in the air, on the ground.
Just one little bee gave Brownie a sting.
Now you can hear poor Brownie sing: /ow/ /ow/ /ow/ /ow/.

Now if you were a cow and a bee found you,
You'd probably jump and shout out too!
(Have the children join in) /ow/ /ow/ /ow/ /ow/.

Pronounce some words and have the children signal thumbs-up if they hear the /ow/ sound. Use the words

now	town	mitten
how	power	down
bake	never	clown

Ask the children to suggest other words that have the /ow/ sound.

* **Blending** Have the children blend the words and sentence, using the suggestions that follow. A complete discussion of the blending process can be found on **Learning Framework Card 3.**

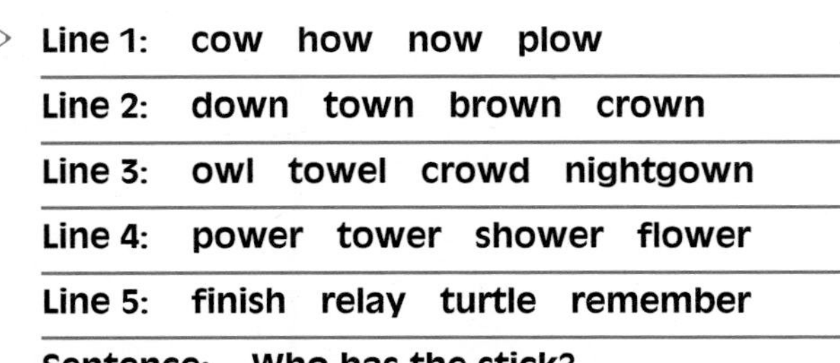

Line 1:	**cow how now plow**
Line 2:	**down town brown crown**
Line 3:	**owl towel crowd nightgown**
Line 4:	**power tower shower flower**
Line 5:	**finish relay turtle remember**
Sentence:	**Who has the stick?**

Words Write the words in line 1 sound by sound and have the children blend them. In lines 2 and 3 write each whole word and have the children blend it. If children have difficulty, return to writing sound by sound. In line 4 have the children blend syllable by syllable *(pow er, power).*

The words in line 5 appear in the story "The Big Team Relay Race" in the student anthology.

To review the word lines, play a number game. Print the numbers 1–4 on separate pieces of construction paper, all the same color. On five pieces of a different-colored construction paper, print the numbers 1–5. Place the set of four numbers in a bag or box labeled *words* and the set of five in a container labeled *lines*. Invite a volunteer to pick two pieces of construction paper—one of each color. The child then uses the two numbers to locate the word in the word lines. For example, if the child chooses 5 and 2, the word to find and read is *relay*. Return the numbers, shake the container, and repeat with other volunteers.

Sentence Introduce the outlaw word *who* by writing the word on the chalkboard, touching the word, and telling the children this is the word *who*. Have several children use the word in sentences. Then write the sentence on the board and underline *who*. Have several children read the sentence.

➤ Reading/Writing Connection, page 11, provides practice reading and writing words with the /ow/ sound spelled *ow*. Help the children complete the page by telling them to copy the words and sentences at the top of the page and to fill in the rhyming word at the bottom of the page.

Reading/Writing Connection, page 11

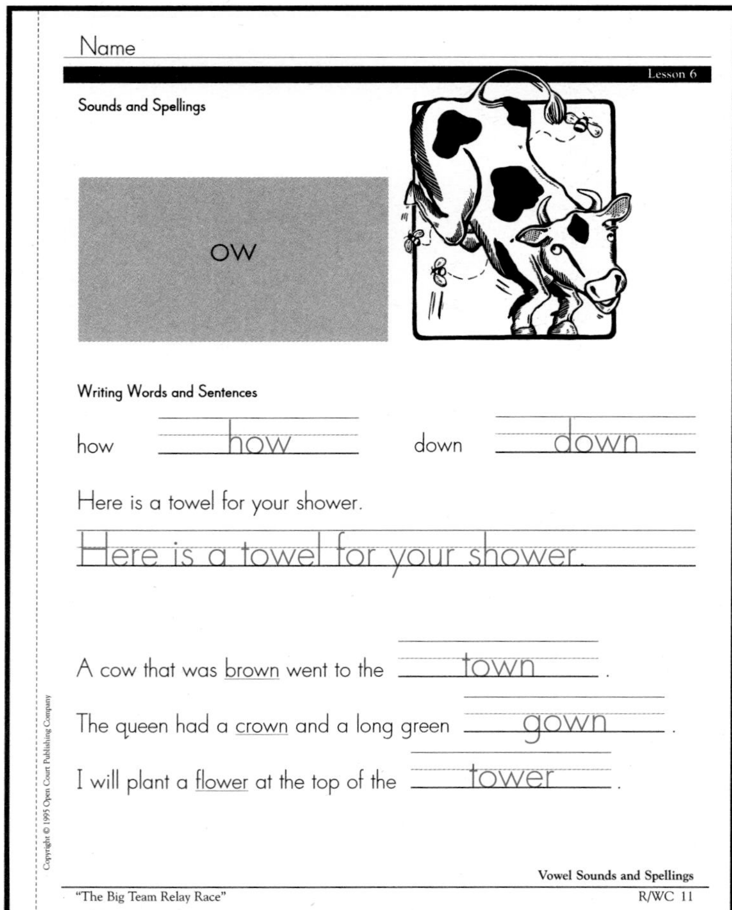
Name

Lesson 6

Sounds and Spellings

ow

Writing Words and Sentences

how how   down down

Here is a towel for your shower.

Here is a towel for your shower.

A cow that was brown went to the town.

The queen had a crown and a long green gown.

I will plant a flower at the top of the tower.

Vowel Sounds and Spellings

"The Big Team Relay Race" R/WC 11

* READING THE STUDENT ANTHOLOGY

"The Big Team Relay Race"

pages 28–31

Note: Because of its length, this selection probably should be read over two class periods. We recommend that on the first day of reading, you stop at the bottom of page 31.

About the Selection

"The Big Team Relay Race" is a humorous story of a relay race involving an unusual assortment of animals. The story has an unexpected hero, a hero who overcomes adversity to cross the finish line first.

Link to the Unit Concept

This story illustrates the importance of team cooperation. Group effort and team spirit are very important in playing certain games successfully.

Activating Prior Knowledge

Have the title of the story read aloud. Ask the children what they know about the type of race called a *relay race*. Call on a volunteer to explain what happens when someone says, "On your mark, get set, go!"

Setting Reading Goals and Expectations

- Have the children browse the first four pages and make any comments about the print and the pictures that come to mind. You might write on the chalkboard the observations the children come up with during browsing.
- If children are having difficulty blending any of the words, remind them to check the Sound/Spelling Cards. If any words cannot be easily blended, pronounce those words for the children.

Recommendations for Reading

- The story will be read in two parts. This lesson will stop at the end of page 31.
- Tell the children that this story was written by Leonard Kessler and illustrated by Linda Kelen. Read the introductory paragraph. Explain that this paragraph sums up what has gone before.
- Have the children read aloud from pages 28 to 31. Discuss with the class anything of interest on a page.

About the Reading Strategies

In reading this selection, children can be encouraged to use strategies for **summing up** and for **predicting** what will happen next. Refer the children to the posters Checking Understanding and Responding to Text, and read the questions that accompany these strategies with the children. Explain that you will use these strategies as you read the selection together.

Think-Aloud Prompts for Use in Oral Reading Notice the think-aloud prompts with the page miniatures. These are merely suggestions. Continue to model using appropriate strategies while reading and continue to encourage children to use the strategies on their own. For a review of information about modeling and generating think-alouds, see **Learning Framework Card 8, Reading the Student Anthologies.** Encourage children to use the blending strategy when they come to regular words that they are having trouble reading.

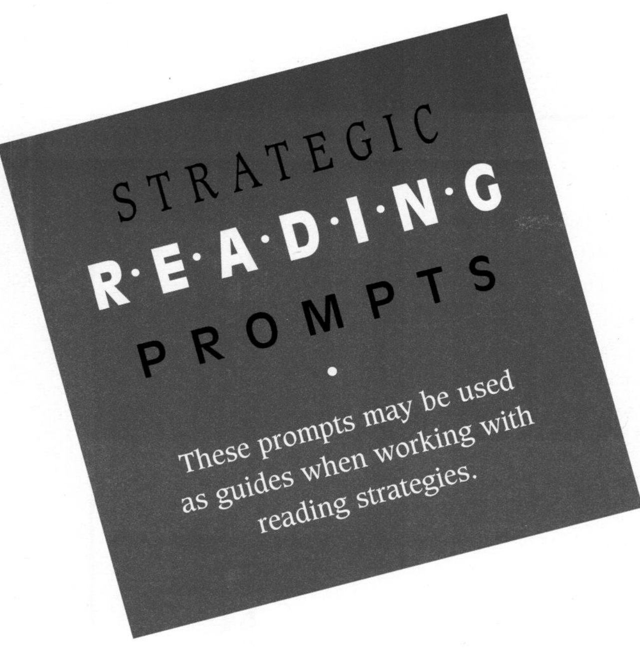
STRATEGIC
R·E·A·D·I·N·G
PROMPTS
These prompts may be used as guides when working with reading strategies.

1 Preface your reading of the introductory paragraph with an explanation such as: *I'll tell you a little about what happens before our story begins. You can follow along as I read this to you. It's in a special print right at the start of the story.*

2 This is a good spot to have the children try to predict what might happen next.

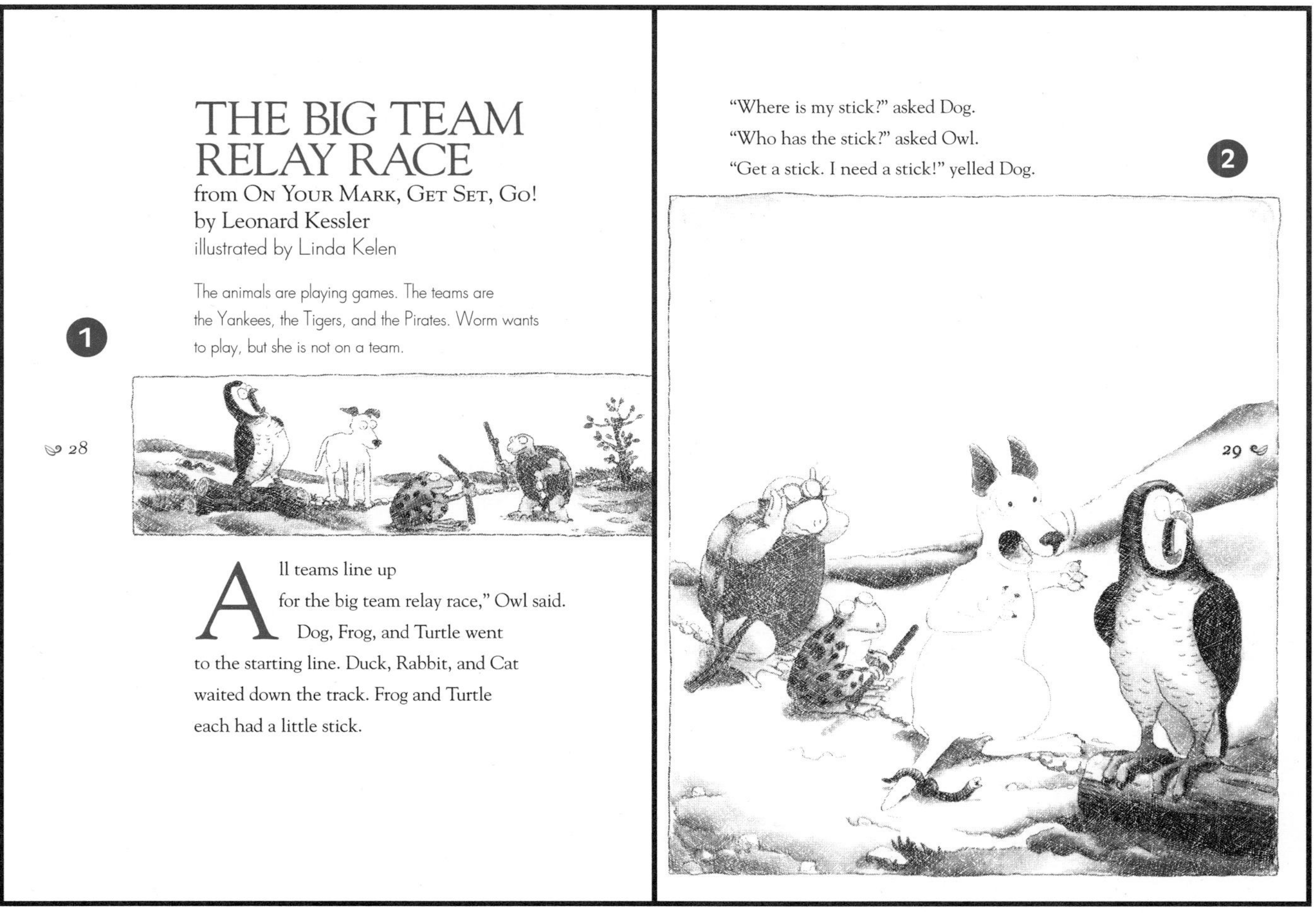

THE BIG TEAM RELAY RACE
from ON YOUR MARK, GET SET, GO!
by Leonard Kessler
illustrated by Linda Kelen

1 The animals are playing games. The teams are the Yankees, the Tigers, and the Pirates. Worm wants to play, but she is not on a team.

28

"All teams line up for the big team relay race," Owl said. Dog, Frog, and Turtle went to the starting line. Duck, Rabbit, and Cat waited down the track. Frog and Turtle each had a little stick.

"Where is my stick?" asked Dog.
"Who has the stick?" asked Owl.
"Get a stick. I need a stick!" yelled Dog. 2

29

Worm wiggled over to Owl.
"I am ready, Coach," said Worm.
"Hey, Worm," said Owl.
"You can be Dog's stick!"
"Wow! I am on a team!" said Worm.
"I'm a Yankee!"
3
30
"Okay," said Owl. "Each of you
must run with your stick. Then pass it on
to your other team member. And remember,"
said Owl, "the stick must cross the finish line."
"Okay," said little Bird.
"On your mark, Get set, Go!"
4
31

3 To make sure that the children understand the action of the story, you might say, *A worm as a stick! What do you think of that?*

4 At the end of page 31, call on a volunteer to sum up the action so far. You might want to ask the children to review names of the teams and their members. You could post team lists on the chalkboard for reference during the next lesson. Ask the children to predict which team seems most likely to win the race.

Responding

- Begin the discussion by observing that this is a very unusual relay race. Allow the children to share any ideas they have and to raise any questions they have about how this race is being carried out. Tell them they will discuss this further after they read the rest of the story.
- Invite the children to discuss how this race is the same as or different from a relay race they have participated in.

➤ Reading/Writing Connection, page 12, provides practice following directions. Help the children read the paragraph at the top and have them use the information to complete the picture.

TEACHING TIP

Have the children do some partner reading daily. Using previously read Phonics Minibooks and Step-by-Step Practice Stories for this purpose will help the children review and solidify their knowledge of the sounds and spellings they have learned. This is a good opportunity to read with children individually and to record their progress.

✱ READING ALOUD

Many versions are available of a classic story about a race, "The Tortoise and the Hare." Choose one that would be an appropriate read-aloud selection.

Reading/Writing Connection, page 12

Name

Lesson 6

Completing a Picture

The Race

Worm is winning the race. Cat is behind worm. Frog watches from the side of the road. Duck is in last place. The sun is high in the sky.

Using Story Clues

12 R/WC "The Big Team Relay Race"

2 WRITING

* DICTATION AND SPELLING

Word-Building Game Have the children use pencil and paper to build the following words:

cow
how
howl
growl
gown
town

INDEPENDENT AND COLLABORATIVE WRITING

Have the children continue working on their game books or posters. For those who want to publish their work, remind them to proofread and revise their work. Refer children to the revising and proofreading charts. Have them rewrite their piece with the corrections. Remind the children to write as legibly as possible, leaving spaces between words, since others will be reading their published work. Remind the children to illustrate their work if they wish. See **Classroom Support Teacher Tool Card 5** for more information about publishing.

Hold conferences with small groups of children who are revising and proofreading their work for publishing.

Have the children share their stories during Seminar. If any new information about games comes up during Seminar, you or the children may wish to add that information to the Concept Board. Some children may wish to post their published books or posters near or on the Concept Board as information to share with the rest of the class.

TEACHING TIP

Remind the children to use the words from the Vocabulary Chart in their writing.

3 GUIDED AND INDEPENDENT EXPLORATION

WORKSHOP

Remind the children that they may use this time to work on projects on their own or in small groups. Be sure that each child knows what projects he or she may choose and how to complete any independent work. Suggestions for teacher-guided, collaborative, and independent activities follow.

Work with the Teacher

- Lead the children in a reading relay. Form two teams of children. Have the players on each team form a line, sitting one behind the other. Make sufficient flash cards so that there is one card for each child. On the flash cards, write words that review the sound /ū/: *few, cue, hue, museum, pure, cure, cute, human, duty, mule, tune, student, pursue, use, flute.* To play the game, the first child on the team picks up a card, reads the word, then takes the card and goes to the end of the line. If a child reads the word incorrectly, the opposite team has an opportunity to say the word. The teams take turns choosing a card and blending and saying the word. The game ends when all the members on one team have successfully read a word.
- Review today's blending lesson with individuals or small groups of children who could benefit from additional practice. The words in line 5 appear in today's reading. Have the children return to the selection and look for the words. The first child to find each word should read aloud the sentence in which the word appears.
- Use flash cards to review outlaw words with those children who are having difficulty remembering them.
- Preteach the remainder of "The Big Team Relay Race" to a small group of children. Include those children with whom you worked yesterday, unless you feel that they read especially well today. In addition, invite any other children who had difficulty with today's reading. Ask the children not to reveal the ending of the story to their classmates.

Collaborative/Independent Activities

- Some children may enjoy playing Go Fish! Before Workshop begins, prepare some new cards for the decks, using the long *o* and long *u* spellings that the children learned in recent lessons. Distribute a deck to each group of children who want to play, and review with them the rules of play. Directions for play can be found on Games and Songs Teacher Tool Card 7.
- Write the following spellings on the chalkboard: *ow, oe, oa, u, u_e, ew,* and *ue.* Challenge children to write one word for each spelling. They can then write and illustrate a sentence using one or more of their words.
- Encourage children to read on their own. Provide a number of books for them to choose from. Children who enjoy reading aloud and can do so independently might like to pick out books to read to groups of two or three listeners. The readers may read alone or take turns reading with a partner.
- Activity Sheet 76 reviews spellings for /ō/. Explain to the children that to complete this activity sheet, they must find the words that are listed at the top of the page within the block of letters below. To get them started, you might want to help them search for and circle the first word, *go*.

Name

Lesson 6

go	flow	note	toe
hoe	coat	blow	soap

w	g	b	z	o	k	m	p
n	o	t	e	c	l	i	s
u	w	c	o	a	t	d	o
f	l	o	w	c	n	t	a
s	a	h	o	e	p	o	p
j	b	l	o	w	w	e	i

Activity Sheet 76

LESSON 7

Lesson Overview

New Learning

- /ow/ spelled *ou*

Materials

- "The Big Team Relay Race," pages 32–37
- Phonics Minibook 14, *The Everybody Club*
- Sound/Spelling Card 39, Cow
- Learning Framework Cards 3, 4, 6, 8
- Reading/Writing Connection, pages 13–14
- Activity Sheet 77

Prepare Ahead

- *ue, u_e, ow* Flash Cards (see page 86)
- Blank index cards (see page 86)

GETTING STARTED

Choose one or more of the following activities to focus the children's attention and to review some of the concepts they have been learning.

Team Words Game Have the children work in groups of equal numbers. Give each group a sheet of paper. Write the letters *ow* on the chalkboard and tell the first person in each group to write a word that contains *ow* as in *cow*. When that child finishes, he or she should pass the paper to the next child, who writes a new word. Continue until every member of each group has written a word. Have the groups read their lists to the class.

Spelling Challenge Divide the class into three or four teams. Explain that you will write a spelling of a long vowel sound on the board and give the teams thirty seconds to one minute to think of words that use that spelling. When time is up, call on each team to say and spell its words. Write them on the board and award one point for each correct word. The team with the most points is the winner. Remind the children to whisper so that those on other teams can't hear overhear their words.

1 READING

PHONICS

Introduce /ow/ spelled *ou* Display Sound/Spelling Card 39, Cow, and ask the children what sound this card stands for and what spelling they have already learned that makes the /ow/ sound. Then direct attention to the spelling *ou* and tell the children that this is another way to spell the /ow/ sound in words.

Blending Help the children blend the following words. A complete discussion of the blending procedure can be found on **Learning Framework Card 3.**

Line 1:	out pout shout about
Line 2:	our sour flour flower
Line 3:	couch pouch house mouse
Line 4:	loud sound playground outside
Line 5:	kindergarten everybody

In line 2, point out and discuss the homophones *flour* and *flower*. To help the children remember the meanings of the words, point to one of them and have a child use it in a sentence. Do this several times for both words.

In line 3, tell the children that the *e* at the end of *house* and *mouse* is silent.

The words in line 5 will appear in *The Everybody Club,* Phonics Minibook 14.

For review, ask the children to find and erase

- a word that rhymes with *ouch*
- a place to play
- the way a lemon tastes
- something you do when you are angry
- an animal

➤ Reading/Writing Connection, page 13, provides practice with the *ou* spelling of the /ow/ sound. Help the children complete the top of the page by reading and copying the words and the sentence.

* READING THE STUDENT ANTHOLOGY

"The Big Team Relay Race"
pages 32–37

Activating Prior Knowledge

Have children sum up what happened in the first part of the story, pages 28–31. If in the previous lesson you wrote the names of the teams and team members on the chalkboard, use them to refresh the children's memories.

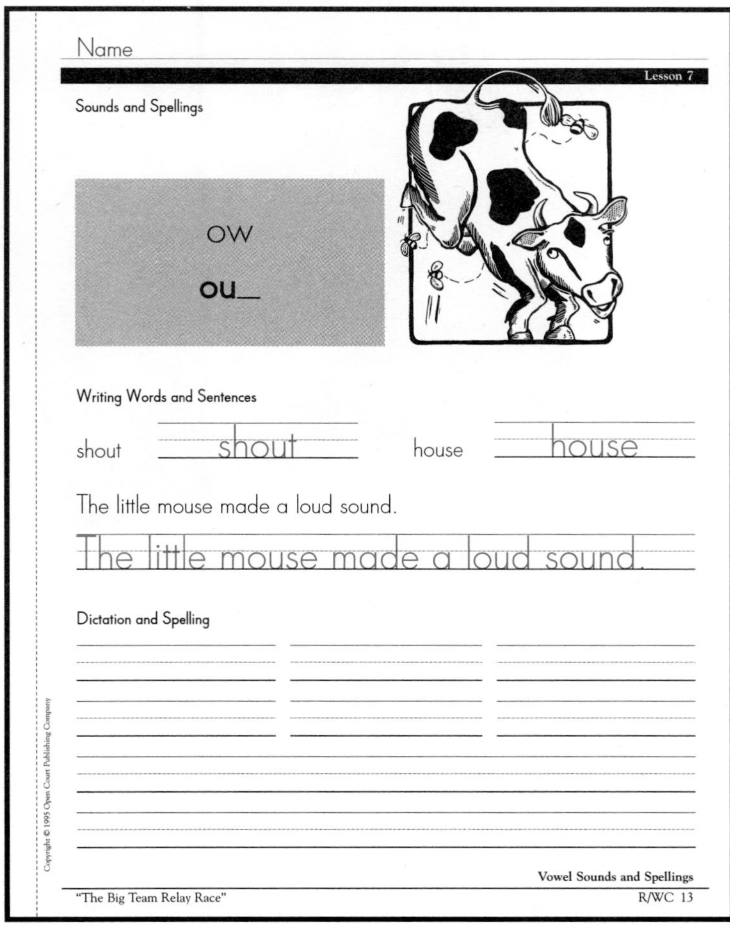
Name

Lesson 7

Sounds and Spellings

ow

ou_

Writing Words and Sentences

shout shout house house

The little mouse made a loud sound.

The little mouse made a loud sound.

Dictation and Spelling

Vowel Sounds and Spellings

"The Big Team Relay Race" R/WC 13

Reading/Writing Connection, page 13

Recommendations for Reading

Have the children read the second part of the story aloud. Encourage wondering, predictions, comments, and questions as the reading progresses.

About the Reading Strategies

In reading this selection, children will find the strategies of **predicting** and **wondering** useful. Explain that you will model these strategies as you read the selection together. Remind the children to use their decoding strategy for unfamiliar words.

Think-Aloud Prompts for Use in Oral Reading Notice the think-aloud prompts with the page miniatures. These are merely suggestions. Continue to model using appropriate strategies while reading and to encourage children to use the strategies on their own. For a review of information about modeling and generating think-alouds, see **Learning Framework Card 8, Reading the Student Anthologies.**

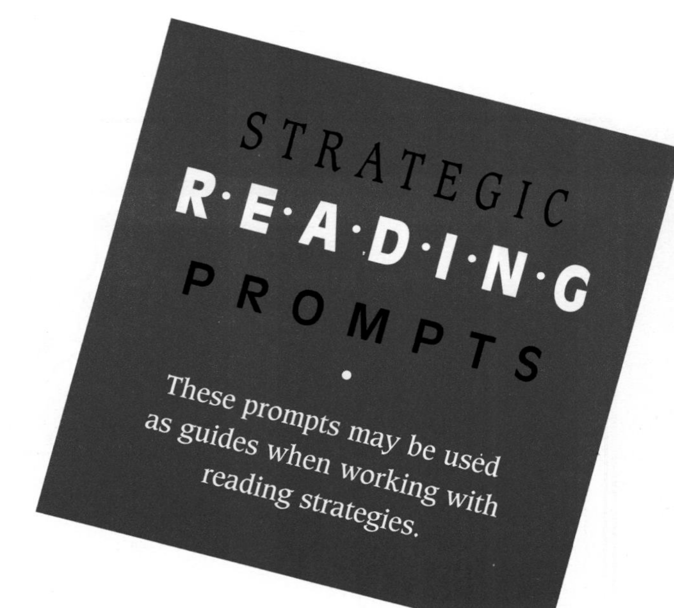
STRATEGIC
R·E·A·D·I·N·G
PROMPTS
These prompts may be used as guides when working with reading strategies.

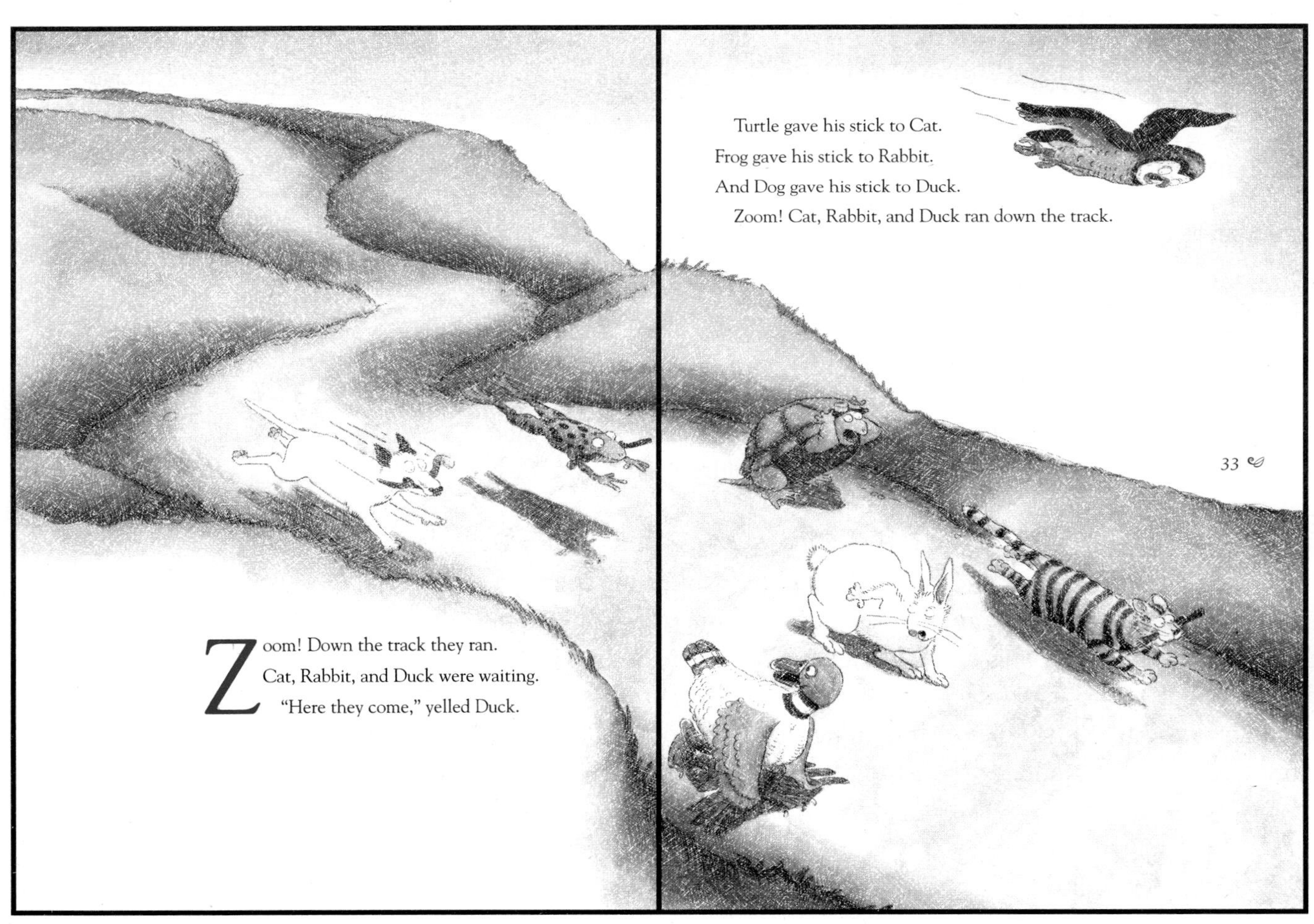
Zoom! Down the track they ran.
Cat, Rabbit, and Duck were waiting.
"Here they come," yelled Duck.
Turtle gave his stick to Cat.
Frog gave his stick to Rabbit.
And Dog gave his stick to Duck.
Zoom! Cat, Rabbit, and Duck ran down the track.
33

1 "Duck is winning, Duck is winning!" yelled Dog.
Duck smiled and waved to the cheering crowd.

34

35

She tripped over her big web feet
and fell into a big mud puddle. Squoosh!
"Get up, Duck," shouted Dog.
"Yikes," yelled Duck, "I am stuck in the mud!"
"Don't worry, Duck," said Worm.
"I will win the race for our team." 2

1. Ask the children what they think might happen now.

2. This is a good spot to predict what might happen. If the children give only one opinion, ask, *What else could happen?*

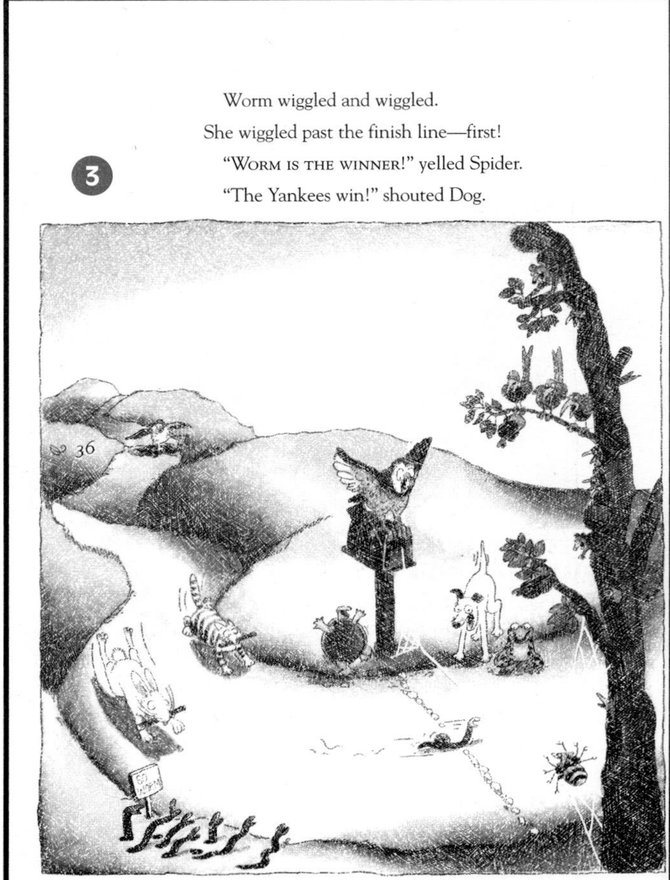

3

Worm wiggled and wiggled.
She wiggled past the finish line—first!
"WORM IS THE WINNER!" yelled Spider.
"The Yankees win!" shouted Dog.

36

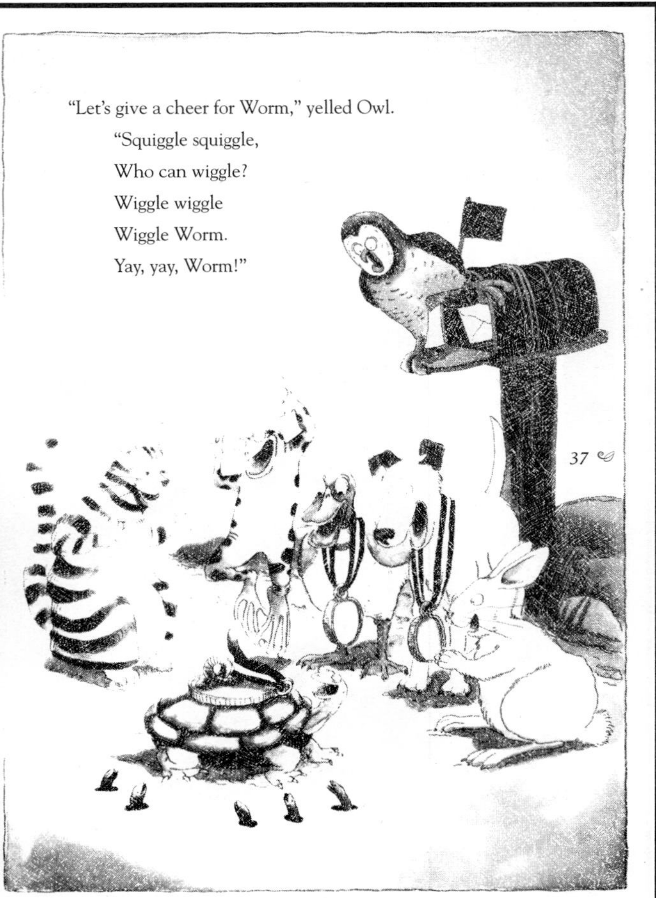

"Let's give a cheer for Worm," yelled Owl.
"Squiggle squiggle,
Who can wiggle?
Wiggle wiggle
Wiggle Worm.
Yay, yay, Worm!"

37

3 You might want to model responding to the story by commenting *Good for Worm!* or by wondering how Worm could have wiggled faster than Cat or Rabbit ran. If any of the children predicted that Worm would win the race, point out that this prediction came true.

Responding

- Invite children to comment on how the race turned out. If any children have participated in relay races, have them share these experiences.
- Have the children discuss relay races, and then you might add this information to the Concept Board.

Vocabulary Discuss with the children any interesting or unusual words from the selection, especially the rhyming words on the last page. Add the words to the class vocabulary chart and have the children write them in their journals. Remind the children to use these words in their own writing.

➤ Have the children complete page 14 in their Reading/Writing Connection book by writing the word that completes each sentence.

TEACHING TIP

Review the postings on the Concept Board with the children. Discuss the kinds of things that have been posted (names of games, pictures, questions about games). Help the children sort these and organize them into different areas of the board.

Reading/Writing Connection, page 14

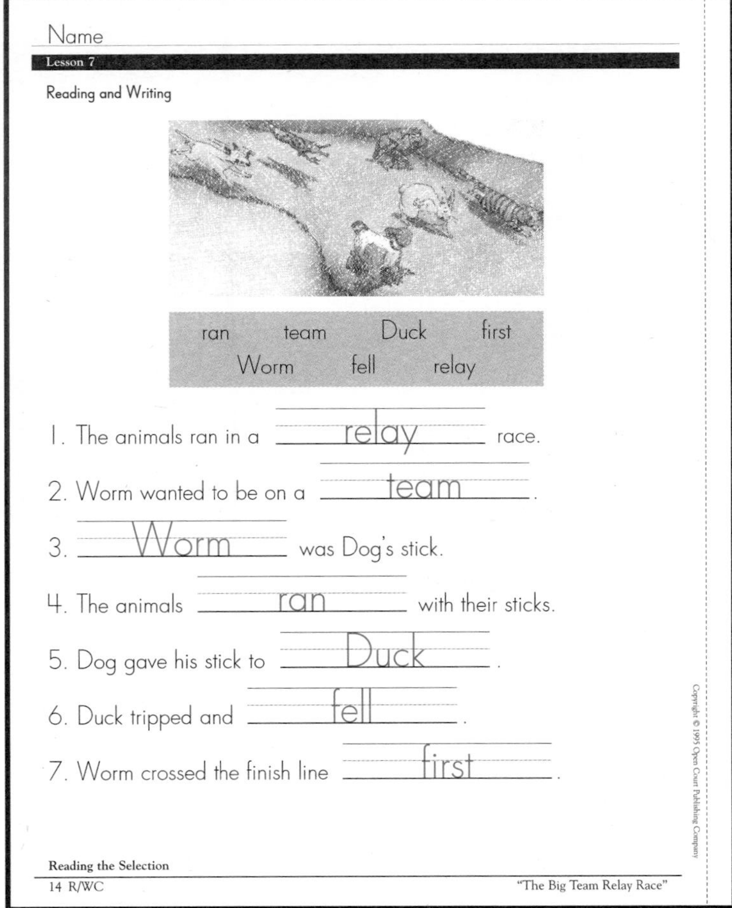

Name

Lesson 7

Reading and Writing

ran team Duck first Worm fell relay

1. The animals ran in a relay race.
2. Worm wanted to be on a team.
3. Worm was Dog's stick.
4. The animals ran with their sticks.
5. Dog gave his stick to Duck.
6. Duck tripped and fell.
7. Worm crossed the finish line first.

Copyright © 1995 Open Court Publishing Company

Reading the Selection

14 R/WC "The Big Team Relay Race"

* READING A PHONICS MINIBOOK

The Everybody Club
Phonics Minibook 14

Getting Ready to Read

Allow the children to look through the book, commenting on what they see in the pictures and what they think the story will be about. They may notice that many of the words in the story have all capital letters.

Recommendations

Have the children read a page of the story to themselves, then call on a different child to read each page of the story aloud. If a child has difficulty with a word, follow the procedures shown on **Learning Framework Card 6.** Reread the story at least twice, calling on different children to read.

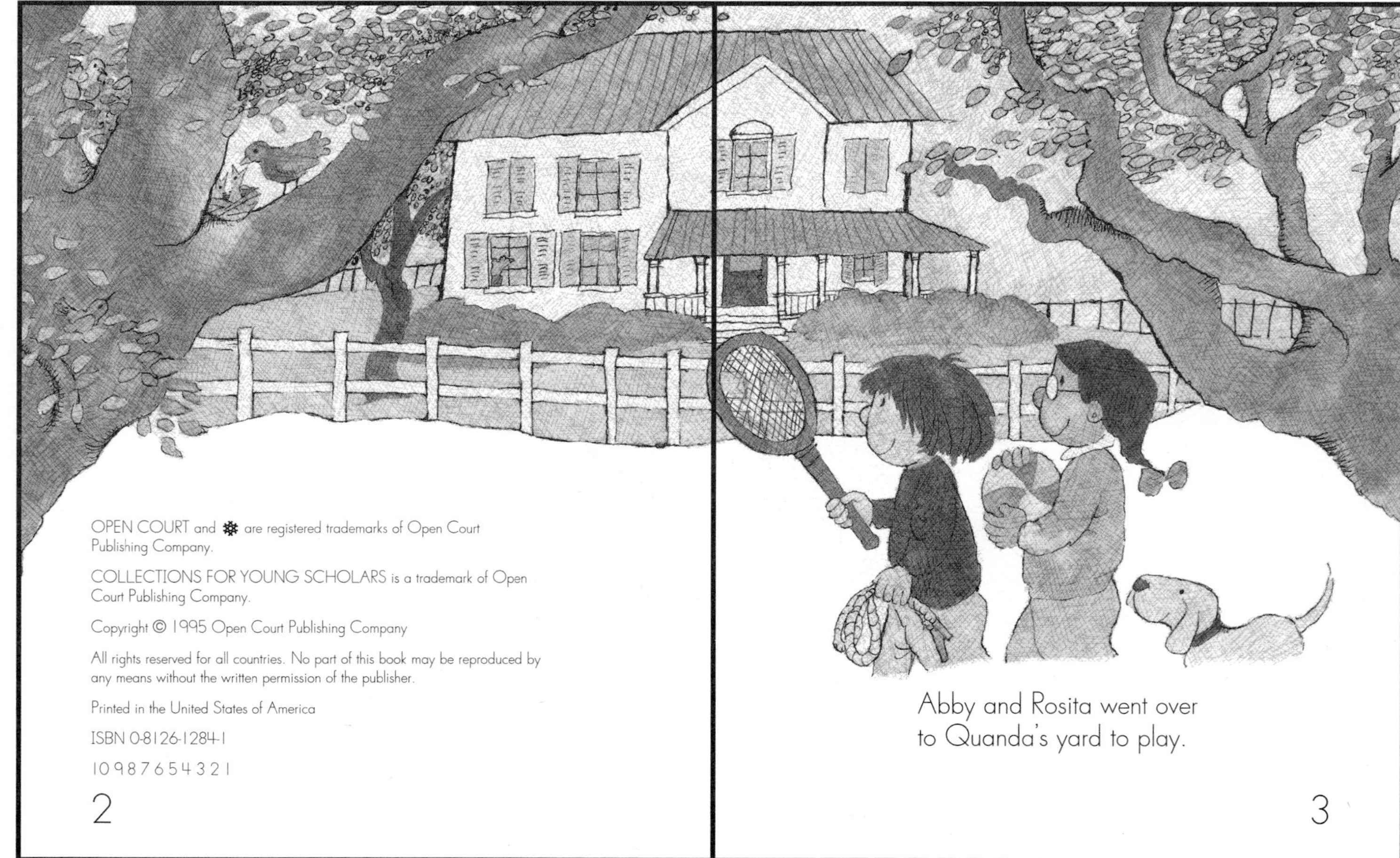

Printed in the United States of America

ISBN 0-8126-1284-1

10 9 8 7 6 5 4 3 2 1

2

Abby and Rosita went over to Quanda's yard to play.

3

"Come on!" called Quanda.
"We can play in the tree house!"

4

"Wow! What a neat place!" said Abby.

"Let's make a club!" said Rosita.
"We can call it the Three Girls Club."

5

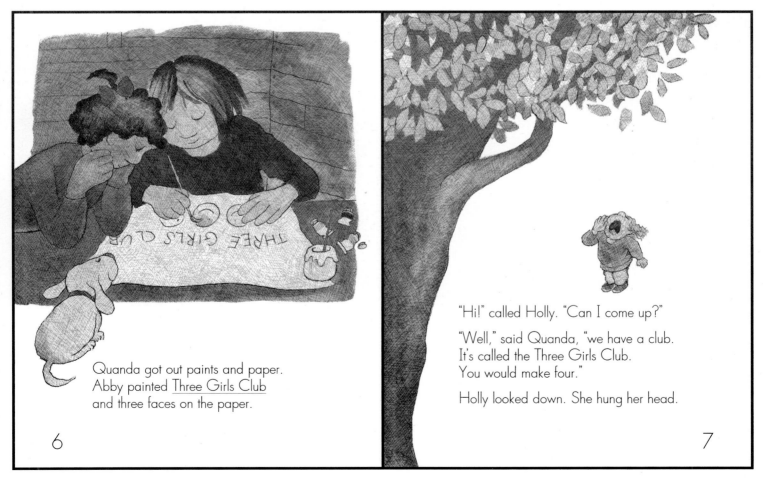

Quanda got out paints and paper.
Abby painted <u>Three Girls Club</u>
and three faces on the paper.

6

"Hi!" called Holly. "Can I come up?"

"Well," said Quanda, "we have a club.
It's called the Three Girls Club.
You would make four."

Holly looked down. She hung her head.

7

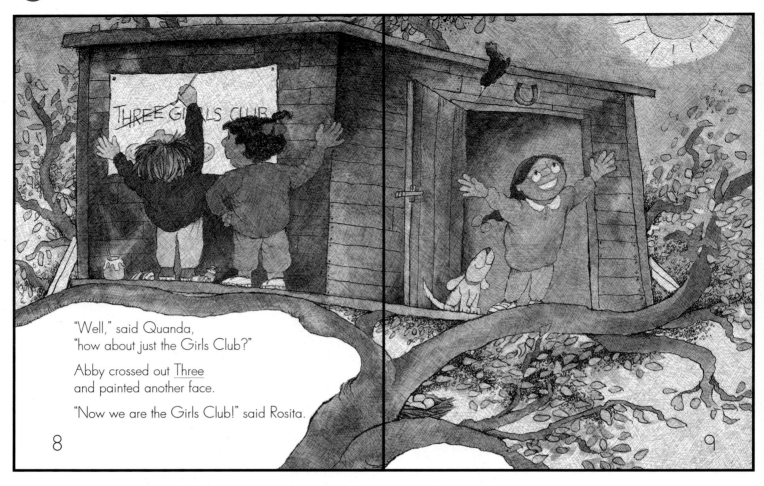

"Well," said Quanda,
"how about just the Girls Club?"

Abby crossed out Three
and painted another face.

"Now we are the Girls Club!" said Rosita.

8

9

"Hi!" called David. "Can I come up?"

"Well," said Quanda, "we have a club.
It's called the Girls Club,
and you aren't a girl."

David frowned. He kicked the dirt.

10

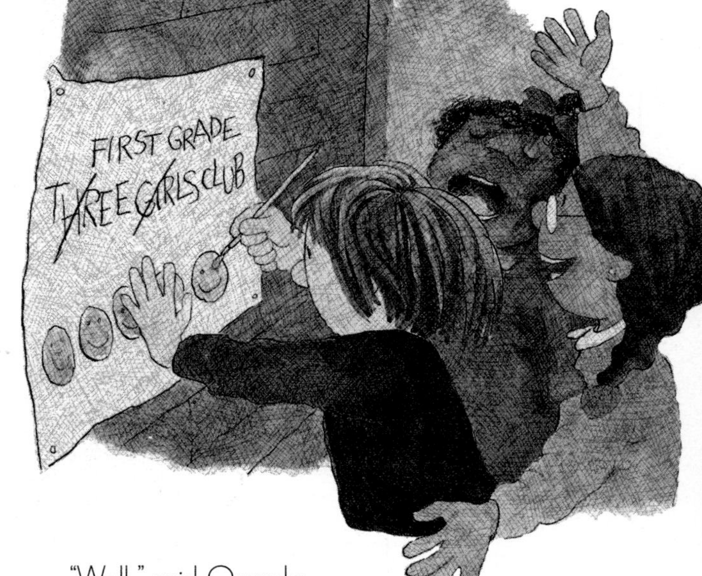

"Well," said Quanda,
"how about the First Grade Club?"

Abby crossed out Girls
and painted First Grade.
Then she painted another face.

"Now we are the First Grade Club!" said Rosita.

11

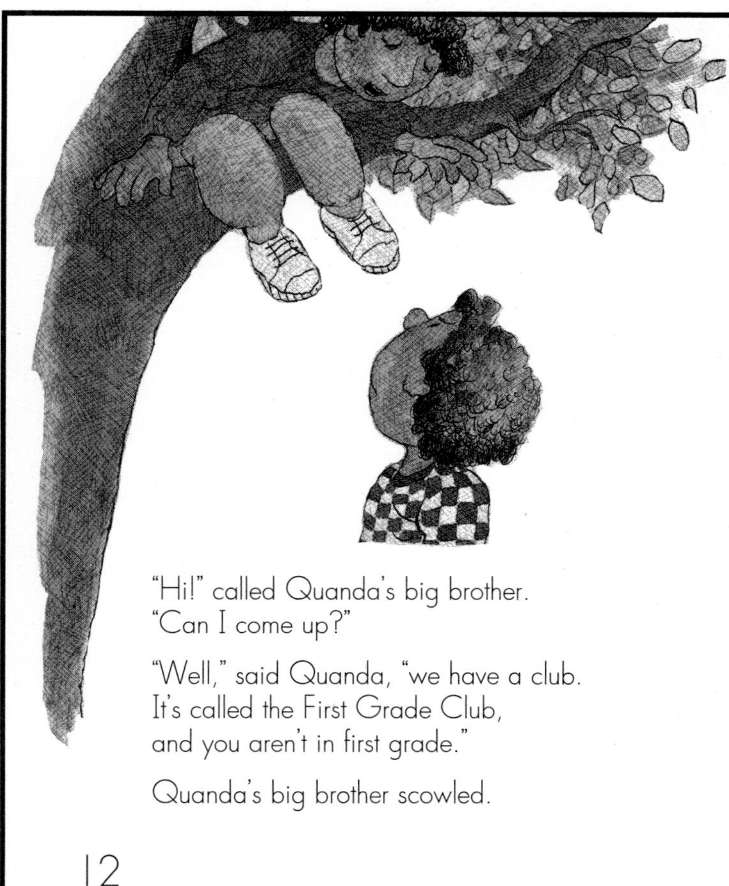

"Hi!" called Quanda's big brother.
"Can I come up?"

"Well," said Quanda, "we have a club.
It's called the First Grade Club,
and you aren't in first grade."

Quanda's big brother scowled.

12

"Well," said Quanda,
"how about the All Grades Club?"

Abby crossed out First,
added an s, and painted All.
Then she painted another face.

"Now we are the All Grades Club!" said Rosita.

13

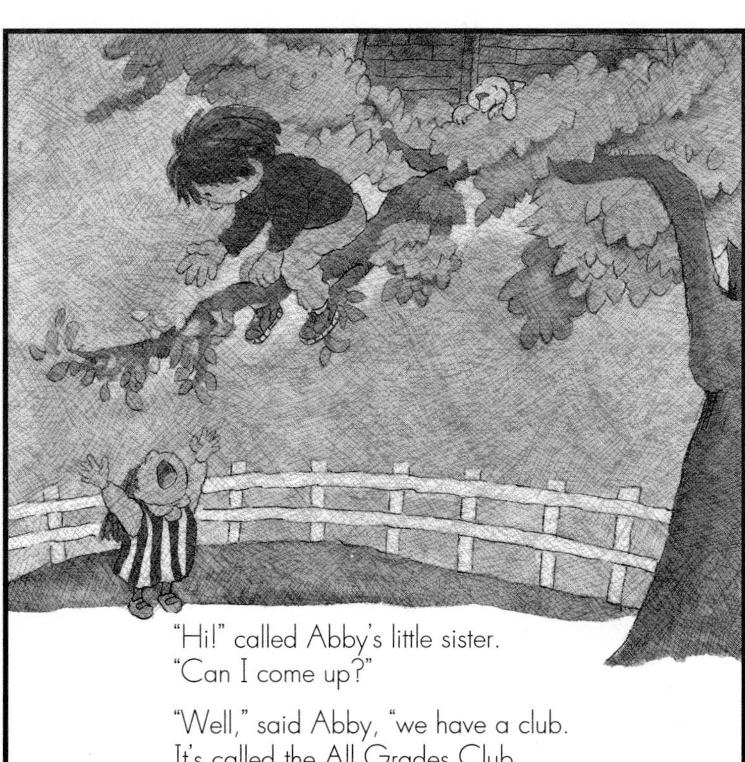

"Hi!" called Abby's little sister.
"Can I come up?"

"Well," said Abby, "we have a club.
It's called the All Grades Club,
and you aren't even in kindergarten!"

14

"It's getting crowded!" said Rosita.
"How about just calling it
the Everybody Club?"

Abby crossed out All Grades
and painted Everybody.
Then she painted lots of faces.

15

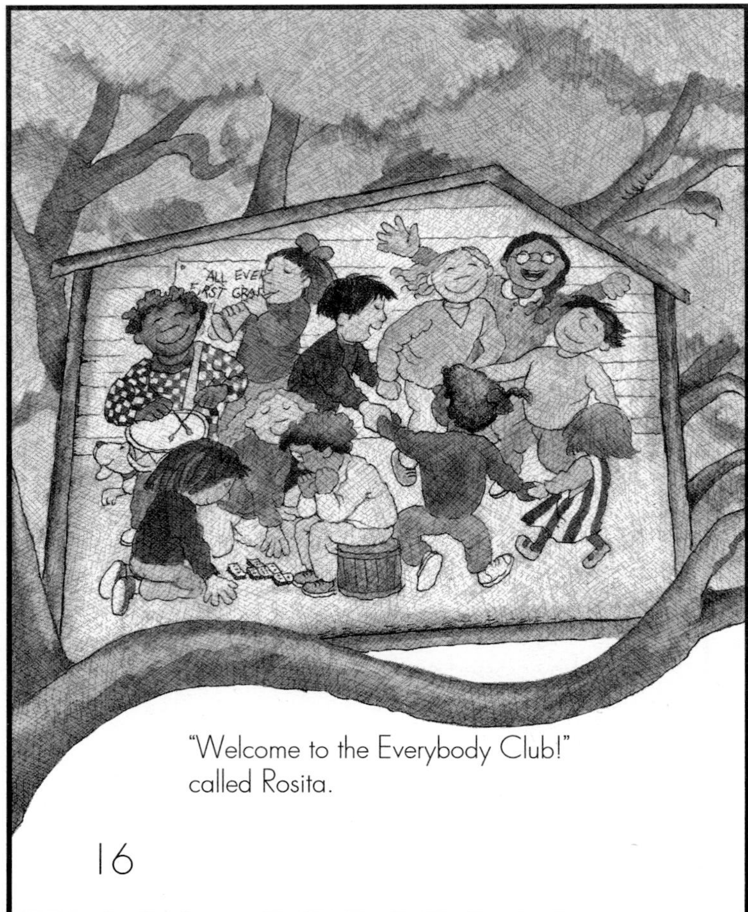
"Welcome to the Everybody Club!"
called Rosita.

16

Responding

After reading, have the children tell in their own words what happened in the story and discuss any difficulties they had while reading the story. To determine that the children are focusing on the words in the story, ask the following questions, having children point to the word in the story that answers each question:

- Where do Abby and Rosita go to play?
- What is the first name of the club?
- What does Quanda get to make a sign for the club?
- What does Holly ask the girls?
- What does David do when the girls say that he isn't a girl?
- What is the club called after David joins?
- What is the club called after Abby's sister joins?

Allow time for children to pair up and reread the story with partners.

TEACHING TIP

Remind the children to read each book twice. When they finish today's book, they should get one from a previous lesson. Reading Assessment Sheets for Phonics Minibooks are available in *Assessment Masters, Grade 1*.

* READING ALOUD

Select one or more versions of "The Tortoise and the Hare." Read these to the children and have them compare what happened in these stories to events in "The Big Team Relay Race." Encourage children to add new ideas and wonderings to the Concept Board.

2 WRITING

* DICTATION AND SPELLING

Have the children open their Reading/Writing Connection book to page 13. Dictate the following words and sentence, using the suggestions for dictation that appear on **Learning Framework Card 4.**

Line 1: how clown flower

Line 2: hope coach pony

Sentence: We drove downtown.

Proofread as usual.

TEACHING TIP

Before dictating line 2, remind the children to use Sound/Spelling Card 35, Long O, to help them find the correct long *o* spelling for each word. Encourage them to ask which spelling to use if they are unsure.

EXPLORING THE WRITER'S CRAFT

Talk about kinds of games based upon the selections that the children have been reading. *Jafta* offers an alternative to the types of games children usually think about. In this story, Jafta plays a game where he pretends that he is a different animal depending on how he feels. This game has no rules or teams. This is in contrast to the "Big Team Relay Race."

Some children may want to continue writing about games from a different perspective. They may want to write about a team sport, a game they attended, a team they participated in, their favorite player, or a fantasy game they play with their friends, toys, or imaginary characters. Some children may enjoy writing in their journal over a period of days about a favorite team or player.

For children who are having trouble coming up with an idea for writing, conference with them at the Concept Board to see if anything stirs their imagination. Children who do not want to write about games are free to select any topic they wish.

TEACHING TIP

When the children write, remind them to date their papers and add them to their folders. This way, they will always have examples of their own writing to work on.

TIP FOR ENGLISH LANGUAGE LEARNERS

Draw English Language Learners into small-group discussions to reinforce that their ideas are valid and worth attention. Encourage the children to express their ideas and help each other with suggestions of where they might need to add an example or rewrite a sentence.

3 GUIDED AND INDEPENDENT EXPLORATION

WORKSHOP

Remind the children that they may use this time to work on projects on their own or in small groups. Be sure that each child knows what projects he or she may choose and how to complete any independent work. Suggestions for teacher-guided, collaborative, and independent activities follow.

Learning Framework Card 11, Workshop, contains a complete discussion of establishing and conducting Workshop and suggestions for helping English Language Learners during Workshop.

Work with the Teacher

- Review Sound/Spelling Card 39, Cow, with children who could benefit from reinforcement of /ow/ spelled *ow.* After reviewing the card, have the children reread Phonics Minibook 14. Rereading provides an opportunity to assess children's progress.
- Before Workshop begins, add to the set of flash cards used during yesterday's Reading Relay. The new cards should include these words: *blow, snow, show, shower, flower, brown, grown, gown, row, towel, tow, owl, how, flow.* Use the cards to work with children who need practice choosing the correct pronunciation of each vowel spelling included in the list above.
- Invite children who are reading independently to choose books to read aloud to you. You might encourage them to select books about races or contests. Invite other children who might enjoy hearing the books to listen in.

Collaborative/Independent Activities

- Pairs of children can reread Phonics Minibook 14, copying down each word in the story that contains /ow/. When they finish reading, they should use each word in a new sentence.
- Have the children work in small groups to create a mural of words with the /ow/ sound. Have each group draw a farm scene, a city scene, or other scene of their choice on poster board or chart paper. Tell them to draw or paste on as many pictures as they can of objects and actions that contain the /ow/ sound. Have them label each object and action with the letters *ow.* Combine the scenes into a mural and display the mural in the classroom.
- Children who enjoy playing the Scrambled Sentences game may want to work alone or in groups to make up some Scrambled Sentences of their own. Provide them with note cards and envelopes. Tell them that they should print one word on each note card and that the first word should have a capital letter, while the last word should be followed by a period. Remind them, also, that they should print an answer key on the inside flap of each Scrambled Sentence envelope. Challenge the children to use /ow/ words in their sentences.
- Activity Sheet 77 reviews the two sounds of the spelling *ow,* as well as /ū/ sounds and spellings. Point out the key at the top of the page and tell the children to use it to help them color the sections of the quilt. They should color those sections with the /ow/ sound red, sections with the /ō/ sound yellow, and sections with the /ū/ sound blue.

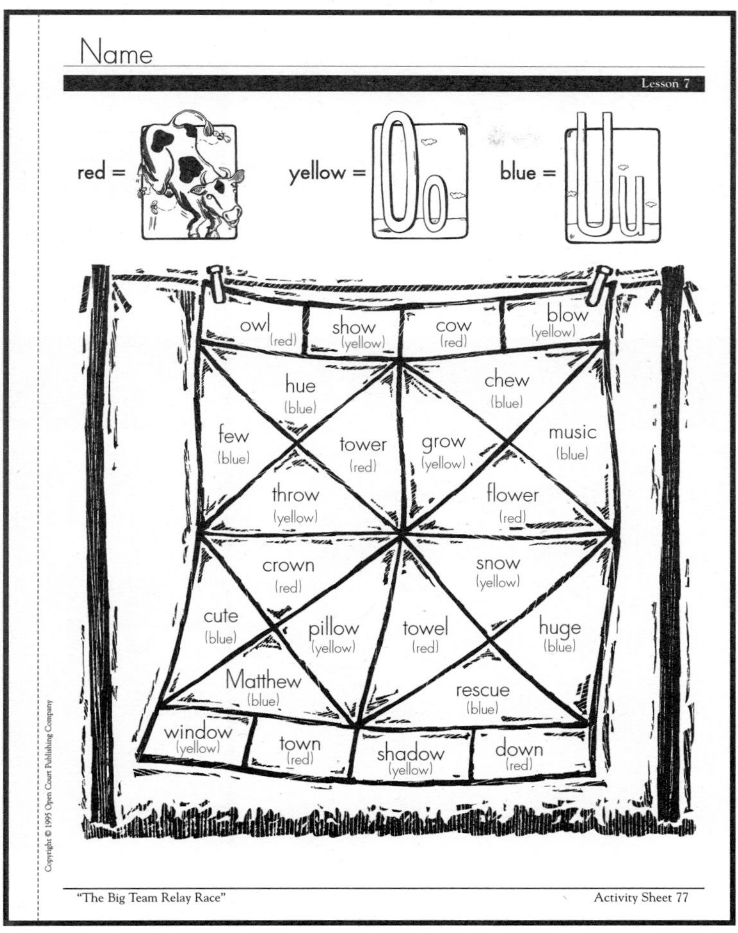
Name
Lesson 7
red =
yellow =
blue =
owl (red)
show (yellow)
cow (red)
blow (yellow)
hue (blue)
chew (blue)
few (blue)
tower (red)
grow (yellow)
music (blue)
throw (yellow)
flower (red)
crown (red)
snow (yellow)
cute (blue)
pillow (yellow)
towel (red)
huge (blue)
Matthew (blue)
rescue (blue)
window (yellow)
town (red)
shadow (yellow)
down (red)
Copyright © 1995 Open Court Publishing Company
"The Big Team Relay Race"
Activity Sheet 77

Activity Sheet 77

LESSON 8

Lesson Overview

New Learning

- Dialogue

Materials

- "The Big Team Relay Race," pages 28–37
- Learning Framework Card 3
- Reading/Writing Connection, pages 15–16
- Activity Sheet 78

Prepare Ahead

- Note cards (see page 93)
- Construction paper, two colors (see page 89)

GETTING STARTED

Choose one or more of the following activities to focus the children's attention and to review some of the concepts they have been learning.

Same Spelling/Different Sound (/ow/ Review) Write one word on the chalkboard at a time. Have the children read the word quietly to themselves. Tell them that if the word contains /ō/, they should hold their arms out from their sides. If the word contains /ow/, they should hold their hands close together in front of them. After the children have done this, ask them to read the word aloud in unison. You might want to use some of the following words:

blow	mow	cow
power	now	
how	low	

Identifying Rhymes On the chalkboard, write three words spaced widely apart. Have the children say the words quietly to themselves and then point to the word that does not rhyme with the others. Ask the children to read the word aloud together. Use these words:

how now low	shower mitten flower
show cow mow	fly round sound
own clown brown	shout think pout

TEACHING TIP

This is an activity in which it is valuable to have the children wait to give a response.

1 READING

PHONICS

* **Blending** Help the children blend the following words. A complete discussion of the blending procedure can be found on **Learning Framework Card 3.**

Line 1:	**frown growl downstairs downtown**
Line 2:	**show grown owner bowl**
Line 3:	**bird turn winner spider**
Line 4:	**worm worry work world**
Line 5:	**fuss fuse full fuel**

After blending line 1, remind the children that they have learned two sounds for the spelling *ow.* If the children do not remember the other sound, point to the Long O Sound/Spelling Card. Blend the words in line 2. Tell the children that if they come across a word they don't know that has this spelling, they should try the /ow/ sound first. If the word is unfamiliar or doesn't make sense, they should try the long *o* sound.

The words in line 3 review the /er/ sound. In line 4, introduce the special pattern *wor.* Tell the children that this pattern also has the /er/ sound.

Line 5 contrasts the long and short sounds of *u.*

To review the word lines, play a number game. Print the numbers 1–4 on separate pieces of construction paper, all the same color. On five pieces of a different-colored construction paper, print the numbers 1–5. Place the set of four numbers in a container labeled *words* and the set of five in a container labeled *lines.* Invite a volunteer to pick two pieces of construction paper—one of each color. The child then uses the two numbers to locate the word. For example, if the child chooses 2 and 5, the word to find and read is the second word in line 5, *fuse.* Put the numbers back in the container and repeat with other students.

➤ Reading/Writing Connection, page 15, reviews the spellings for the /ow/ sound and contrasts the sounds of words spelled with *ow.* Help the students finish the page by selecting the correct word to complete each sentence. At the bottom of the page have them list the words with the /ow/ sound and the words with the long *o* sound.

Name

Lesson 8

how sound snow crow crown show

1. The queen has a crown with a big round ruby.

2. Do you know how to play checkers?

3. The class put on a puppet show.

4. The balloon made a loud sound when it popped.

5. The snow made the ground white.

6. A crow is a big, black bird.

crown	show
how	snow
sound	crow

Vowel Sounds and Spellings

"The Big Team Relay Race" R/WC 15

Reading/Writing Connection, page 15

✱ READING THE STUDENT ANTHOLOGY

"The Big Team Relay Race"
pages 28–37

Activating Prior Knowledge

Review the story briefly by calling on volunteers to sum up its main events.

Recommendations for Reading

- Begin work on expressive reading. Tell the children that they should try to read as though they were reading a story to a younger sister or brother. If a student reads without expression, model reading a sentence or two and ask the student to read again with more expression.
- The children might enjoy acting out the story. Assign a narrator and players for each story character. To allow more children an opportunity to read, you may wish to change players for the second part of the story. Remind the children who are playing parts to read only the words within the quotation marks.

Note: Reading the story with a partner is a good option for Workshop.

TEACHING TIP

Set aside ten minutes for partner reading every day. During this time, you should read with individuals, recording their progress.

Responding

- Ask the children to comment on their favorite parts or on what they liked best.
- Call on volunteers to name the characters in the story and to tell what each character did.
- Discuss whether this story is real or make-believe and why. Have the children compare this to other fantasy stories they have read.

Vocabulary Discuss with the children any interesting or unusual words from the selection. Have several children use these words in oral sentences. Add these to your class vocabulary chart and have children write them in their journals. Possible words are *cheering, remember, squoosh, team, wiggle,* and *winner.* Remind children to use these in their own writing.

2 WRITING

* DICTATION AND SPELLING

Word-Building Game Have the children use paper and pencil to build the following words:

out
ouch
couch
pouch
pound
hound
house

Minilesson

Dialogue

Previous lessons introduced the use of dialogue bubbles as a way of showing who is talking. In addition the children have read many selections that use bubbles and quotation marks. "The Big Team Relay Race" has excellent examples of dialogue. Writers use dialogue to make the story more interesting and to make the characters seem real. Remind the children that when writers use dialogue, they let the reader know by putting the words the character says in quotation marks.

"Where is my stick?" asked Dog.
"Get up, Duck," shouted Dog.
"Wow! I am on a team!" said Worm.

Have the children look through "The Big Team Relay Race" to find and read other examples of dialogue.

▶ Reading/Writing Connection, page 16, asks the children to find statements made by the characters in "The Big Team Relay Race." Have them find a statement made by the character and write the dialogue within the quotation marks. To the side, they should write the number of the page on which they found the dialogue. Provide time for the children to compare their pages.

After the children have finished page 16 in the Reading/Writing Connection book, have them look at their own stories and try to include dialogue in their writing about games. For example, if the children are writing about a team game they attended, they may want to add dialogue such as: "Go, Tigers!" yelled the crowd.

TEACHING TIP

Remind the children to use the words from the Vocabulary Chart in their own writing.

Reading/Writing Connection, page 16

Name

Lesson 8

Quotation Marks

"All teams line up," said Owl.

(Student answers will vary.)

" ______________________________
______________________________," yelled Dog. page ______

" ______________________________
______________________________," said Worm. page ______

" ______________________________
______________________________," yelled Duck. page ______

" ______________________________," said little Bird. page ______

Using Dialogue

16 R/WC "The Big Team Relay Race"

3 GUIDED AND INDEPENDENT EXPLORATION

WORKSHOP

Remind the children that they may use this time to work on projects on their own or in small groups. Be sure that each child knows what projects he or she may choose and how to complete any independent work. Suggestions for teacher-guided, collaborative, and independent activities follow.

Work with the Teacher

- Use the flash cards from yesterday's lesson to play the Reading Relay game with two teams of four or five children each. To make the teams even and the game fun, make sure each team includes children of varying abilities.
- Play the Word-Building game for additional spelling practice. Repeat today's word list or choose a previous list, according to the children's needs.
- With your help, some of the children might enjoy creating a poster that tells how a "good sport" should behave. Begin by having the children brainstorm for ideas that they might want to include on the chart. As new ideas are raised, write them down on the chalkboard or a sheet of chart paper where all the children can see them. Save them to use during tomorrow's Workshop. This project should take three to five days to complete.

Collaborative/Independent Activities

- If some of the children made Scrambled Sentences games yesterday, other children may want to solve them now. Remind them to check their work against the answer keys and to recopy their unscrambled sentences onto scratch paper for you to see.
- Pairs of children can make new cards for the Go Fish! game, using words that contain /ow/ spelled *ou* or *ow*. When one child thinks of an /ow/ word, his or her partner should think of another word that rhymes with it. Each child should write on scratch paper all the words that she or he generates. When the children have completed five or six pairs of words, they should trade lists and proofread each other's words making any necessary corrections. Tomorrow they can copy the words onto note cards to include in the Go Fish! deck.
- Pairs of children may want to work on adding dialogue to their own stories.
- Activity Sheet 78 focuses on the /ow/ sound and spellings. Explain to the children that only one word in each of the sentences on this activity sheet has the /ow/ sound. They should find this word, circle it, then draw a picture of the circled word in the corresponding box at the bottom of the page.

Name

Lesson 8

1. Let's pick a flower to show Mom.
2. The little mouse ate the yellow cheese.
3. Do cows grow by eating grass?
4. Each king has his own crown.
5. Do you know which house is Tom's?
6. The crow flies in the clouds.

(Student art as indicated)

flower	mouse	cows
1.	2.	3.
crown	house	clouds
4.	5.	6.

Activity Sheet 78 "The Big Team Relay Race"

Activity Sheet 78

LESSON 9

Lesson Overview

Materials

- "Mary Mack," pages 38–39
- Learning Framework Cards 3, 4
- Reading/Writing Connection, pages 17–18
- Alphabet Flash Cards
- Activity Sheet 79

Prepare Ahead

- Charades Word Cards (see page 96)
- Chart paper with ladder (see page 96)

GETTING STARTED

Choose one or more of the following activities to focus the children's attention and to review some of the concepts they have been learning.

Before and After Game Have the children sit in a circle. Shuffle the Alphabet Flash Cards and go around the circle, showing a card to each child. The child should name the letter shown and then tell the letter that comes after the one on the card. Vary the game by having the children name the letter that comes before and after theirs.

TEACHING TIP

Start the game by having the children name the letter that comes after, as it is much easier than naming the letter that comes before. Remind them they can use the Sound/Spelling Cards.

Team Words Game Have the children work in teams and give the first child in each team a sheet of paper. Write the spelling *ou* on the chalkboard and have each child write a word with this spelling. Have the teams read their completed list of words.

1 READING

PHONICS

No new sounds are introduced in this lesson. Choose one of the following review activities, or review those sounds and spellings that you feel would be most beneficial for your students.

What Am I? What Am I Doing? Play a game of Charades with word cards that contain the /ow/ sound.

bounce	count	cow	owl	spout
mouse	growl	crouch	frown	shout

Place the cards in an empty container and invite a child to pick a word. Have the child whisper the word in your ear, then act it out for the class. For example, if the child chooses *spout*, he or she could pretend to be a teapot tipping its spout. The other children guess what the word is. The child shows the card and blends the word with the class. Have one of the children then write the word on the board.

Up the Ladder Game The Up the Ladder game reviews words with double consonants and reinforces the rule that double consonants make only one sound.

Draw a ladder on a piece of chart paper. On each step of the ladder print a word with double consonants. Example words include the following:

ladder	hammer	giggle	button
allow	middle	worry	cinnamon
pillow	zipper	rabbit	happy

Cover each word with construction paper and have the children climb the ladder by blending the word as it is revealed.

When the children reach the top, ask what they notice about all the words. Have them circle the double consonant spellings and congratulate them for recognizing that these spellings make only one sound.

* **Blending** Help the children blend the following words. A complete discussion of the blending procedure can be found on **Learning Framework Card 3.**

Line 1:	**cloud scout around surround**
Line 2:	**clown allow chowder powder**
Line 3:	**check cheek shack shake**
Line 4:	**other mother brother**
Line 5:	**cent centipede fence cinnamon**

Line 1 focuses on words in which /ow/ is spelled *ou,* while line 2 reviews the spelling *ow* for the same sound. In line 3, words with short and long vowels are contrasted.

Line 4 contains a spelling pattern where the *o* does not make the short *o* sound. These are common words found in children's literature.

Line 5 reviews words in which *c* followed by *e* or *i* represents the /s/ sound. The children may need some help blending *centipede.* Blend the word syllable by syllable.

To review the words, use them in oral sentences, emphasizing the target word. Ask a child to find, read aloud, and erase the word each time. You might use the following example sentences:

The *scout* learned how to make a campfire.
Eva sprinkled *cinnamon* on her toast.
Joseph ate fish *chowder* for dinner.
Brick walls *surround* the city.

To vary the activity, point to one line of words and invite a child to choose a word and give a sentence clue for it.

➤ Reading/Writing Connection, page 17, provides practice blending and reading words. Help the children fill in the blanks to complete the top part of the page at this time.

✱ READING THE STUDENT ANTHOLOGY

"Mary Mack"
pages 38–39

About the Selection

"Mary Mack," pages 38–39, is an easy-to-understand clapping rhyme that the children should learn quickly and enjoy.

Reading/Writing Connection, page 17

Name

Lesson 9

Reading and Writing

outside down around counts
shout found out

We play hide and seek outside.

"Not It!" Rose and I shout.

Steve is It. He counts to ten. Rose hides under the picnic table. I hide behind a tree. Steve hunts around the yard. I feel a tug down on my sneaker. It's my pup.

"Cut that out," I say.

It's too late. Steve has found me. Now I'm It.

Dictation and Spelling

Vowel Sounds and Spellings

"Mary Mack" R/WC 17

Activating Prior Knowledge

Have children turn to pages 38–39 and call on a volunteer to read the title. Discuss clapping games or other rhyming games the children know.

Setting Reading Goals and Expectations

- Before reading the selection, invite the children to browse the two pages and comment on anything they like. From the illustrations, they will probably conclude that this is a clapping game. On the chalkboard, write in brief note form the questions and observations the children come up with.

Recommendations for Reading

- Allow children time to read the pages to themselves. Then call on children to read two sentences each. If children have difficulty blending any of the words, remind them to check the Sound/Spelling Cards. If any words cannot be easily blended, pronounce the words for the children.
- Demonstrate the clapping routine that goes with the rhyme and let everyone do it as you read the poem.
- Since this is a short rhyme, read the selection twice, then let everyone read it together.

Note: Having the children read the selection in pairs is a good option for Workshop.

MONITORING READING During the next five days, observe children as they read a sentence or two from "Mary Mack." Note children who have difficulty blending words. Record your observations in Teacher's Observation Log 3.

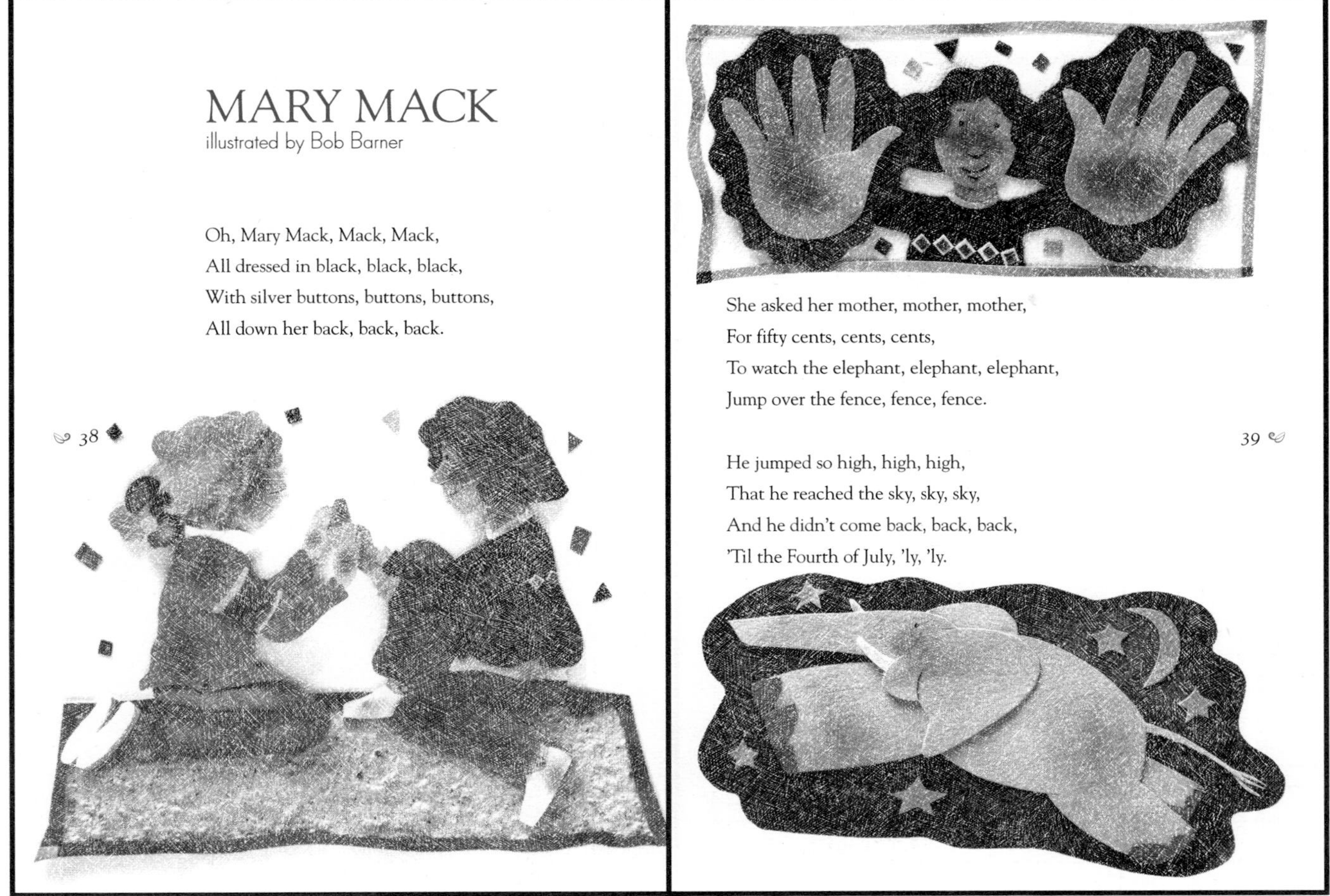
MARY MACK
illustrated by Bob Barner

Oh, Mary Mack, Mack, Mack,
All dressed in black, black, black,
With silver buttons, buttons, buttons,
All down her back, back, back.

38

She asked her mother, mother, mother,
For fifty cents, cents, cents,
To watch the elephant, elephant, elephant,
Jump over the fence, fence, fence.

He jumped so high, high, high,
That he reached the sky, sky, sky,
And he didn't come back, back, back,
'Til the Fourth of July, 'ly, 'ly.

39

Responding

- Encourage the children to discuss other rhymes this selection might remind them of, such as "Pease Porridge Hot," "Eensy Weensy Spider," or "I'm a Little Teapot."
- On the chalkboard, note other rhymes or rhyming games the children may be familiar with. Suggest the children copy these onto sheets of paper and add these to the Concept Board.

➤ Have the children complete page 18 in their Reading/Writing Connection book by writing the rhyming word that completes each sentence.

✱ READING ALOUD

A number of children's books provide rhyming fun. You may want to share one or more of the books that follow:

There's a Wocket in My Pocket by Dr. Seuss
Lazy Blackbird and Other Verses by Jack Prelutsky
My Mama Is a Llama by Steven Kellogg

TIP FOR ENGLISH LANGUAGE LEARNERS

Encourage English Language Learners to practice using and producing language to express their ideas. Have the children reread the story in a choral reading. Group English Language Learners with native English-speaking children in groups of four. Have two children in the group read the first page of the poem together and the other two children read the next page. After the children have finished reading, have them pair off. Encourage partners to talk about what they liked about the poem.

Reading/Writing Connection, page 18

Name

Lesson 9

Reading and Writing

July black cents high Mack back fence sky

Miss Mary Mack,
All dressed in black,
With silver buttons all down her back.

She asked her mother for fifty cents,
To watch the elephant jump over the fence.

He jumped so high,
That he reached the sky,
And he didn't come back until the Fourth of July.

Reading the Selection

18 R/WC "Mary Mack"

2 WRITING

* DICTATION AND SPELLING

Have the children return to page 17 in their Reading/Writing Connection book. Dictate the following words and sentence, using the suggestions for dictation that appear on **Learning Framework Card 4.** Remind the children to ask for help if they are unsure of which vowel spelling to use.

Line 1: **gown frown powder**

Line 2: **shout mouth found**

Sentence: **The brown dog growled.**

Proofread as usual.

INDEPENDENT AND COLLABORATIVE WRITING

Begin with Seminar. If any of the children have used dialogue in their stories, have them share their work. If none of the children have put dialogue in their stories, you may want to discuss where dialogue might be used in their work.

Have the children continue working on their writing. Remind those who are keeping track of a favorite team or player in their journal to make an entry.

This is a good time to meet with small groups of children who would like to include dialogue in their stories.

Remind the children to put the date on the papers before placing their work in their folders.

TEACHING TIP

You may want to share your own writing that includes some dialogue.

3 GUIDED AND INDEPENDENT EXPLORATION

WORKSHOP

Remind the children that they may use this time to work on projects on their own or in small groups. Be sure that each child knows what projects he or she may choose and how to complete any independent work. Suggestions for teacher-guided, collaborative, and independent activities follow.

Learning Framework Card 11, Workshop, contains a complete discussion of establishing and conducting Workshop and suggestions for helping English Language Learners during Workshop.

Work with the Teacher

- Repeat today's Blending lesson with children who need additional practice.
- Use flash cards to review outlaw words with a group of children. You might divide the children into two teams and have a Reading Relay.
- Reread "The Big Team Relay Race" with children. Use the rereading as an opportunity to assess their progress.
- Continue to assist children who are working on a "good sport" poster. Engage them in a review of the ideas they listed yesterday and help them to decide which ideas to use. Make a check mark next to each idea they decide to keep. Then discuss with them how they would like to present their ideas on the poster. Possible options include writing the ideas one after another in a numbered list, making separate lists for *Do* and *Don't,* or illustrating each idea and writing a caption beneath each illustration.

Collaborative/Independent Activities

- Children who began work on Go Fish! cards during yesterday's Workshop can complete their work today. Provide them with notecards and colored pencils. Tell them to first finish any proofreading and revising that they were unable to complete yesterday. They should then carefully copy each word onto a notecard, using their best handwriting. When they finish, they may add the cards to the deck.

Note: If the deck is becoming too large, you may want to go through it later and remove some of the cards containing words that the children have already mastered. Alternatively, you could remove a group of cards of differing levels of difficulty and make an additional deck.

- Some of the children may enjoy drawing pictures of Mary Mack, according to the description given in the rhyme. Have them print the first verse of "Mary Mack" beneath her picture and underline all the rhyming words.
- Activity Sheet 79 provides practice for reading and writing words. Tell the children to read each group of words and choose a word from the box that belongs to the group, then write that word on the line.

Home/School Connection

Send home the take home version of Phonics Minibook 13, *The Snow Game,* and encourage the children to read it to their families.

Name

Lesson 9

dime	grapes	thousand	flower
ring	couch	brown	tea

1. necklace pin bracelet — ring
2. peaches cherries apples — grapes
3. yellow black blue — brown
4. thirteen twenty hundred — thousand
5. chair bench rocker — couch
6. nickel penny dollar — dime
7. milk coffee soda — tea
8. grass tree weed — flower

"Mary Mack" Activity Sheet 79

Activity Sheet 79

LESSON 10

Lesson Overview

Materials

- "Mary Mack," pages 38–39
- Learning Framework Card 3
- Reading/Writing Connection, pages 19–20
- Activity Sheet 80
- Home/School Connection 15

Prepare Ahead

- Bingo grids with two- and three-letter clusters (see page 103)
- Beans, buttons, or counters to cover grid squares
- Poster board (see page 108)

GETTING STARTED

Choose one or more of the following activities to focus the children's attention and to review some of the concepts they have been learning.

Bingo For this activity, each child will need a sheet with a Bingo grid drawn on it and something to cover the squares (beans, buttons, counters or such). Each square should contain one of the following two- or three-letter clusters: *str-, scr-, -tch, spl-, shr-, -nch, -nth, sk-, -mp, bl-.* As you say a word with a consonant cluster, have the children cover that cluster on the grid. Repeat with additional words until one (or more) of the children covers all of the squares and calls "Bingo!" Use the following words:

blue	street	tenth	strawberry
scrap	skin	scrape	skip
lunch	shrivel	splinter	shred
watch	lamp	bloom	bump
bench	splatter	butterscotch	month

Spelling Challenge Divide the class into 3 or 4 teams. Explain that you will write a spelling of a long vowel sound on the board and give the teams 30 seconds to 1 minute to think of words that use that spelling. When time is up, call on each team to say and spell its words. Write them on the board and award 1 point for each correct word. The team with the most points is the winner. Remind the children to whisper so that those on other teams can't overhear their words.

1 READING

PHONICS

Review Spellings for /ow/ Recite the following rhyme, pausing at the blanks to have the children supply the rhyming word.

A family of pigs
Sitting on a **mound.**

The first one said,
"I don't hear a ______." (sound)

The second one said,
"I see a little **mouse.**"

The third one said,
"It's making a little ______." (house)

The fourth one said,
"Look! A spotted **cow.**"

The fifth one said,
"It's taking a _____." (bow)

Write the rhyme on the board, on chart paper, or on a transparency. Have the children read the rhyme and fill in the rhyming words.

Encourage the children to suggest other rhyming couplets using the words *owl* and *howl* or *found* and *ground*. For example, *The sixth one said, "Listen to the owl." The seventh one said, "What a scary (howl)!"* Write these on the board.

* **Blending** Help the children blend the following words. A complete discussion of the blending procedure can be found on **Learning Framework Card 3.**

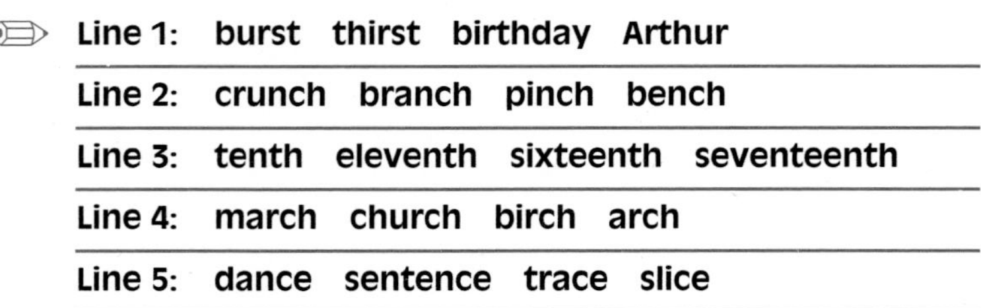

Line 1:	**burst**	**thirst**	**birthday**	**Arthur**
Line 2:	**crunch**	**branch**	**pinch**	**bench**
Line 3:	**tenth**	**eleventh**	**sixteenth**	**seventeenth**
Line 4:	**march**	**church**	**birch**	**arch**
Line 5:	**dance**	**sentence**	**trace**	**slice**

To help the children with the consonant clusters, blend the words as follows:

/b/ /ur/ /st/ = *burst*

/cr/ /u/ /nch/ = *crunch*

/t/ /e/ /nth/ = *tenth*

/m/ /ar/ /ch/ = *march*

Have the children point out the various spellings for /er/ in the first line. Also, ask why *Arthur* begins with a capital letter.

Line 5 reviews words with *ce* pronounced /s/.

Review the words using a sponge die labeled with the numbers 1–4 and two stars. The children choose a word line and roll the die. They read the word that matches the number they roll within the line they have chosen. For example, if a child chooses line 2 and rolls a 3, the word to say is *pinch*. If they roll a star, they can read any word in the line. If they roll a number for a word already read, they must roll again.

➤ Reading/Writing Connection, page 19, provides practice with reading and blending. Help the children read the page and fill in the correct words to complete the sentences.

Reading/Writing Connection, page 19

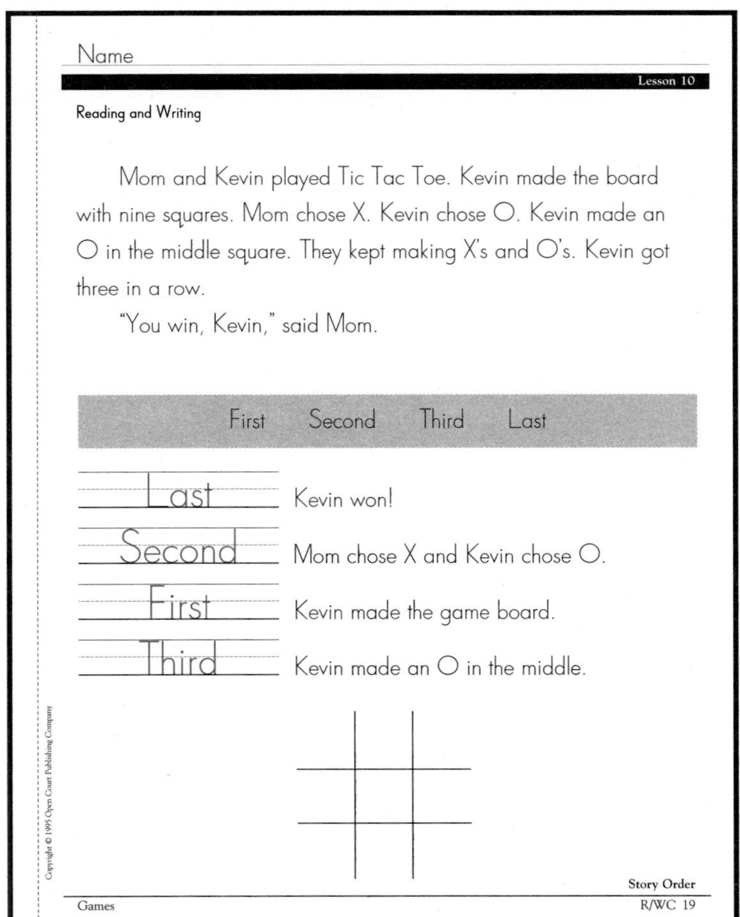

Name

Lesson 10

Reading and Writing

Mom and Kevin played Tic Tac Toe. Kevin made the board with nine squares. Mom chose X. Kevin chose O. Kevin made an O in the middle square. They kept making X's and O's. Kevin got three in a row.

"You win, Kevin," said Mom.

First Second Third Last

Last Kevin won!

Second Mom chose X and Kevin chose O.

First Kevin made the game board.

Third Kevin made an O in the middle.

Story Order

Games R/WC 19

✱ READING THE STUDENT ANTHOLOGY

"Mary Mack"
pages 38–39

Activating Prior Knowledge

Briefly review the selection by asking children what they remember about the rhyme.

Recommendations for Reading

Have the children reread the selection by doing a choral reading.

Responding

Encourage the children to speculate about what other activities, besides clapping, might be performed to this rhyme (for example, jumping rope).

➤ Reading/Writing Connection, page 20, may be completed at this time. Have the children write the sentence that means almost the same as the first sentence.

MONITORING READING Continue to observe children as they read "Mary Mack" aloud. Record your observations in Teacher's Observation Log 3.

TEACHING TIP

Have the children do some partner reading daily. Using previously read Phonics Minibooks and Step-by-Step Practice Stories for this purpose will help the children review and solidify their knowledge of the sounds and spellings they have learned. This is a good opportunity to read with children individually and to record their progress.

Reading/Writing Connection, page 20

Name

Lesson 10

Reading and Writing

1. **The crown was bright yellow.**
   The crown was big and heavy.
   The crown was shiny gold.

   The crown was shiny gold.

2. **Martha gave Mitch a present.**
   Martha gave Mitch a party.
   Martha gave Mitch a gift.

   Martha gave Mitch a gift.

3. **Everybody looked at the clown.**
   Everybody watched the clown.
   Everybody liked the clown.

   Everybody watched the clown.

4. **Place the cup on the table.**
   Throw the cup at the table.
   Put the cup on the table.

   Put the cup on the table.

Paraphrasing

20 R/WC Games

✱ READING ALOUD

A number of children's books provide rhyming fun. You may want to share one or more of these books:

Lazy Blackbird and Other Verses by Jack Prelutsky

Miss Mary Mack and Other Children's Street Rhymes by Joanna and Philip Cole

2 WRITING

✱ DICTATION AND SPELLING

Word-Building Game Have the children use pencil and paper to build the following words:

inch
pinch
punch
bunch
bench
lunch

Challenge the children to build a new word by changing one sound and spelling in the last word.

INDEPENDENT AND COLLABORATIVE WRITING

Have the children continue their work in progress. Encourage the children to work together to revise and proofread their work. Children may write in their journals. This is a perfect time to hold small group conferences with children who share common interests or who need additional support in some aspect of the writing process. Allow time for children to share their work.

TEACHING TIP

You may prefer to have Seminar at the beginning of Writing so that children will have an opportunity to make changes based on class input. If the children have included words in their work that are interesting or unusual, add these to the class vocabulary chart.

3 GUIDED AND INDEPENDENT EXPLORATION

WORKSHOP

Remind the children that they may use this time to work on projects individually or in small groups. Be sure that each child knows what projects he or she may choose and how to complete any independent work. Suggestions for teacher-guided, collaborative, and independent activities follow.

Work with the Teacher

- Use an oral spelling game to review three-letter final consonants. Write the word at the top of each column on the chalkboard, have the children blend it, then have them tell you how to spell the next two words in the column. Use the following words:

pit	rat	bus	bus	Ted	bid
pinch	rant	bun	bust	ten	bird
pin	ranch	bunch	burst	tenth	birth

- Continue to work with those children who are making a "good sport" poster. Have them think of a title for the chart and then print that title across the top of a sheet of poster board. Help them to print their ideas on the poster board, using the format agreed upon in the previous lesson. You may want to have each child take a turn printing one sentence, providing her or him with any necessary help. Leave enough room for the children to illustrate the chart tomorrow.
- Listen to children read Phonics Minibook 14, *The Everybody Club.* This can be done with individuals or small groups.

Collaborative/Independent Activities

- Write the final clusters *-rth, -nth, -rst,* and *-nch* on the chalkboard. Challenge children to see how many words they can write that contain one of the clusters. Have them trade their finished lists with a partner for proofreading. Tell them to save the lists for tomorrow's Workshop.
- Some of the children may want to play Go Fish! using the deck of cards for which they or their classmates have made /ow/ cards.
- Invite some of the fluent readers to read a book of their choice to a small group of classmates.
- Activity Sheet 80 reviews the spellings for the /ow/ sound. Tell the children to choose a word from the box to complete each sentence, then to write the word a second time in the corresponding puzzle boxes.

Home/School Connection

Distribute Home/School Connection 15, which asks children to learn games and/or songs from other family members.

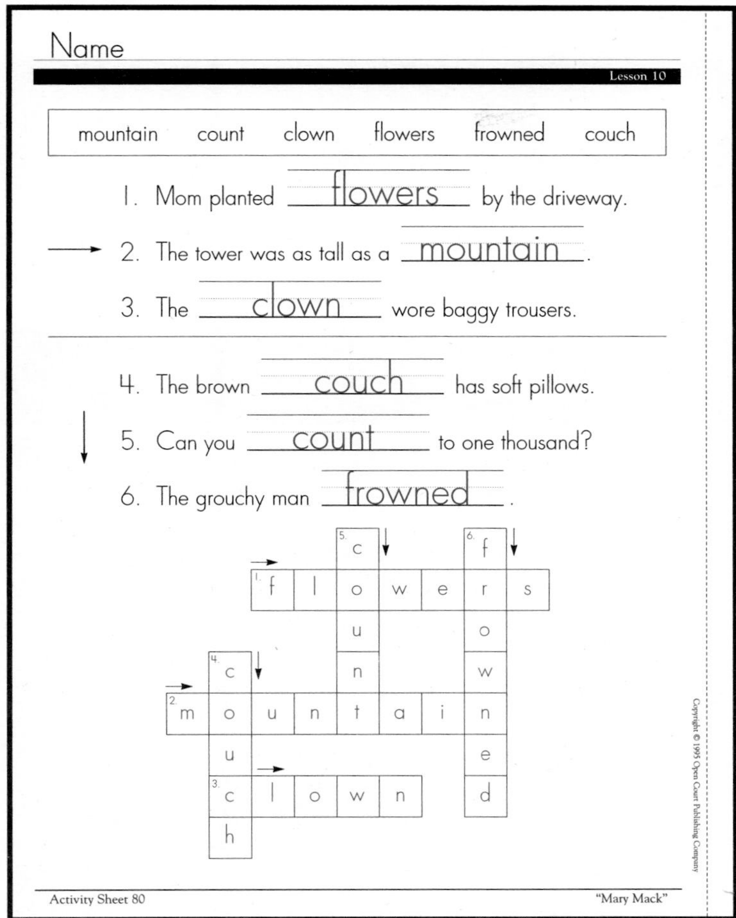
Name

Lesson 10

mountain count clown flowers frowned couch

1. Mom planted flowers by the driveway.

→ 2. The tower was as tall as a mountain.

3. The clown wore baggy trousers.

4. The brown couch has soft pillows.

↓ 5. Can you count to one thousand?

6. The grouchy man frowned.

Copyright © 1995 Open Court Publishing Company

Activity Sheet 80 "Mary Mack"

Activity Sheet 80

LESSON 11

Lesson Overview

New Learning

- Review compound words

Outlaw Words

break, friend

Materials

- Fine Art, pages 40–41
- Learning Framework Cards 3, 4, 5
- Reading/Writing Connection, pages 21–22
- Classroom Support Teacher Tool Card 2
- Activity Sheet 81

Prepare Ahead

- Compound Word Riddle Cards (see page 117)

GETTING STARTED

Choose one or more of the following activities to focus the children's attention and to review concepts they have been learning.

Review Sounds and Spellings Have one child name a Sound/Spelling Card and call on a second child. The second child must pronounce the sound, give a word that has the sound, name the next card, and call on another child.

Long Sound/Short Sound Spellings On the chalkboard, write several words containing long or short vowel sounds. Touch one word at a time and ask the children to respond by holding their arms out from their sides if the word contains a long vowel sound or by holding their hands close together in front of themselves if the word contains a short vowel sound. These words will help you get started:

pink	judge	peach	spring
splash	page	squeeze	
face	skunk	flight	

Remember to use wait time and have everyone respond together.

1 READING

PHONICS

Review Compound Words Copy the two word lists that follow on the chalkboard.

dragon	fly
some	time
butter	where
every	ground
play	side
black	day
in	bird

Have the children make compound words by choosing a word from each list. They should write their words on paper. Have children share their words and write the words they made on the board. You may add other words to the lists if you like or ask children to share any compound words they know.

* **Blending** Have the children blend the following words. For reference and additional suggestions for blending, see **Learning Framework Card 3.**

Line 1:	**upstairs downstairs inside everything**
Line 2:	**herself himself playmate baseball**
Line 3:	**sold cone slow store**
Line 4:	**square lady piece rescue**
Line 5:	**gentle register large stage**
Sentence 1:	**Tilly is Matthew's friend.**
Sentence 2:	**Did you break my crayon?**

Words Many of the compound words in lines 1 and 2 appear in the selection *Matthew and Tilly*. Ask the children which two words they see in each long word. Invite them to think of other compound words that contain one of these small words. For example, they could use *down* in *downstairs* to make *downtown* or *play* in *playmate* to make *playground*.

Lines 3 and 4 review words from *Matthew and Tilly* that have long vowel spellings. Have the children identify the long vowel sounds they hear and name or circle the spellings.

In line 5, the children review words in which *g* makes the sound /j/ when it is followed by an *e* or *i*. Some children may be unfamiliar with the word *register*. If so, explain the word and use it in a sentence.

To review the words, use them in oral sentences, emphasizing the word from the word lines. Ask a child to find, read aloud, and erase the word each time. Example sentences to use include the following:

Antonio ate a double-scoop ice cream *cone*.
Marta was *gentle* with her baby kitten.
Rebecca paid at the cash *register*.

To vary the activity, point to one line of words and invite a child to choose a word and give a sentence clue for it.

Sentences Introduce the outlaw words *friend* and *break* before writing the sentences on the board. Write the word *friend* on the board and read it to the children. Call on children to use the word in sentences. Then write the first sentence on the board, underlining the new word *friend*. Have children read the sentence. Repeat the procedure with the word *break*.

➤ Reading/Writing Connection, page 21, provides practice with reading compound words. Help the children complete the top part of the page by circling the compound word in each sentence and then writing the two words from the compound on the lines provided.

Reading/Writing Connection, page 21

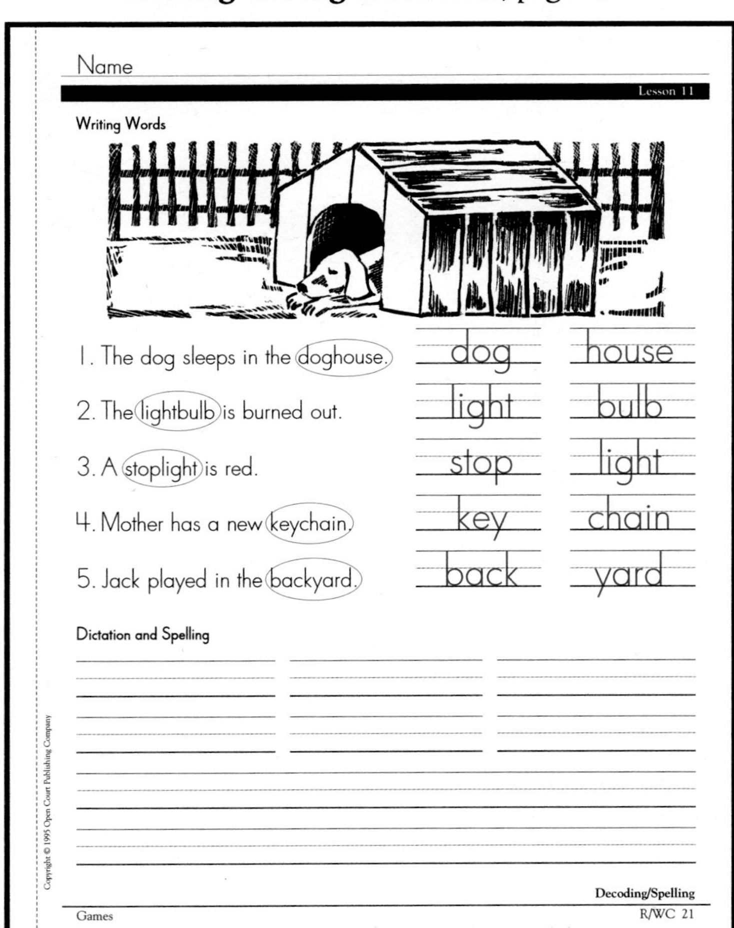
Name

Lesson 11

Writing Words

1. The dog sleeps in the doghouse. dog house
2. The lightbulb is burned out. light bulb
3. A stoplight is red. stop light
4. Mother has a new keychain. key chain
5. Jack played in the backyard. back yard

Dictation and Spelling

Decoding/Spelling

Games R/WC 21

✱ READING THE STUDENT ANTHOLOGY

Fine Art
pages 40–41

Discussing Fine Art

Each fine-art spread in *Collections for Young Scholars* represents a variety of media and cultures. You should encourage the children to freely share their feelings and opinions. Especially encourage them to tell what they think each piece has to do with the unit concept. The following are some typical questions that can initiate discussion of all types of art:

- Do you like it? Why?
- What is interesting about it?
- How does it make you feel?
- What does it make you think about?

For additional information on discussing fine art, refer to **Classroom Support Teacher Tool Card 2.**

Information for the Teacher

Have the children turn to the reproductions of fine-art pieces on pages 40–41. Invite them to tell anything they care to mention about the pieces of art. You might want to share some of the following information about each piece.

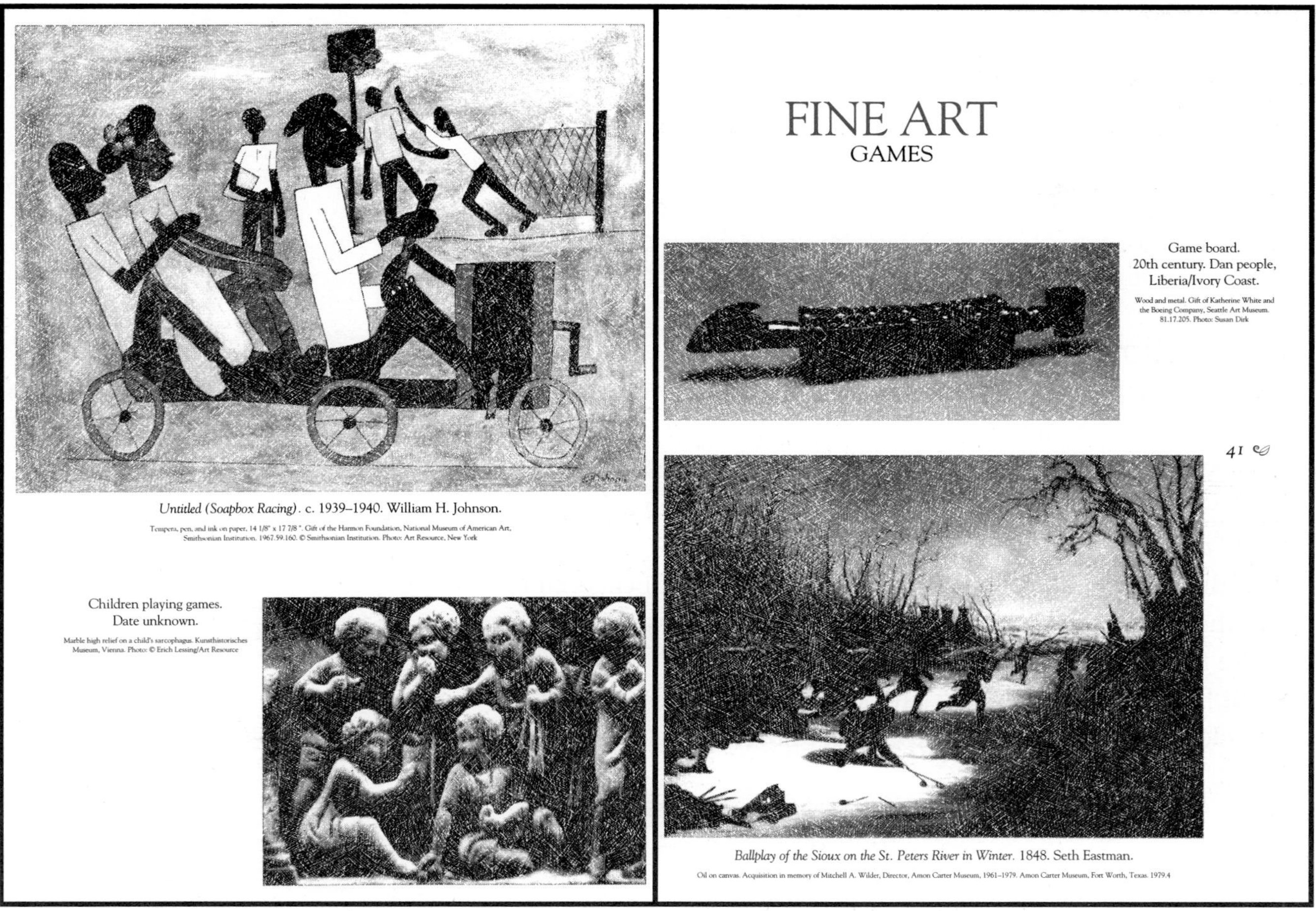

FINE ART
GAMES
Untitled (Soapbox Racing). c. 1939–1940. William H. Johnson.
Tempera, pen, and ink on paper, 14 1/8" x 17 7/8 ". Gift of the Harmon Foundation, National Museum of American Art, Smithsonian Institution. 1967.59.160. © Smithsonian Institution. Photo: Art Resource, New York
Children playing games. Date unknown.
Marble high relief on a child's sarcophagus. Kunsthistorisches Museum, Vienna. Photo: © Erich Lessing/Art Resource
Game board. 20th century. Dan people, Liberia/Ivory Coast.
Wood and metal. Gift of Katherine White and the Boeing Company, Seattle Art Museum. 81.17.205. Photo: Susan Dirk
41
Ballplay of the Sioux on the St. Peters River in Winter. 1848. Seth Eastman.
Oil on canvas. Acquisition in memory of Mitchell A. Wilder, Director, Amon Carter Museum, 1961–1979. Amon Carter Museum, Fort Worth, Texas. 1979.4

Untitled (*Soapbox Racing*). c. 1939–1940.
William H. Johnson. Tempera, pen, and ink on paper.

William H. Johnson (1901–1970) was born in Florence, South Carolina. Living in Harlem, Johnson began to use the life of the African-American community as the central theme of his work. He created paintings that dealt with the social and political realities of Harlem, as well as his youth in the South. *Soapbox Racing* depicts one of the small, motorless cars that are used in downhill coasting races.

Children playing games. Date unknown.
Marble high relief on a child's sarcophagus.

The relief shown here is from the Roman Empire. Roman children had many toys and games with which to occupy themselves. Babies played with terra-cotta rattles filled with pebbles. Carts, tops, rolling hoops, marbles, and balls were all favorite playthings. Games of tag, blindman's bluff, tug of war, and hide-and-seek were popular.

Game board. 20th century.
Dan people, Liberia/Ivory Coast. Wood and metal.

The Dan people live in inland Liberia along the Ivory Coast of Africa. In the Dan tradition, the game generally known as *mankala* or *owari* is very important. To the Dan people, game boards are an important form of sculpture and are commissioned from well-known wood carvers.

Ballplay of the Sioux on the St. Peters River in Winter. 1848.
Seth Eastman. Oil on canvas.

Seth Eastman (1808–1875) was born in Brunswick, Maine. Eastman, a graduate of the U.S. Military Academy, became interested in recording the way of life of Native Americans while serving at a number of frontier posts. *Ballplay of the Sioux on the St. Peters River in Winter* is among the finest of Eastman's more than four hundred oil paintings, watercolors, and drawings of Native-American life and of the Minnesota landscape.

Recommendations

- Invite the children to discuss the pieces of art as you provide the background information and title.
- Discuss ways the game board and the carved marble piece showing children playing games are different from *Soapbox Racing* and *Ballplay of the Sioux on the St. Peters River in Winter.*
- Ask what the children like about each piece. Invite several children to point out their favorite part of the piece. How does looking at the piece make them feel? What does it make them think of?
- Talk about how these pieces are related to the unit concept, Games. Add new ideas or wonderings to the Concept Board.

TEACHING TIP

Have the children do some partner reading daily. Using previously read Phonics Minibooks and Step-by-Step Practice Stories for this purpose will help the children review and solidify their knowledge of the sounds and spellings they have learned. This is a good opportunity to read with children individually and to record their progress.

Name

Lesson 11

Completing a Picture

Games

Megan plays with marbles. Jordan jumps rope. Mitch throws a ball at a basket.

Using Story Clues

22 R/WC Games

Reading/Writing Connection, page 22

➤ Reading/Writing Connection, page 22, may be completed at this time. Have the children read the sentences at the top of the page and use the information to add the missing parts to the picture.

✱ READING ALOUD

The first of the following books takes children on a journey through an art museum, while the other two selections tell about creating art with line and color. You may want to share one or more of these books with your class.

Visiting the Art Museum by Laurene Krasny Brown and Marc Brown
Mouse Paint by Ellen Stoll Walsh
I Can Draw Myself by Me, Myself by Dr. Seuss

After reading, ask the children questions such as, "What did you find most interesting in this book? Why?" and "What did this book tell you that you didn't know before?"

See **Learning Framework Card 5** for additional suggestions for reading aloud.

2 WRITING

* DICTATION AND SPELLING

Have the children turn to page 22 of their Reading/Writing Connection. Dictate the following words and sentence, using the suggestions for dictation that appear on **Learning Framework Card 4.**

Line 1: lunch ranch bench

Line 2: pitch catch scratch

Sentence: Mom can patch the jeans.

Help the children proofread each line.

MONITORING DICTATION Collect students' Reading/Writing Connection books. Scan them to see how the children are doing with writing words and sentences as well as proofreading. Record your observations and keep them in the students' folders.

EXPLORING THE WRITER'S CRAFT

Remind the children of the fine art they looked at in today's lesson. Three of the four pieces of art show people playing together. One of the points the artists were showing is that games are fun when you share that fun with others. Have children share special times that they have had while playing games with friends. This may naturally expand into special things they like to do with friends. Brainstorm and generate a list of activities that children enjoy and that they may like to write about. Feel free to add things that you as an adult like to do or that you remember doing as a child. Save this list to refer to tomorrow. Children may note that sometimes friends disagree when they play together. This is a good opportunity to talk about what happens when you're playing a game and there is a disagreement. How can this be resolved? Children may want to write about this topic in stories or in their journals.

Reread the list of ideas and have children think about what they want to write about. While the unit is on games and the discussion has been about games and friends, children are free to write about something else.

As an additional resource, you may want to have other books about games, friendship, and related topics available for the children to browse through for good writing ideas. Possible books might include

Best Friends by Steven Kellogg
Three Wishes by Lucille Clifton
Addie Meets Max by Joan Robins

Conference with children, helping them decide on a topic they would like to write about. If children come up with an idea but do not know what to write about it, brainstorm with them or suggest that they draw a picture just as the artists in the fine-art section did. Posters also are a way to share information.

Provide time at the end for Seminar for children to share their ideas or plans.

TIP FOR ENGLISH LANGUAGE LEARNERS

Give English Language Learners a chance to share their experiences and provide new knowledge to other children. Encourage the children to draw a picture or make a poster of a familiar game. Invite them to describe the game to the other children and to use their illustration or poster to point out some of the details of the game.

3 GUIDED AND INDEPENDENT EXPLORATION

WORKSHOP

Remind the children that they may use this time to work on projects on their own or in small groups. Be sure that each child knows what projects he or she may choose and how to complete any independent work. Suggestions for teacher-guided, collaborative, and independent activities follow.

Work with the Teacher

- In preparation for tomorrow's lesson on base word + *-er* and *-est* endings, review with children the endings *(-ing, -ies)* that they have already learned.
- Preteach the first half of *Matthew and Tilly,* pages 42–55 in the student anthology, to those children who may have difficulty during tomorrow's lesson. Stop reading at the bottom of page 50, unless you plan to teach the entire selection tomorrow.
- Review the concept of blending words by component parts, rather than by syllables. Have the children read the compound words, word by word. Possible words include

airplane	frostbite
basketball	mousetrap
catnap	outside
doghouse	superman

  and any of the compound words from today's Blending exercise.
- Continue to work with those children who are making a "good sport" poster. Help them to finish printing their list of rules or ideas on the poster. When the writing is finished, provide time for the children to illustrate the poster. Display the completed poster in the classroom.

Collaborative/Independent Activities

- For additional practice with compound words, small groups of children can solve Compound Word Riddles. Prepare the game pieces before Workshop begins. Cut several "stocking caps" and an equal number of left- and right-hand "mittens" from construction paper. On each cap, write a simple question or riddle that can be answered with a compound word. Write the first half of each compound-word answer on a right-hand mitten. Write the second half of each answer on a left-hand mitten. You may want to make several sets of game pieces, using a different color paper for each set. Place each set in a resealable envelope or Ziploc™ bag. Distribute a set to each group and make sure all players are familiar with the procedure for playing Compound Word Riddles. Players should lay the caps and mittens face down on the floor or table. They should take turns turning over a cap and reading the riddle, and then work together to solve the riddle. To enliven the game, two or more groups of children might compete to see who can answer all of the riddles in their set first. If they finish early, the groups can trade game sets and play again.
- Children who listed words ending in three-letter clusters during yesterday's Workshop should take out their lists at this time. Provide the children with notecards and colored pencils. Tell them that after they finish making any necessary spelling corrections, they should circle all the rhyming words on their lists. They can then copy the words onto notecards, using their best handwriting, and add the cards to the Go Fish! deck.
- Children who were intrigued by the fine-art pieces, pages 40–41 in the student anthology, may want to revisit them at this time. Invite the children to use available art supplies to create and title their own unit-related art pieces. They may continue their work during tomorrow's Workshop.
- Activity Sheet 81 provides practice for reading and writing compound words. Tell the children to read each group of words, then choose a compound word from the box that belongs to the group and write it on the line.

Name

Lesson 11

popcorn	newspaper	sunflower	afternoon	lumberjack
airplane	flashlight	butterfly	basketball	

1. ladybug grasshopper ant — butterfly
2. morning evening night — afternoon
3. baseball football bowling — basketball
4. chips candy pretzels — popcorn
5. daisy pansy rose — sunflower
6. teacher doctor firefighter — lumberjack
7. boat train helicopter — airplane
8. candle lamp lantern — flashlight

"Mary Mack" Activity Sheet 81

Activity Sheet 81

LESSON 12

Lesson Overview

New Learning

- Comparatives with *-er, -est*

Outlaw Words

enough, look

Materials

- ***Matthew and Tilly***, pages 42–55
- Phonics Minibook 15, ***Superhero to the Rescue***
- Learning Framework Cards 3, 5, 8
- Reading/Writing Connection, pages 23–24
- Activity Sheet 82

GETTING STARTED

Choose one or more of the following activities to focus the children's attention and to review some of the concepts they have been learning.

Long Vowel Spelling Review This activity reviews some of the spellings of long vowel sounds the children have learned so far. Divide the class into two teams. On both ends of the chalkboard, write ten words containing long vowel sound spellings you would like to review. (If you have more than 20 students, you should include additional words with long vowel sound spellings.) Tell the children that you will say a sound and that one child from each team should go to the board, circle a word with that sound, and underline the letters that spell that sound. For each sound that the children identify correctly, their team receives a point. At the end of the activity, call on different children to read each word on the list. A sample list follows:

stage	show	high	road
music	street	peace	smile
might	space		

Spellings with the Same Letter Tell the children that you want to see how quickly they can remember the sounds by different spellings that use a specific letter, for example, *o*. On the chalkboard, one at a time write the spellings listed below. As you write each one, have the children name it and say it aloud. Then say two words, one with and one without the target sound. The children should repeat the word that contains the sound. The word with the sound is underlined.

Spelling	**Words**
oa	boat, boot
_oe	toe, too
o_e	rot, rose

1 READING

PHONICS

Introduce Comparatives with *-er* and *-est* Write the following sentences on the chalkboard:

Tim runs fast.
Tom runs faster.
Sally runs the fastest.

Ask volunteers to read the examples aloud. Explain to the children that the endings *-er* and *-est* are sometimes added to base words in order to compare one person or thing to other persons or things. The ending *-er* means *more,* as in "one person is *more fast* than another." The ending *-est* means *most* as in "one person is the *most fast* of all." Invite the children to give other examples of *-er* and *-est* comparison words.

Now write the following example sentences on the board (or ask volunteers to generate example sentences using the base word *hot).*

The pan is hot.
The stove is hotter.
The fire is the hottest.

Ask volunteers to read the sentences aloud. Remind the children that when they learned about *-ing* they learned that it is sometimes necessary to double the last letter in the base word before adding *-ing.* Explain that this is also true when adding *-er* and *-est.* Point out that without the double *t, hotter* and *hottest* would be spelled *hoter* and *hotest.* To illustrate why this would be a problem, write *hoter* and *hotest* on the chalkboard and ask a volunteer to blend them.

Next write these example sentences on the board and select a child to read each one aloud.

The puppy is funny.
The monkey is funnier.
The clown is the funniest.

Point out that when you added *-er* and *-est* to *funny,* you first changed the *y* at the end of *funny* to an *i.* Explain that when adding *-er* and *-est* to a base word ending in *y,* it is usually necessary to change the *y* to an *i.* Point out that the sound of the *i* in these cases is the same as the sound of the *y* in the base words.

For further practice use the words *loud, wet,* and *sunny.*

* **Blending** Have the children blend the following words. For reference and additional suggestions for blending, see **Learning Framework Card 3.**

Line 1:	**play player played playing**
Line 2:	**grouch grouchy grouchier grouchiest**
Line 3:	**slip slipped slipping slippery**
Line 4:	**crab crabby crabbier crabbiest**
Line 5:	**late later latest lately**
Sentence 1:	**Matthew had enough to eat.**
Sentence 2:	**I like to look at the stars at night.**

Words Lines 1–5 focus on various endings that can be added to words and the types of spelling changes that occur. Talk with the children about the meaning of each ending. You might ask:

Which ending shows that something happened in the past?
What little word do we find in *slippery?*
Which ending do we use to show that something is the most?

Have the children use some of the words in sentences to contrast the differences among the various endings. As well, invite the children's comments about spelling changes. For example, they might say that to go from *grouchy* to *grouchier*, we change the *y* to *i* and add *-er.*

Review the words by giving the children clues and asking them to find and erase:

- the word in line 4 that means "the most crabby"
- the word in line 3 that means "slick" or "slithery"
- the word in line 1 that fills in the blank:
  The children are ______ baseball.
- the word in line 5 that is the opposite of *early*

Sentences Introduce the outlaw words *enough* and *look* before writing the sentences on the board. Write the word *enough* on the board and read it to the children. Use the word in a sentence, then call on children to make their own sentences with the word. Write the first sentence on the board, underlining *enough,* and call on children to read the sentence. Follow the same procedure for the word *look.*

➤ Reading/Writing Connection, page 23, provides practice making words with the endings *-er* and *-est.* Help the children complete the page by adding the two endings to each word.

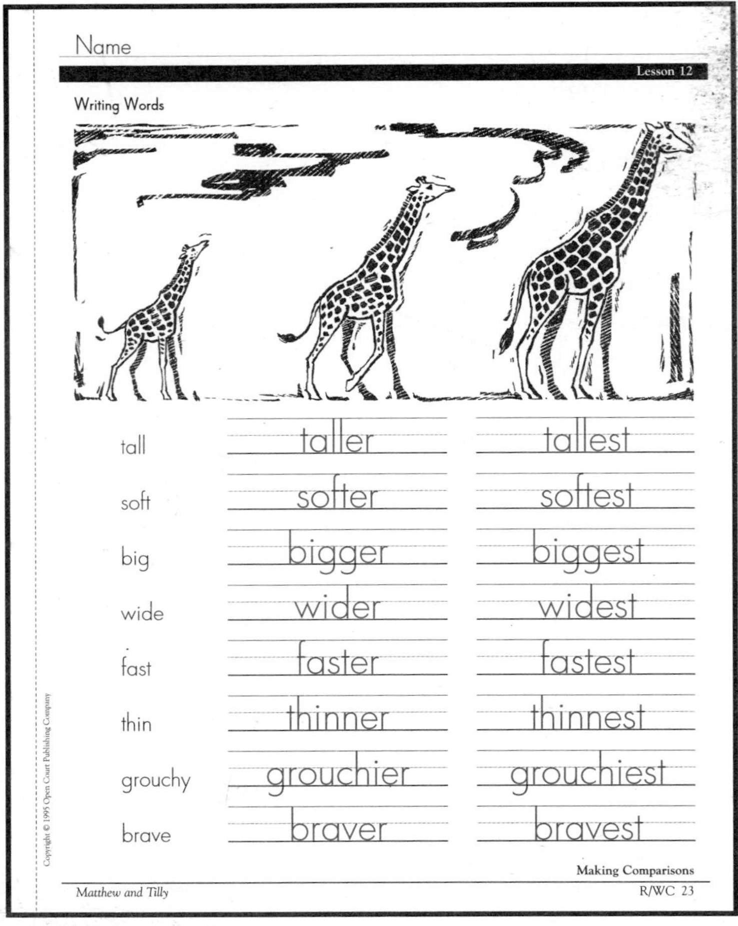
Name

Lesson 12

Writing Words

tall	taller	tallest
soft	softer	softest
big	bigger	biggest
wide	wider	widest
fast	faster	fastest
thin	thinner	thinnest
grouchy	grouchier	grouchiest
brave	braver	bravest

Making Comparisons

Matthew and Tilly R/WC 23

Reading/Writing Connection, page 23

✱ READING THE STUDENT ANTHOLOGY

Matthew and Tilly
pages 42–55

Note: Because of its length, this selection probably should be read over two class periods. We recommend that on this first day of reading, you stop at the bottom of page 50.

About the Selection

Together, Matthew and Tilly play games, do business, and even perform acts of bravery. Then one day, a broken crayon leads them into a terrible fight. Will this youthful duo be reunited? Find out when you read Rebecca C. Jones's poignant tale of childhood friendship.

Link to the Unit Concept

In *Matthew and Tilly,* pages 42–55, two children discover that they have more fun playing games together than alone. Readers may recognize that in sharing games, the children have become good friends.

About the Author

Rebecca C. Jones says, "I was sick a great deal between the ages of nine and sixteen, and I missed a lot of 'normal life.' During that time I created great imaginary characters to keep me company in the sickroom. Today I'm fascinated by children, and many of those imaginary characters sit down with me at the typewriter to tell their stories."

Ms. Jones has written a number of books for children, including *Germy Blew It* and other "Germy" books.

About the Illustrator

Beth Peck lived for a time in New York City. She used the Washington Heights neighborhood as the model for her drawings in *Matthew and Tilly.*

Activating Prior Knowledge

Invite the children to read the title, helping them with *Matthew,* if necessary. Encourage them to talk about what it is like to have best friends and to be best friends.

Setting Reading Goals and Expectations

- Have the children browse the story through page 50. Ask them to look for words that may be hard to read and then tell you on which page each of these words appears. Write the words and page numbers on the chalkboard. Invite children to try to figure out these words as they read.
- If children are having difficulty blending any of the words, remind them to check the Sound/Spelling Cards. If any words cannot be easily blended, pronounce those words for the children.

Recommendations for Reading

- This story will be read in two parts. This lesson will cover pages 42–50.
- Have the children read the story aloud.
- Encourage children to ask for help to clarify the meaning of words they don't understand and to share their reactions to the story.

Note: Reading this selection in pairs is a good option for Workshop.

About the Reading Strategies

In reading this selection, children will need strategies for decoding unfamiliar words. Explain that you will model strategies for clarifying unfamiliar words and passages.

Think-Aloud Prompts for Use in Oral Reading Notice the think-aloud prompts with the page miniatures. These are merely suggestions. Continue to model using appropriate strategies while reading and continue to encourage children to use the strategies on their own. For a review of information about modeling and generating think-alouds, see **Learning Framework Card 8, Reading the Student Anthologies.**

TEACHING TIP

Tell the children the following words as they come to them: *business, money, machines, chewed, though, voice, new,* and *stupid.* These words contain irregular spellings or sounds and spellings the children have not yet learned.

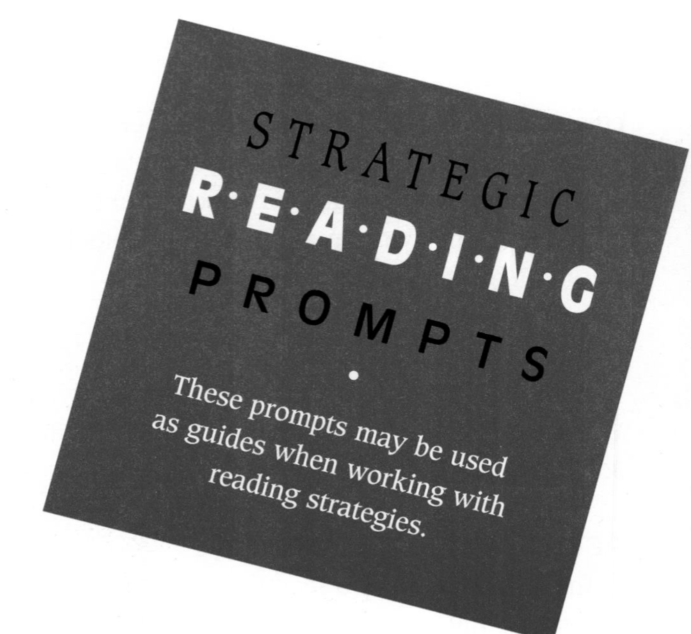

1. If a reader has difficulty with *lemonade,* suggest that it be broken into parts. Break it into parts for the child if necessary.

2. Do not ask children to blend *business.* If the word presents difficulty, simply explain that it is an outlaw and pronounce it for the children. Ask if anyone knows the meaning of the word. If no one does, explain that *business* means selling things for money.

3. If children have difficulty with *sidewalk,* encourage them to find the two little words in the big word. If necessary, show them how.

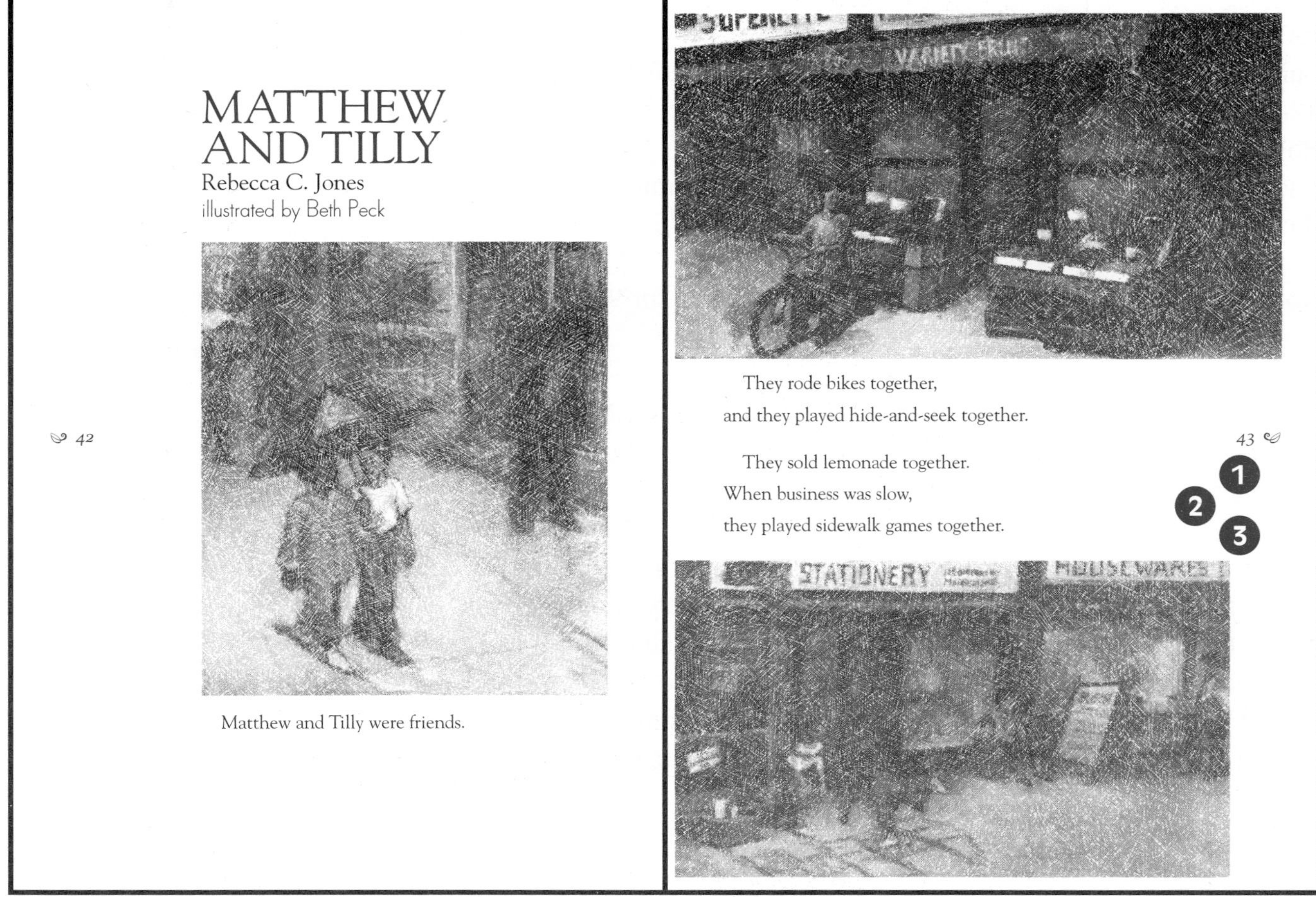

MATTHEW AND TILLY
Rebecca C. Jones
illustrated by Beth Peck
Matthew and Tilly were friends.
42
They rode bikes together,
and they played hide-and-seek together.
43
They sold lemonade together.
When business was slow,
they played sidewalk games together.
1
2
3
STATIONERY

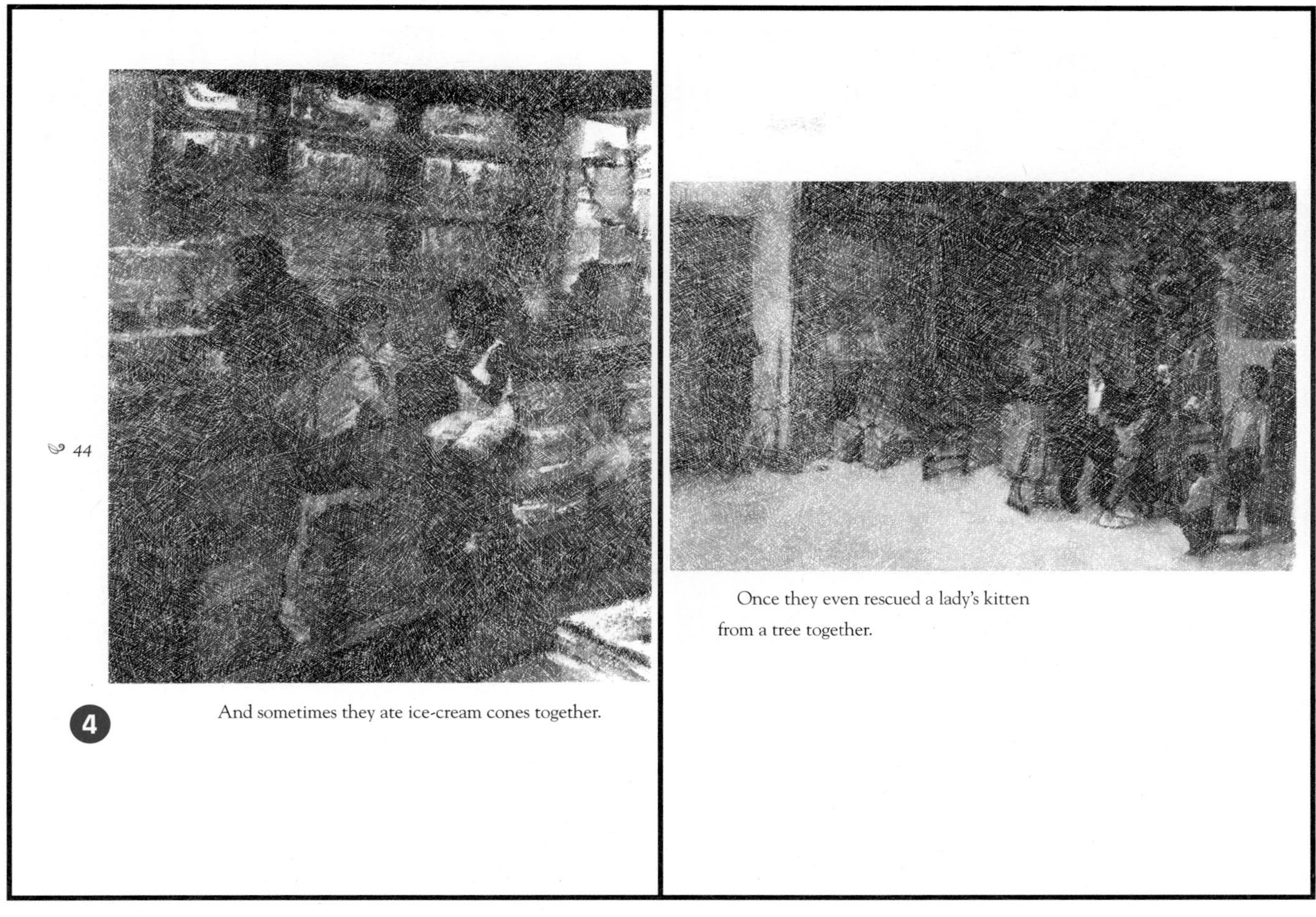

44

And sometimes they ate ice-cream cones together.

Once they even rescued a lady's kitten from a tree together.

4

4 Say, *They never seemed bored, did they?*

46

The lady gave them money
for the bubble-gum machines.

5

So later they chewed gum together
and remembered how brave they had been.

6

47

5 If children have difficulty with *bubble-gum,* suggest that they break it into parts. They may try the same technique for *machines,* but the *ch* spelling of /sh/ and the *i_e* spelling of /ē/ may present difficulties; in this case, just tell them the word.

6 Have the reader break *remembered* into parts if necessary.

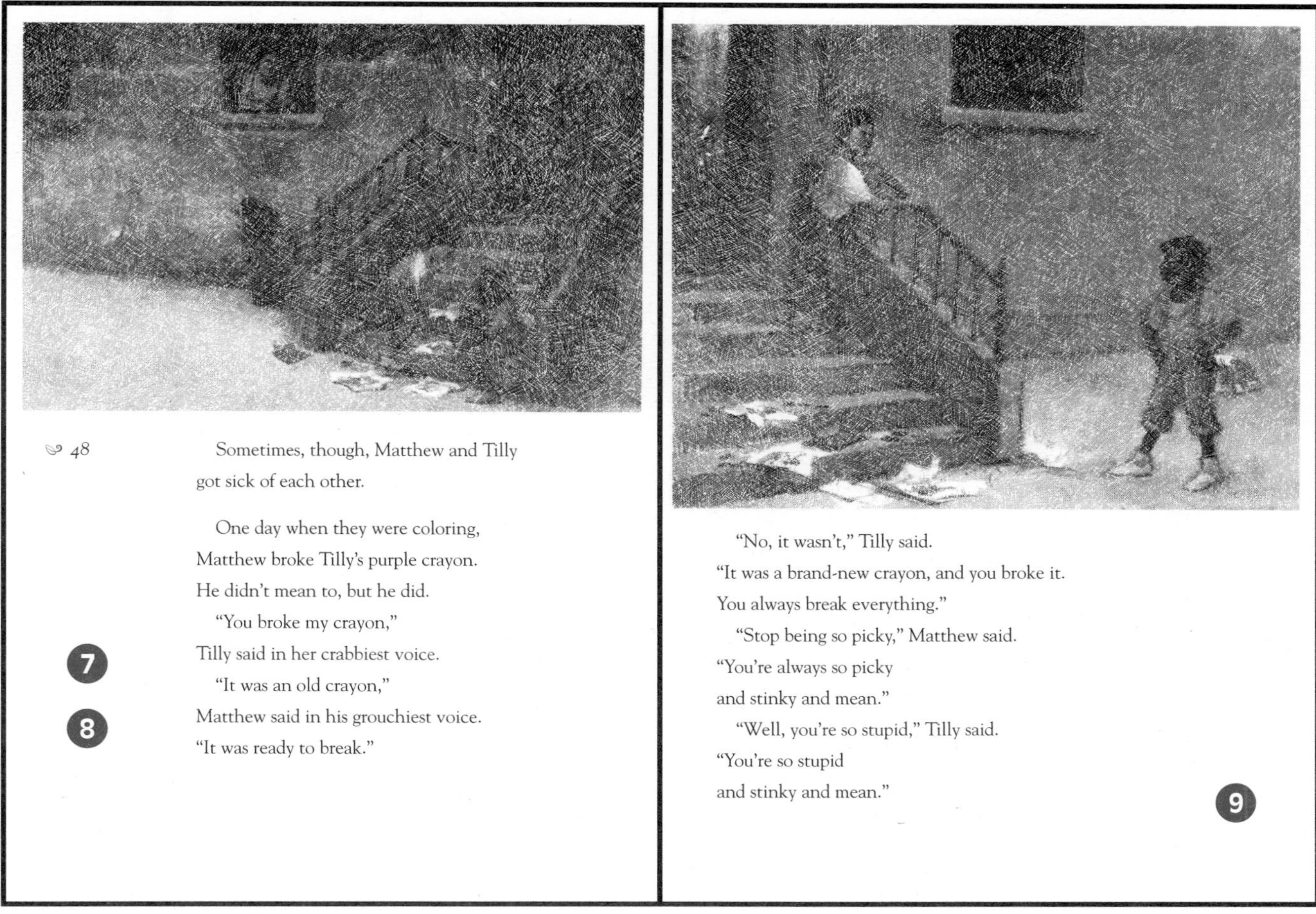

48

Sometimes, though, Matthew and Tilly
got sick of each other.

One day when they were coloring,
Matthew broke Tilly's purple crayon.
He didn't mean to, but he did.
"You broke my crayon,"
7 Tilly said in her crabbiest voice.
"It was an old crayon,"
8 Matthew said in his grouchiest voice.
"It was ready to break."

"No, it wasn't," Tilly said.
"It was a brand-new crayon, and you broke it.
You always break everything."
"Stop being so picky," Matthew said.
"You're always so picky
and stinky and mean."
"Well, you're so stupid," Tilly said.
"You're so stupid
and stinky and mean." 9

7 The reader can break *crabbiest* into parts if necessary.

8 Have the reader break *grouchiest* into parts if necessary.

9 Ask how Matthew and Tilly are treating each other.

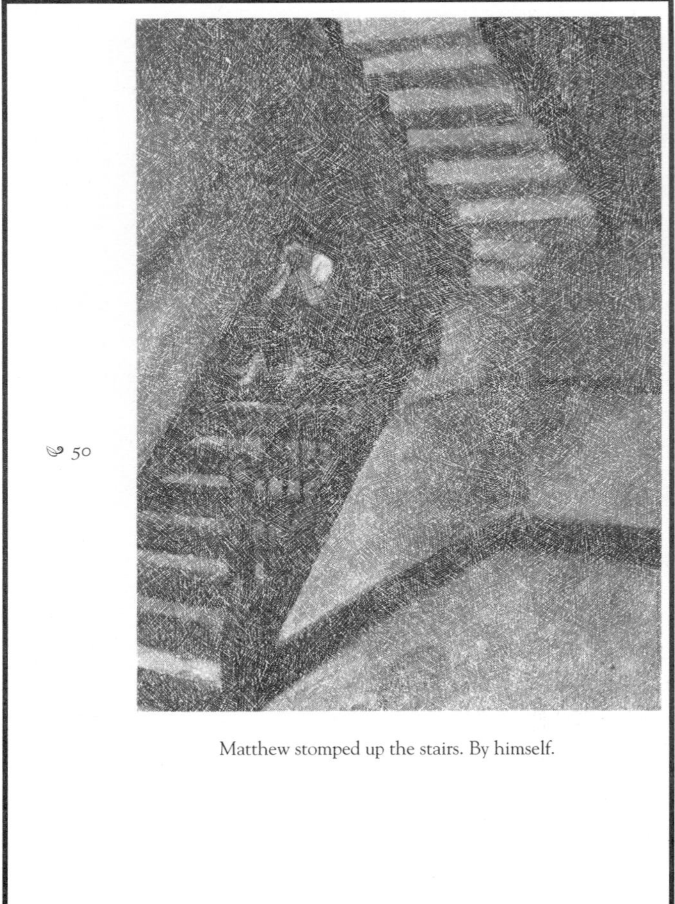

50

Matthew stomped up the stairs. By himself.

Responding

- Let the children discuss the selection in any way they want. If no one comments on the changes in the characters' behavior, ask the children to compare what Matthew and Tilly are like when they are getting along with what they are like when they are fighting.
- Ask if anyone in the class has ever argued with a friend the way that Matthew and Tilly argue. Encourage the children to tell what they think about the way the characters are acting. Be sure to allow for the expression of differing opinions. In fact, if only one point of view is offered, you may want to ask who has a different idea.
- Return to the words on the board to see which actually gave children trouble. Ask the children how they figured out these words.

➤ Reading/Writing Connection, page 24, requires the children to think about comparing objects. Tell the children to use the words at the bottom of each box to complete the sentences in the box.

Name

Lesson 12

Completing Sentences

A cat is bigger than a mouse. mouse cat	A dog is smaller than a house. dog house
Sally is fast. A dog is faster. A car is fastest. car dog	A rope is thin. A shoelace is thinner. A thread is thinnest. shoelace thread
Jon is tall. A tree is taller. A skyscraper is tallest. skyscraper tree	A snake is long. A rope is longer. A road is longest. rope road

Making Comparisons

24 R/WC Matthew and Tilly

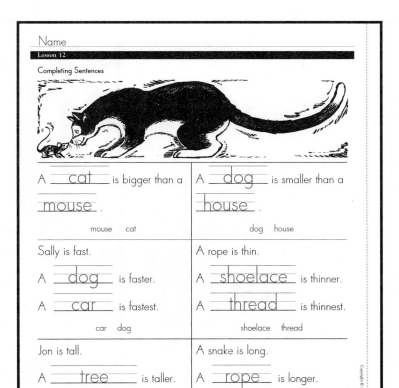

Reading/Writing Connection, page 24

✱ READING A PHONICS MINIBOOK

Superhero to the Rescue
Phonics Minibook 15

Getting Ready to Read

- Have volunteers read the title, the author's name, and the illustrator's name. Offer help as needed.
- Have the children browse the book as usual, commenting on what they see in the illustrations and what they think the story will tell them.

Recommendations

Follow the standard procedure for reading a Phonics Minibook:

- Have the class read each page of the story to themselves, then call on a child to read the page aloud. Clarify any difficulties on the page, then have a different child reread it before going on.
- Have the children reread the story aloud at least twice, calling on different children to read each time.

TEACHING TIP

As the children read, it might be helpful to have them find the little words within compound words such as *downstairs, naptime,* and *superhero.* Breaking these words into parts will help the children tackle the decoding.

OPEN COURT and ❋ are registered trademarks of Open Court Publishing Company.

COLLECTIONS FOR YOUNG SCHOLARS is a trademark of Open Court Publishing Company.

Printed in the United States of America

ISBN 0-8126-1285-X

10 9 8 7 6 5 4 3 2 1

Lenny wanted to be a superhero.

Lenny put on his cape.
"Superhero to the rescue!"
he shouted.
He raced downstairs.

Lenny landed on top
of his little sister Nikki.
"Ouch!" shouted Nikki.
She began to cry.

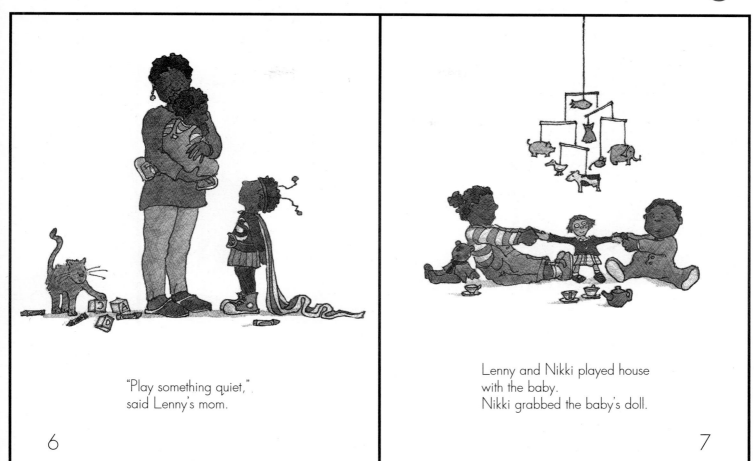

"Play something quiet,"
said Lenny's mom.

6

Lenny and Nikki played house
with the baby.
Nikki grabbed the baby's doll.

7

"Superhero to the rescue!"
shouted Lenny.
He pushed Nikki out of the way.

8

Nikki and the baby
both began to cry.

9

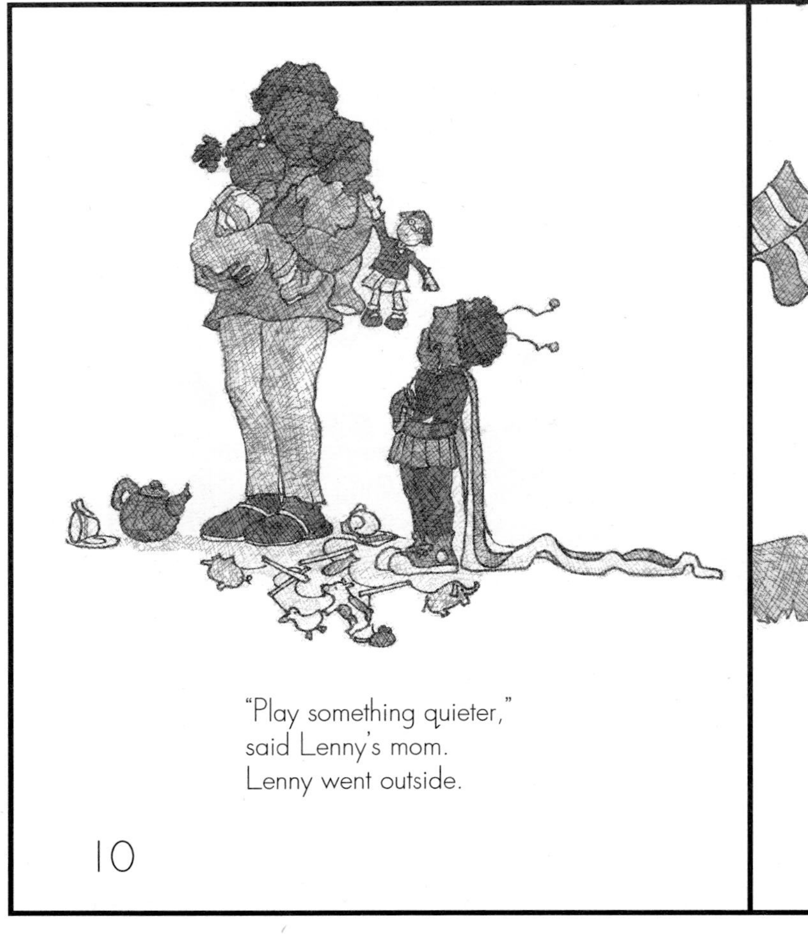

"Play something quieter,"
said Lenny's mom.
Lenny went outside.

10

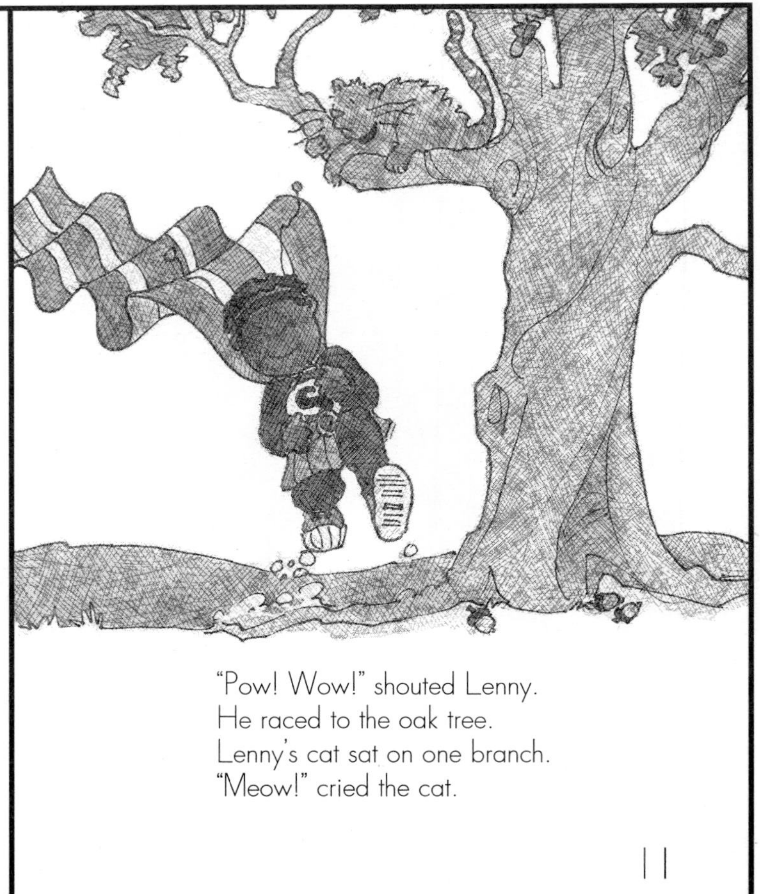

"Pow! Wow!" shouted Lenny.
He raced to the oak tree.
Lenny's cat sat on one branch.
"Meow!" cried the cat.

11

"Superhero to the rescue!"
shouted Lenny.
He reached for a branch.

12

Lenny's mom found him in the tree.
She helped him get down.
"Play something safer," she said.
They went back inside.

13

At naptime Lenny was bored.
His mom had put Nikki
and the baby to bed.

14

Lenny went upstairs.
The baby was crying.
His bunny had fallen out of the crib.

15

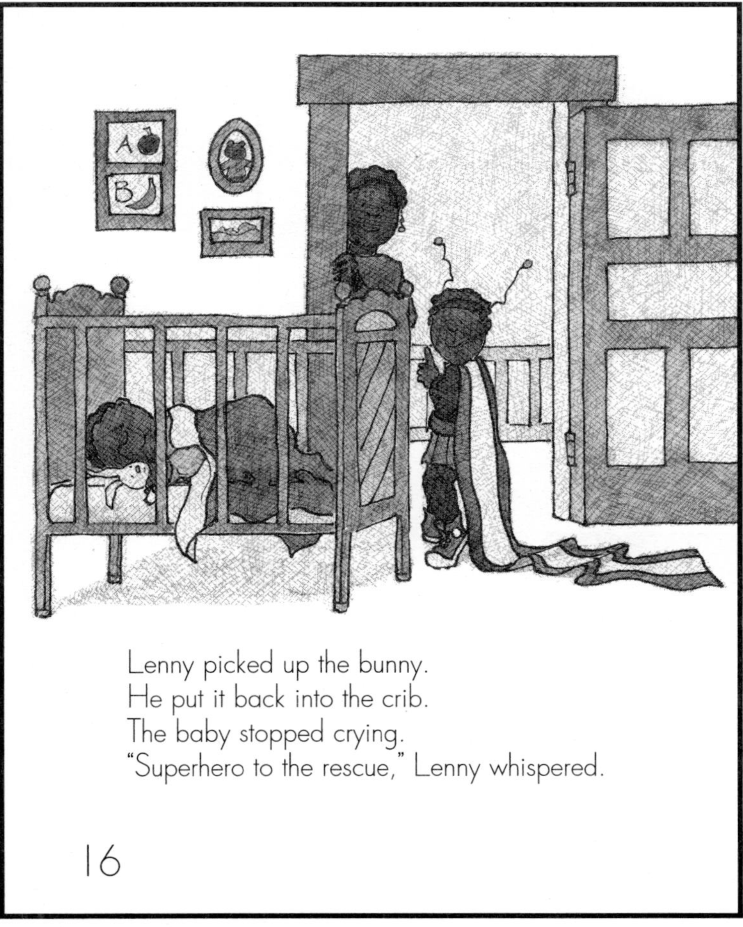

Lenny picked up the bunny.
He put it back into the crib.
The baby stopped crying.
"Superhero to the rescue," Lenny whispered.

16

Responding

- Have the children point out words in the story that were hard to read and tell how they figured them out.
- To make sure the children are reading the words in the story, have them answer the following questions by pointing to and reading aloud the word or sentence that answers each question:
  What did Lenny's sister say when he landed on her?
  Where did Lenny go after he made Nikki and the baby cry?
  What did Lenny's mother tell him when she helped him get down from the tree?
  How did Lenny feel when it was naptime?
  How did Lenny say "Superhero to the rescue" the very last time he said it?
- Invite a few volunteers to read the sentence of their choice from the story, pointing to the sentence as they read.
- Encouage the children to tell in their own words what happened in the story and to discuss what they liked best about it.

Finally, have the children pair up and read the story to each other.

TEACHING TIP

Set aside ten minutes for partner reading every day. During this time you should read with individuals, recording their progress. Reading Assessment Sheets for Phonics Minibooks are available in *Assessment Masters, Grade 1*.

* READING ALOUD

Many children's books have been written about friendship. The following books offer great opportunities to discuss what it means to be a friend. You may want to share one or more of the books with your class.

The Giving Tree by Shel Silverstein
We Are Best Friends by Aliki
Three Wishes by Lucille Clifton
Bob and Jack: A Boy and His Yak by Jeff Moss
Best Friends by Miriam Cohen

Remember to respond aloud as you read, relating the text to something that has happened to you, or empathizing with the characters.

For other suggestions for reading aloud, see **Learning Framework Card 5.**

2 WRITING

* DICTATION AND SPELLING

Word-Building Game Have the children take out paper and pencil for today's Word-Building game. The word list follows:

owl
out
ouch
couch
grouch
grouchy

Follow the established procedure for playing the game. Have the children write the words in list form, one under the other. Remind them to refer to the Sound/Spelling Cards for help. Model for them by writing along with them.

EXPLORING THE WRITER'S CRAFT

Review the list that the children generated in the previous lesson. Have the children talk about what kinds of things Matthew and Tilly like to do together. Discuss some of the problems they encountered and how they felt. Since this is a piece of realistic fiction, many children may be able to relate to this story, and it may suggest some good ideas for writing.

If a number of children are having trouble getting started, do a class story. Have the children review the list generated in Lesson 11 and decide on a topic. You may want to suggest other ideas such as "Things That I Do with Friends During the Summer," or "Winter," and so on. Brainstorm what might go into the story and then have the children write or draw what they would like to include in the story. Let children start sharing their contributions tomorrow.

Hold conferences with children who are still having problems coming up with a topic to write about. If you are doing a class story, then meet with children and talk about what they want included in the story.

TEACHING TIP

Remind the children to use the words from the Vocabulary Chart in their writing.

3 GUIDED AND INDEPENDENT EXPLORATION

WORKSHOP

Remind the children that they may use this time to work on projects on their own or in small groups. Be sure that each child knows what projects he or she may choose and how to complete any independent work. Suggestion for teacher-guided, collaborative, and independent activities follow.

Work with the Teacher

- With a small group of children, review base words + *-er* and *-est* endings. Practice with one base word ending in *e* and one ending in *y*. Use as examples words found in *Matthew and Tilly* and *Superhero to the Rescue*.
- Practice finding little words with small groups of children who are having problems with compound words. Again, find sample compound words in the readings for today.
- Preteach Sound/Spelling Card 40, Hawk, to those children who might need some extra help learning /aw/ spelled *aw*.
- Read the second half of *Matthew and Tilly* with those children who may have difficulty during tomorrow's lesson. Begin reading at the top of student anthology, page 51, or wherever you left off today.

Collaborative/Independent Activities

- Small groups of children might enjoy making comparison word posters. Have each group choose a base word. Provide each group with a large sheet of poster board divided, with light pencil lines, into three sections. At the tops of the sections, the children should print their base word, the base word plus *-er* and the base word plus *-est*. They can then illustrate each section appropriately and write a sentence at the bottom of the section describing what is happening in that scene.
- Challenge children to write and illustrate sentences using words from today's Blending exercise. Encourage them to write sentences that demonstrate their understanding of comparison words; for example, a child might choose to write sentences telling about a *crabby* person, a *crabbier* person, and the *crabbiest* person of all.
- Children who began games-related art pieces during yesterday's Workshop may finish their work today. They may want to add these to the Concept Board.
- Activity Sheet 82 is a game board. Pairs of children can play the Sidewalk game to reinforce their knowledge of long vowel sounds and spellings. Provide a die and two markers (markers from a generic game board would be fine) to each interested pair. Tell the children that they will take turns rolling the die and moving forward as many spaces as indicated on the die. Once a child has landed on a space, he or she must blend the word printed on that space and identify the long vowel found in that word. If successful, he or she may remain on that space; if not, the player must return to his or her previous space. The first player to reach *finish* wins.

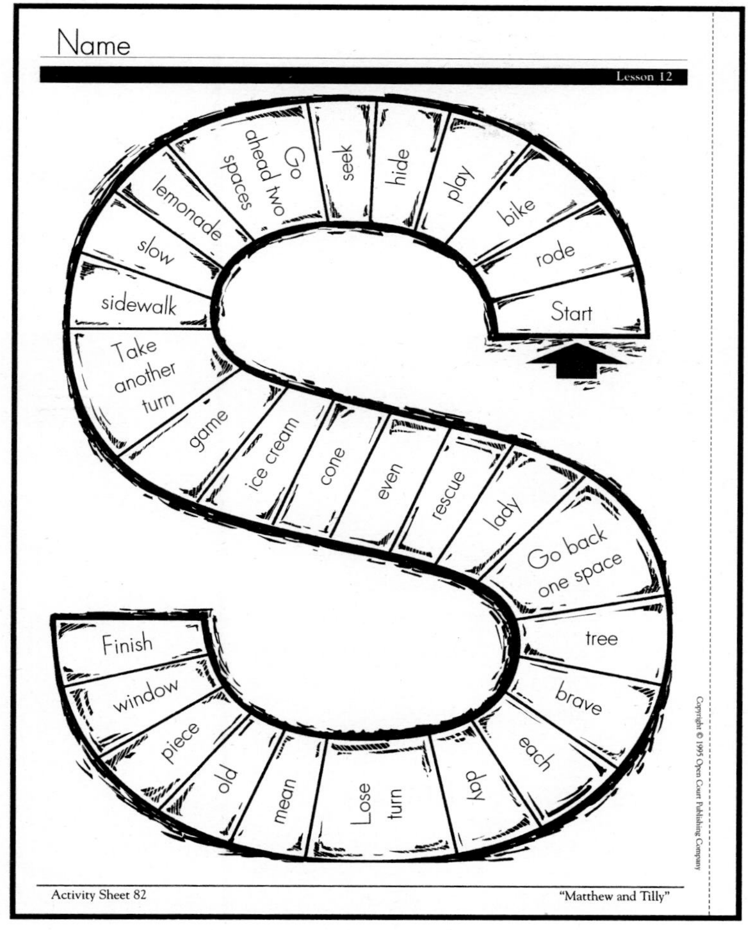
Name
Lesson 12
Go ahead two spaces
seek
hide
play
bike
rode
Start
lemonade
slow
sidewalk
Take another turn
game
ice cream
cone
even
rescue
lady
Go back one space
tree
brave
each
day
Lose turn
mean
old
piece
window
Finish
Copyright © 1995 Open Court Publishing Company
Activity Sheet 82
"Matthew and Tilly"

Activity Sheet 82

LESSON 13

Lesson Overview

New Learning

- /aw/ spelled *aw, au*

Outlaw Word

anyone

Materials

- ***Matthew and Tilly***, pages 51–55
- Sound/Spelling Card 40, Hawk
- Learning Framework Cards 2, 3, 4, 5, 8
- Reading/Writing Connection, pages 25–26
- Outlaw Word Flash Cards
- Activity Sheet 83

Prepare Ahead

- Compound Word Riddle Game (see page 147)

GETTING STARTED

Choose one or more of the following activities to focus the children's attention and to review some of the concepts they have been learning.

Spelling Challenge Divide the class into three or four teams. Explain that you will write a spelling of a long vowel sound on the board and give the teams thirty seconds to one minute to think of words that use that spelling. When time is up call on each team to say and spell its words. Write them on the board and award one point for each correct word. The team with the most points is the winner. Remind the children to whisper so that the other teams won't hear their words.

Keep the Card Game Place in a paper bag Outlaw Word Flash Cards and/or index cards with words containing spellings you want to review. Divide the class into teams of five children each. Tell the children that they will be playing a new game called Keep the Card. Explain that a player on each team will draw a card out of the paper bag and look at it. (The player's team members will also see the card.) If the player says the word correctly, he or she may put the card on the table in front of his or her team. If the player misses, the card will go back in the bag. The teams take turns. The team with the most cards at the end of about five to ten minutes wins the game.

1 READING

PHONICS

* **Introduce /aw/ spelled *aw, au*** Display Sound/Spelling Card 40, Hawk, and tell the children that this bird is a hawk. Ask the children what they may know about this bird. Explain that a hawk uses its claws and beak to hunt other animals and is called a bird of prey.

Point to the two different spellings and tell the children that today they will talk about both ways to spell the /aw/ sound. Ask them to listen for the /aw/ sound as you read the Hawk story.

A discussion of the procedure for introducing new sounds and spellings can be found on **Learning Framework Card 2.**

> Hazel the hawk never cooks her food,
> instead, she eats it raw.
> And when she thinks of dinnertime
> she caws: /aw/ /aw/ /aw/ /aw/.
>
> Hazel the Hawk likes rabbits and mice
> and catches them with her claws.
> In August, she flies high above the fields
> and spies them below, in the straw.
> Sometimes she even snatches a snake!
> And when she's caught one, she caws: /aw/ /aw/ /aw/ /aw/.
>
> If you were a hawk thinking of dinnertime,
> what do you think ***you'd*** say?
> (Have the children answer) /aw/ /aw/ /aw/ /aw/.

Read the story again. Each time you say a word with the sound /aw/, have the children say /aw/. Ask children to explain how they can use the Hawk card to help them remember this sound.

* **Blending** Have the children blend the following words. For reference and additional suggestions for blending, see **Learning Framework Card 3.**

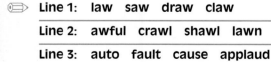

Line 1:	**law saw draw claw**
Line 2:	**awful crawl shawl lawn**
Line 3:	**auto fault cause applaud**
Line 4:	**August saucer pause paws**
Line 5:	**walk sidewalk chalk**
Sentence:	**Tilly didn't have anyone to play with.**

Words As the children sound and blend the words in the word lines, invite them to circle the various spellings for /aw/.

In line 4, point to *August* and ask the children why it begins with a capital letter. Explain the meanings of the homophones in *pause* and *paws.* Tell the children that *pause* is an action word meaning to take a short break or stop whatever you are doing for a while. *Paws,* as the children likely know, refers to the feet of an animal such as a dog or cat. Invite the children to use each word in a sentence to show its meaning.

Note that line 5 includes the word *sidewalk,* which the children encountered yesterday in *Matthew and Tilly.* Remind them that *walk* is a little word contained within *sidewalk*. Point out that *walk, sidewalk,* and *chalk* all contain the /aw/ sound. Explain that *alk* is a special spelling pattern that contains the /aw/ sound. You may want to compare this pattern to the *all* pattern that also contains the /aw/ sound.

You might want to ask a volunteer to give a clue, then send another child to the board to locate and erase the correct word. When he or she has successfully erased the right word, the child can give the next clue. Continue the review until most or all of the words have been erased.

Sentence Introduce the outlaw word *anyone* before you write the sentence on the board. Write the word *anyone* on the chalkboard and tell the children what it is. Call on children to use the word in sentences. Write the sentence on the board, underlining the new word *anyone.* Have the children read the sentence.

➤ Reading/Writing Connection, page 25, provides practice with words with the /aw/ sound. Help the children complete the top of the page by reading and copying the words and the sentence.

* READING THE STUDENT ANTHOLOGY

Matthew and Tilly
pages 51–55

Activating Prior Knowledge

Ask the children to think back to yesterday's reading. Call on volunteers to sum up what happened in the first part of the story.

Setting Reading Goals and Expectations

- Invite the children to browse the second half of the story. Once again, ask them to point out words that might be difficult to read. Write each page number and word on the board and invite children to try to figure out these words during the reading.

Recommendations for Reading

- To lead into today's reading, ask a child to read the sentence on page 50 that ended the first half of the story.

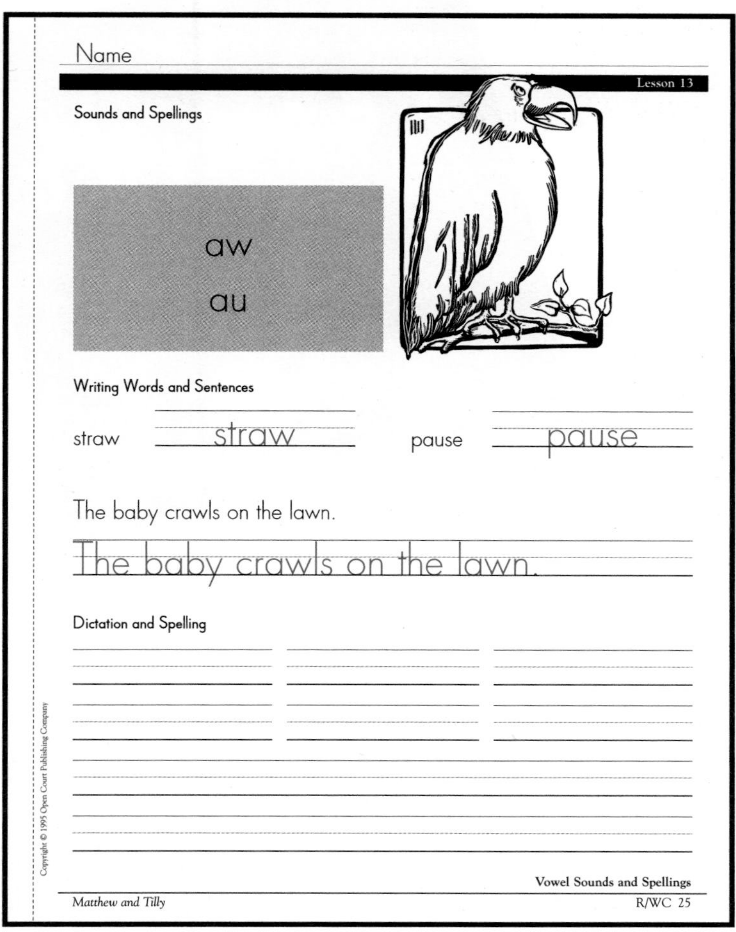
Name

Lesson 13

Sounds and Spellings

aw
au

Writing Words and Sentences

straw straw pause pause

The baby crawls on the lawn.

The baby crawls on the lawn.

Dictation and Spelling

Copyright © 1995 Open Court Publishing Company

Vowel Sounds and Spellings

Matthew and Tilly R/WC 25

Reading/Writing Connection, page 25

- Have the children take turns reading aloud. Have each child read a sentence or a whole page, depending on the length of the page. If children are having difficulty blending any of the words, remind them to check the Sound/Spelling Cards. If any words cannot be easily blended, pronounce the words for the children.

Note: Having the children read the story in pairs is a good option for Workshop.

MONITORING TIP Finish observing children as they read *Matthew and Tilly*. Record your observations in Teacher's Observation Log 3.

About the Reading Strategies

In reading this selection, children should use strategies for decoding unfamiliar words, responding, and predicting what will happen next. Refer the children to the posters on Clarifying Unfamiliar Words and Passages, Checking Understanding, and Responding to Text. Explain how using these strategies as you read helps you understand the story.

Think-Aloud Prompts for Use in Oral Reading Notice the think-aloud prompts with the page miniatures. These are merely suggestions. Continue to model using appropriate strategies while reading, and encourage the children to use the strategies on their own. For a review of information about modeling and generating think-alouds, see **Learning Framework Card 8, Reading the Student Anthologies.**

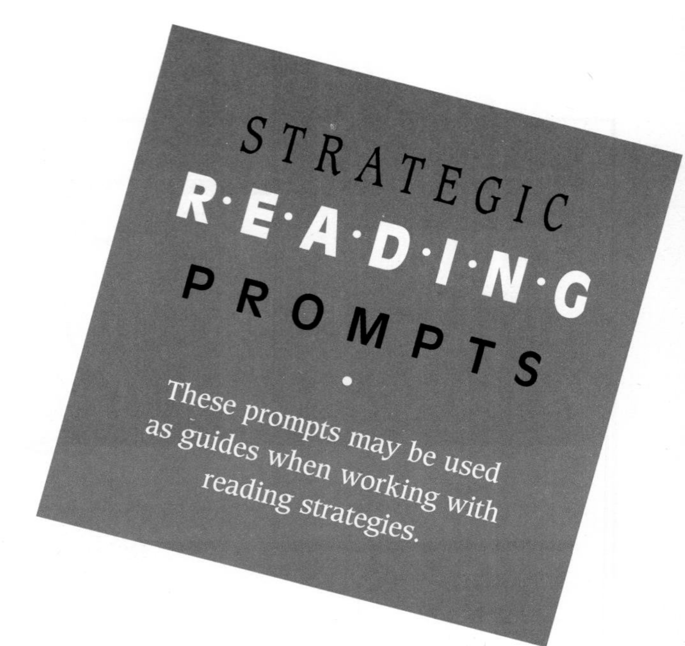

1 After reading the word *herself,* you might model responding by saying, *Poor Matthew. Poor Tilly.*

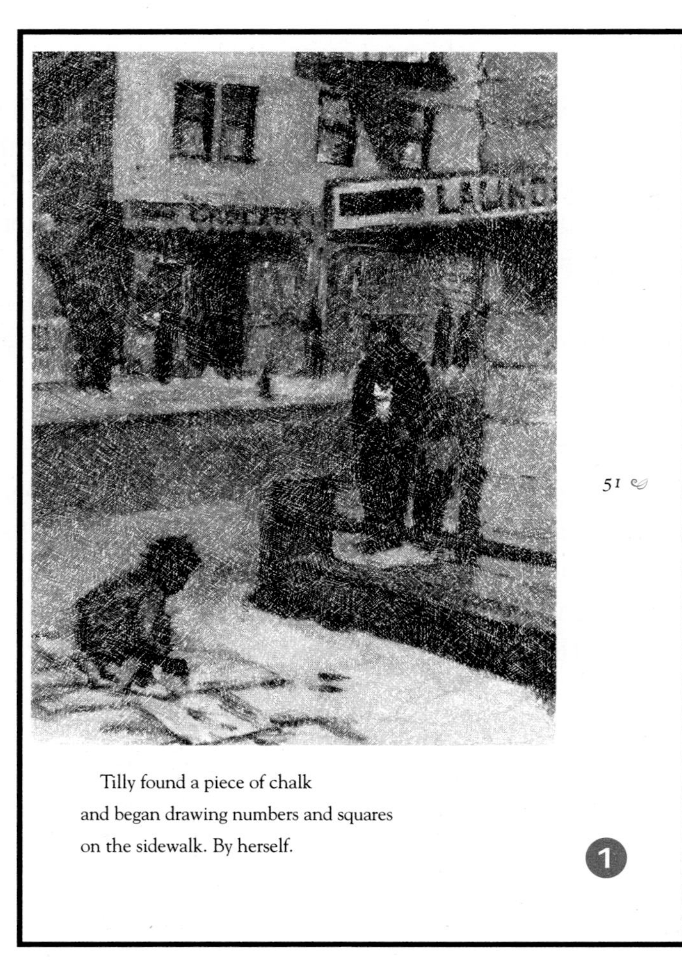

Tilly found a piece of chalk
and began drawing numbers and squares
on the sidewalk. By herself.
51
1

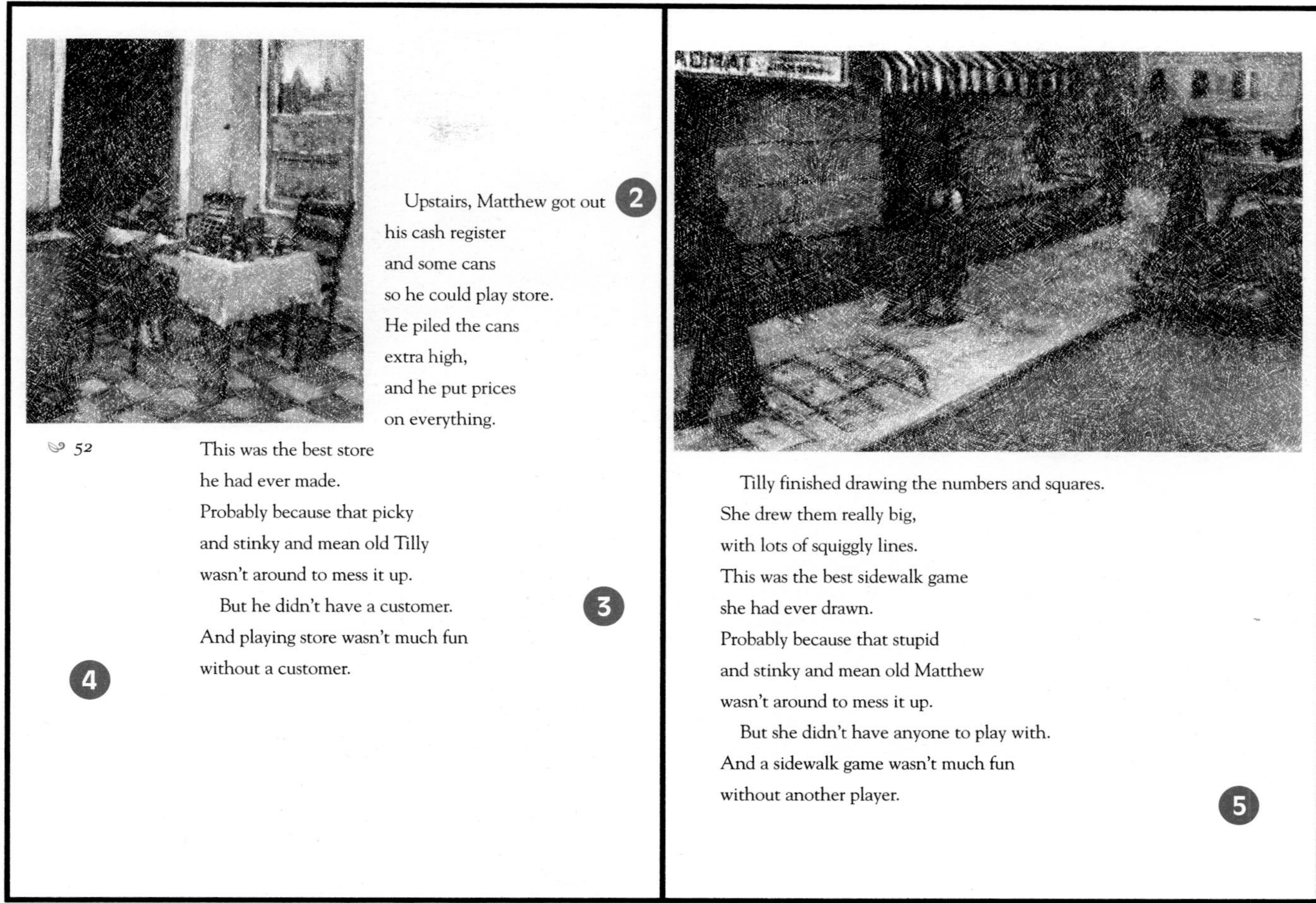

Upstairs, Matthew got out (2)
his cash register
and some cans
so he could play store.
He piled the cans
extra high,
and he put prices
on everything.

52

This was the best store
he had ever made.
Probably because that picky
and stinky and mean old Tilly
wasn't around to mess it up.
But he didn't have a customer. (3)
And playing store wasn't much fun
without a customer.

(4)

Tilly finished drawing the numbers and squares.
She drew them really big,
with lots of squiggly lines.
This was the best sidewalk game
she had ever drawn.
Probably because that stupid
and stinky and mean old Matthew
wasn't around to mess it up.
But she didn't have anyone to play with.
And a sidewalk game wasn't much fun
without another player. (5)

2 If children need help with *upstairs,* encourage them to look for the little words in the big word.

3 If the children have trouble with *register* and *customer,* have them break the words into parts. If necessary, remind them about the sound /j/ spelled *gi.*

4 At the end of the page, ask the children to predict what they think might happen.

5 At the end of the page, tell the children that this is a good place to predict and ask them what they think will happen next.

Matthew looked out the window
and wondered what Tilly was doing.
Tilly looked up at Matthew's window
and wondered what he was doing.
She smiled, just a little.
That was enough for Matthew.
"I'm sorry," he called.
"So am I," said Tilly. 6

55

And Matthew ran downstairs so they could play.
Together again. 7

6 At the end of the page, you might want to model responding by saying, *They're being nice.*

7 Remind a child having difficulty that *downstairs* should be treated the same way as *upstairs.*

Responding to the Selection

- Encourage the children to discuss any new games they learned about in this story.
- Have the children return to the words you wrote on the chalkboard during Browsing. Have them tell which words they actually had trouble with and explain how they figured out the words.
- Let the children discuss anything that interests them about the selection. Again, have them compare Matthew and Tilly when they got along with Matthew and Tilly when they fought. Discuss what Matthew and Tilly did by themselves. Ask what the children thought of the story, how it made them feel, and what it reminds them of.
- Have the children compare this story to a fantasy story, such as "The Big Team Relay Race," and discuss how this story is different. Point out that Matthew and Tilly might be real children and that this story might really have happened. Have the children talk about some of the things that could really happen.
- Discuss what new ideas or questions should be added to the Concept Board.
- To assess the children's understanding of the story, you might ask them how they can tell that Matthew and Tilly are true friends.

Vocabulary Ask children if there are any interesting words in this story that they want to add to the unit vocabulary list. Have the children use these words in oral sentences; then add the words to the class vocabulary chart. Possible words might include *friends, wondered, sorry, together.*

➤ Reading/Writing Connection, page 26, can be completed at this time. Have the children use the words in the box to complete the paragraph about *Matthew and Tilly.*

TIP FOR ENGLISH LANGUAGE LEARNERS

Provide opportunities for English Language Learners to clarify their understanding of the idea of the story and to express their feelings about it. Have them try to explain the story to themselves. Then pair English Language Learners with native English-speaking partners. Encourage partners to talk about the important ideas in the story. Informally monitor the children's conversations to assess their understanding and to check that each child is participating.

* READING ALOUD

Angry words sometimes pass between friends. After discussing this sort of experience, which many children will be able to identify with, you may want to share one or more of the following books:

No Fighting, No Biting by Else Homeland Minarek
I'll Fix Anthony by Judith Viorst
Peter's Chair by Ezra Jack Keats

Remember to ask the children questions about how the story made them feel and what they thought was most important in the story. For additional suggestions, see **Learning Framework Card 5, Reading Aloud.**

Name

Lesson 13

Reading and Writing

fight yelled sidewalk friends sorry
together played crayon himself

Matthew and Tilly were friends. They played together all the time. One day, they had a fight because Matthew broke Tilly's crayon. Tilly yelled at Matthew, and Matthew yelled at Tilly. Matthew went upstairs to play by himself. Tilly stayed on the sidewalk by herself. After a while, they were sorry. At the end they played together again.

Reading the Selection

26 R/WC *Matthew and Tilly*

Reading/Writing Connection, page 26

2 WRITING

✱ DICTATION AND SPELLING

Have the children open their Reading/Writing Connection book to page 25. Dictate the following words and sentences, using the suggestions for dictation that appear on **Learning Framework Card 4.**

Line 1: round growl shout

Line 2: louder fastest harder

Sentence: The mouse is brown.

Remind the children to proofread their work.

INDEPENDENT AND COLLABORATIVE WRITING

Have the children continue working on their stories. Conference with children. Remind them of how authors use dialogue to make stories more interesting. Select a story to use tomorrow as you review revision. Be sure you have the author's permission.

If you are doing a class story, have children discuss what they want in the story, after talking about how to organize the story. Using chart

TEACHING TIP

Remind the children to use the words from the Vocabulary Chart in their own writing.

paper, have children dictate what to write. Some children may be able to come up and write their own contributions. As this is being done, encourage children to elaborate on their ideas by extending sentences. Also encourage children to use dialogue just as the author did in *Matthew and Tilly.* If you are doing the writing, make it look like a draft that will need changes.

3 GUIDED AND INDEPENDENT EXPLORATION

WORKSHOP

Remind the children that they may use this time to work on projects on their own or in small groups. Be sure that each child knows what projects he or she may choose and how to complete any independent work. Suggestions for teacher-guided, collaborative, and independent activities follow.

Work with the Teacher

- Review Sound/Spelling Card 40, Hawk, and today's Blending exercise, with those children who could use extra practice.
- In the second half of *Matthew and Tilly,* there are several words containing /aw/, and /aw/ followed by /k/ (page 51, *chalk, drawing, sidewalk;* page 53, *drawing, sidewalk, drawn*). Have a few children return to the selection and race to locate each word. The first child to find a word should read aloud the whole sentence containing the word, and then tell which letters made the /aw/, or /aw/ followed by /k/ sound.
- Ask a few independent readers to read with you. You might suggest that they select books that tell about friendship and playing with friends. Invite other children to listen to the reading.
- Have children read Phonics Minibook 15, *Superhero to the Rescue.* This can be done with individuals or small groups of students.

ASSESSMENT Give students the written test. See assessment booklet for instructions.

Collaborative/Independent Activities

- Play Bingo. Use Bingo cards that include the spellings *ow, ou, aw,* and *au,* as well as the final consonant clusters *-rth, -nth, -nch,* and *-rst.* Make sure that the list of words you call out includes words with the /ow/ and /aw/ sounds. Check recent Blending lessons for word ideas.
- Encourage pairs of children to reread previous Phonics Minibooks or student anthology selections. Introduce peer tutoring by pairing less fluent readers with children who read confidently.
- Invite groups of two or three children to play the Compound Word Riddle game. Provide each group with an envelope of game materials and review the rules of play. Before Workshop begins, you may want to make up some new riddles for the children to solve.
- Some children might enjoy drawing pictures of themselves and their best friends, playing the games they most enjoy playing together. Encourage each child to write a sentence or two at the bottom of his or her drawing which tells what is happening in the drawing. Children may also want to include dialogue in the sentences that explain their picture.
- Activity Sheet 83 focuses on the spellings of /aw/. Tell the children to choose the word that completes each sentence and write it in the blank, then illustrate their favorite sentence in the box at the bottom of the page.

Name

Lesson 13

1. Lightning caused the forest fire.
called/caused

2. April is the month after March.
August/April

3. The tall man juggled three balls.
saw/tall balls/hawks

4. The cat's milk is in the saucer.
saw/saucer

5. The dog's paws got dirty in the mud.
paws/walk

6. The hawk has long claws.
hall/hawk chalk/claws

"Matthew and Tilly" Activity Sheet 83

Activity Sheet 83

LESSON 14

Lesson Overview

Materials

- Student Anthology, Games unit, pages 10–57
- Sound/Spelling Card 40, Hawk
- Learning Framework Cards 3, 5
- Reading/Writing Connection, pages 27–28
- Activity Sheets 82, 84

Prepare Ahead

- /aw/ words on index cards (see page 155)
- Sidewalk Game (see page 155)

GETTING STARTED

Choose one or more of the following activities to focus the children's attention and to review some of the concepts they have been learning.

Riddle Me This Tell the children that you are thinking of a word you can make from the sounds on the Sound/Spelling Cards. Say *Sausages* and *Hawk* and ask the children to guess your riddle *(saw)*. Repeat the process for other riddles.

Popcorn, Long A, Nose, Timer *(paint)*
Dinosaur, Robot, Long I, Vacuum *(drive)*
Jump rope, Long O, Camera *(joke)*
Timer, Long E, Chipmunk, Bird *(teacher)*
Camera, Armadillo, Dinosaur *(card)*

Team Words Game Divide the class into several teams and give each team a sheet of paper. Write the spelling *oa* on the board and have each member of the team write a word with this spelling. Have the teams read their lists of words to the group.

1 READING

PHONICS

Review /aw/ spelled *aw* and *au* Write *aw* and *au* on the chalkboard. Point to Sound/Spelling Card 40, Hawk, and ask what sound these spellings make. Give clues for words with this sound and have children guess the words. As the children guess each word, write it beneath the correct spelling and have the guesser come to the board and underline the spelling within the word.

Use clues such as the following:

- the month after July
- what you do when you clap
- a person who writes a book
- another name for a car
- use this to cut wood

* **Blending** Have the children blend the following words. For reference and additional suggestions for blending, see **Learning Framework Card 3.**

Line 1:	**because saucer laundry automatic**
Line 2:	**fawn yawn dawn awning**
Line 3:	**red black pink yellow**
Line 4:	**white green brown purple**
Line 5:	**sorry squiggly customer probably**

Lines 1 and 2 review words with the sound /aw/. Ask the children where in the word they hear the sound and invite them to circle the spelling.

Lines 3 and 4 focus on color words. Have the children give other color words. Print these words on chart paper and point out that the children may want to use these words in their writing. Add to the list as the children learn other spellings, for example, *ue* in *blue.*

Line 5 reviews vocabulary from the story, *Matthew and Tilly*. After the children sound and blend the words, you may want them to read the sentences from the story in which these words are found. You may wish to write the sentences ahead of time either on chart paper or on the chalkboard.

Review the word lines with the number game. Put slips of paper with numbers 1–4 in a container labeled *words,* and numbers 1–5 in a second container labeled *lines*. Children choose a number from each container and find the correct word, such as the second word in line 3, to read.

➤ Reading/Writing Connection, page 27, provides practice reading words with the /aw/ sound. Have the children select the word to complete each sentence.

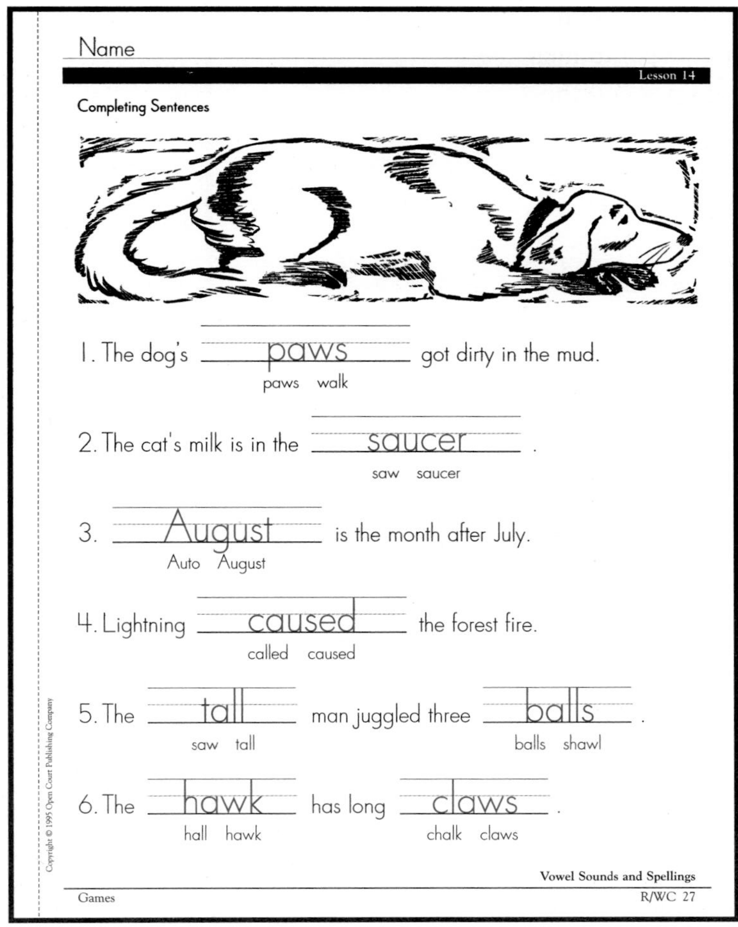
Name

Lesson 14

Completing Sentences

1. The dog's paws got dirty in the mud.
paws walk

2. The cat's milk is in the saucer.
saw saucer

3. August is the month after July.
Auto August

4. Lightning caused the forest fire.
called caused

5. The tall man juggled three balls.
saw tall balls shawl

6. The hawk has long claws.
hall hawk chalk claws

Copyright © 1995 Open Court Publishing Company

Vowel Sounds and Spellings

Games R/WC 27

Reading/Writing Connection, page 27

✱ READING THE STUDENT ANTHOLOGY

Reread Favorite Games Unit Selection

Recommendations for Reading

- Ask children to identify a story they would like to read again. Develop groups based upon student interests. Have the students read the stories in groups or pairs. If children have difficulty, have classmates come to their assistance in breaking up the word, finding little words, or blending. If children have difficulty with meaning, encourage them to reread the sentence and use the context to find meaning.

Responding

- Let the children discuss anything related to the selections. Have the children tell in their own words what happened in the selection and discuss any difficulties they had. Again, refer to the original lesson.

Unit Discussion

In reading the Games unit, several interesting questions have surfaced, "What shall we play?" in "A Game Called Piggle," and "Can everybody be on the team?" in "The Big Team Relay Race." Ask some children to draw from their personal experiences. You may wish to mention some of the following concepts, but these certainly do not end the conversations that can come from looking closely at the stories and relating them to the children's real life experiences.

- "A Game Called Piggle"—Some games involve imagination and imitation.
- *Jafta* deals not only with imagination, but also shows that some games can be played alone.
- "The Big Team Relay Race"—Being little doesn't mean I can't play, and maybe win!
- *Matthew and Tilly*—I can do things by myself, but it's nice to share and play with a friend.

Other concepts that you might explore in these selections include treating boredom with creative invention and the idea that anything can be a game.

Direct the children's attention to the Concept Board and discuss what they have learned as they read selections and discussed this unit. Review some of the drawings and wonderings that the children have contributed to the board and have them tell what they may know about games and playing now that they were only wondering about before.

➤ Reading/Writing Connection, page 28, provides an opportunity for the children to draw or write about what they have learned through their reading and discussions during this unit. Have them refer back to page 2 and discuss what they drew or wrote about as they began the unit. Then have them draw or write about what they have learned.

Celebrating the Unit

Celebrate the completion of the unit. You might want to encourage the children to play their favorite games, to teach friends to play games, or to teach games to younger children. You may want to set aside a part of a day as Game Day. Children could invite parents to visit and play along.

* READING ALOUD

Many books for children involve games and playing. You may want to share one of the following books with your class:

Is Susan Here? by Janice May Udry
Stella and Roy by Ashley Wolff
The Chase by Béatrice Tanaka

Remember to ask the children questions about their favorite parts of the story and about the new ideas they learned from the story. See **Learning Framework Card 5** for more suggestions for reading aloud.

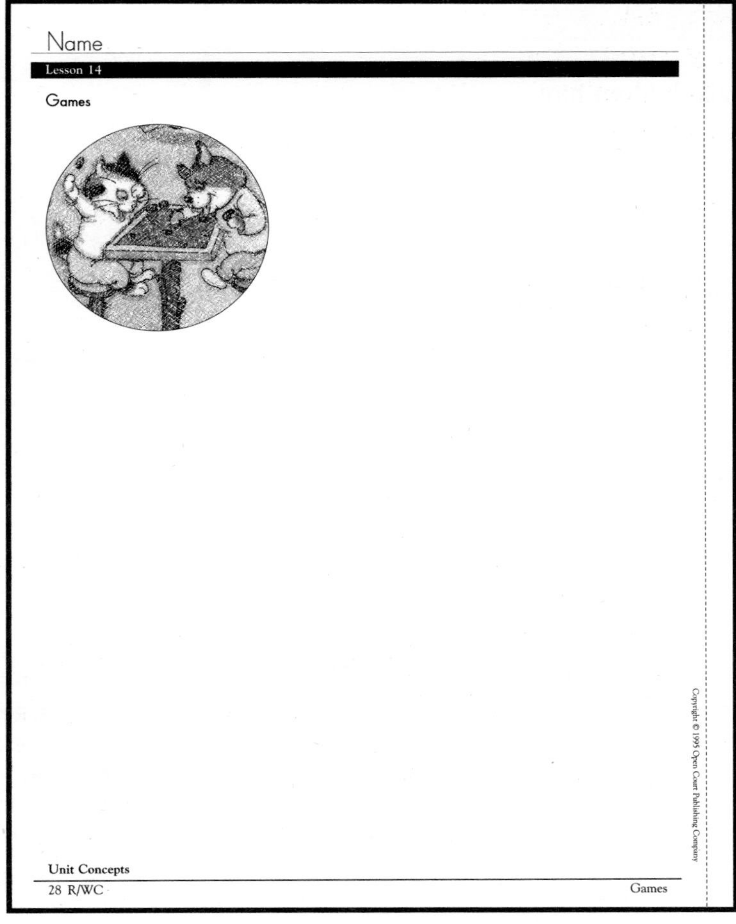

Name

Lesson 14

Games

Unit Concepts

28 R/WC Games

Reading/Writing Connection, page 28

2 WRITING

✱ DICTATION AND SPELLING

Word-Building Game Have the children use pencil and paper for the Word-Building game in this lesson. The list of words follows:

law
lawn
yawn
yawning
dawn
draw

Follow the established procedures for the game. Have the children write the words in a list, one under the other. The children should isolate the sounds in succession and check the Sound/Spelling Cards for spellings. Write along with the children to provide a model.

INDEPENDENT AND COLLABORATIVE WRITING

If you are working on a group story, make sure that all children have had an opportunity to share their ideas. If you have posted a chart of these points, refer to it. Then go back and reread the story. Remind children that good writers revisit or revise their work by checking to see whether it makes sense, whether anything needs to be added, or whether anything needs to be taken out. Be sure to use a caret when you insert something or a line through word(s) you want to delete.

Even if children are working on individual stories, talk about revision and what writers do to make their stories better. Using the story you selected yesterday, write it on the board or chart paper, or make a transparency. Read the story aloud and then talk about how to revise it. Give the final copy to the author to use in reworking the story. Suggest that some children who are ready may want to work on revising their stories during the remainder of writing time. Workshop too may be a good time to continue work on their writing.

Hold conferences with those children who are ready to revise their stories. This can be done individually or in small groups.

TEACHING TIP

Revise using a colored pencil. This makes changes easier to see when you are rewriting. Have the children do the same.

TEACHING TIP

Not all children will be writing sentences. Revision for these children may be simply adding describing words or just more labels to their work. Posters too can be revised by making sure that all the important information has been included.

Activity Sheet 84

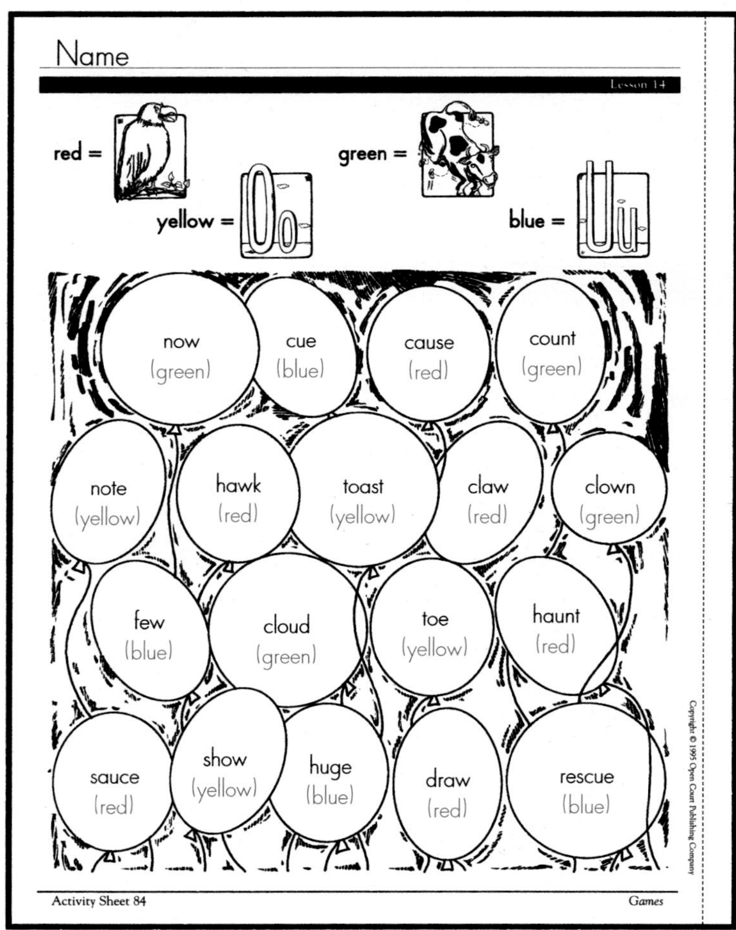

3 GUIDED AND INDEPENDENT EXPLORATION

WORKSHOP

Remind the children that they may use this time to work on projects on their own or in small groups. Be sure that each child knows what projects he or she may choose and how to complete any independent work. Suggestions for teacher-guided, collaborative, and independent activities follow.

Work with the Teacher

- Review the blending activity from today's or previous lessons.
- Hold a Reading Relay between two teams of children. Use flash cards containing compound words and /aw/ words. Words you might choose include

dawn	crawl	fault
inside	hawk	paws
chalk	doghouse	lawn
pause	talk	catnap
law	jaws	baseball
superhero	claw	sawed
sidewalk	anteater	draw
August	upstairs	drawing
sauce	downstairs	drawn
saucer	outside	

You might also include words containing three-letter final consonant clusters, such as

munch	pinch	first
crunch	thirst	tenth
branch	burst	eleventh

- Review base word + *-ing, -er,* and *-est* endings with a small group of children. Use this session to assess the children's progress.
- Preteach Sound/Spelling Card 41, Hoot owl, or preview "The Gingerbread Man," student anthology pages 60–69, with those children who may need extra help with the new sound/spelling.

Collaborative/Independent Activities

- Encourage children to illustrate their favorite character from a selection in the Games unit.
- You may want to create a new version of the Sidewalk game, Activity Sheet 82, filling in the squares with *-er* and *-est* words or words containing /aw/ spelled *aw* and *au.* Make several photocopies of the game and distribute one, along with a die and two markers, to each interested pair of children. Before they begin, remind them of the rules of play.
- Children may use this time to work in their journals or put the finishing touches on pieces they began during the Games unit.
- Activity Sheet 84 reviews the sounds and spellings of /aw/, /ow/, /ō/, and /ū/. Tell the children to use the key at the top of the page to help them color the balloons. They should color those balloons with the /aw/ sound red, balloons with the /ow/ sound green, balloons with the /ō/ sound yellow, and balloons with the /ū/ sound blue.

Folk Tales

UNIT INTRODUCTION

BACKGROUND INFORMATION FOR THE TEACHER

Explorable Concepts

Folk tales began as stories that were told before many people learned to read and write. Often these stories illustrate qualities and values held dear by the people of each culture: honesty, kindness, hard work, and obedience are rewarded; goodness overcomes obstacles; evil is punished. Particular lessons about human nature may be taught.

Children are a natural audience for folk tales. The tales are generally short and concise. They are packed with action. Frequently they include rhyme and repetition, animal characters, and humor. In most folk tales, each character represents one particular quality—goodness, evil, cleverness, or stupidity—that is easily recognized by children. The plots are simple; the conclusions, satisfying.

By reading folk literature from around the world, the children are exposed to the similarities among cultures. They come to understand that people everywhere share many of the same feelings, experience the same problems, and appreciate the same kind of humorous events. In addition, the children are also introduced to cultural differences in language, food, traditions, and interests.

UNIT 2

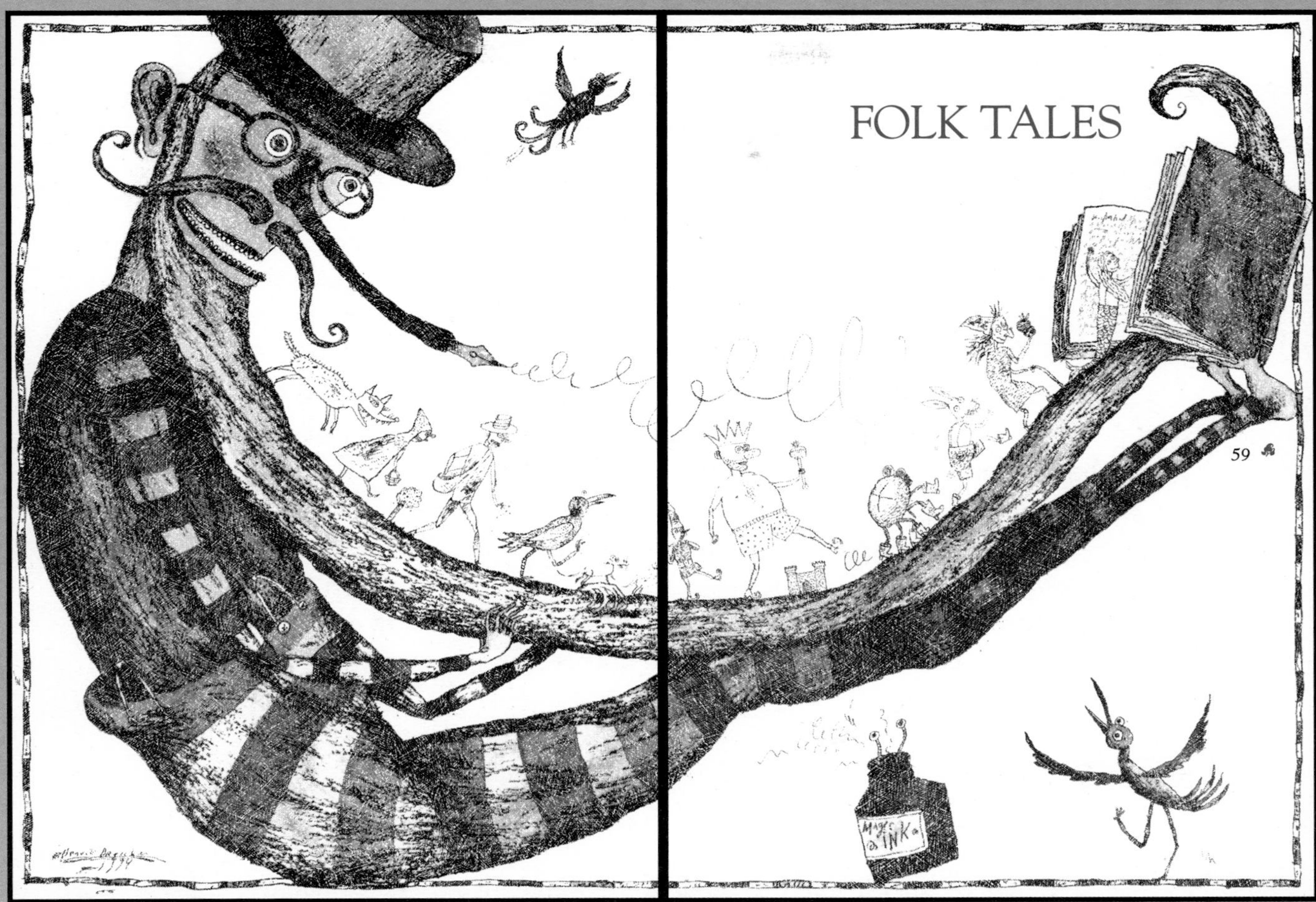

As you proceed through this unit with your class, you may find it useful to think about the following questions:

- What may be learned from folk tales or fables?
- Why are these stories still enjoyable?
- Do the children know other versions of the stories?

Resources

Among the following resources are professional reference books, audiovisual materials, and community/school resources. The reference books are intended to help you develop the concepts and organize information to share with the children in whatever way you choose. The community/school resources include people, agencies, and institutions that may be helpful in your exploration.

In addition to the resources listed here, a bibliography appears in the student anthology. The children may want to use the bibliography to find other folk tales to read.

Professional Reference Books

Bosma, Betty. *Fairy Tales, Fables, Legends, and Myths: Using Folk Literature in Your Classroom.* Teachers College Press, 1992. In this handy resource, teachers will find many ways of using folk literature in the classroom.

Jacobs, Joseph. *English Folk and Fairy Tales.* Dover Reprint, 1967. This is a fine source of classic fairy and folk tales. Jacobs has also edited other anthologies of folk tales.

Sierra, Judy. *The Flannelboard Storytelling Book.* H.W. Wilson, 1987. Songs, poems, and folk tales, each accompanied by patterns for flannelboard figures.

———, and Kaminski, Robert. *Multicultural Folktales: Stories to Tell Young Children.* Oryx Press, 1991. A collection of folk tales from many cultures with suggestions for telling the stories, flannelboard patterns, and suggestions for children to put on puppet plays.

Yolen, Jane. *Touch Magic: Faerie and Folklore in the Literature of Childhood.* Putnam, 1981. A collection of fairy and folk tales.

Read-Alouds

Brett, Jan. *Goldilocks and the Three Bears.* Dodd, Meade and Company, 1987. In this lavishly illustrated classic tale, a curious little girl helps herself to the three bears' food and then falls asleep in their cottage.

Clark, Margaret. *The Best of Aesop's Fables.* Little, Brown and Company, 1990. In these simply told fables, the morals have been omitted.

Galdone, Paul. *Puss in Boots.* Clarion, 1976. A poor young man meets a beautiful princess and gains a fortune after his crafty cat outwits a giant.

Mosel, Arlene. *Tikki Tikki Tembo.* Henry Holt and Company, 1968. In this humorous Chinese folk tale, we learn why the Chinese give their children short names.

Willard, Nancy. *The Sorcerer's Apprentice.* Scholastic, 1993. The magician's apprentice steals a magic spell and creates havoc.

Yolen, Jane. *The Sleeping Beauty.* Alfred A. Knopf, 1986. When she is not invited to the princess's christening, a wicked fairy casts a spell.

Zelinsky, Paul O. *Rumpelstiltskin.* E. P. Dutton, 1986. Zelinsky retells a favorite Grimm fairy tale about a miller's daughter who is asked to spin straw into gold.

Audiovisual Materials

Beauty and the Beast. Lightyear Entertainment/Video, 1988. A faithful daughter agrees to become the companion of a frightening beast in order to save her father. 27 minutes; videocassette.

The Nightingale. Platypus Productions, 1983. A kitchen maid finds a nightingale for an emperor who has everything. 54 minutes; videocassette.

Peachboy. Rabbit Ears Productions, Inc., 1991. A peasant couple finds a little boy inside a giant peach. 54 minutes; videocassette.

The Princess and the Pea. Platypus Productions, 1983. A domineering queen insists on testing the sensitivity of all the princesses who try to marry her son. 50 minutes; videocassette.

The Snow Queen. Platypus Productions, Inc., 1983. A young girl and boy travel to an ice palace, where they learn the value of love and warmth. 48 minutes; videocassette.

The Three Billy Goats Gruff and *The Three Little Pigs.* Rabbit Ears Productions, 1989. In *The Three Billy Goats Gruff,* three billy goats encounter a greedy troll under the bridge. In *The Three Little Pigs,* three little pigs battle with a wolf. 30 minutes (combined); one videocassette.

Community/School

- Librarian
- Storytellers

Concept Board

Provide a space in your classroom where you and the children can share your ideas, questions, and wonderings as you read and respond to the selections in the unit. This area will be called the Concept Board. It might be a bulletin board or a large sheet of chart paper attached to a wall. The Concept Board will be a place where you and the children can post any information about folk tales that they gather and wish to share with their classmates. This information might include written notes or stories, drawings, magazine or newspaper pictures and articles, or whatever they wish to add to illustrate their growing knowledge about folk tales. From time to time you should direct the children's attention to the Concept Board and discuss the materials that are on it. After reading each selection, you should discuss what the children have learned that might be new or that they might not have thought of before. In addition, encourage them to express anything that they wonder about because of what they have read. Have them write, illustrate, or dictate their ideas and post them on the board. Review earlier information, particularly any questions that the children had, to determine whether they have new information to add.

Learning Unit: Folk Tales

SELECTION	LINK TO THE UNIT CONCEPT	LESSON	NEW LEARNING	WRITING
The Gingerbread Man, pages 162–184 folk tale retold by Jo Olson, illustrated by Nelle Davis	Like other folk tales, this story has been retold many times by many different storytellers.	15	/o͞o/ spelled ***oo, ue, u_e, u, _ew***	Independent and Collaborative Writing
		16	/oo/ spelled ***oo***	Exploring the Writer's Craft
A Shared Reading Story ▲ ■ Anansi and the Talking Melon, pages 185–221 folk tale retold by Eric A. Kimmel, illustrated by Janet Stevens	Folk tales in many cultures include a trickster—someone who is always tricking other characters either for fun or to get out of tough situations.	17	/n/ spelled ***kn***	Independent and Collaborative Writing
		18		Independent and Collaborative Writing
		19	/oy/ spelled ***oy*** and ***oi***	Minilesson: Story Elements
FINE ART pages 222–229 ***Sinbad the Sailor***, Paul Klee; ***Peter and the Wolf***, Ben Shahn; Bunraku Performance in Osaka, Japan; ***The Sleeping Beauty***, Sir Edward Burne-Jones	Children will recognize some of the folk tales illustrated here.	20		Minilesson: Using Describing Words
The Lion and the Mouse, pages 230–244 fable by Aesop, retold by Christine Crocker, illustrated by Alexi Natchev	Telling stories is one of the universal ways that people have discovered for expressing the values and traditions of their culture.	21		Exploring the Writer's Craft
		22		Independent and Collaborative Writing
The Wolf in Sheep's Clothing, pages 245–260 fable by Aesop, retold by Christine Crocker, illustrated by Normand Chartier	Timeless truths—such as actions speak louder than words, looks can be deceiving—occur frequently in folk literature.	23		Minilesson: Speaker Tags
		24		Independent and Collaborative Writing
■ The Three Billy Goats Gruff, pages 261–283 folk tale retold by Christine Crocker, illustrated by Cat Bowman Smith	Folk tales often illustrate how good wins over evil.	25		Independent and Collaborative Writing
		26	/r/ spelled ***wr_***	Independent and Collaborative Writing
		27	/f/ spelled ***ph***	Independent and Collaborative Writing
Little Green Riding Hood, pages 295–311 from ***Telephone Tales*** by Gianni Rodari, rewritten as a play, illustrated by Nadine Bernard Westcott	Folk tales were originally passed on from storyteller to audience, changing as they passed from one generation to the next and traveled from one country to another.	28		Exploring the Writer's Craft
		29		Independent and Collaborative Writing
Unit Review, pages 312–318		30		Independent and Collaborative Writing

▲ Full-length trade books ■ Dramatized on audiocassette

LESSON 15

Lesson Overview

New Learning

- Introduction to Folk Tales unit
- /o͞o/ spelled ***oo, ue, u, u_e, _ew***

Outlaw Word

woman

Materials

- "The Gingerbread Man," pages 60–69
- Sound/Spelling Card 41, Hoot owl
- Learning Framework Cards 2, 3, 4 , 8
- Reading/Writing Connection, pages 29–31
- Outlaw Word Flash Cards
- Activity Sheet 85
- Home/School Connection 16

Prepare Ahead

- Go Fish! Cards (see page 171)

GETTING STARTED

Choose one or both of the following activities to focus the children's attention and to review some of the concepts they have been learning.

Spelling Challenge Divide the group into several teams and give each team a sheet of paper. Write the word *train* on the board. Challenge the teams to form as many two-letter words as they can, using the letters in *train*. (Possibilities include *at, it, in,* and *an.*) Stop them after a few minutes, ask for volunteers to share their words, and write them on the board. Next, tell them to make three-letter words (*Art, ant, ran, rat, tin, tan,* and *tar* are possibilities) and follow the same procedure. Finally, challenge the groups to find the four-letter word inside *train (rain).*

Keep the Card Game In a paper bag, place Outlaw Word Flash Cards and/or index cards with words containing spellings you want to review. Divide the children into teams of five children each. Tell the children that they will be playing a new game called Keep the Card. Explain that a player on each team will draw a card out of the paper bag and look at it. (The player's team members will also see the card.) If the player says the word correctly, he or she may put the card on the table in front of his or her team. If the player misses, the card will go back in the bag. The teams take turns, and players on each team take turns. The team with the most cards at the end of 5 to 10 minutes wins the game.

1 READING

PHONICS

There are a number of new spellings for /o͞o/ introduced in this lesson. Some of your students may have trouble remembering all the spellings or using them in blending. This is normal. Do not worry about mastery in this lesson. Students will have many opportunities to practice using the sound and multiple spellings in reading and writing.

* **Introducing /o͞o/ Spelled *oo, ue, u, u_e, _ew*** Display Sound/Spelling Card 41, Hoot owl. Tell the children that all these spellings can stand for the /o͞o/ sound. Then read the Hoot owl story.

You can find the procedure for introducing a new sound/spelling on **Learning Framework Card 2.**

/o͞o/ /o͞o/ /o͞o/ /o͞o/ /o͞o/ /o͞o/!
What can be making that hooting sound?
Could it be a flute?
No, it's Scooter, the Hoot owl.
/o͞o/ /o͞o/ /o͞o/ /o͞o/ /o͞o/ /o͞o/!

When the sky is dark blue
And the new moon is bright,
Scooter the Hoot owl
Calls out through the night:
/o͞o/ /o͞o/ /o͞o/ /o͞o/ /o͞o/ /o͞o/!

He stoops in a yew tree
And sleeps there at noon,
But he swoops silently
By the light of the moon:
/o͞o/ /o͞o/ /o͞o/ /o͞o/ /o͞o/ /o͞o/!

Could Scooter the Hoot owl be calling to you?
If you think he is, then hoot to him too!
(Have the children say:) /o͞o/ /o͞o/ /o͞o/ /o͞o/ /o͞o/ /o͞o/!

Reread the story and invite the children to clap when they hear words with the sound /o͞o/. As you say the words *flute, yew,* and *blue* write them on the chalkboard and point to the different spellings used in the words. Ask the children to tell how this card will help them read words with the /o͞o/ sound.

* **Blending** Have the children blend the following words and sentences. For reference and additional suggestions for blending, see **Learning Framework Card 3.**

Line 1:	**food stool spoon gloomy**
Line 2:	**true glue blue cruel**
Line 3:	**truth tuna super rubies**
Line 4:	**rude flute rule include**
Line 5:	**blew grew stew crew**
Sentence:	**The little old woman lived in a little old house.**

Words These lines focus on the various spellings for /o͞o/. After blending the words in lines 2–5, point to Sound/Spelling Card 36, Long U, and have the children compare the spellings for /o͞o/ with those for long *u*. Once the children notice that the spellings are the same, explain that the sounds /o͞o/ and /ū/ are very similar.

Some children may be unfamiliar with words such as *rubies, include,* and *crew.* If so, children who know the words could use them in sentences. Have the children find the homophones *blue* and *blew* (line 2 and line 5). Explain that *blue* is the color while *blew* is the past tense of *blow.* Have children use each of these words in a sentence.

Review the words by having the children fill in the blank in sentences such as:

He sat on a ______ by the table.
It's ______ to talk with your mouth full.
The dark sky made it feel ______.
A ______ is a kind of fish.
The girl ______ out the candles on her cake.
The color of the sky is usually ______.

Sentences Introduce the outlaw word *woman* by writing the word on the chalkboard, touching the word, and telling the children that this is the word *woman*. Have several children use the word in sentences. Then write the sentence on the board and underline *woman*. Have several children read the sentence.

➤ Reading/Writing Connection, pages 29–30, provides practice with the /o͞o/ sound and spellings. Help the children complete the pages by copying the words and sentences and filling in the words to complete the sentences.

* READING THE STUDENT ANTHOLOGY

UNIT PREVIEW BY THE CHILDREN

Activating Prior Knowledge

Talk about folk stories that were read to you or that you read as a child, for example, "Little Red Riding Hood," or "The Three Little Pigs."

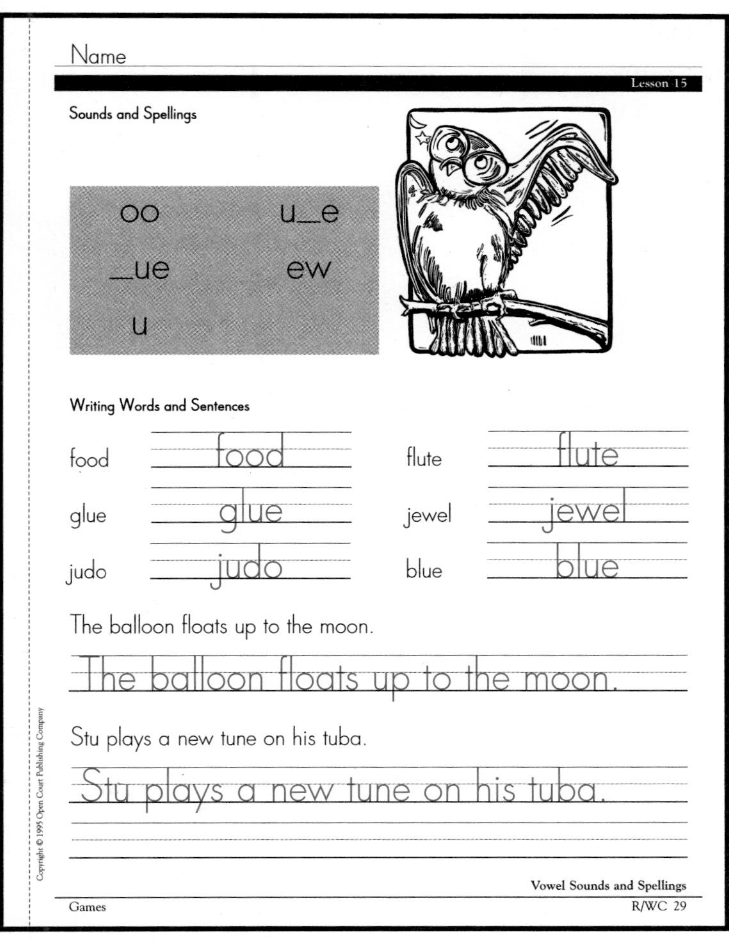
Name

Lesson 15

Sounds and Spellings

oo u_e
_ue ew
u

Writing Words and Sentences

food food
flute flute
glue glue
jewel jewel
judo judo
blue blue

The balloon floats up to the moon.

The balloon floats up to the moon.

Stu plays a new tune on his tuba.

Stu plays a new tune on his tuba.

Vowel Sounds and Spellings

Games R/WC 29

Reading/Writing Connection, page 29

Name

Lesson 15

Writing Words

1. He huffed and he puffed and he blew the house down. blew
2. The farmer's goose honked at me. goose
3. I saw a cocoon on a leaf. cocoon
4. She made a house for bluebirds. bluebirds
5. Do you know the rules of the game? rules

Dictation and Spelling

Vowel Sounds and Spellings

30 R/WC Folk Tales

Reading/Writing Connection, page 30

Ask the children to share folk tales that they are familiar with, either from their reading or from filmed versions of the tales. Encourage them to discuss what they know about folk tales, for example, that they may have talking animals in them or that they often begin "Once upon a time . . ." Children may not realize that they have been exposed to many such stories in their lives.

Setting Reading Goals and Expectations

Procedures for Browsing the Unit

- Turn to the unit opener on pages 58–59. Read the unit title and ask the children what it means and what kind of selections will be in the unit.
- Look at the illustration on the opener pages. Children may recognize some familiar characters from stories they know, Red Riding Hood, the Big Bad Wolf, Johnny Appleseed, and the Pied Piper. The unit opener also suggests that folk tales contain real characters and animals that have a fantastic quality about them. Tell the children that these characters and ideas are all found in stories we call folk tales. List the children's observations on the chalkboard and then decide which ones they want to put up on the Concept Board for this unit.
- Turn to the selections in the unit. Read the titles and quickly browse the selections, looking briefly at the illustrations and the print. Let

TEACHING TIP

Label your Concept Board *Folk Tales.* The children may want to decorate the board with pictures of their favorite folk tale characters.

the children report on and discuss things that they have noticed in their browsing and that they feel are important. Let them raise any questions. Help them post their pictures, questions, and ideas on the Concept Board.

For a review of the procedures for browsing a unit, see **Learning Framework Card 8, Reading the Student Anthologies.**

Explain to the children that throughout this unit they will be participating in activities that will extend their experiences and deepen their knowledge of folk tales. These activities may include writing, drama, art, and discussions.

➤ Have the children find page 31 in the Reading/Writing Connection. Tell them to use this page to draw or write about folk tales they may know. They might want to list favorite stories, favorite characteristics, or anything they wonder about.

"The Gingerbread Man"
pages 60–69

Note: Your class may require two days to read this selection. We recommend that on the first day the children read through page 63.

Reading/Writing Connection, page 31

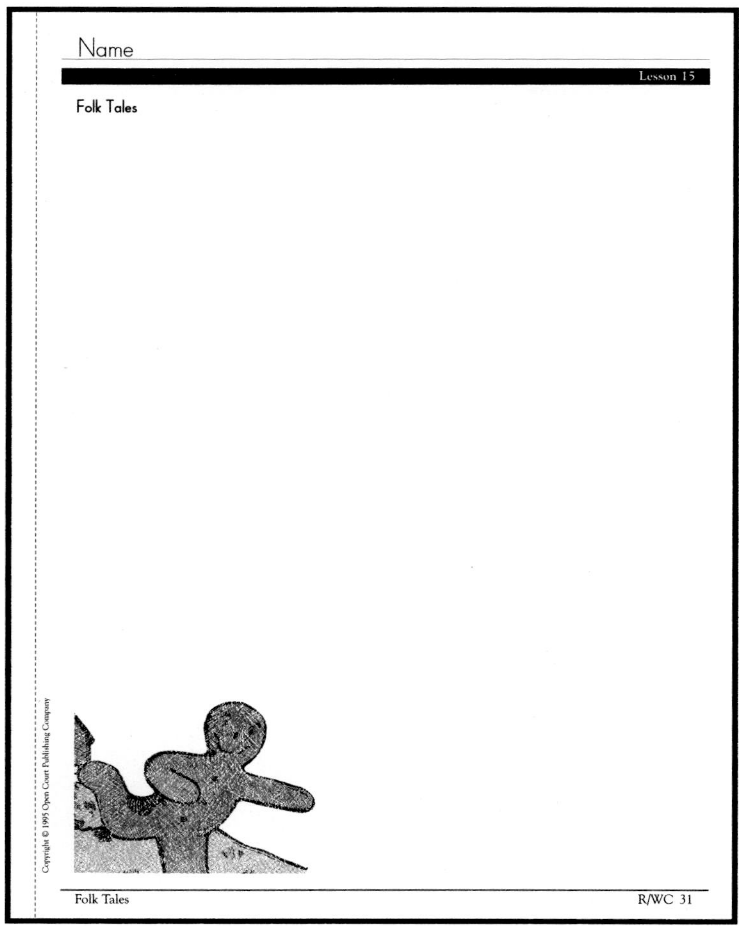

Name

Lesson 15

Folk Tales

Folk Tales R/WC 31

About the Selection

A clever gingerbread man comes to life and escapes the little old couple who baked him. Away he runs, so fast that no one in his village can catch him—until he meets up with a creature even craftier than himself. Young readers will particularly enjoy the humorous illustrations that accompany this version of the classic cumulative tale.

Link to the Unit Concept

This story, like the others in the unit, is a folk tale. It has been retold many times by many different storytellers.

Activating Prior Knowledge

Read the title of the story to the children. Ask them if anyone has ever seen a gingerbread man or a gingerbread house. Ask if anyone in the class has read or heard this story before. It is likely that some of the children have. Ask those children to think, as they read, about ways in which this version is similar to and different from other versions they have read. Tell them not to give away the ending to their classmates.

Setting Reading Goals and Expectations

- Have the children browse the first half of the story. Ask them to mention anything that they notice about it, particularly as concerns the print. For a review of the browsing procedure, see **Learning Framework Card 8, Reading the Student Anthologies.**

Recommendations for Reading

- Call on children to read the story aloud. Have each child read a sentence or two. Continue in this manner through the bottom of page 63. If children are having difficulty blending any of the words, remind them to check the Sound/Spelling Cards. If any words cannot be easily blended, pronounce the words for the children. You might have the whole class chime in on "Run, run, as fast as you can. . . ."
- You might have the children sum up the story at the bottom of page 63.

About the Reading Strategies

Invite the children to wonder about and remark on anything that interests them as they read. Encourage them to pause to clarify the meaning of words that puzzle them. Model surprise at some of the events in the story, as suggested in the page miniatures.

Think-Aloud Prompts for Use in Oral Reading Notice the think-aloud prompts with the page miniatures. These are merely suggestions. Continue to model using appropriate strategies while reading and to encourage children to use the strategies on their own. For a review of information about modeling and generating think-alouds, see **Learning Framework Card 8, Reading the Student Anthologies.**

TIP FOR ENGLISH LANGUAGE LEARNERS

To encourage English Language Learners to predict what might be coming next in the story, have them explain the sentence or the passage in the text to themselves before they predict from it. They can predict what's next after they discuss and understand how the vocabulary of a sentence or passage fits into the larger text.

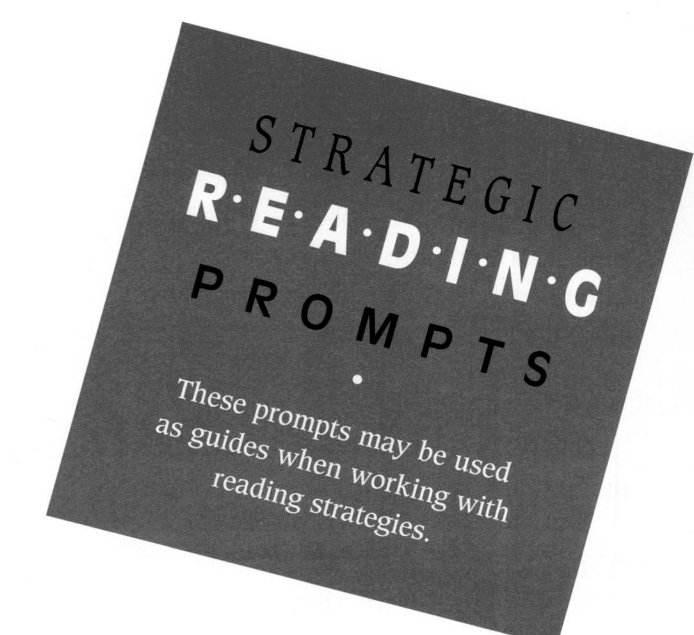
STRATEGIC
R·E·A·D·I·N·G
PROMPTS
These prompts may be used as guides when working with reading strategies.

1 Ask children if they know what the word *popped* means.

2 After the words *to bake,* ask children if they know other stories that begin with "Once upon a time . . ." and if so, how many?

3 Model wondering by saying, *I wonder why he is running away.*

4 You might ask the children to **predict** what will happen next.

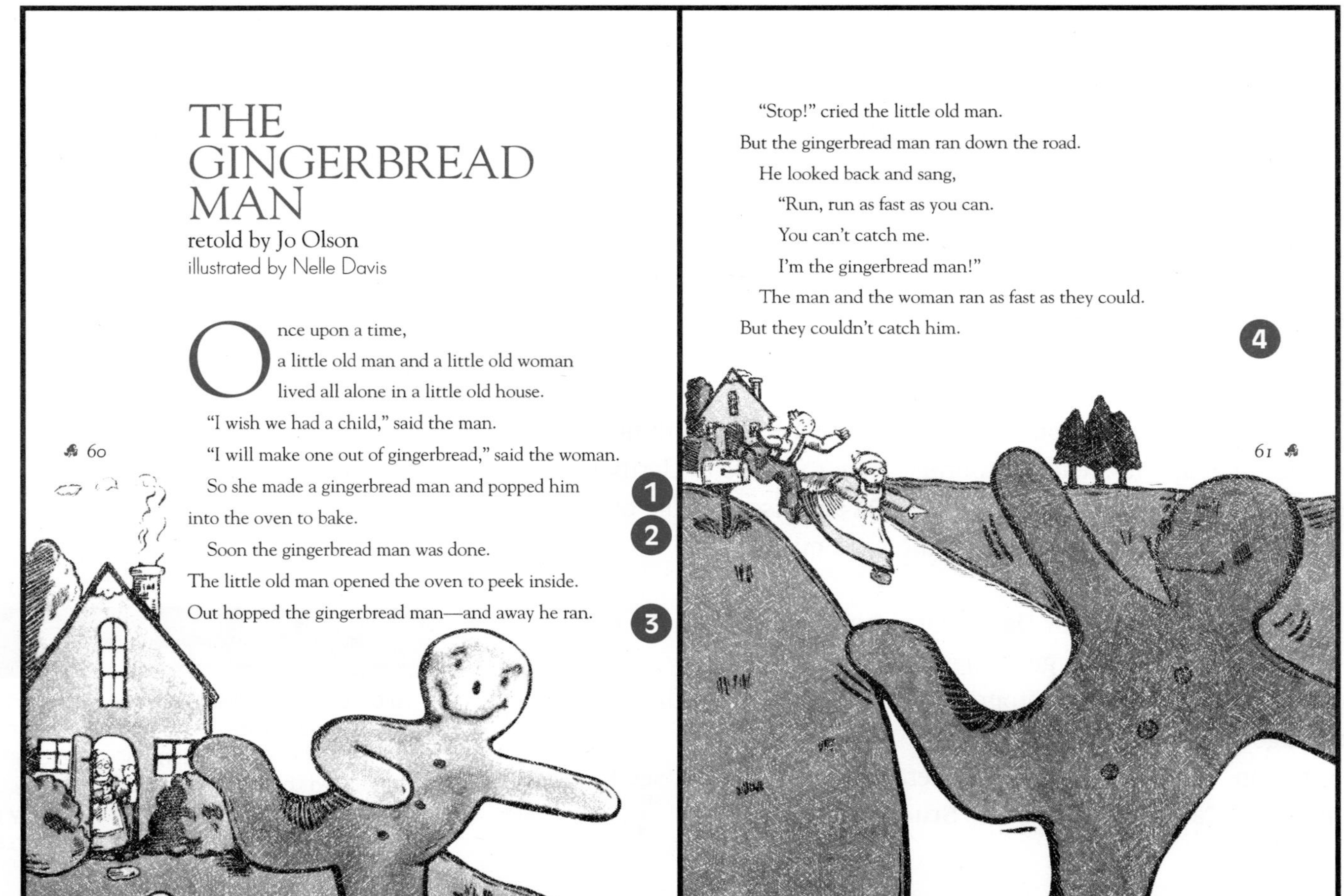

THE GINGERBREAD MAN

retold by Jo Olson
illustrated by Nelle Davis

Once upon a time,
a little old man and a little old woman
lived all alone in a little old house.

"I wish we had a child," said the man.

"I will make one out of gingerbread," said the woman.

So she made a gingerbread man and popped him into the oven to bake. 1 2

Soon the gingerbread man was done.
The little old man opened the oven to peek inside.
Out hopped the gingerbread man—and away he ran. 3

60

"Stop!" cried the little old man.
But the gingerbread man ran down the road.

He looked back and sang,

"Run, run as fast as you can.
You can't catch me.
I'm the gingerbread man!"

The man and the woman ran as fast as they could.
But they couldn't catch him. 4

61

Soon the gingerbread man saw a cow.
"Stop!" said the cow. "You look good to eat."
"No," said the gingerbread man.
"I have run away from a man and a woman.
I will run away from you, too."
The cow ran after the gingerbread man.
He sang,
"Run, run as fast as you can.
You can't catch me.
I'm the gingerbread man!"
And the cow couldn't catch him.

62

5

Soon the gingerbread man saw a horse.
"Stop!" said the horse. "You look good to eat."
"No," said the gingerbread man.
"I have run away from a man and a woman
and a cow. I will run away from you, too."
The horse ran after the gingerbread man.
He sang,
"Run, run as fast as you can.
You can't catch me.
I'm the gingerbread man!"
And the horse couldn't catch him.

63

5 Say, *What a surprise! I didn't know cows ate cookies.*

Responding

- Discuss briefly with the children the nature of folk tales. They are short, repetitive, and humorous. The animals talk and the stories are full of action. Make a list of these characteristics and add them to the Concept Board. Look back at the unit introduction for more information about the characteristics of folk tales.
- Invite the children to share their responses to the story so far. Ask them what they think of the gingerbread boy and how this version of the tale compares with others they may have heard.

TEACHING TIP

Have the children do some partner reading daily. Using previously read Phonics Minibooks and Step-by-Step Practice Stories for this purpose will help the children review and solidify their knowledge of the sounds and spellings they have learned. This is a good opportunity to read with the children individually and to record their progress.

* READING ALOUD

Children are already familiar with many folk tales, whether or not they are familiar with the term. "Cinderella," "Snow White," and "Beauty and the Beast" are all examples of such tales that children probably know. A cumulative folk tale such as "The House that Jack Built" provides a good comparison to "The Gingerbread Man." You might read one of these tales, or another one of which you are especially fond, to the children.

After reading, remember to ask the children questions concerning what they liked best and what they found most interesting. If any new ideas are discussed you may want to add these to the Concept Board.

2 WRITING

* DICTATION AND SPELLING

Have the children open their Reading/Writing Connection books to page 30. Dictate the following words and sentence, using the suggestions for dictation that appear on **Learning Framework Card 4.**

Line 1: law draw fawn

Line 2: sauce cause August

Sentence: The baby can crawl.

As the children proofread the words in line 2, remind them that *August* begins with a capital letter because it is the name of a month.

INDEPENDENT AND COLLABORATIVE WRITING

While not all children will want to publish the story or piece they have been working on, review proofreading—checking for spelling, capitals, and punctuation. Encourage children to work with a partner to proofread their work. You can proofread using either a piece of student writing or the class story. As with making revisions, use a colored pencil so changes can be easily seen. Encourage children to do the same.

Have children work in pairs to proofread.

If children do not have time to complete the proofreading, encourage them to continue working on their writing during Workshop. This is also an ideal time to recopy their revised and proofread stories if they are going to publish them. If you are working on a class book, then have pairs of children take responsibility for recopying and illustrating different pages from this story and for making a cover. Take a few minutes at the end to put the pages together to make a book.

Those children who wish to share their stories should be encouraged to do so.

ASSESSMENT Collect student stories and use the Writing Rubric for "The Gingerbread Man" to judge the students' writing.

3 GUIDED AND INDEPENDENT EXPLORATION

WORKSHOP

Remind the children that they may use this time to work on projects on their own or in small groups. Be sure that each child knows what projects he or she may choose and how to complete any independent work. Suggestion for teacher-guided, collaborative, and independent activities follow.

Learning Framework Card 11, Workshop, contains a complete discussion of establishing and conducting Workshop and suggestions for helping English Language Learners during Workshop.

Work with the Teacher

- The /o͞o/ sound has several spellings. Review them with children. Use the /o͞o/ words from the Hoot owl story.
- Review the /o͞o/ words from Blending. Have children read the words, use them in sentences, and then extend the sentences.
- Work on breaking long words into parts with children who could use some extra practice. Reread with them the first part of "The Gingerbread Man," pages 60–69 in the student anthology. Stop reading at the bottom of page 63, or wherever the class stopped during today's lesson.

Collaborative/Independent Activities

- Small groups can play Go Fish! or a memory game like Concentration, using the decks of rhyming-word game cards. You may want to add /aw/ cards to the decks before Workshop begins. Check recent blending lessons and anthology selections for word ideas.
- Before Workshop starts, write the following verse on the chalkboard:

  ______, ______ as fast as you can.
  You can't catch me.
  I'm the gingerbread man!

  Have children copy the verse and fill in the blanks with the action words of their choice. They may then illustrate their versions of the verse. Have them share their verses and pictures with the class.
- Activity Sheet 85 focuses on the /o͞o/ sound and spellings. Tell the children to circle the one word in each sentence that has the /o͞o/ sound. They should then draw a picture of each word they circled in the corresponding boxes at the bottom of the page.

Home/School Connection

Home/School Connection 16 introduces the Folk Tales unit and includes a list of library books parents might like to share with their children.

Name

Lesson 15

1. Dad cleaned the kitchen with a broom.
2. The old cat ate a can of tuna.
3. Robin found a jewel in the river.
4. The balloon floated up to the sky.
5. Bud dropped his spoon.
6. I need glue for my class project.

(Student art as indicated)

broom	tuna	jewel
1.	2.	3.
balloon	spoon	glue
4.	5.	6.

Activity Sheet 85

LESSON 16

Lesson Overview

New Learning

- /oo/ spelled *oo*

Materials

- "The Gingerbread Man," pages 64–69
- Sound/Spelling Card 42, Brook
- Learning Framework Cards 2, 3, 5, 8
- Reading/Writing Connection, pages 32–33
- Activity Sheet 86

Prepare Ahead

- Long and short *oo* Flash Cards (see page 183)

GETTING STARTED

Choose one or more of the following activities to focus the children's attention and to review some of the concepts they have been learning.

Review /o͞o/ Spelled *oo* To review the sound /o͞o/ spelled *oo,* which the children learned yesterday, reread the Hoot owl story and have the class chime in on each chorus of /o͞o/'s. After the first reading, divide the class in half according to seating arrangement and read the Hoot owl story again. Each time you come to the /o͞o/ chorus, point to the half that you want to have join in. Finally, read the story a third time and have the children chime in each time you come to an /o͞o/ word. An example follows:

Teacher: What could be making that curious sound? Could it be a . . .
Children: Flute

Fill in the Blank Print the spellings *aw*, *au*, *ow*, and *ou* on the chalkboard. Point to the spellings one at a time and have the children identify what sound each one makes. Then tell the children that you are going to print some words on the chalkboard with some of the spellings missing.

The children have to decide which spelling belongs in the blanks: *aw*, *au*, *ow*, or *ou*. Have the children write down the answer as you point to each word. Ask for volunteers to share their answers and fill in the blanks on the board as they respond.

1. dr__ (*draw*)
2. ab__t (*about*)
3. c__se (*cause*)
4. t__er (*tower*)
5. th__ (*thaw*)
6. cr__n (*crown*)
7. p__se (*pause*)
8. cl__d (*cloud*)
9. s__nd (*sound*)
10. __ful (*awful*)

1 READING

PHONICS

* **Introduce /oo/ Spelled *oo*** Turn Sound/Spelling Card 42, Brook. You can find the procedure for introducing a new sound/spelling on **Learning Framework Card 2.**

Once I took my coat and hood
And went out walking in the wood.
And there I came upon a brook
That made this sound: /oo/ /oo/ /oo/ /oo/.

I tied a string onto a hook
And threw the hook into the brook.
The good, cold, babbling, bubbling brook
Said: /oo/ /oo/ /oo/ /oo/ /oo/ /oo/ /oo/.

A minute, then, was all it took.
A lovely fish was on my hook!
I pulled the fish out of the brook.
/oo/ /oo/ /oo/ /oo/ /oo/ /oo/ /oo/.

That fine fish wiggled, looked, and shook.
I couldn't take it home to cook!
I threw it back into the brook.

What did the good brook say?
(Have the children answer:) /oo/ /oo/ /oo/ /oo/ /oo/ /oo/ /oo/.

Ask the children what words they recall in the story with the sound /oo/. Then write *oo* on the chalkboard. Ask a child to use these letters to make the word *hood.* Proofread the word with the child. Then repeat with other words from the story. Vary the activity by writing *oo* and inviting the children to choose an /oo/ word they would like to make.

* **Blending** Have the children blend the following words and sentences. For reference and additional suggestions for blending, see **Learning Framework Card 3.**

Line 1:	**look took cookie crooked**
Line 2:	**good wood hood stood**
Line 3:	**cool moonlight bedroom foolish**
Line 4:	**stung study student ruler**
Line 5:	**few pure flew clue**

As the children sound and blend the words in lines 1–3, let them talk about the patterns in each line. Have them circle the *oo* spelling in each word and tell what sound this spelling makes. The children will notice that *oo* makes two sounds: long *oo* and short *oo.*

- Ask the children to tell the compound words they see in line 3. The children could suggest other compound words with *moon, light, bed,* or *room;* for example, *moonbeam, lighthouse, bedbug,* or *bathroom.*
- Line 4 reviews words with *u* pronounced /u/ and /o͞o/. If the children are unsure of which pronunciation to choose, encourage them to try both sounds to see which is correct.
- Line 5 focuses on words with the /ū/ and /o͞o/ sounds. Have the children print other words they know with these sounds on the chalkboard, using the Sound/Spelling Cards as a guide.
- To review the words, ask the children to give each other clues. Each child who thinks of the correct word to "answer" a clue should go to the chalkboard, locate the word, and erase it. Continue the game until several or all of the words have been erased.

➤ Reading/Writing Connection, page 32, practices reading and writing words with the /oo/ sound. Help the children complete the page.

* READING THE STUDENT ANTHOLOGY

"The Gingerbread Man"
pages 64–69

Activating Prior Knowledge

Review the first half of the story with the children. Ask volunteers to sum up the story so far. Encourage other children to help them by adding any important details they remember.

Recommendations for Reading

- Have the children browse the second half of the story. Encourage them to comment on anything they notice; for example, that the same lines are repeated in this part of the story.
- Have the children read the story aloud.
- When they have finished reading the second half of the story, have the children sum up the entire story. Remind them to use their own words and to focus on the most important parts of the story.

Name

Lesson 16

Sounds and Spellings

oo

Writing Words and Sentences

brook brook hood hood

cook cook wool wool

The woodpecker shook his foot.

The woodpecker shook his foot.

She took a look at the book.

She took a look at the book.

Vowel Sounds and Spellings

32 R/WC "The Gingerbread Man"

Reading/Writing Connection, page 32

About the Reading Strategies

As with the first half of the selection, encourage the children to wonder about and comment on anything that interests them during the reading. Invite them, also, to remark on anything in the story that surprises them and, again, model these responses. Remind the children to ask for help in clarifying words that puzzle them and to use their decoding strategy.

Think-Aloud Prompts for Use in Oral Reading Notice the think-aloud prompts with the page miniatures. These are merely suggestions. Continue to model using appropriate strategies while reading and to encourage children to use the strategies on their own. For a review of information about modeling and generating think-alouds, see **Learning Framework Card 8, Reading the Student Anthologies.**

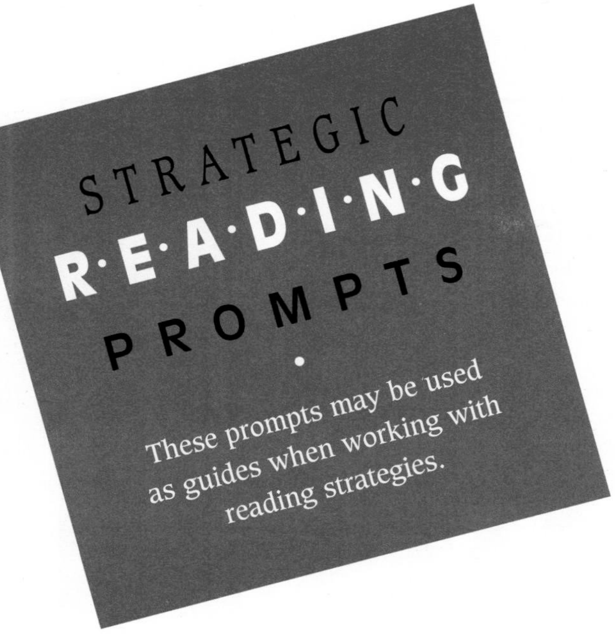
STRATEGIC
R·E·A·D·I·N·G
PROMPTS
These prompts may be used as guides when working with reading strategies.

Soon the gingerbread man saw
some workers raking hay.
"Stop!" said the workers.
"You look good to eat."
"No," said the gingerbread man.
"I have run away from a man and
a woman and a cow and a horse.
I will run away from you, too."
64
The workers ran after the gingerbread man.
He sang,
"Run, run as fast as you can.
You can't catch me.
I'm the gingerbread man!"
And the workers couldn't catch him.
65

66

Soon the gingerbread man saw a fox sitting by the edge of the river.

"I'm not afraid of you," the gingerbread man said to the fox. "I have run away from a man and a woman and a cow and a horse and some workers. I can run away from you, too." ❶

"I don't want to catch you," said the fox. "I will help you run away. Jump on my back. I will take you across the river." ❷

❶ Say, *I wonder if the gingerbread man is as fast as this fox?*

❷ *This is a surprise. I didn't expect the fox to be so helpful. I wonder what will happen?*

68
So the gingerbread man hopped up
on the fox's back. The fox began to swim.
"It's too wet on my back," said the fox.
"Jump on my nose. I will hold you
out of the water."
3
The gingerbread man jumped
on the fox's nose. The fox opened his mouth.
Snip, snap, gulp!
That was the end of the gingerbread man.
69

3 *I wonder if the fox really cares if the gingerbread man gets wet?*

Responding

- Allow the children to discuss anything that interests them about the selection. Ask them to share their opinions about the gingerbread man and about the other characters in the story.
- Ask the children whether they have read or heard "The Gingerbread Man" before. Was it the same as or different from this story?
- Connect the story to the unit concept by discussing how children can tell this is a folk tale—animals and things talk and act like people, an action or dialogue is repeated three or more times.
- Add any new ideas about folk tales to the Concept Board.
- If time permits, the children may enjoy acting out the story in a Reader's Theater format. They may want to do this outdoors if the weather allows.

Vocabulary Remember to have the children point out interesting or unusual words from the selection. Have them use these words in oral sentences; then add the words to the Vocabulary Chart.

Possible words and phrases include the following:
catch; peek; run, run as fast as you can

➤ Reading/Writing Connection, page 33, reviews "The Gingerbread Man." Help the children read the page and fill in the blanks.

Reading/Writing Connection, page 33

Name

Lesson 16

Paraphrasing

An old woman wanted a child so she made one out of gingerbread.

✓ An old woman wanted a son so she baked one.

___ An old woman wanted to make gingerbread cookies.

The gingerbread man hopped up and ran away.

___ The gingerbread man hoped to fly away.

✓ The gingerbread man jumped up and ran.

Everyone chased the gingerbread man.

✓ They all ran after the gingerbread man.

___ Everyone liked the gingerbread man.

The fox tricked the gingerbread man.

___ The fox tried to find the gingerbread man.

✓ The fox fooled the gingerbread man.

What happened to the gingerbread man?

(Student answers will vary.)

Reading the Selection

"The Gingerbread Man" R/WC 33

TEACHING TIP

Have the children do some partner reading daily. Using previously read Phonics Minibooks and Step-by-Step Practice Stories for this purpose will help the children review and solidify their knowledge of the sounds and spellings they have learned. This is a good opportunity to read with children individually and to record their progress.

* READING ALOUD

Be sure to set aside time in the day for reading aloud. You may want to share other folk tales with the children. *The Adventures of Pinocchio* has some features in common with "The Gingerbread Man." Both Pinocchio and the Gingerbread Man were created by an adult character who wanted a child, and both came to life.

After reading, find out what the children like best or find most interesting about the selection. If you chose to read a folk tale, ask the children if they could tell it was a folk tale, and if so, how. For additional suggestions, see **Learning Framework Card 5, Reading Aloud.**

2 WRITING

* DICTATION AND SPELLING

Have the children use their own paper and pencils for today's Word-Building game. Use the following words:

book
took
cook
hook
hood
good
wood
wool

Follow the established procedure for the game. Have the children write the words in a list, one under the other. The children should isolate the sounds in succession and check the Sound/Spelling Cards for spellings. Write along with the children to provide a model.

EXPLORING THE WRITER'S CRAFT

Stories like "The Gingerbread Man" have the repetitive characteristics found in so many folk tales. This is a good time to revisit "The House That Jack Built" in the Big Book *Look Who's Reading!* When this was first read at the beginning of the year, you read it to the children. Now have the children read it along with you in the Big Book or in the smaller student versions. Talk about what was repeated in this story as compared to what was repeated in "The Gingerbread Man." This cumulative characteristic has been used by contemporary writers in such stories as

Jump, Frog, Jump! by Robert Kalan
The Rose in My Garden by Arnold Lobel
At Mary Bloom's by Aliki

You may want to share some of these with the children as well. This can be done in a Seminar situation in which you read the story and the children comment on and discuss special aspects of the story, what they liked about it, and how they might use it in their own writing.

Children not only love the predictability and repetition in reading cumulative stories but also enjoy using this in their own writing. While folk tales may be hard for children of this age to write, the cumulative story is something children can explore in their own writing. A cumulative story is ideal for a shared group story. All children can participate and have some fun.

To help the children understand this cumulative quality, start with something obvious. Write on the board, chart paper, or a transparency, "My grandmother had a very old trunk, and in it was a ______." You can fill in the first noun, *an old brown book,* for example, and read the whole sentence aloud. Now ask a child to tell you something else that might be in the trunk. Write the next sentence, "My grandmother had a very old trunk, and in it was an old brown book and ______" (whatever the child suggests). Now have the whole class read the first and second sentence. You may want to have all the children contribute to this or, after several other examples, have children write down what they found in the trunk. Then build the story from their written suggestions. If children write or draw their suggestions, they can stand up in front of the class after their idea has been given in the order in which the cumulative story should be retold.

As a writing option children may want to write a retelling of one of their favorite folk tales.

TEACHING TIP

If children have books at home that have a cumulative quality to them, have them bring them in and share them during Seminar. Or you may want to hold a special Seminar during which the librarian shares cumulative stories.

TEACHING TIP

Remind the children to use the words from the Vocabulary Chart in their writing.

3 GUIDED AND INDEPENDENT EXPLORATION

WORKSHOP

Remind the children that they may use this time to work on projects on their own or in small groups. Be sure that each child knows what projects he or she may choose and how to complete any independent work. Suggestions for teacher-guided, collaborative, and independent activities follow.

Work with the Teacher

- Print a variety of long and short *oo* words on flash cards. Use the cards to have children practice reading words with various long and short *oo* spellings. For word ideas, return to today's and yesterday's Blending lessons.
- Reread the second half of "The Gingerbread Man," pages 64–69 in the student anthology, with children who could use extra help. Use the rereading session to assess the children's progress.
- Some of the children might be interested in working with you to write their own version of a favorite folk tale or to write an original story into which they will incorporate some of the elements of a folk tale. Remind them that during the introduction to the Folk Tales unit they learned about some of the common characteristics of a folk tale. Have them tell everything that they can remember about the genre. Begin an information web on the chalkboard. Write *folk tales* in the center of the web and, around it, list those things that the children know about folk tales. Save the web for use during tomorrow's Workshop.

Collaborative/Independent Activities

- A small group of children might enjoy acting out "The Gingerbread Man" for the rest of the class. They will probably need several Workshop periods to prepare for their performance. Today the children should reread the story. As they read, one child can make a list of all the characters in the story. After reading, they should decide who will play each part and who will be the narrator. If there are more children than parts, some children can work on scenery and props. If there are too few children, some of them can play more than one part.
- Pairs or small groups of children can make *oo* posters. Have the children outline the letters *oo* on a large sheet of poster board. Tell them to fill in the first *o* with pictures of words that contain the long *oo* sound and the second *o* with pictures of words that contain the short *oo* sound. As usual, they may draw the pictures themselves or cut pictures out of magazines. Beneath each *o*, they should print the name of as many of the long and short *oo* pictures as they can.
- Distribute Activity Sheet 86 and tell the children to follow the directions at the bottom to color the shapes.

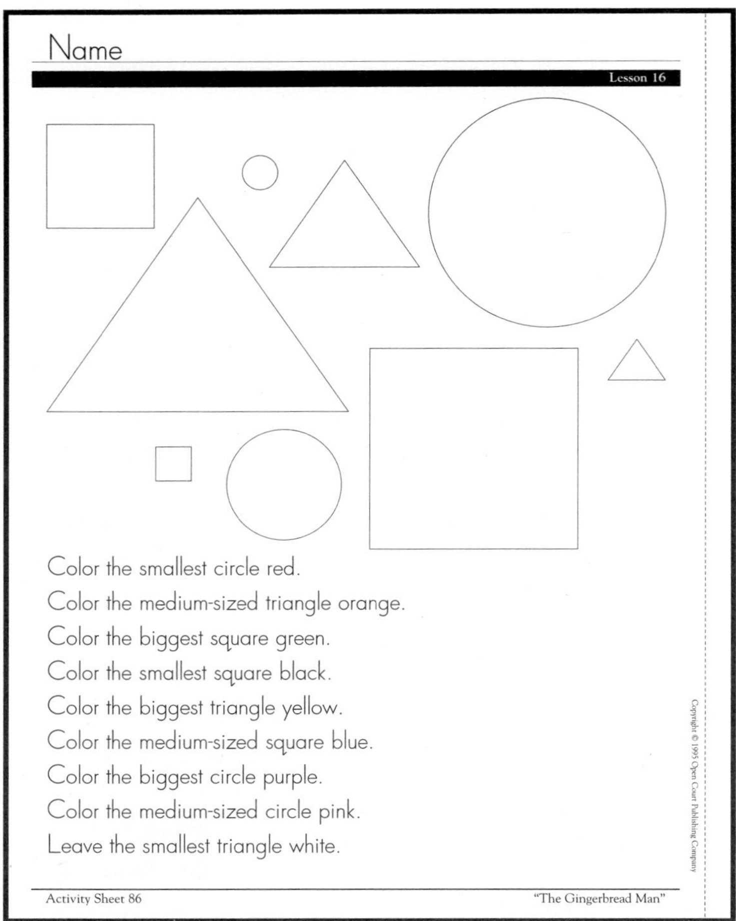

Name

Lesson 16

Color the smallest circle red.
Color the medium-sized triangle orange.
Color the biggest square green.
Color the smallest square black.
Color the biggest triangle yellow.
Color the medium-sized square blue.
Color the biggest circle purple.
Color the medium-sized circle pink.
Leave the smallest triangle white.

Activity Sheet 86 "The Gingerbread Man"

Activity Sheet 86

LESSON 17

Lesson Overview

New Learning

- /n/ spelled *kn*

Materials

- ***Anansi and the Talking Melon***, pages 70–87
- Phonics Minibook 16, ***Mr. Lee***
- Sound/Spelling Card 14, Nose
- Learning Framework Cards 4, 8, 10
- Reading/Writing Connection, pages 34–35
- Letter Cards
- Activity Sheet 87

GETTING STARTED

Choose one or more of the following activities to focus the children's attention and to review some of the concepts they have been learning.

Long Sound/Short Sound Spellings Write one word on the chalkboard at a time. Have the children read the word quietly to themselves. Tell them that if the word contains the /o͞o/ sound, they should hold their arms out from their sides. If the word contains the /oo/ sound, they should hold their hands close together in front of them. After the children have done this, ask them to read the word aloud together. You might want to use the following words:

true	tube	zoo
crook	look	book
broom	new	
glue	hook	

TEACHING TIP

Remember to use wait time so all children have time to read the word before responding.

Before and After Have the children sit in a circle. Give each child a Letter Card for one of the alphabet letters from *b* to *y*. Walk around the outside of the circle and tap a child on the shoulder. Ask, "What letter do you have? What letter comes after yours in the alphabet?" After the child answers, he or she can walk around the circle, tap someone else, and repeat the game. The child takes the new traveler's place in the circle. Vary the game by having the children name the letter that comes *before* their letter or name the letter that comes both before *and* after.

1 READING

PHONICS

Review /o͞o/ Words On the chalkboard, draw a picture of a train with four or five cars and a caboose. In each car, write several words with the sound /o͞o/. Some words are: *cartoon, ruby, balloon, clue, flute, zoo, tooth, judo, truth, crew, moon, chew, noodle, glue, prune.* In the caboose, print the word *kangaroo* or *poodle.* Cover the animal name with a card.

Tell the children that there's an animal loose in the caboose. To find out what it is, they read the words on the cars of the train. When the children come to the caboose, ask if they can think of an animal whose name has the /o͞o/ sound. Remove the card and read the word together.

Read the words on the cars again and ask the children what similarity in sound they notice among the words. Invite them to circle the spellings that make the /o͞o/ sound. They can use Sound/Spelling Card 41, Hoot owl, as a guide.

/n/ spelled *kn* Review the sound /n/ by pointing to Sound/Spelling Card 14, Nose, and ask the children to tell what sound the picture stands for. Tell the children that today they will learn the other spelling for /n/ and indicate the *kn* spelling on the card. Tell the children that when *k* comes before letter *n,* the *k* is silent.

* **Blending** Have the children blend the following words and sentences. For reference and additional suggestions for blending, see **Learning Framework Card 4.**

Line 1:	knock knee kneel knit knuckle
Line 2:	no know new knew
Line 3:	night knight not knot
Line 4:	hungry command hundred excitement
Line 5:	bounced louder replied exclaimed

Point to the word *kneel* in line 1 and ask the children what smaller word they see in the bigger one. What connection do they notice between the meaning of *knee* and *kneel?*

In line 2, point out the homophones *no* and *know.* Ask the children which spelling means the opposite of *yes,* and which means to be sure of something. Invite the children to use each word in a sentence. Repeat with the other homophones in lines 2 and 3. You might also ask the children what they notice about the words *know* and *knew.* Elicit that *knew* is the past tense of *know.* Lines 4 and 5 review vocabulary from *Anansi and the Talking Melon.*

Review the words by asking the children to find and erase:

- another word for *answered*
- something you do with yarn
- two body parts
- a number
- the opposite of *day*

➤ Reading/Writing Connection, page 34, provides additional practice with the *kn* spelling. Have the children read and copy the words and the sentence.

Reading/Writing Connection, page 34

Name

Lesson 17

Sounds and Spellings

n

kn__

Writing Words and Sentences

knit knit knot knot

The knight knocked on the door.

The knight knocked on the door.

Dictation and Spelling

Consonant Sounds and Spellings

34 R/WC *Anansi and the Talking Melon*

Anansi and the Talking Melon
pages 70–87

About the Selection

Tell the children that Anansi the Spider is the hero of many African folk tales. The little spider Anansi is well known for getting into trouble, and for being a trickster.

Link to the Unit Concepts

Folk tales in many cultures include tricksters such as trolls, brownies, leprechauns, and coyotes. These characters are always tricking other characters either for fun or to get out of tough situations.

Activating Prior Knowledge

Ask the children if they have read or heard any stories in which a character tricks other characters, or any stories in which the main characters are animals. Talk about "The Gingerbread Man" and who did the tricking.

Setting Reading Goals and Expectations

- Browse the story before beginning to read, encouraging the children to comment freely.

Recommendations for Reading

- Read the story to the children as they follow along in their books.
- Invite the children to tell what they think about the story as it is being read and to ask questions about story words and ideas.

About the Reading Strategies

In reading this selection, children can use the strategies of wondering, word clarification, and predicting. Explain that you will use these strategies as you read the selection.

Think-aloud Prompts for Use in Oral Reading Notice the think-aloud prompts with the page miniatures. These are merely suggestions. Continue to model using appropriate strategies while reading and to encourage children to use the strategies on their own. For a review of information about modeling and generating think-alouds, see **Learning Framework Card 8, Reading the Student Anthologies.**

STRATEGIC
R·E·A·D·I·N·G
PROMPTS

These prompts may be used as guides when working with reading strategies.

1 You might comment, *I never heard of a thorn tree before. It must be the one in the picture. I can see how it got its name—look at all those thorns.*

ANANSI AND
THE TALKING
MELON
A Shared Reading Story
retold by Eric A. Kimmel
illustrated by Janet Stevens
One fine morning Anansi the Spider
sat high up in a thorn tree
looking down into Elephant's garden.
Elephant was hoeing his melon patch.
The ripe melons seemed to call out to Anansi,
"Look how juicy and sweet we are!
Come eat us!"
1
70
71

Anansi loved to eat melons,
but he was much too lazy to grow them himself.
So he sat up in the thorn tree, watching and waiting,
while the sun rose high in the sky and the day grew warm.
By the time noon came, it was too hot to work.
Elephant put down his hoe
and went inside his house to take a nap.
Here was the moment Anansi had been waiting for.
He broke off a thorn and dropped down into the melon patch.
He used the thorn to bore a hole
2 in the biggest, ripest melon.

Anansi squeezed inside
and started eating. He ate and ate
until he was as round as a berry.
"I'm full," Anansi said at last.
"Elephant will be coming back soon.
It is time to go."

But when he tried
to squeeze through the hole,
Anansi had a surprise.
He didn't fit!
The hole was big enough
for a thin spider,
but much too small
for a fat one.

"I'm stuck!" Anansi cried. "I can't get out.
I will have to wait until I am thin again."
Anansi sat down on a pile of melon seeds
and waited to get thin.
Time passed slowly.
"I'm bored," Anansi said.
3 "I wish I had something to do."

73

2 *I wonder what* bore *means? How can you tell?* Explain how the sentence and picture help to show the meaning of the word, if necessary. Also, at end of page, *This is a good spot to predict. What do you think might happen next? What else?* Later, confirm the children's ideas if the story turns out as they predicted.

3 Ask what the children think might happen next. Later, confirm children's ideas if their predictions are correct.

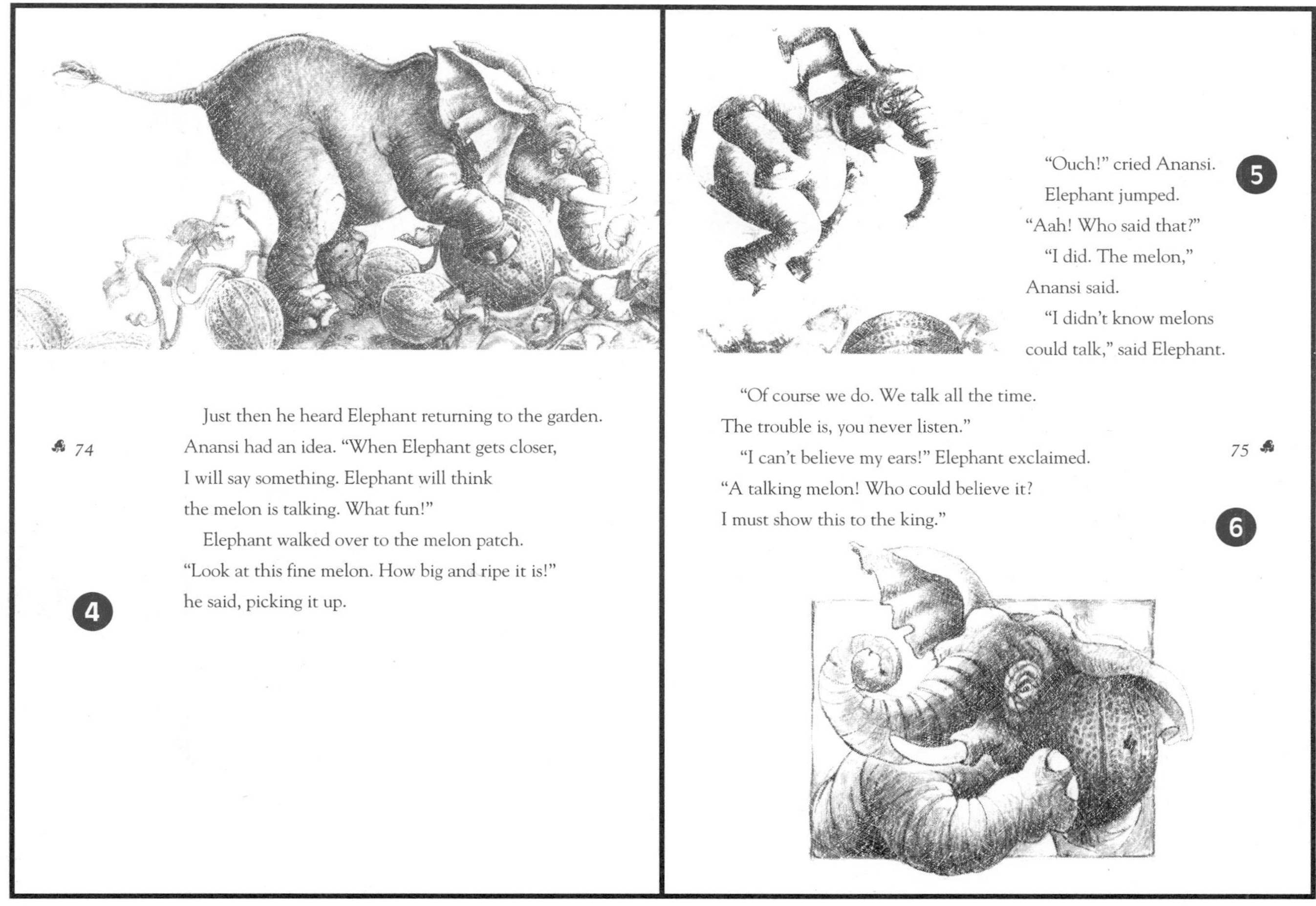

74

Just then he heard Elephant returning to the garden. Anansi had an idea. "When Elephant gets closer, I will say something. Elephant will think the melon is talking. What fun!"

Elephant walked over to the melon patch. "Look at this fine melon. How big and ripe it is!" he said, picking it up. **4**

"Ouch!" cried Anansi. **5**

Elephant jumped. "Aah! Who said that?"

"I did. The melon," Anansi said.

"I didn't know melons could talk," said Elephant.

"Of course we do. We talk all the time. The trouble is, you never listen."

"I can't believe my ears!" Elephant exclaimed. "A talking melon! Who could believe it? I must show this to the king." **6**

75

4 *Do you think Elephant will find him? Why?*

5 *I wonder why he says 'Ouch!'?*

6 Ask what the children think of Anansi so far, and what they think of Elephant.

Elephant ran down the road,
carrying the melon with Anansi inside.
Along the way, he ran into Hippo.

"Where are you going with that melon?" Hippo asked.

"I'm taking it to the king," Elephant told him.

"What for? The king has hundreds of melons."

"He doesn't have one like this," Elephant said. "This is a talking melon."

Hippo didn't believe Elephant. "A talking melon? What an idea! That's as ridiculous as . . ."

". . . a skinny hippo," the melon said.

Hippo got so angry his face turned red.

"Who said that? Did you say that, Elephant?"

"It wasn't me. It was the melon," Elephant said. "I told you it talks. Do you believe me now?"

"I do!" Hippo exclaimed. "I want to go with you.
I want to hear what the king says
when you show him this talking melon."

"Come along, then," said Elephant.

So Elephant and Hippo went down the road together, carrying the melon.

78

7

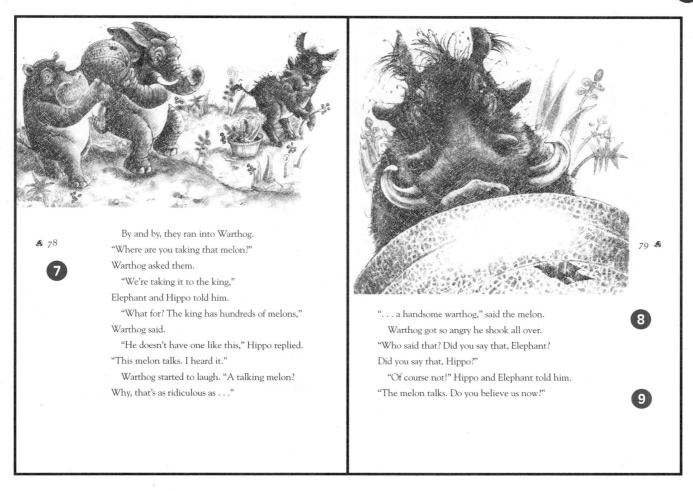

By and by, they ran into Warthog.
"Where are you taking that melon?"
Warthog asked them.
"We're taking it to the king,"
Elephant and Hippo told him.
"What for? The king has hundreds of melons,"
Warthog said.
"He doesn't have one like this," Hippo replied.
"This melon talks. I heard it."
Warthog started to laugh. "A talking melon?
Why, that's as ridiculous as . . ."

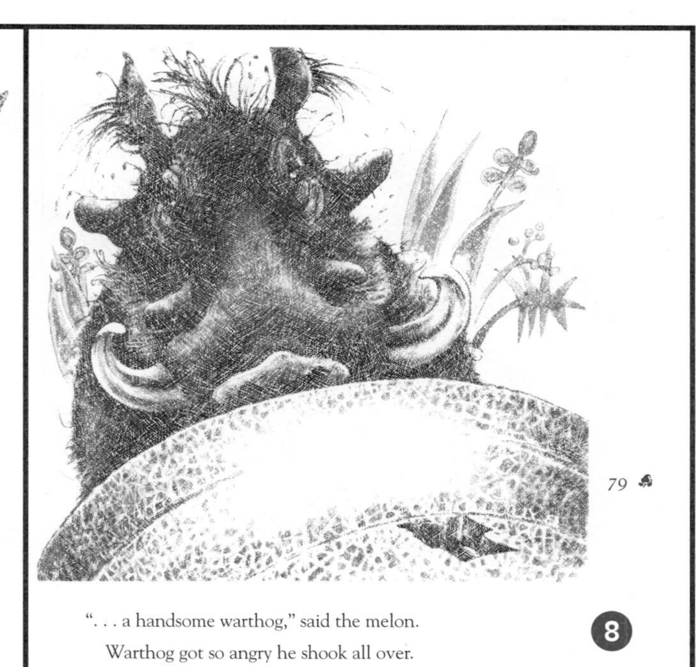

79

". . . a handsome warthog," said the melon. 8
Warthog got so angry he shook all over.
"Who said that? Did you say that, Elephant?
Did you say that, Hippo?"
"Of course not!" Hippo and Elephant told him.
"The melon talks. Do you believe us now?" 9

7 *Do you know what a warthog is? How do you know?* If students do not recall the warthog from *Jafta*, remind them. In addition, they should be able to describe the animal from the picture.

8 *That's funny. There's nothing handsome about a warthog.*

9 This is a good spot to predict. Ask what the children think will happen next. Be sure to confirm the children's ideas later if the story turns out as they predicted.

"I do!" cried Warthog. "Let me go with you.
I want to see what the king does
when you show him this talking melon."

So Warthog, Elephant, and Hippo went
down the road together, carrying the melon.

Along the way, they met Ostrich, Rhino, and Turtle.

They didn't believe the melon could talk either
until they heard it for themselves.
Then they wanted to come along too.

The animals came before the king.
Elephant bowed low as he placed the melon at the king's feet.
The king looked down.
"Why did you bring me a melon?" he asked Elephant.
"I have hundreds of melons growing in my garden."
"You don't have one like this," Elephant said.
"This melon talks."

"A talking melon? I don't believe it. Say something, Melon."
The king prodded the melon with his foot. 10
The melon said nothing.
"Melon," the king said in a slightly louder voice,
"there is no reason to be shy. Say whatever you like.
I only want to hear you talk."

83

10 Prodded . . . *how can we tell what that means?* Students should be able to tell from the picture, although the sentence also helps. If necessary, explain how you would figure out the word.

The melon still said nothing. The king grew impatient. "Melon, if you can talk, I want you to say something. I command you to speak."

The melon did not make a sound.

11 The king gave up. "Oh, this is a stupid melon!" he said.

84

Just then the melon spoke. "Stupid, am I? Why do you say that? I'm not the one who talks to melons!"

The animals had never seen the king so angry. "How dare this melon insult me!" he shouted. The king picked up the melon and hurled it as far as he could.

85

11 *I wonder if the king really believes melons can talk? What do you think? Why do you think so?*

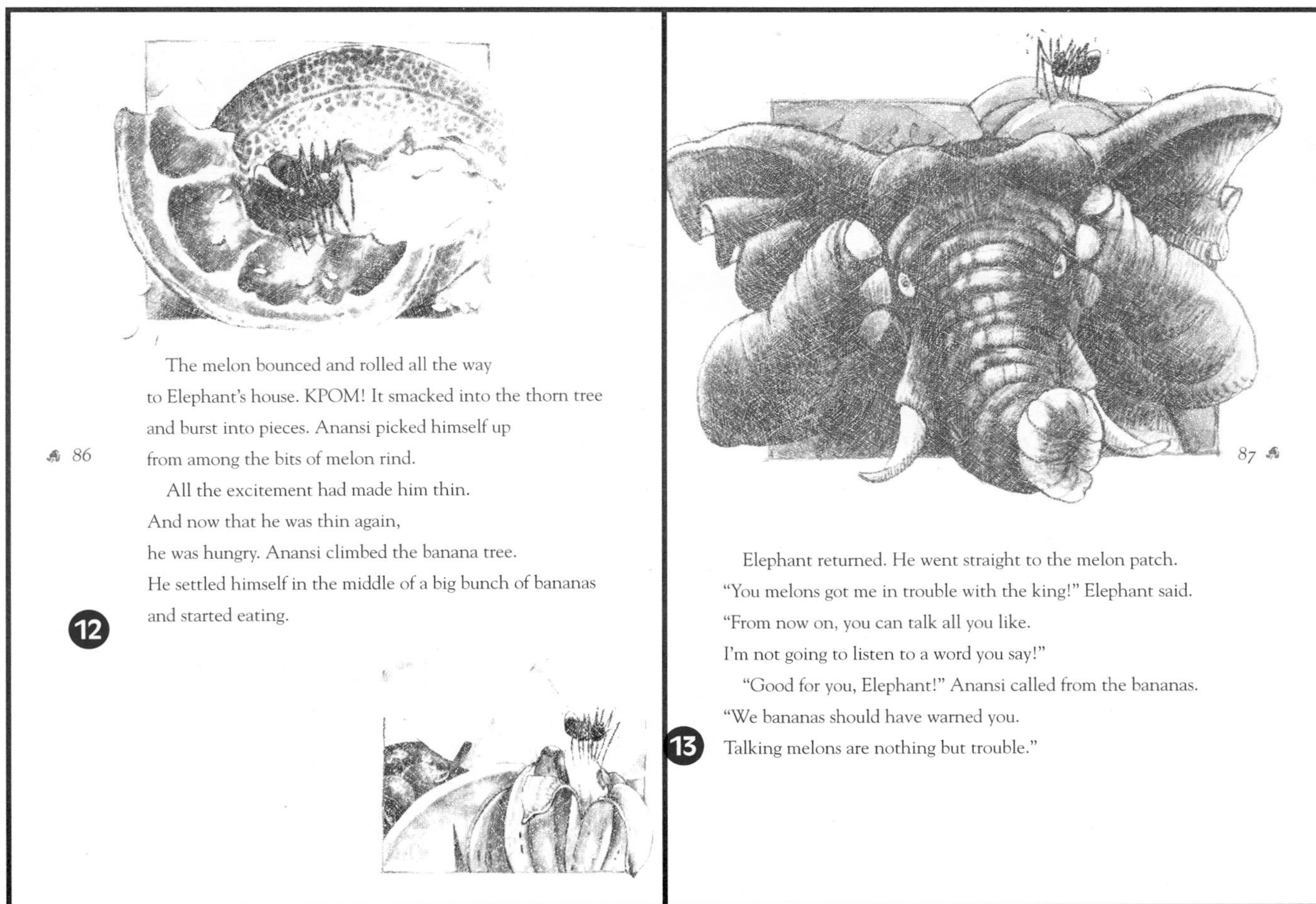

The melon bounced and rolled all the way to Elephant's house. KPOM! It smacked into the thorn tree and burst into pieces. Anansi picked himself up from among the bits of melon rind.

86

All the excitement had made him thin. And now that he was thin again, he was hungry. Anansi climbed the banana tree. He settled himself in the middle of a big bunch of bananas

12 and started eating.

87

Elephant returned. He went straight to the melon patch. "You melons got me in trouble with the king!" Elephant said. "From now on, you can talk all you like. I'm not going to listen to a word you say!"

"Good for you, Elephant!" Anansi called from the bananas. "We bananas should have warned you.

13 Talking melons are nothing but trouble."

12 *Anansi has just gotten into a bunch of bananas. I wonder what will happen now?*

13 Again, confirm children's predictions if possible.

Responding

- Encourage the children to tell what they liked about the story.

➤ Reading/Writing Connection, page 35, reviews this story. Work with the children to read the page and fill in the blanks. Have them reread the completed page.

TIP FOR ENGLISH LANGUAGE LEARNERS

Provide opportunities for conversational practice. Pair English Language Learners with each other or with native English-speaking partners. Encourage them to talk about Anansi's problem in the story. Have the children suggest other ways Anansi might have been able to solve his problem. Conversational practice promotes using language as a social activity and as a means of personal discovery.

* READING ALOUD

Many folk tales have a trickster such as Anansi as the hero of the story. You may want to share some of these. Suggested collections are:

The People Could Fly by Virginia Hamilton

And It Is Still That Way: Legends Told by Arizona Indian Children by Byrd Baylor

Reading/Writing Connection, page 35

Name

Lesson 17

Reading and Writing

talking again stuck burst trouble
squeezed bananas threw inside
fooled Anansi king angry

Anansi squeezed into a melon. He ate so much that he got stuck. "I can trick Elephant," said Anansi. "I will speak and he will think the melon is talking."

Elephant was fooled. He took the melon to show the king. Anansi talked to the king from inside the melon. The king was angry. He threw the melon and it burst open.

Then Anansi hid in the bananas. "You got me into trouble," Elephant said to the melons. This time Anansi pretended to be a talking banana. He tricked Elephant again.

Reading the Selection

Anansi and the Talking Melon R/WC 35

* READING A PHONICS MINIBOOK

Mr. Lee
Phonics Minibook 16

Getting Ready to Read

- Allow the children to look through the book, commenting on what they see in the illustrations and what they think the story will tell them.

Recommendations

Follow the standard procedure for reading a Phonics Minibook:

- Call on a different child to read each page of the story aloud. Clarify any difficulties on a page, then have a different child reread the page before going on.
- Reread the story at least twice, calling on different children to read.

Printed in the United States of America

ISBN 0-8126-1286-8

10 9 8 7 6 5 4 3 2 1

2

Mr. Lee was a timid man.
He was also an artist.
Mr. Lee made stained glass windows.
His glass made rainbows dance in rooms.

3

One day, Mr. Lee made
a window pane for an inn.
He took the window pane to the inn.
The inn was far away.
Timid Mr. Lee walked and walked.

4

5

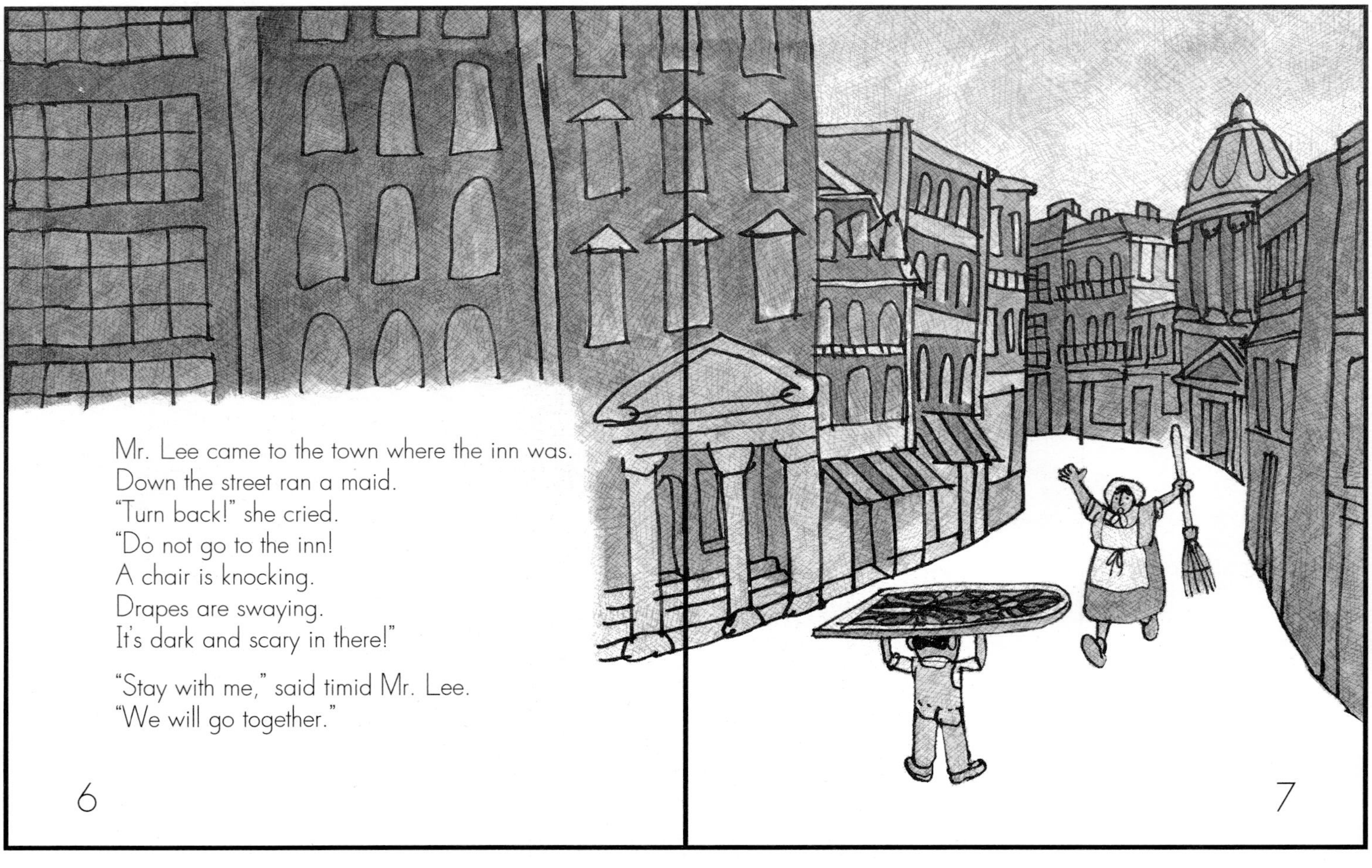

Mr. Lee came to the town where the inn was.
Down the street ran a maid.
"Turn back!" she cried.
"Do not go to the inn!
A chair is knocking.
Drapes are swaying.
It's dark and scary in there!"

"Stay with me," said timid Mr. Lee.
"We will go together."

6

7

Mr. Lee and the maid came to a gate.
Out ran a cook waving a spoon.
"Turn back!" cried the cook.
"A chair is knocking.
Drapes are swaying.
A tablecloth is floating.
It's dark and scary in there!"

"Stay with me," said timid Mr. Lee.
"We will go together."

8

9

Mr. Lee, the maid, and the cook
came to the front door.
Out ran the innkeeper.
"Turn back!" she cried.
"A chair is knocking.
Drapes are swaying.
A tablecloth is floating,
and a hat is tipping.
It's dark and scary in there!"

"But what about the window?" asked Mr. Lee.
"I am a timid man,
but this is my best window ever.
I will put in my window no matter what."

10

11

Timid Mr. Lee walked in.
It was dark and scary.
A chair was knocking,
drapes were swaying,
a tablecloth was floating,
a hat was tipping.

12

13

Mr. Lee felt a breeze.
He found a broken window.
He put in the new window.
It was a perfect fit.

14

Mr. Lee turned around.
The chair was not knocking.
The drapes were not swaying.
The tablecloth was not floating.
The hat was not tipping.
It was not dark and scary in there.
Rainbows danced in the room.

15

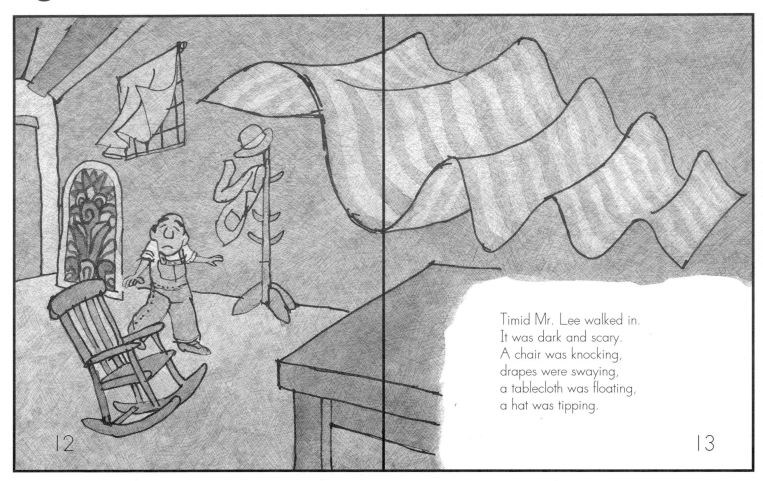

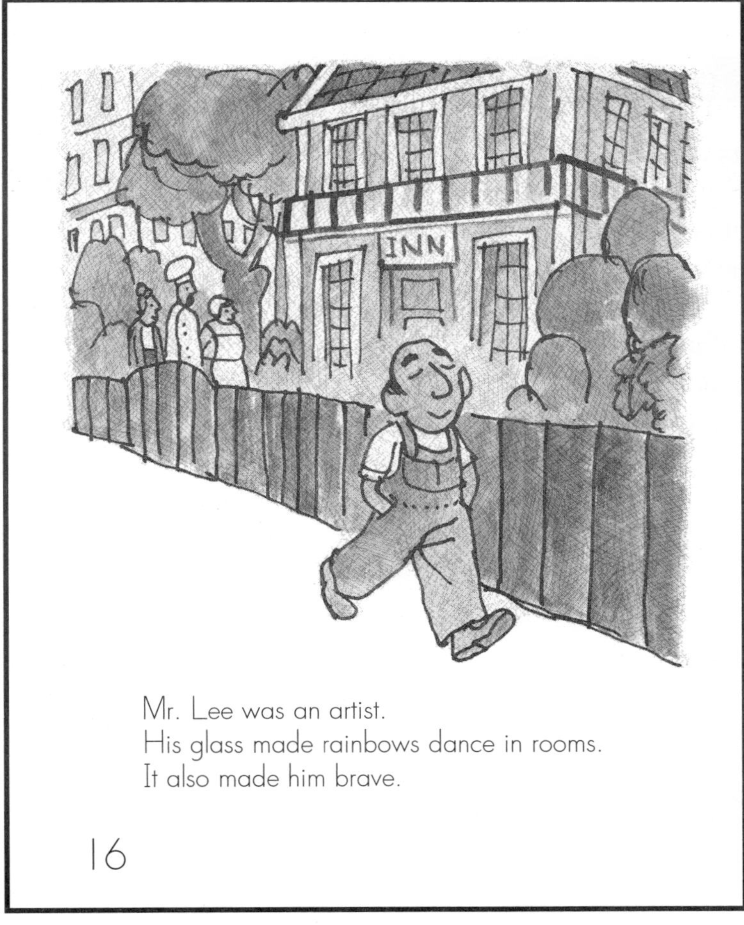

Mr. Lee was an artist.
His glass made rainbows dance in rooms.
It also made him brave.

16

Responding

- Ask the children to talk about any hard words they came across in their reading and how they figured out the words.
- Have the children answer questions such as the following by reading words or sentences in the story that supply the answer:
  What kind of person was Mr. Lee?
  Why was Mr. Lee going to the inn?
  What did the maid tell Mr. Lee?
  Who else told Mr. Lee to turn back?
  How did Mr. Lee's window change the inn?
  Was Mr. Lee timid or brave?
- Call on volunteers to point out new words that they can read.
- Invite children to tell what they like best about the story.

Have the children read the story with a partner. Observing the partner reading is a good way to assess student progress. As you observe the children reading, record their progress.

ASSESSMENT Listen to several students individually read from a Phonics Minibook. Record your observations on the Reading Rubric and keep in the student's folder.

2 WRITING

* DICTATION AND SPELLING

During Dictation and Spelling, some of your students may still show some confusion using the different spellings for the long vowels. This is natural. It is important that you not wait for mastery of each spelling. Students will have many opportunities to work with the various vowel spellings patterns in reading and writing.

Have the children turn to page 34 of their Reading/Writing Connection book. Dictate the following words and sentence, using the suggestions for dictation that appear on **Learning Framework Card 4.**

Line 1: soon noon balloon

Line 2: blue glue tube

Sentence: The owl hooted at the moon.

Help the children proofread each line, following the guidelines on **Learning Framework Card 10.** For lines 1 and 2, ask what patterns they notice.

INDEPENDENT AND COLLABORATIVE WRITING

If the children enjoyed doing the cumulative story as a group, you may want to do another one with the class. This time have the class change the topic. For example, "When I go walking in my neighborhood, I see ______." "When I was so hungry, I ate ______." "When I was a bird flying on high, I looked down below and spied a ______." Children should be encouraged to use more than one-word responses. For example, the bird might spy a large fat worm, a big wide river, and a group of children playing. Children may want to take time to illustrate this class book.

Alternatively, some children may want to work on their own or in pairs to create a cumulative story. If children are working in pairs or alone, hold conferences with them to help them identify themes for their cumulative stories. For those children having problems, suggest a list with a single sentence at the beginning, such as "When I went to the beach, I saw ______." "For supper, I like to eat ______."

TEACHING TIP

Write your own cumulative story to share with the class tomorrow or choose a student as a partner and together write a cumulative story.

3 GUIDED AND INDEPENDENT EXPLORATION

WORKSHOP

Remind the children that they may use this time to work on projects on their own or in small groups. Be sure that each child knows what projects he or she may choose and how to complete any independent work.

Learning Framework Card 11, Workshop, contains a complete discussion of establishing and conducting Workshop and suggestions for helping English Language Learners during Workshop.

Work with the Teacher

- Review today's Blending with children.
- Reread Phonics Minibook 16 with individuals or pairs of children. Use these rereading sessions to assess the children's progress.
- Continue to work with children who are writing their own version of a folk tale. Return to the planning web they began yesterday and review it with them, finding out if there is anything they would like to add to or delete from the web. They might, for example, want to add that folk tales often feature a "trickster" such as Anansi from today's selection. If they are ready, you can help the children to make a new web to plan their own story. Write "our story" in the center of the web and extend from the center the children's story ideas. Save both webs for use during tomorrow's Workshop.

Collaborative/Independent Activities

- Those children who are working on a performance of "The Gingerbread Man" should meet at this time to continue their work. They may want to do a practice run of the performance. Provide them with adequate space to do so. Remind them that the parts of the story that are in quotation marks should be said by the actors, while the rest of the story should be read by the narrator. Each actor might want to write down his or her lines before beginning the practice run. The narrator, who will be reading from the student anthology, can prompt the actors if they forget when to say their lines. They should listen to the story for cues as to what actions to perform. The children will probably not get all the way through the story today and can finish tomorrow.
- Write the words *hoot* and *brook* on the chalkboard. Have children copy these words onto scratch paper. Beneath each word they should list all the words they can think of that contain the same vowel sound. They should then underline the letter or letters in each word that make the vowel sound. Finally, each child should write a sentence using one word from each list.
- A small group of children can play Fish-for-a-Spelling. Review the procedure with them before they play. Add an *oo* card to the set of cards.
- Activity Sheet 87 provides practice with *oo* words. Have the children color the flowers with words that have the /oo/ sound red and those with the /o͞o/ sound blue.

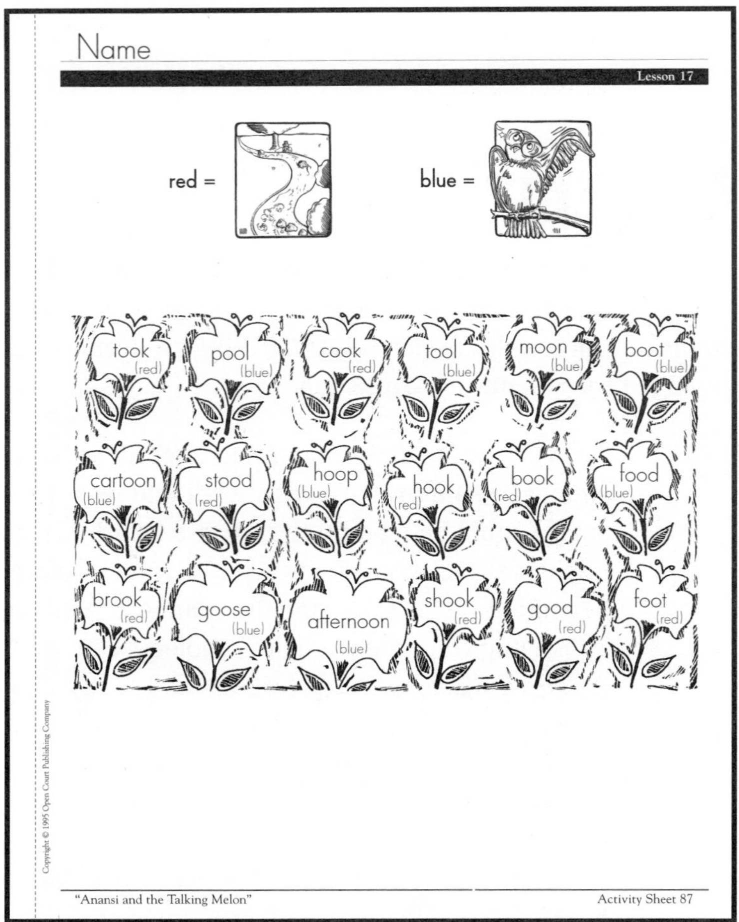
Name
Lesson 17
red =
blue =
took (red)
pool (blue)
cook (red)
tool (blue)
moon (blue)
boot (blue)
cartoon (blue)
stood (red)
hoop (blue)
hook (red)
book (red)
food (blue)
brook (red)
goose (blue)
afternoon (blue)
shook (red)
good (red)
foot (red)
Copyright © 1995 Open Court Publishing Company
"Anansi and the Talking Melon"
Activity Sheet 87

Activity Sheet 87

LESSON 18

Lesson Overview

Materials

- ***Anansi and the Talking Melon***, pages 70–77
- Learning Framework Card 3
- Reading/Writing Connection, pages 36–37
- Activity Sheets 82, 88

Prepare Ahead

- Reading Relay Flash Cards (see page 207)
- Wonder Word Flash Cards (see page 208)
- Bingo Cards (see page 212)
- Sidewalk Game sheets (see page 212)

GETTING STARTED

Choose one or more of the following activities to focus the children's attention and to review some of the concepts they have been learning.

Reading Relay Game Form two teams of children and have the players on each team sit one behind the other. Make sufficient flash cards of /n/ words so that there is at least one card for each child. Words that review the /n/ sound/spellings include: *doorknob, knot, know, knee, knuckle, nose, number, November, nine, knock, knit, night, knight, nothing, noodle, kneel, needle.* To play the game, the first child on the team picks up a word card, reads the word, then takes the card and goes to the end of the line. If a child reads the word incorrectly, the opposite team has an opportunity to say the word. The teams take turns choosing a card and blending and saying the word. The game ends when all the members on one team have successfully read a word.

Spellings with the Same Letter Tell the children that you want to see how quickly they can give you the spellings for different sounds. Say each word and have the children repeat the word. Then have them tell you how to spell the vowel sound. Example words are:

food	few	cue	flute	tuba
flood	new	glue	cute	turtle

1 READING

PHONICS REVIEW

Choose one of the following review activities.

Review /o͞o/ and /o͝o/ Play the Wonder Word game to review words with the *oo* spelling. Print the following words on cards: *book, brook, wool, cook, good, hook, hood, look, wood, shook, cookie, took, stood, food, spoon, moon, balloon, gloomy, boot, cool.* Say this verse as you pass a card around the circle.

The wonder word goes round and round.
To pass it quickly you are bound.
If you're the one to have it last,
Then you must read it rather fast.

The child who has the card when the verse ends reads the word. This child picks the next card from the center of the circle and continues the game. The game ends once the children have read all the cards.

Review /n/ Spellings Use homophones to review words that begin with *n* or *kn.* Print the following pairs of words on the chalkboard:

new knew night knight not knot nose knows

Point to the first pair of homophones and use one of the words in a sentence. Invite a child to use the second word in a sentence. Continue the activity with the other pairs of homophones.

* **Blending** Have the children blend the following words and sentences. For reference and additional suggestions for blending, see **Learning Framework Card 3.**

Line 1:	**slowly slightly quickly closely**
Line 2:	**skinny jumpy lazy wavy**
Line 3:	**believe squeeze reason angry**
Line 4:	**clock cloak block bowl**
Line 5:	**brook boot clown cloud**

Line 1 reviews words with the *-ly* ending. Have the children use the words in sentences.

Line 2 reviews words with the *-y* ending. Invite the children to complete these phrases:

a skinny ______
a jumpy ______
a lazy ______
a wavy ______

The words in line 3 review different long *e* spellings.

TEACHING TIP

You can use the words from this game for an independent activity. Write the words on cards and give them to a small group of children to sort according to whether they contain the *boot* sound or the *book* sound. Encourage the children to look for spelling patterns in each group.

As the children sound and blend the words in line 4, have them listen for the vowel sound they hear in each word. Help them note that the line compares short *o* and long *o*. After the children blend the words in line 5, point out that *brook* and *boot* have the same vowel spelling but different vowel sounds, while *clown* and *cloud* have the same vowel sound but different vowel spellings.

To review the words, have volunteers go to the chalkboard, read, and erase a word.

➤ Reading/Writing Connection, page 36, reviews words with /o͞o/ and /oo/. Help the children read the story and then list the /o͞o/ and /oo/ words in the correct column.

✱ READING THE STUDENT ANTHOLOGY

Anansi and the Talking Melon
pages 70–77

Activating Prior Knowledge

Review the story by asking children to tell what they remember from yesterday's reading.

Reading/Writing Connection, page 36

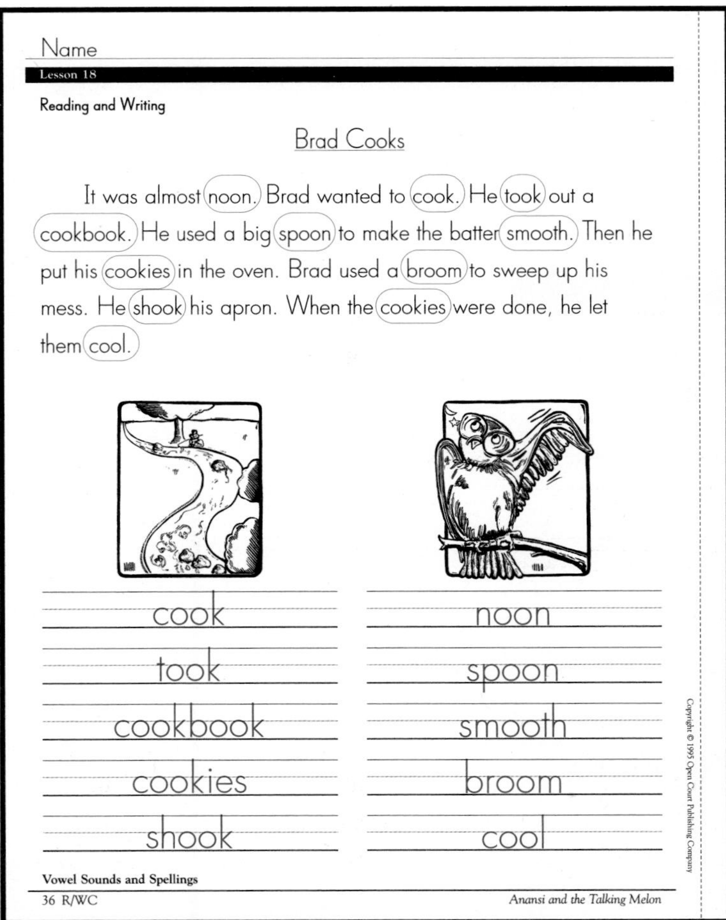

Name

Lesson 18

Reading and Writing

Brad Cooks

It was almost noon. Brad wanted to cook. He took out a cookbook. He used a big spoon to make the batter smooth. Then he put his cookies in the oven. Brad used a broom to sweep up his mess. He shook his apron. When the cookies were done, he let them cool.

cook	noon
took	spoon
cookbook	smooth
cookies	broom
shook	cool

Vowel Sounds and Spellings

36 R/WC *Anansi and the Talking Melon*

Recommendations for Reading

- Focus on reading fluently.
- Reread the first part of *Anansi and the Talking Melon,* pages 70–77. Have the children follow along in their books. This time pause in your reading when you come to a place where a character speaks, and ask children to read the dialogue.
- Stop to ask children to sum up at various points in the story.

About the Reading Strategies

In reading this selection, children will need the strategies of wondering, word clarification, and predicting. Explain that you will model using these strategies.

Responding

- Have the children sum up the story so far.
- Have children discuss the characteristics of a folk tale they noticed in this story, such as talking animals, silly characters, and humor.
- Discuss whether or not the children have any ideas or anything they wonder about to add to the Concept Board.

Vocabulary Discuss any interesting or unusual words from the first part of the story that the children might want to add to the Vocabulary Chart or to their journals for use in their writing. Have the children use these words in oral sentences. Possible words include the following:

aah, juicy, ouch, ridiculous, squeeze, sweet

➤ Reading/Writing Connection, page 37, may be completed at this time. Help the children read the story and answer the questions.

TEACHING TIP

Have the children do some partner reading daily. Using previously read Phonics Minibooks and Step-by-Step Practice Stories for this purpose will help the children review and solidify their knowledge of the sounds and spellings they have learned. This is a good opportunity to read with children individually and to record their progress.

2 WRITING

* DICTATION AND SPELLING

Word-Building Game Have the children use pencil and paper to build the following words:

knee
knew
no
knots
knot
net
new

Use the words in sentences to differentiate between homophones.

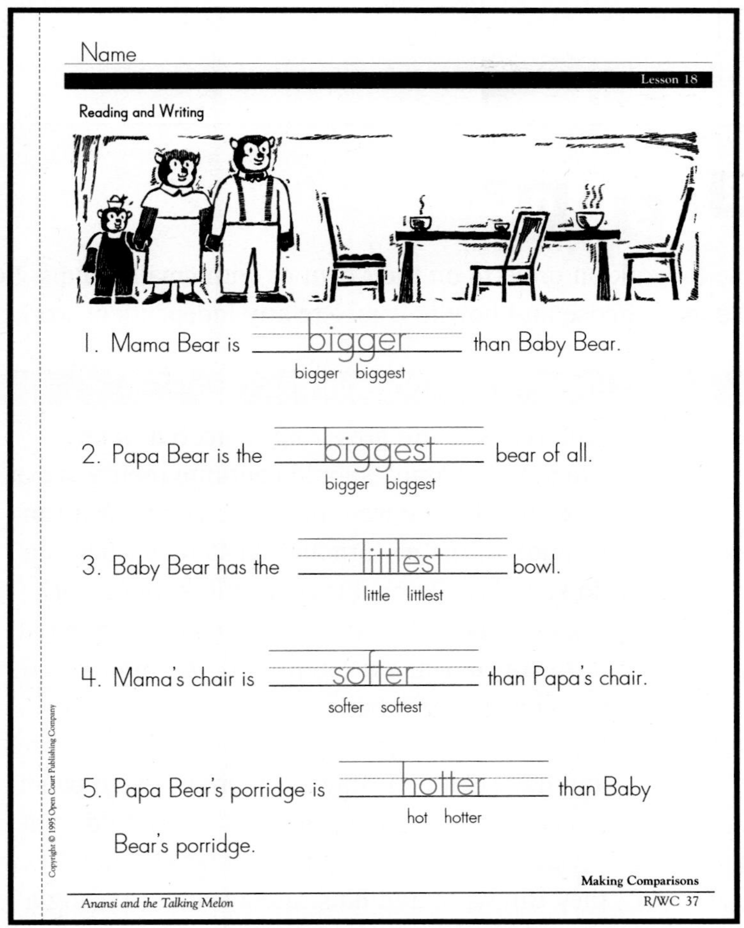

Name

Lesson 18

Reading and Writing

1. Mama Bear is bigger than Baby Bear.
bigger biggest

2. Papa Bear is the biggest bear of all.
bigger biggest

3. Baby Bear has the littlest bowl.
little littlest

4. Mama's chair is softer than Papa's chair.
softer softest

5. Papa Bear's porridge is hotter than Baby Bear's porridge.
hot hotter

Making Comparisons

Anansi and the Talking Melon R/WC 37

Reading/Writing Connection, page 37

INDEPENDENT AND COLLABORATIVE WRITING

Since all children will probably have written some form of cumulative story, take time to have as many as possible share their stories. Children may want to do some predicting once the author has read his or her first sentence. If you have written a cumulative story, take a turn as Seminar leader and share yours.

3 GUIDED AND INDEPENDENT EXPLORATION

WORKSHOP

Remind the children that they may use this time to work on projects on their own or with small groups. Be sure that each child knows what projects she or he may choose and how to complete any independent work.

Work with the Teacher

- Play Bingo with a small group of children. Add the spellings *kn-* and *oo* to some of the Bingo cards and add some words that contain those spellings to the stack of word cards you will read to the Bingo players. Check recent Blending lessons for word ideas.
- Play the Word-Building game with children who need to work on their spelling. Repeat today's list or choose a previous list, based on the children's needs.
- Continue to work with those children who are writing a folk tale. Return to the planning web they began yesterday. Review the ideas in the web and find out if the children would like to add or delete ideas. Tell them that the ideas in the web should answer questions such as, Who are the characters in the story? What will happen to them? If the children are retelling a story, how will their version be different from other versions and how will it be the same?

ASSESSMENT Listen to eight to ten students individually read from a Phonics Minibook. Record your observations on the Reading Rubric and keep it in the student's folder.

Student Collaboration

- Children who are preparing to act out "The Gingerbread Man" should continue their work at this time. If they were unable to complete a run-through of the performance yesterday, they can do so today. Remind them to think about such issues as how the gingerbread man will pop out of the oven, run out the front door, and cross the river on the fox's back.
- Write the spellings *n* and *kn-* on the chalkboard and have children copy them onto scratch paper. Beneath each spelling, the children should write several words that begin with that spelling. Then they can write and illustrate a sentence using a word from each list.
- Prepare and photocopy a Sidewalk Game sheet (Activity Sheet 82), including some *kn-* and *-ly* words. Distribute a sheet, a die, and markers to each pair or group of interested children.
- Activity Sheet 88 focuses on the *kn-* spelling. Tell the children to complete each sentence with the correct word, then write the words again in the corresponding puzzle boxes. You might want to point out that in this puzzle, some numbers have both horizontal and vertical answer boxes. The children can use the arrows to help them write their answers in the puzzle correctly.

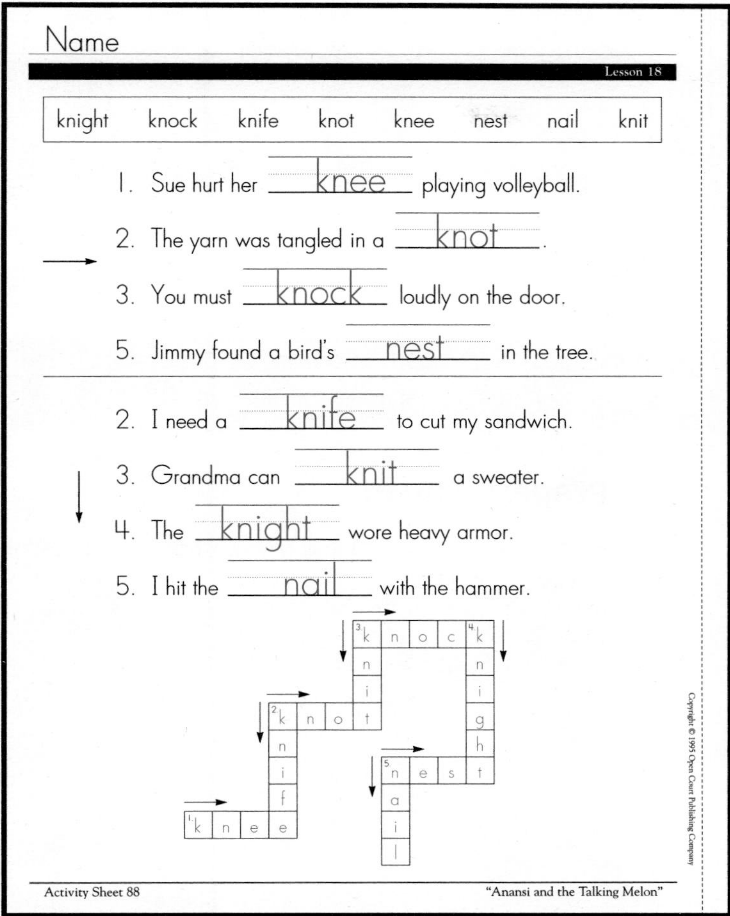

Name

Lesson 18

knight knock knife knot knee nest nail knit

→

1. Sue hurt her knee playing volleyball.
2. The yarn was tangled in a knot.
3. You must knock loudly on the door.
5. Jimmy found a bird's nest in the tree.

↓

2. I need a knife to cut my sandwich.
3. Grandma can knit a sweater.
4. The knight wore heavy armor.
5. I hit the nail with the hammer.

Activity Sheet 88 "Anansi and the Talking Melon"

Activity Sheet 88

LESSON 19

Lesson Overview

New Learning

- /oi/ spelled ***oi*** and ***oy***
- Story Elements

Materials

- ***Anansi and the Talking Melon,*** pages 78–87
- Sound/Spelling Card 43, Coil
- Learning Framework Cards 2, 3, 4
- Reading/Writing Connection, pages 38–39
- Activity Sheet 89

Prepare Ahead

- Supplies for Gingerbread Man costumes and scenery (see page 220)

GETTING STARTED

Choose one or more of the following activities to focus the children's attention and to review some of the concepts they have been learning.

Write a Word Game Ask one child to go to the chalkboard and have a second child name any Sound/Spelling Card. The child at the chalkboard should write any word that contains the sound of the named card. Continue with other children.

Identifying Rhymes Write three words on the chalkboard. Then have the children say the words quietly to themselves and write the word that does not rhyme with the others. Have the children hold up their answer and ask them to say the word aloud together. Use these groups of words:

wood rude food
put foot boot
spoon moon mood
good rude hood
took true clue
cook book spook
stewed brood good

1 READING

PHONICS

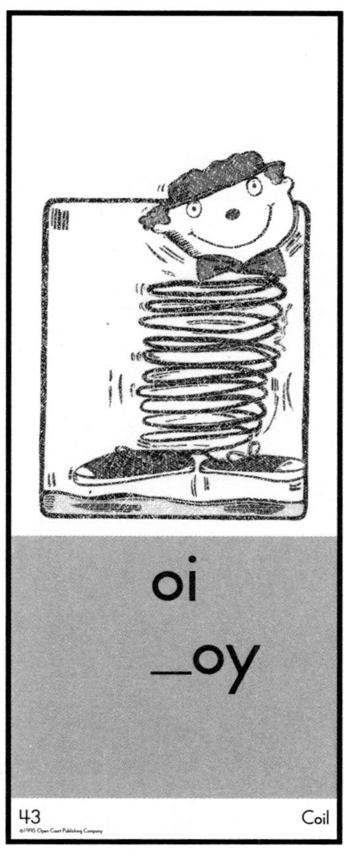

* **Introducing /oi/ Spelled *oi, oy*** Turn Sound/Spelling Card 43, Coil, and tell the children this is the Coil card. Have the children identify the two spellings on the card. Write the words *toy* and *coil* on the board and read each. Then tell the children to listen for the /oy/ sound as you read the Coil story.

A complete discussion of the procedure for introducing sounds and spellings can be found on **Learning Framework Card 2.**

Boing! Boing! Boing! Boing!
Roy the Coil is a bouncing toy,
and this is the sound of his bounce:
/oi/ /oi/ /oi/ /oi/ /oi/.

Doing! Doing! Doing! Doing!
Roy the Coil just dances for joy.
This is the sound of his dance:
/oi/ /oi/ /oi/ /oi/ /oi/.

Ke-boing! Ke-boing!
Roy the Coil springs over a boy.
What springing sound does he make?
(Have the children join in) /oi/ /oi/ /oi/ /oi/ /oi/.

Have the children suggest words that contain the /oy/ sound.

* **Blending** Have the children blend the following words and sentences. For reference and additional suggestions for blending, see **Learning Framework Card 3.**

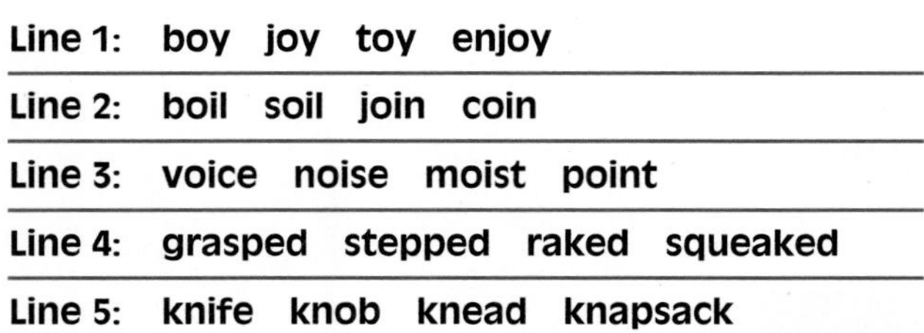

Line 1:	**boy**	**joy**	**toy**	**enjoy**
Line 2:	**boil**	**soil**	**join**	**coin**
Line 3:	**voice**	**noise**	**moist**	**point**
Line 4:	**grasped**	**stepped**	**raked**	**squeaked**
Line 5:	**knife**	**knob**	**knead**	**knapsack**

Lines 1–3 review words with the sound /oi/. As the children sound and blend each word, ask where they hear the target sound and have them circle the spelling for /oi/.

Line 4 focuses on words with the *-ed* ending. Ask the children what this ending tells about the word. How would they say each word if the action were happening today? Have the children tell how the past tense of each word is formed.

Line 5 review the *kn-* spelling for /n/. Point out the word *knead* and use it in a sentence. Print *need* on the chalkboard and have a volunteer use it in a sentence.

Name

Lesson 19

Sounds and Spellings

oi

_oy

Writing Words and Sentences

noise noise enjoy enjoy

The boy has a nice voice.

The boy has a nice voice.

Dictation and Spelling

Vowel Sounds and Spellings

38 R/WC *Anansi and the Talking Melon*

Reading/Writing Connection, page 38

As a review, use the words from the lines in oral sentences. The children find, say, and erase the word each time. To vary the activity, point to a line and invite a child to use one of the words in a sentence.

➤ Reading/Writing Connection, page 38, provides a review of /oi/ spelled *oi* and *oy.* Have the children read and copy the words and the sentence.

* READING THE STUDENT ANTHOLOGY

Anansi and the Talking Melon
pages 78–87

Recommendations for Reading

- Continue reading the story aloud with the children, stopping to have them read the dialogue. You may want to have groups of children read a character's part, for example, all the boys or all the girls.
- During reading, children may continue to comment on the selection.

Responding

- Ask children which parts of the story they thought were the funniest.

- Discuss the characters' feelings in different parts of the story. You might ask, "How did Elephant feel when he first heard the melon talk? How did Hippo and Warthog feel when they heard the melon? Were they more than just surprised? How do you think Elephant felt at the end?"
- Ask children how they can tell this is a folk tale. How is it like other folk tales they've heard or read?
- Discuss whether or not the children have any new ideas they would like to add to the Concept Board, including favorite characters or anything they might wonder about.

Vocabulary Discuss any words the children found interesting or unusual. They may want to add these to the Vocabulary Chart or to their journals. Have the children use the words in oral sentences. Possible words are *angry, handsome, hurled, trouble.*

TIP FOR ENGLISH LANGUAGE LEARNERS

Give English Language Learners a chance to share folk tales with the other children. In small groups or in pairs, allow English Language Learners to tell a story or talk about a folk tale that is like *Anansi and the Talking Melon.* Praise their language efforts. Allowing opportunities for English Language Learners to provide a model for other children helps to increase their confidence in using language.

ASSESSMENT Listen to the final eight to ten students individually read one of the stories in Phonics Minibook 16, *Mr. Lee.* Record your observations and put results in the student's folder.

* READING ALOUD

Children will enjoy hearing another Anansi story if time permits.

2 WRITING

* DICTATION AND SPELLING

Have the children open their Reading/Writing Connection book to page 38. Dictate the following words and sentence, using the suggestions for dictation that appear on **Learning Framework Card 4.**

Line 1: **knot knock knife**

Line 2: **good hook stood**

Sentence: **I know how to knit.**

As the children proofread the words in line 1, point out the *kn-* spelling at the beginning of each word.

Minilesson

Story Elements

The selection *Anansi and the Talking Melon* offers a good opportunity to talk about characters, problems, and solutions—elements that writers incorporate into stories. When most children write stories, they usually have a character in mind but little for the character to do. By beginning with a problem and a solution, most children should be able to improve their writing.

Write the words *character, problem,* and *solution* on the chalkboard. Explain to the children that in a story, the people or, as in *Anansi,* the animals are called the characters. Have the children name some of the other characters (animals) in the story. Then write *Anansi* and any other characters under the heading *character.* Explain that often a story is mostly about only one character, a person or animal, and this character usually has a problem. In this story, Anansi is the main character. Ask the children what problem Anansi had. (He got stuck in the melon.) Write their replies below the heading *problem.* Finally tell the children that in stories, there is usually a solution to a problem. Have the children talk about how Anansi's problem was solved. You may want to read the last section of the story to the children if they seem unsure of Anansi's solution. Write their reply on the chalkboard. (The angry king hurled the melon, and it broke.)

In *Anansi and the Talking Melon* there is a suggestion at the end of the story that Anansi may have another problem. The story refers to a talking banana. Have the children talk about who the character would be in that story, what the problem might be, and how the character might solve the problem. Or you may want to revisit *Matthew and Tilly,* a story in which two main characters have a problem.

➤ To provide additional work with story elements, have the children complete Reading/Writing Connection, page 39. Work with the children to complete the page. Have them read the paragraph and then answer the questions.

If time permits, children may want to start writing a new Anansi story about Anansi being caught in a bunch of bananas or anything else they wish to use as a problem for the spider. Children should feel free to continue this project during Workshop.

TEACHING TIP

Remind the children to use the words from the Vocabulary Chart in their writing.

Name

Lesson 19

Identifying Story Elements

Jenny wanted some flowers for Mother's Day. She went to the flower store. It was closed. On her way home Jenny found some nice flowers in a field. She picked them for her mother.

(possible answers)

Who is the main character? Jenny

What is the problem? She wants flowers, but the store is closed.

How is the problem solved? Jenny picks some flowers in a field.

Story Elements

Anansi and the Talking Melon R/WC 39

Reading/Writing Connection, page 39

3 GUIDED AND INDEPENDENT EXPLORATION

WORKSHOP

Remind the children that they may use this time to work on projects on their own or with small groups. Be sure that each child knows what projects he or she may choose and how to complete any independent work.

Learning Framework Card 11, Workshop, contains a complete discussion of establishing and conducting Workshop and suggestions for helping English Language Learners during Workshop.

Work with the Teacher

- Reteach Sound/Spelling Card 43, Coil, and today's Blending lesson to children who had trouble with /oi/ spelled *oi* and *oy*.
- On the chalkboard, write the endings *-er, -est,* and *-ly.* Write the following sentences beneath them:

  Jill runs very slow__
  Tom is slow__ than Jill.
  Mike is the slow__ of all.

  Peter Rabbit is the quick__ rabbit in the woods.
  He hops very quick__ down the rabbit trail.
  There is no rabbit quick__ than Peter.

  The sun shines very bright__ in the sky.
  Noon is the bright__ time of day.
  At night, the moon is bright__ than the sun.

  Work with a small group of children. Have one child at a time go to the board, select and fill in the appropriate ending to complete a sentence, and read the entire sentence aloud.
- Continue to work with those children who are writing a folk tale. Review the planning web and make any additional changes that the children suggest. By now, the children may be ready to begin writing. On a sheet of chart paper, write down the story as the children dictate it to you. Encourage them to tell the entire tale as it comes to their minds. Remind them that this is only a first draft of the story and that tomorrow they will have the opportunity to revise their work.

Collaborative/Independent Activities

- Children who are planning to act out "The Gingerbread Man" should continue their work at this time. The children may want to work on scenery and costumes for their performance. One good way to create a background scene is to draw a scene on a transparency and project it on a wall or screen behind the performance space. You may want to provide the children with transparency sheets and magic markers for this purpose. They might also want to make a construction-paper river for the fox and gingerbread man to cross. Provide them with the necessary art supplies.
- Ask children to look through magazines and catalogs to find pictures of words that contain these sounds: /oo/, /oi/, /n/. Allow them to work in pairs to see if they can correctly write the words for their pictures.
- Have children take out their papers from today's Dictation lesson. Challenge them to form as many words as they can by starting with a word from line 2 *(good, hook, stood)* and changing or adding one letter at a time. Tell them to finish by using two or more of the new words in a sentence and illustrating the sentence.
- Activity Sheet 89 provides practice for reading and writing words. Tell the children to read the words and write them in the correct column depending on whether the word is a color, a number, or a feeling.

Home/School Connection

Send home the take-home version of Phonics Minibook 15, *Superhero to the Rescue,* and encourage the children to read it to their parents.

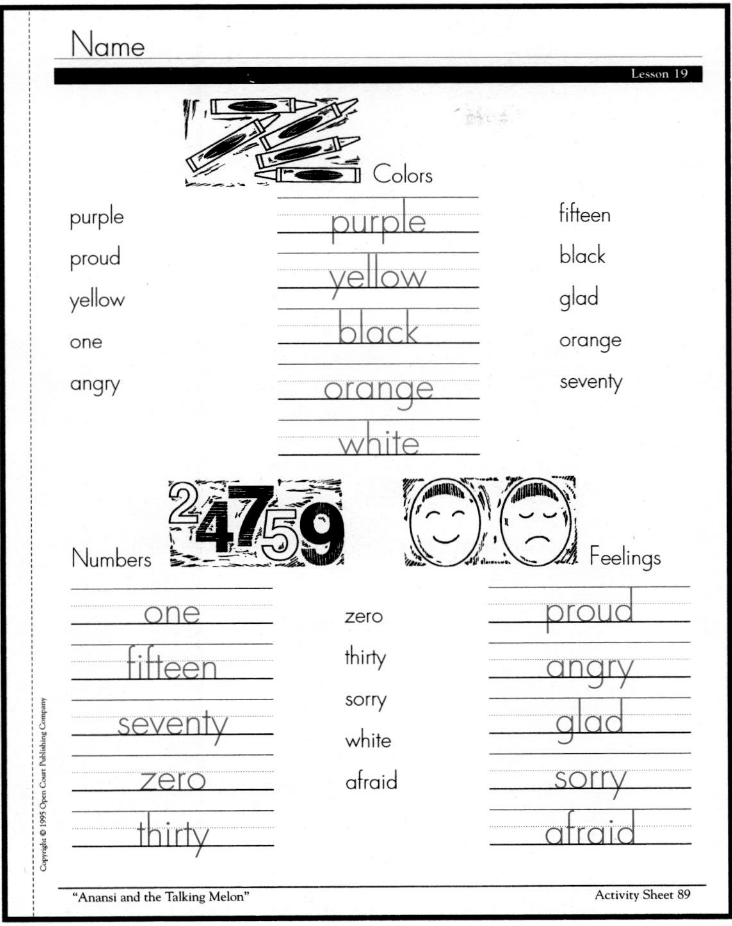

Name

Lesson 19

Colors

purple	purple	fifteen
proud	yellow	black
yellow	black	glad
one	orange	orange
angry	white	seventy

Numbers

Feelings

one	zero	proud
fifteen	thirty	angry
seventy	sorry	glad
zero	white	sorry
thirty	afraid	afraid

"Anansi and the Talking Melon" Activity Sheet 89

Activity Sheet 89

LESSON 20

Lesson Overview

New Learning

- Describing Words

Materials

- Fine Art, pages 88–89
- Learning Framework Card 3
- Reading/Writing Connection, pages 40–41
- Classroom Support Teacher Tool Card 2
- Activity Sheet 90

Prepare Ahead

- Compound Word Puzzle (See page 228)

GETTING STARTED

Choose one or more of the following activities to focus the children's attention and to review some of the concepts they have been learning.

Riddle Me This: (A Variation) Give the children clues such as, "I'm thinking of something you play with." The children think of words that fit the clue. They respond by naming the cards that stand for the sounds of the word, for example Timer, Coil (toy). The rest of the class tells the word.

Dictate to the Teacher Write the word *oil* on the board. Have the children read the word. Then ask how to make the word *coil.* Write the new word. Continue having the children tell you how to make the following words:

soil boy
toil foil
toy

1 READING

PHONICS

Practice Reading Compound Words Write the following compound words on the board:

staircase	windmill	scarecrow
bedroom	underground	popcorn
football	tugboat	bulldozer
schoolyard	supermarket	horseshoe
spaceship	shoelace	hamburger

Have the children read the words and then tell what two words make up each compound.

* **Blending** Have the children blend the following words and sentences. For reference and additional suggestions for blending, see **Learning Framework Card 3.**

Line 1:	**hunt hunter hunted hunting**
Line 2:	**cry crying cries cried**
Line 3:	**sunny funny bunny tummy**
Line 4:	**yawn applaud claw pause**
Line 5:	**caught taught daughter**

Lines 1 and 2 review different endings added to a base word. Ask the children to tell what ending was added and have them use the words in sentences. Discuss how the base word changes when each ending is added.

The children may notice several patterns among the words in line 3: all the words end in /ē/ spelled *y*; they all contain the /u/ sound; and they all have a double consonant.

Lines 4 and 5 contain words with the sound /aw/. The children review the spellings *aw* and *au* in line 4. Tell them that *augh* is another spelling for this sound. Have the children sound and blend the words in line 5, then use them in sentences.

Review the words by having the children fill in the blank in sentences such as the following:

The baby lies on her ______.
If you like the movie, ______ loudly.
I ______ when I'm tired.
The opposite of son is ______.
A baby rabbit is a ______.

➤ Reading/Writing Connection, page 40, can be completed at this time. Have the children circle the word that does not belong in each sentence. Then have them write a word that could replace the circled word.

TEACHING TIP

If you have kept a list of compound words on chart paper, you might cut these charts apart to play the game.

Name

Lesson 20

Reading and Writing

1. Dolls, yo-yos, and chickens are toys.
2. Noodles, crayons, and cookies are food.
3. Root, trunk, and hook are parts of a tree.
4. Five, foot, and elbow are body parts.
5. A goose, boot, and balloon can fly.
6. Oil, dimes, and pennies are coins.
7. Foil, boil, and bake are ways to cook.
8. A baboon, moose, and book are animals.

(Answers will vary.)

Vowel Sounds and Spellings

40 R/WC Folk Tales

Reading/Writing Connection, page 40

✱ READING THE STUDENT ANTHOLOGY

Fine Art
pages 88–89

Information for the Teacher

Following is some background information about the fine-art pieces that appear on pages 88–89 of the student anthology.

Battle scene from the frontispiece to *Sinbad the Sailor.* 1923.
Paul Klee. Watercolor.

Paul Klee (1879–1940) was born in Berne, Switzerland. His work included drawings, watercolors, oil paintings, and paintings on glass. His art was one of emotion and rhythm; he likened it to making music, for he was also an accomplished musician. Klee's output as an artist is estimated at about 8,000 works. Approximately 500 of these were inspired by the world of opera and theater, his subjects sometimes surrounded by or depicted as stage settings, as with the piece shown here.

Peter and the Wolf. 1943. Ben Shahn. Tempera.

Ben Shahn (1898–1969), born in Kovno, Lithuania, was an American painter and graphic artist. His work was primarily concerned

Battle scene from the frontispiece to *Sinbad the Sailor*. 1923. Paul Klee.

Watercolor. Durst-Haase Collection, Muttenz. Photo: Giraudon/Art Resource

88

Peter and the Wolf. 1943. Ben Shahn.

Tempera. 6 1/2" x 10". Private collection. © 1994 Estate of Ben Shahn/VAGA, NY. Photo: SCALA/Art Resource

FINE ART

FOLK TALES

Bunraku performance in Osaka, Japan.

Photo: Werner Forman Archive/Art Resource

89

The Sleeping Beauty from a series illustrating the *Legend of the Briar Rose*. Series painted 1871–1890. Sir Edward Burne-Jones.

Oil on canvas, 61 x 82.5 cm. Faringdon Collection, Buscot, Oxfordshire, Great Britain. Photo: Bridgeman/Art Resource

with social commentary and criticism until the mid-1950s, when he began to reveal more personal reflections. Shahn also illustrated a number of books, particularly several works on Jewish festivals and Hebrew script. The painting shown here illustrates the musical composition *Peter and the Wolf,* created by Sergey Sergeyevich Prokofiev for a children's theater in Moscow in 1936.

Bunraku performance in Osaka, Japan.

Bunraku, named for eighteenth-century puppet master Uemura Bunrakuken, is a major theatrical form in Japan. It is derived from the combination of the ancient arts of puppet theater and storytelling. The puppets are one-half to one-third life size, and the more important characters are smaller than the less important ones. The eyes of each puppet can open and close, and their arms, hands, and legs are fully jointed. The operators stand on stage and are on view throughout the performance; up to three operators are needed to manipulate each puppet. The assistants to the principal operator are dressed completely in black, including black hoods fitted with eye slits, but the principal operator, considered an important artist, remains unmasked. The story is narrated by a chanter who sits in an alcove at stage left with his script on a small stand in front of him.

The Sleeping Beauty, from a series of paintings illustrating the *Legend of the Briar Rose.* (1871–1890). Sir Edward Burne-Jones. Oil on canvas.

The British artist Sir Edward Burne-Jones (1833–1898) turned away from the growing technology of nineteenth-century England toward the romantic ideals of his imagination. In his art he portrayed many scenes of history and legend, his images often dreamlike and faintly sad. The series illustrating the *Legend of the Briar Rose* consists of four large canvases which, as Burne-Jones wrote in a letter to a friend, were intended as a "beautiful romantic dream of something that never was, never will be."

Recommendations

- Have the children turn to pages 88 and 89. Encourage them to talk about what they see in the pictures and anything else they want to discuss about the art shown here.
- Invite the children to respond to each work by asking whether they like it, and why they feel as they do. Ask whether it reminds them of anything they have done.

See Classroom Support **Teacher Tool Card** 2 for additional suggestions for discussing fine art.

TEACHING TIP

Have the children do some partner reading daily. Using previously read Phonics Minibooks and Step-by-Step Practice Stories for this purpose will help the children review and solidify their knowledge of the sounds and spellings they have learned. This is a good opportunity to read with children individually and to record their progress.

* READING ALOUD

A number of books have been written about art and artists. You may want to share one of the following suggestions or another of your own choosing:

The Art Lesson by Tomie dePaola
The Adventures of the Three Colors by Annette Tison and Talus Taylor
Visiting the Art Museum by Laurene Krasney Brown

2 WRITING

* DICTATION AND SPELLING

Word-Building Game Have the children use paper and pencil to play the Word-Building game. The words to use are as follows:

boy
joy
toy
toil
coil
coin
join

At the end of the game, challenge children to build a new word by changing one or more of the sounds in the last word.

Minilesson

Using Describing Words

In *Anansi and the Talking Melon*, the author uses describing words to make this story interesting and fun to read. Describing words tell something about characters or things in the story. Read some phrases from the story that contain good describing words, for example, "skinny hippo" (page 77), "handsome warthog" (page 79) or "stupid melon" (page 84). Identify the describing words, pointing out that *warthog* by itself is less interesting than *handsome warthog*. (Many consider warthogs to be quite unattractive so in this case the description adds humor. Don't worry if the children miss this subtlety.) Describing a melon as *stupid*, a warthog as *handsome*, or a hippo as *skinny* all add to our enjoyment of the story. Then have the children look through any of the stories in their anthologies to find other examples of describing words and have them share these words and phrases with the class. Suggest that the children may want to use describing words in their writing.

TEACHING TIP

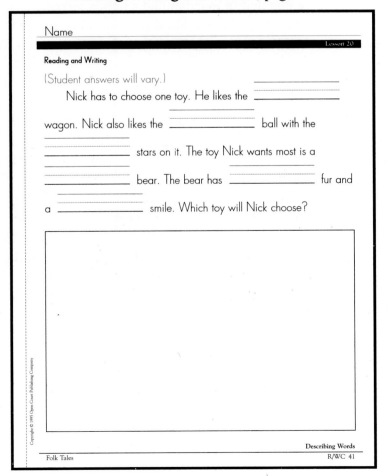

If you made a Revision Chart, you may want to add Using Dialogue and Using Describing Words to the list of things that writers think about when they revise their work.

TEACHING TIP

Remind the children to refer to the Vocabulary Chart for word ideas.

➤ Have the children complete Reading/Writing Connection, page 41, by adding describing words to the story, then have them draw a picture to go with the story.

Reading/Writing Connection, page 41

Name ____________________

Lesson 20

Reading and Writing

(Student answers will vary.)

Nick has to choose one toy. He likes the ________ wagon. Nick also likes the ________ ball with the ________ stars on it. The toy Nick wants most is a ________ bear. The bear has ________ fur and a ________ smile. Which toy will Nick choose?

Folk Tales — Describing Words — R/WC 41

3 GUIDED AND INDEPENDENT EXPLORATION

WORKSHOP

Remind the children that they may use this time to work on projects on their own or in small groups. Be sure that each child knows what projects he or she may choose and how to complete any independent work.

Work with the Teacher

- Play a spelling game with a small group of children. Print the word *coin* on the chalkboard. Blend it, then ask a child to use the word in a sentence. Using scratch paper have the children build the following words. Remind them to use the Sound/Spelling Cards to help them sound the word before they write it. If children are having problems, ask them to identify which sounds need to change. After each change, have a child say the new word and use it in a sentence.

  coil
  cool
  spool
  spoon
  spoil

- Reread *Anansi and the Talking Melon* with the children. Use this opportunity to assess their progress. Since this is a long story, have them read a funny or favorite part.
- Continue to work with the children who are writing a folk tale. Reread to them what they wrote yesterday and ask them for suggestions about how the tale might be revised. They may, for example, want to add some of the describing words that they talked about during today's Writer's Craft lesson. Remind them that the revising poster can help them think of ways to revise their writing. If they seem confused about what to do, you might review the poster with them and prompt them by asking questions about what they might want to add, delete, move, or clarify. Insert their revisons on the draft.

Collaborative/Independent Activities

- The children who are working on a performance of "The Gingerbread Man" should use this time to finish making any scenery, costumes, and props that they have been working on. The children can do a dress rehearsal of their performance during tomorrow's or the next day's Workshop. Set aside some time within the next few days for them to perform for the class.
- **Compound Word Puzzle** Print compound words on cards or strips of paper, then cut the compound words between their smaller words in a puzzle pattern. Give small groups of children several compound word puzzles. Challenge them to make compound words by finding the two smaller words that fit together like a jigsaw puzzle. Encourage them to blend the two words together and then write the words.
- Some of the children may want to return to writing that they have done in their journals and add describing words to some of their pieces.
- Children who have drafted stories about Anansi may want to exchange papers with a partner to critique or proofread each other's work. Remind them to refer to the posters on revising and proofreading.
- Activity Sheet 90 reviews spellings for /oi/ and the *kn* spelling for /n/. Tell the children to find the words that are listed at the top of the page within the cowboy hat. You might want to help them search for and circle the first word, *cowboy*.

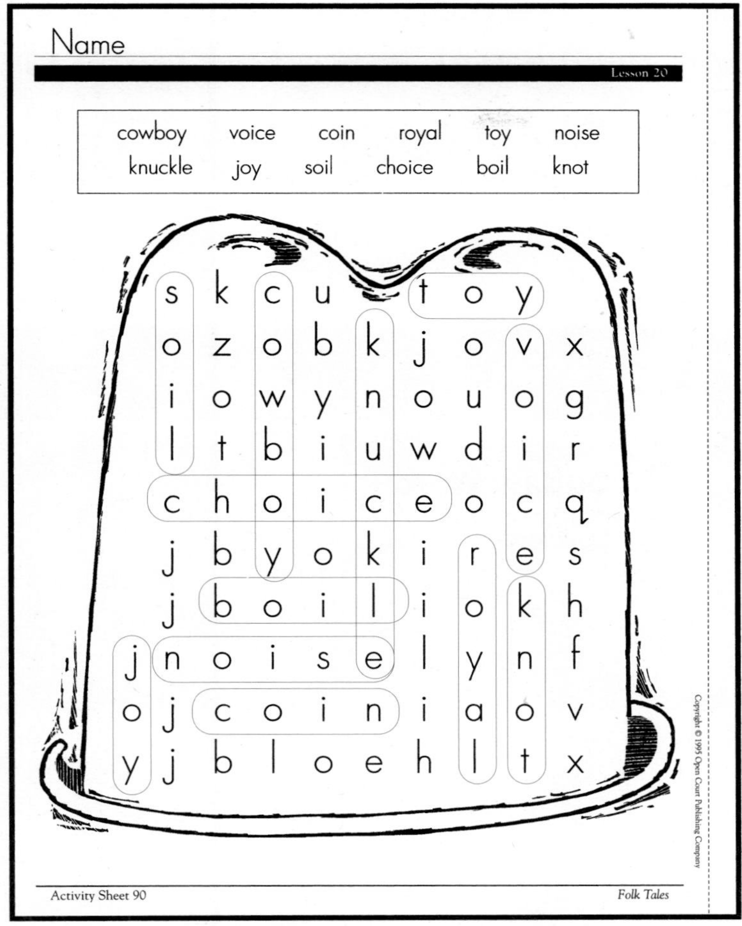
Name

Lesson 20

cowboy voice coin royal toy noise
knuckle joy soil choice boil knot

s k c u t o y
o z o b k j o v x
i o w y n o u o g
l t b i u w d i r
c h o i c e o c q
j b y o k i r e s
j b o i l i o k h
j n o i s e l y n f
o j c o i n i a o v
y j b l o e h l t x

Activity Sheet 90 *Folk Tales*

Activity Sheet 90

LESSON 21

Lesson Overview

Materials

- "The Lion and the Mouse," pages 90–91
- Learning Framework Cards 2, 3, 4, 5, 8
- Reading/Writing Connection, pages 42–43
- Activity Sheet 91

Outlaw Word

trouble

GETTING STARTED

Choose one or both of the following activities to focus the children's attention and to review some of the concepts they have been learning.

Alphabet Game Shuffle the Alphabet Flash Cards and show two cards at a time to the children. Have the children tell which letter comes first. You can vary the activity by holding up three cards at a time.

Fill in the Blank Print the spellings *aw, au, oi,* and *oy* on the chalkboard. Point to one spelling at a time and have the children identify the sound it makes. Then tell the children that you are going to print some words on the chalkboard that are missing some of their letters. The children have to decide which letters belong in the blanks: *aw, au, oi,* or *oy.* Have them write the word with the correct spelling on scratch paper and then tell you how to finish spelling the word.

cl__ ann__ p__se l__n
b__l th__ j__ c__ght
c__se cr__l sp__l j__

1 READING

PHONICS

Adding Endings to Words That End in *y* Print the word *baby* on the chalkboard. Tell the children that you want to change *baby* to *babies* to show there is more than one baby. Ask the children how you should make the new word. Print the new word on the chalkboard. Repeat with other singular and plural words. Example words include *party/parties, lily/lilies, family/families, city/cities*.

Then print the word *try* on the chalkboard. Tell the children that you want to change this word to *tried*. Again, invite a volunteer to print the new word on the chalkboard. Repeat with *cry/cried, worry/worried*, and *hurry/hurried*.

* **Blending** Have the children blend the following words. For reference and additional suggestions for blending, see **Learning Framework Card 3**.

Line 1:	gnaw gnat gnash gnarled
Line 2:	tickle jungle grumble tackle
Line 3:	long strong king string
Line 4:	grateful smile bite rope
Line 5:	green purple brown yellow blue
Sentence:	You'd be in big trouble if it weren't for me.

Words Line 1 introduces the children to /n/ spelled *gn*. Explain that the *g* in *gn* is silent, just like the *k* in *kn*. Together, sound and blend each of the words. If some of the words are unfamiliar to the children, have the children use these words in sentences.

Line 3 contains words that end in *ng*. Invite the children to give other words that follow this pattern. Line 4 reviews vocabulary from "The Lion and the Mouse." Have children use these words in sentences. Line 5 reviews color words.

As a review, point to a word and have a child read it. If the child reads the word correctly, he or she points to a word and asks another child to read it.

Sentence Introduce the outlaw word *trouble*. Write the word on the board and read it. Have the children use the word in sentences. Then write the sentence on the board and have the children read it.

➤ Reading/Writing Connection, page 42, can be completed at this time. Help the children complete the page by reading and copying the words and the sentence.

Name

Lesson 21

Writing Words and Sentences

gnaw gnaw gnat gnat

sign sign design design

The old tree was gnarled.

The old tree was gnarled.

Stop at the sign.

Stop at the sign.

Dictation and Spelling

Consonant Sounds and Spellings

42 R/WC "The Lion and the Mouse"

Reading/Writing Connection, page 42

* READING THE STUDENT ANTHOLOGY

"The Lion and the Mouse"
pages 90–91

About the Selection

How can someone who is very small be a powerful friend to someone who is much larger? "The Lion and the Mouse" illustrates the idea that everyone—no matter how small or weak or young—has special abilities.

Link to the Unit Concept

Telling stories is one of the universal ways in which people express the values and traditions of their cultures. Students will probably be interested to know that people were telling stories more than two thousand years ago. You might discuss the idea that stories that were told long ago in faraway places may still be meaningful to us.

About the Author

Legend has it that Aesop, who lived from about 620 to 560 B.C., was born a slave in Greece and was an entertainer at the court of King Croesus of Lydia, in Asia Minor. Aesop is remembered for writing many fables in which he shows human strengths and weaknesses through the actions and thoughts of animal characters.

Activating Prior Knowledge

Read aloud the title and the name of the author of the selection on page 90. Ask whether students have already heard this story. If so, invite them to listen to see whether the story is the same as the one they have heard. Ask the children what they already know about lions and mice. Remind them that thinking about what they already know can help them understand what they are about to read.

Setting Reading Goals and Expectations

- Have the children browse the selection, looking for words that might be difficult to read or to understand. Invite the children to try to figure out these words as they read.
- Tell the children that this selection is a special kind of folk tale called a fable. Explain that a fable is a short tale that has only a few characters and that often these characters are animals. Fables also teach a lesson about how people should act or think. Review what the children already know about fables. Ask whether they can remember reading any other fables.

Recommendations for Reading

- Have the children read the selection aloud. Call on volunteers to each read two or three sentences as the other children follow along.
- If children are having difficulty reading any of the words, remind them to check the Sound/Spelling Cards, then sound and blend the word. If any words cannot be easily blended, pronounce the words for the children.

Note: Reading the story with a partner is a good option for Workshop.

TEACHING TIP

Set aside ten minutes for partner reading every day. During this time, you should read with individuals, recording their progress.

About the Reading Strategies

In reading this selection, children will need to use the strategies for clarifying unfamiliar words and summarizing. Refer the children to the poster Clarifying Unfamiliar Words and Passages. Explain that you will model using these strategies as you read the selection.

Think-Aloud Prompts for Use in Oral Reading Notice the think-aloud prompts with the page miniatures. These are merely suggestions. Continue to model using appropriate strategies while reading and to encourage children to use the strategies on their own. For a review of information about modeling and generating think-alouds, see **Learning Framework Card 8, Reading the Student Anthologies.**

STRATEGIC
R·E·A·D·I·N·G
PROMPTS
These prompts may be used as guides when working with reading strategies.

1 Encourage the children to wonder about the lion's words. You might say, *The idea that a tiny mouse could help a big lion seems pretty funny to me, too. What do you think?*

2 Have the children summarize the story so far.

3 Ask the children what the word *gnaw* means and how they can tell. Encourage them to use sentence context and/or illustrations.

4 Ask whether anyone knows what *grateful* means. This word is not easily understood from context. Tell the children the meaning of the word if they are unable to figure it out.

5 Invite the children to summarize what happened in the story.

THE LION AND THE MOUSE

Aesop

illustrated by Alexi Natchev

A large lion was napping in the shade
when a little mouse ran across his tummy.
This tickled the lion,
so he grabbed the little mouse.
The mouse squeaked with fear.
"Oh, please don't eat me," squeaked the mouse.
"I'm so small I wouldn't even make one good bite.
Let me go, and some day I could help you."
"Now that's funny!" roared the lion.
"How could a little thing like you
1 ever help me, the king of the jungle?"
2 But the lion let the mouse go.

90

Weeks and weeks went by.

One day the mouse heard the lion
roaring. The lion seemed to be in pain.
The mouse ran to the lion.
He had been caught by hunters.
His paws were tied with rope.
3 The mouse began to gnaw the rope
with his sharp little teeth.
He worked a long, long, time.
At last the lion was free!
The mouse said, "There, you see!
You'd be in big trouble if it weren't for me."
The grateful lion smiled. "So I see, 4
my little friend. So I see." 5

91

Responding

- Ask the children what lesson they have learned from this story. They might suggest several morals, such as the following: When you do something good, something good comes back to you. Even small creatures can do big favors. You can find a friend where you least expect one. Even the small are powerful.

Accept all ideas that fit the story.

- Ask the children how this story is like the other folk tales that they have read in this unit.
- During Workshop, partners may collaborate to make lion and mouse stick puppets and to reenact the story with the puppets.

➤ Reading/Writing Connection, page 43, reviews this selection. Help the children read and complete the page.

TIP FOR ENGLISH LANGUAGE LEARNERS

Provide conversational opportunities for English Language Learners to use creative language. Encourage the children to have a conversation about the illustrations. Pair English Language Learners with each other or native English-speaking children. Encourage partners to talk about the illustrations. Praise the children's efforts at using language.

Reading/Writing Connection, page 43

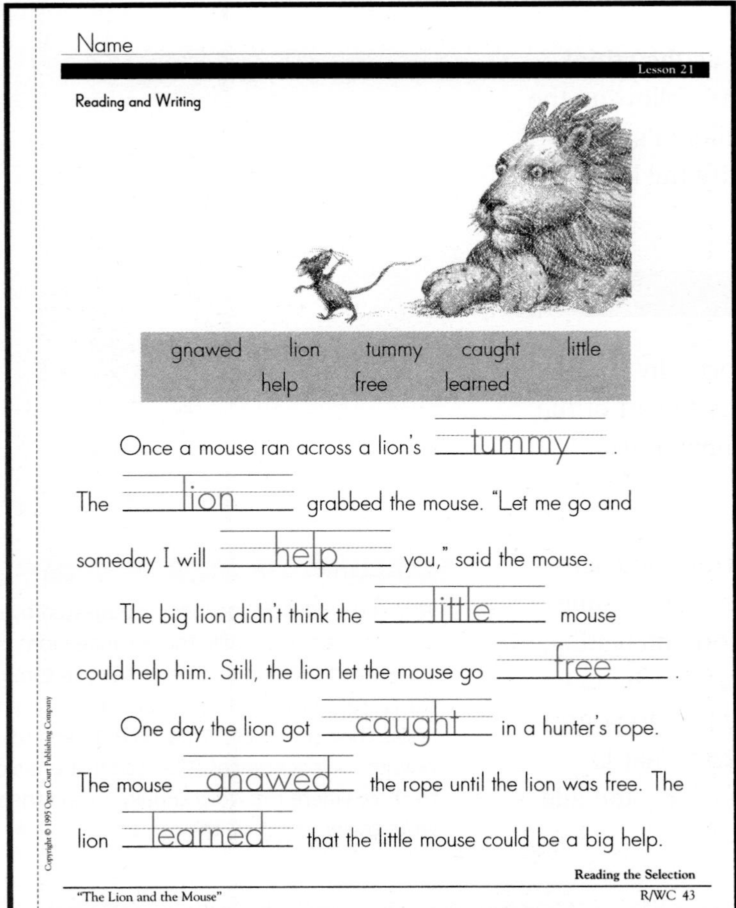

Name

Lesson 21

Reading and Writing

gnawed lion tummy caught little
help free learned

Once a mouse ran across a lion's tummy.

The lion grabbed the mouse. "Let me go and someday I will help you," said the mouse.

The big lion didn't think the little mouse could help him. Still, the lion let the mouse go free.

One day the lion got caught in a hunter's rope. The mouse gnawed the rope until the lion was free. The lion learned that the little mouse could be a big help.

Copyright © 1995 Open Court Publishing Company

Reading the Selection

"The Lion and the Mouse" R/WC 43

* READING ALOUD

"The Lion and the Mouse," demonstrates that even a little mouse can be a hero in the right situation. The children might enjoy hearing other stories of unlikely heroes, such as the following:

A Hero by Mistake by Anita Brenner
The Steadfast Tin Soldier by Hans Christian Andersen, translated by M. R. James
The Velveteen Rabbit by Margery Williams

See **Learning Framework Card 5** for suggestions for modeling as you read aloud.

2 WRITING

* DICTATION AND SPELLING

Have the children turn to page 42 of their Reading/Writing Connection. Dictate the following words and sentence, using the suggestions for dictation that appear on **Learning Framework Card 4.**

Line 1: coin boil toy

Line 2: slowly softly mostly

Sentence: The boy played quietly.

Remind the children to use the Sound/Spelling Cards as they think about the spellings. Help the children proofread each line, following the guidelines on **Learning Framework Card 2.** Call the children's attention to the words *played* and *quietly*. Ask them to identify the base words and the endings.

EXPLORING THE WRITER'S CRAFT

Using *Anansi and the Talking Melon* or any other stories in the anthology, have the children draw a picture of their favorite part of the story and write a sentence about that picture. Remind them to use describing words.

During Seminar have several children share their pictures and sentences. When the students have finished, make comments or ask questions that will help the children make their sentences more interesting, for example, "What else can you tell us about your picture?" "In your picture, you have a long, fat worm. You may want to add *fat* to your sentence." "What is special about the animal you drew?" "What is funny about your animal?" Leave time for children to go back and add their describing words to their sentences.

TEACHING TIP

Write down describing words suggested by the class or the author. Give these suggestions to the author and suggest that he or she use some of the words in the sentence. Have the children revise their sentences. They do not need to rewrite their sentences. They can just use a caret to show where the word should go and then write the word above the caret.

3 GUIDED AND INDEPENDENT EXPLORATION

WORKSHOP

Remind the children that they may use this time to work on projects on their own or in small groups. Be sure that each child knows what projects he or she may choose and how to complete any independent work. Suggestions for teacher-guided, collaborative, and independent activities follow.

Learning Framework Card 11, Workshop, contains a complete discussion of establishing and conducting Workshop and suggestions for helping English Language Learners during Workshop.

Work with the Teacher

- Hold a Reading Relay between two teams of children. Include among the flash cards a number of words ending in *-ly,* as well as some words that contain the sound /oi/ spelled *oi* or *oy.* Words you might use include *slowly, quickly, quietly, closely, nicely, sadly, gladly, boy, toy, joyful, enjoy, annoy, noisy, coil, boil,* and *coin.*
- To review /n/ spelled *kn* and *gn,* write words that begin with *kn, gn, n, k,* and *g* on the chalkboard. Words you might use include *gnarled, gnat, gnash, gnaw, grateful, girl, garden, grow, know, kneecap, knot, knight, knife, nightmare, need, noisy, nasty, nicely, kite, king, kettle.* Have the children read the words.
- Conference with the children who are writing a folk tale. Reread the children's tale with them and help make any additional revisions that they suggest. If they are satisfied with the tale, have them begin proofreading it. Review the steps on the proofreading poster.

Collaborative/Independent Activities

- Children who are preparing a performance of "The Gingerbread Man" may be ready to do a final rehearsal before performing for the class.
- Pairs of children might enjoy making stick puppets of the lion and the mouse and use them to reenact the story.
- Encourage the children to read independently or with a partner. Make available some collections of Aesop's fables that have been retold especially for young children. *The Best of Aesop's Fables,* retold by Margaret Clark and illustrated by Charlotte Voake, is one such collection.
- Distribute Activity Sheet 91 and tell the children to complete each statement by adding words that answer the question.

ASSESSMENT Give the students the multiple choice written test. See the Assessment Booklet for instructions.

Name

Lesson 21

(Student answers will vary.)

1. Mother was happy

(Why?)

2. We found the hidden prize

(Where?)

3. A kitten ran away

(When?)

4. The children surprised their teacher

(How?)

"The Lion and the Mouse" Activity Sheet 91

Activity Sheet 91

LESSON 22

Lesson Overview

Materials

- "The Lion and the Mouse," pages 90–91
- Learning Framework Cards 3, 5
- Reading/Writing Connection, pages 44–45
- Activity Sheet 92

Prepare Ahead

- Scrambled Sentences (see page 243)

GETTING STARTED

Choose one or both of the following activities to focus the children's attention and to review some of the concepts they have been learning.

Which Doesn't Belong? Write the words *noodle, knot,* and *poodle* on the chalkboard. Blend all three words, then ask the children to write on a piece of paper which word doesn't belong in the group. Call on several students to show which word they wrote down and explain why they decided that word didn't belong. Repeat with other sets of words, such as: *good, food, goof; gnaw, know, claw;* and *knew, clue, crude.*

TEACHING TIP

Accept any response the children can justify. Some may say that *knot* is different because it doesn't rhyme with the other two. Others may decide that *poodle* doesn't belong because it doesn't begin with /n/.

Add to the Pattern Review the Coil and Hawk Sound/Spelling Cards. To help the children become more confident writing words for which there are various possible spellings, print *oi, oy, aw,* and *au* on the chalkboard. Print the following words in another area of the board: *oil, coin, boy, loyal, claw, hawk, August, applaud.* Then invite children to read any word and write it under the correct spelling. Ask children to suggest words to add to each list.

Review the words by asking, "Which word is *loyal*?" Have a child touch the word, read it, and circle the target spelling. That child should then choose another word and ask a classmate to find it. Continue with different children selecting the word each time.

1 READING

PHONICS

* **Blending** Have the children blend the following words and sentences. For reference and additional suggestions for blending, see **Learning Framework Card 3.**

Line 1:	**crackle pickle tingle tangle**
Line 2:	**tremble stumble simple sample**
Line 3:	**enjoyment fantastic responsible**
Line 4:	**mound count frown growl**
Line 5:	**ought bought brought fought thought**

Lines 1 and 2 review short vowel words that end in *-le*. Have the words used in sentences.

The children may need some help decoding three- and four-syllable words in line 3. Help the children blend the words syllable by syllable.

Line 4 focuses on words with the sound /ow/.

In line 5, the words contain the *ough* spelling for /aw/. Review the spellings the children have already learned: *aw, au,* and *augh.* Tell the children that sometimes the spelling pattern *ough* makes the same sound. Write the words and help the children sound and blend the words. Have the children use them in sentences.

Review the words by giving clues such as the following, and then having the children erase each word they read:

- rhymes with *tickle*
- an upside-down smile
- another word for *wonderful*

➤ Ask volunteers to give clues to their classmates for the remaining words. Reading/Writing Connection, page 44, can be completed at this time.

* READING THE STUDENT ANTHOLOGY

"The Lion and the Mouse"

pages 90–91

Activating Prior Knowledge

Ask the children to turn to page 90 in their readers. Then ask them what they remember about this fable from their previous reading.

Recommendations for Reading

- Call on volunteers to read the selection aloud, a few sentences at a time, as the other children follow along.

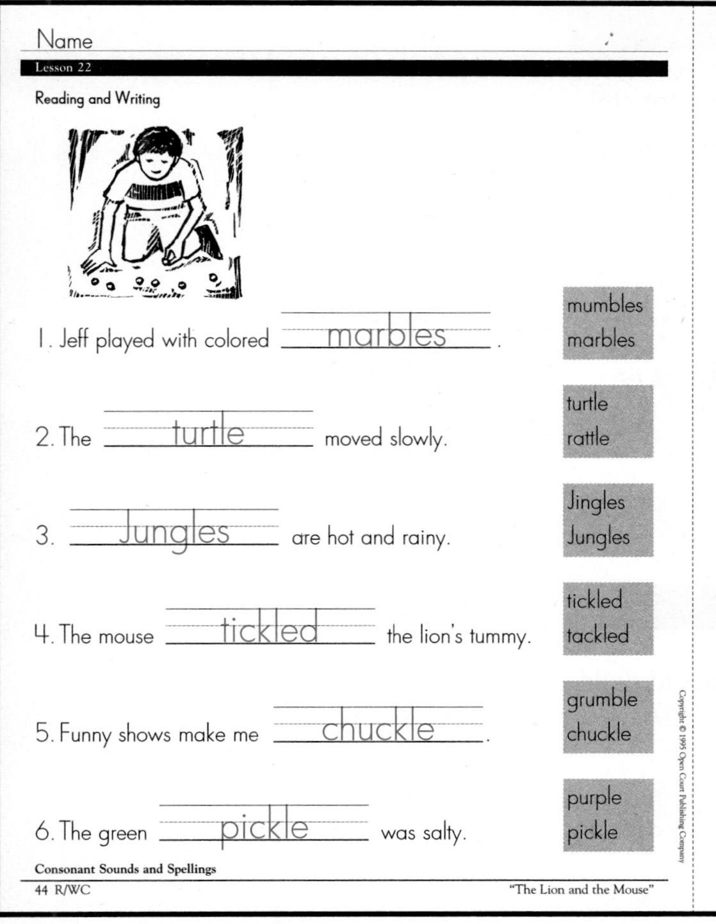
Name

Lesson 22

Reading and Writing

1. Jeff played with colored marbles. (mumbles / marbles)

2. The turtle moved slowly. (turtle / rattle)

3. Jungles are hot and rainy. (Jingles / Jungles)

4. The mouse tickled the lion's tummy. (tickled / tackled)

5. Funny shows make me chuckle. (grumble / chuckle)

6. The green pickle was salty. (purple / pickle)

Consonant Sounds and Spellings

44 R/WC "The Lion and the Mouse"

Copyright © 1995 Open Court Publishing Company

Reading/Writing Connection, page 44

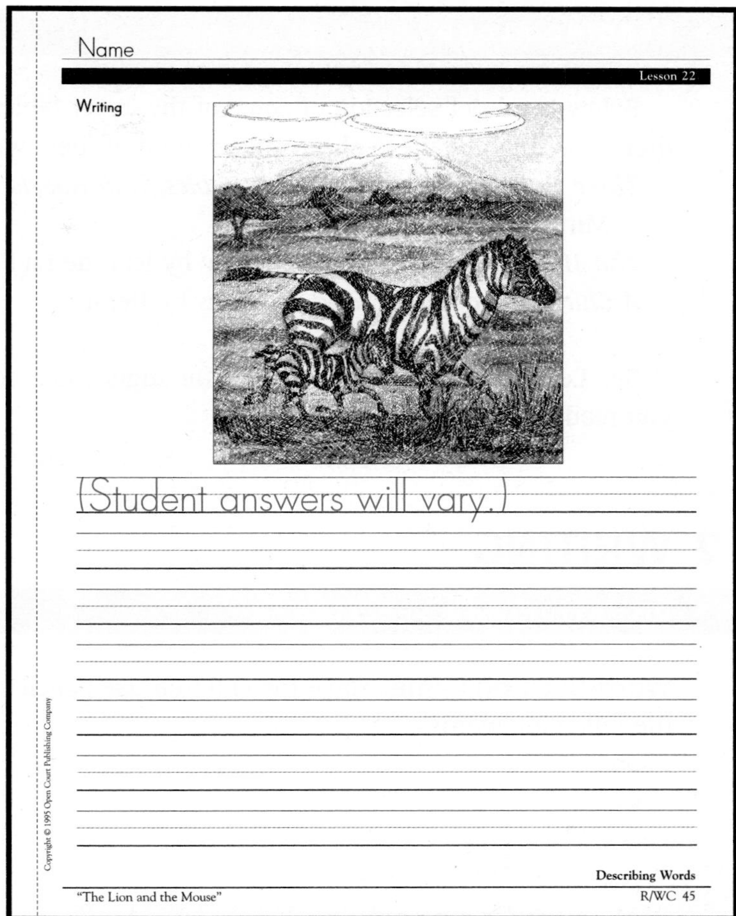
Name

Lesson 22

Writing

(Student answers will vary.)

Describing Words

"The Lion and the Mouse" R/WC 45

Copyright © 1995 Open Court Publishing Company

Reading/Writing Connection, page 45

Responding

- Ask the children what they like about this story and why.
- Help the children connect what they have read to what they thought about lions and mice before reading the selection. Ask in what ways the lion and the mouse acted as a real lion and mouse would.
- Discuss any new ideas or questions that the children might like to add to the Concept Board. Review the information on the board.
- Review why this selection is a fable. The children may mention that a fable teaches a lesson, has only a few characters, and often uses animals as characters.

Vocabulary Discuss any interesting or unusual words from the selection that the children might want to use in their writing. Add these words to the Vocabulary Chart and have children use them in oral sentences. Possible words are *squeaked* and *grateful.*

➤ Reading/Writing Connection, page 45, can be completed at this time. Discuss the picture and have children suggest describing words they would use. Have them write sentences to describe the picture.

TEACHING TIP

Have the children do some partner reading daily. Using previously read Phonics Minibooks and Step-by-Step Practice Stories for this purpose will help the children review and solidify their knowledge of the sounds and spellings they have learned. This is a good opportunity to read with children individually and to record their progress.

* READING ALOUD

Below is a brief selection of some of the many fables written for children. You might want to share one or more of them with your class.

Three Rolls and One Doughnut: Fables from Russia by Mirra Ginsburg
The Miller, the Boy and the Donkey by Jean de La Fontaine
A Chinese Zoo: Fables and Proverbs by Demi

See **Learning Framework Card 5** for suggestions for modeling as you read aloud.

2 WRITING

* DICTATION AND SPELLING

Word-Building Game Have the children use pencil and paper to build the following words:

gnaw
jaw
raw
paw
pause (give a sentence)
cause (give a sentence)
claws (give a sentence)
crawl

INDEPENDENT AND COLLABORATIVE WRITING

Start with Seminar. Continue having children share their describing sentences, asking questions and making comments that lead students to adding describing words. Since you modeled these in Lesson 21, encourage the children to ask the questions and make the comments to help each other.

Have children revise their sentences. If several children have described animals from the same story, they may want to work together to make a poster with their pictures and sentences on it. Have them make a title for the poster, for example "The Special Animals in Anansi," and then paste their pictures with sentences on a large sheet. As an alternative, children may want to cut their pictures apart from their sentences and play a game in which they match the picture to the sentence.

TEACHING TIP

Children do not have to redraw their pictures when they rewrite their sentences. Simply have them cut their sentence off the page, paste the picture to a clean sheet, and then rewrite the revised sentence.

3 GUIDED AND INDEPENDENT EXPLORATION

WORKSHOP

Remind the children that they may use this time to work on projects of their own or in small groups. Be sure that each child knows what projects he or she may choose and how to complete any independent work. Suggestions for teacher-guided, collaborative, and independent activities follow.

Work with the Teacher

- Play the Word-Building game with those children who have been having difficulty during Dictation and Spelling. Repeat today's game, or choose a previous game, depending on the children's needs.
- Obtain a collection of Aesop's fables written for a first-grade reading level and have children read them to you. Invite other children to listen in.
- Continue to work with the children who are writing a folk tale. If the proofreading is finished, the children should be ready to publish their tale. They may want to publish the tale as a Big Book, using chart paper for the pages, and alternating each page of print with a page of illustrations. You can help each child to recopy one or two sentences of the tale onto the chart paper, reminding him or her to print as neatly as possible. While one child writes with you, the others can work on the illustrations.
- Read "The Wolf in Sheep's Clothing" with children to help them prepare for the next lesson.

TEACHING TIP Encourage the children to read to each other. You, too, should choose children to read with. As you read with each child, note his or her progress.

Collaborative/Independent Activities

- Children who have been working on a performance of "The Gingerbread Man" should finish any remaining work at this time. If the children are ready, you might want to set aside all or part of today's Workshop session for them to perform, or set aside some time later in the day or week.
- Children who made Lion and Mouse puppets might want to act out the fable for small groups of classmates.
- Some of the children can play Scrambled Sentences. Prepare some new sentences for them, incorporating the spellings they have learned recently. Suggest that when they have unscrambled their sentences, the children can write their own scrambled sentences for others to solve.
- To review *-le* words, write the following words on cards:

kettle	bubble	fiddle	apple	whistle
eagle	table	candle	beetle	wriggle
castle	icicle	tickle	jungle	freckle
pickle	bottle	uncle		

  Have two children pick one word each. Each child should read his or her word, then they should work together to make up a sentence that contains both words. Encourage the children to make their sentences as funny as possible. As an extra challenge, groups of three might create a sentence using their words. Have the children write their sentences.
- Activity Sheet 92 provides practice reading. Tell the children to read the sentences and to paste them under the correct pictures.

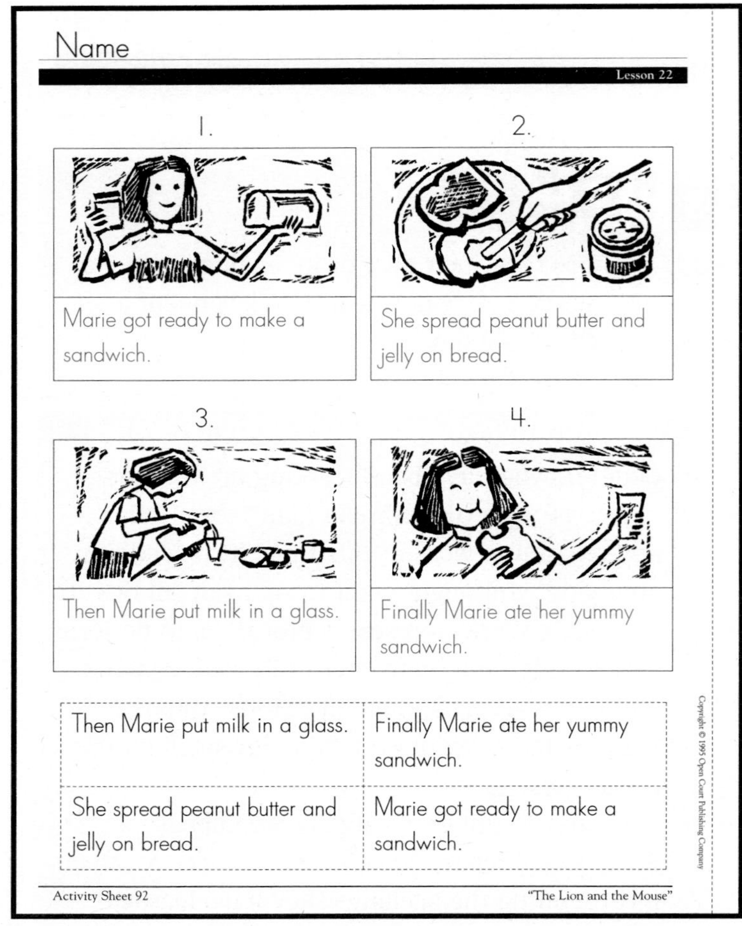

Name
Lesson 22
1.
Marie got ready to make a sandwich.
2.
She spread peanut butter and jelly on bread.
3.
Then Marie put milk in a glass.
4.
Finally Marie ate her yummy sandwich.
Then Marie put milk in a glass.
Finally Marie ate her yummy sandwich.
She spread peanut butter and jelly on bread.
Marie got ready to make a sandwich.
Copyright © 1995 Open Court Publishing Company
Activity Sheet 92
"The Lion and the Mouse"

Activity Sheet 92

LESSON 23

Lesson Overview

New Learning

- Speaker Tags

Materials

- "The Wolf in Sheep's Clothing," pages 92–93
- Learning Framework Cards 3, 4, 5, 8
- Reading/Writing Connection, pages 46–47
- Alphabet Flash Cards
- Activity Sheet 93

Prepare Ahead

- Word Flash Cards (see page 245)
- Bingo Cards (see page 252)

GETTING STARTED

Choose one or both of the following activities to focus the children's attention and to review some of the concepts they have been learning.

Alphabet Game Shuffle the Alphabet Flash Cards and display two at a time to students. The student should tell which of the two letters comes first. Make the activity more challenging by showing three cards at a time.

Tic-Tac-Toe This game reviews words with the /ow/ sound and focuses the children's attention on the different spellings of this sound.

Print the following words on the chalkboard: *round, cow, owl, shout, crown, mouth, ounce, towel, shower, count, growl, trousers, pouch, brown, spout, crowded, frown, cloud, bounce, flower*. Blend each word with the children.

Have pairs of children draw a Tic-Tac-Toe grid on a sheet of paper or on a slate and fill in the grid with some of the words on the chalkboard. The children place the words wherever they choose, using each word only once.

Read the words and have the children cross out each one on their grid. The goal is to cross out a straight line.

1 READING

PHONICS

✱ **Blending** Have the children blend the following words and sentences. For reference and additional suggestions for blending, see **Learning Framework Card 3.**

Line 1:	**jumped dressed raced grabbed**
Line 2:	**quick queen squawk squirt**
Line 3:	**wink blink shrink twinkle**
Line 4:	**shepherd clothing**
Line 5:	**sheep retrieve secret theme puppy**

Line 1 reviews words with *-ed* endings. Ask the children what happens to the base word in each word. For example, for *jumped* you simply add *-ed* to the base word and for *grabbed* you double the final consonant on the base word, then add *-ed.*

Line 3 focuses on the *nk* spelling. Invite them to suggest words in which *nk* is preceded by *a, o,* and *u* (for example, *bank, honk,* and *skunk*).

Line 4 presents vocabulary from "The Wolf in Sheep's Clothing."

After the children sound and blend the words in line 5, call individual children to tell which spelling of long *e* is represented in each word. You may want to have them underline each spelling. Encourage them to refer to Sound/Spelling Card 37, Long E.

Words such as *squawk, retrieve,* and *theme* may be unfamiliar to the children. Ask volunteers to use these words and any others in sentences.

To review the words, call out a line number and word number, for example, line 2, word 3, and have volunteers read the word.

➤ The top portion of Reading/Writing Connection, page 46, can be completed at this time. Have the children select the correct word to complete each sentence.

✱ READING THE STUDENT ANTHOLOGY

"The Wolf in Sheep's Clothing"
pages 92–93

About the Selection

A wolf decides to disguise himself as a sheep. Will anyone see through his actions?

Link to the Unit Concept

This brief fable illustrates timeless truths that occur frequently in folk literature—actions speak louder than words, looks can be deceiving, and so forth.

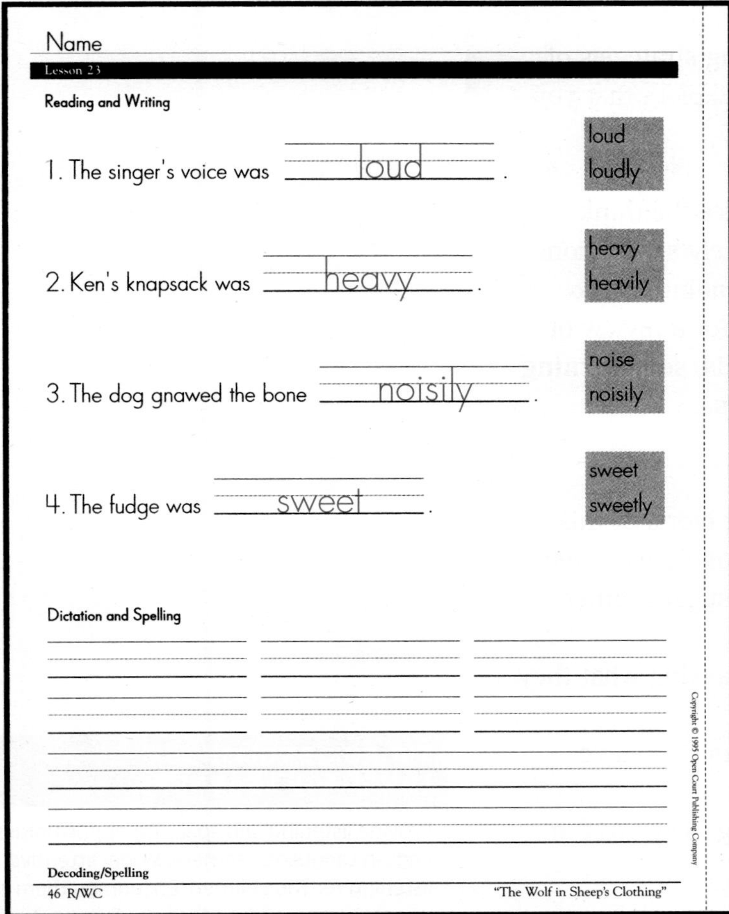
Name

Lesson 23

Reading and Writing

1. The singer's voice was loud. (loud / loudly)

2. Ken's knapsack was heavy. (heavy / heavily)

3. The dog gnawed the bone noisily. (noise / noisily)

4. The fudge was sweet. (sweet / sweetly)

Dictation and Spelling

Decoding/Spelling

46 R/WC "The Wolf in Sheep's Clothing"

Reading/Writing Connection, page 46

Activating Prior Knowledge

Read aloud the title of the selection and the author on page 92. Have the children tell what they remember about the fable they read in the previous lesson. Ask if anyone has already heard this story. If so, invite them to listen to see whether the story is the same as the one they have already heard.

Setting Reading Goals and Expectations

- Have the children browse the selection and point out any words that may be difficult to read or understand. Encourage the children to try to figure out these words as they read.

Recommendations for Reading

- Have the children read the selection aloud. If children are having difficulty blending any of the words, remind them to check the Sound/Spelling Cards. If any words cannot be easily blended, pronounce the words for the children.
- Invite the children to tell what they think about the story as it is being read, and to ask questions about story words and ideas.

Note: Reading this selection in pairs is a good option for Workshop.

TEACHING TIP

You, too, should choose children to read with. As you read with each child, note his or her progress.

About the Reading Strategies

In reading this selection, children will find the reading strategies of wondering, clarifying words, and summing up useful. Explain that you will model these strategies as you read the selection.

Think-Aloud Prompts for Use in Oral Reading Notice the think-aloud prompts with the page miniatures. These are merely suggestions. Continue to model using appropriate strategies while reading and to encourage children to use the strategies on their own. For a review of information about modeling and generating think-alouds, see **Learning Framework Card 8, Reading the Student Anthologies.**

Responding

- Encourage the children to discuss what the lesson or moral of this story might be. The children may suggest that you can't always tell what something is by the way it looks, or they may suggest other morals. Accept all ideas that fit with the story.
- Encourage the children to express their opinions by asking what they thought about the characters in the story.
- Have the children discuss how this fable is like others they have read. How is it different?
- During Workshop, the children may enjoy illustrating "The Wolf in Sheep's Clothing."

TIP FOR ENGLISH LANGUAGE LEARNERS

Provide listening and speaking opportunities for English Language Learners. Model attentive listening for the children. Encourage them to sum up what some of the other children have said about the fable during the classroom discussion. Then ask them to add anything they want to about their own ideas about the fable. Praise the children's listening and speaking efforts.

* READING ALOUD

The children might enjoy hearing more fables. You might share one or more of the following with them during the time set aside for reading aloud:

Doctor Coyote: A Native American Aesop's Fable by John Bierhorst
Old Man Whickutt's Donkey by Mary Calhoun
The Town Mouse and the Country Mouse by Janet Stevens

See **Learning Framework Card 5** for suggestions for modeling as you read aloud.

STRATEGIC
R·E·A·D·I·N·G
PROMPTS
These prompts may be used as guides when working with reading strategies.

1 Encourage the children to wonder about the wolf's actions. You might say, *I wonder what the wolf is up to?*

2 Model wondering by saying something like, *I wonder how the shepherd could tell that he was a wolf?*

3 Ask the children what *drove* means in this sentence and how they can tell. Then ask volunteers to sum up the story.

THE WOLF IN SHEEP'S CLOTHING

Aesop
illustrated by Normand Chartier

Once upon a time a hungry wolf saw some sheep in a pen. "If I could live in that pen, I would never have to hunt for my dinner again," said the wolf.

The wolf found an old sheep's skin.
1 He put it over him and jumped into the pen.

Quick as a wink, the wolf grabbed a nice, fat sheep.

The shepherd saw what the wolf was doing. He raced over with a big stick in his hand.

"Stop!" he cried.

"Don't yell at me," said the wolf. I'm just one of your sheep."

2 "No," said the shepherd. "You are a wolf."

"How do you know?" asked the wolf.

"You may be dressed like a sheep," said the shepherd, "but you act like a wolf."

Then the shepherd drove the wolf away. 3

93

2 WRITING

* DICTATION AND SPELLING

Have the children turn to page 46 of their Reading/Writing Connection book. Dictate the following words and sentence, using the suggestions for dictation that appear on **Learning Framework Card 4.**

MONITORING DICTATION Collect students' Reading/Writing Connection books. Scan them to see how the children are doing both in writing the words and sentences as well as in proofreading. Record your notes and place them in the students' folders.

Line 1: **gnat knock nurse**

Line 2: **bring stung strong**

Sentence: **The rat gnaws on the string.**

Help the children proofread each line, following the guidelines on **Learning Framework Card 4.** As the children proofread line 1 and the sentence, draw their attention to the *gn* spelling.

Minilesson

Speaker Tags

Speaker tags are those statements that let the reader know who is speaking—"said the duck," for example. Children often repeat the same word—usually "said" in their own writing. Yet these can easily be made more descriptive. In "The Lion and the Mouse" the author used terms like "roared the lion" and "squeaked the mouse." These are more descriptive, letting us know how the animals spoke. These words often express feelings as well; for example, "cheered the crowd." Have the children revisit stories they have read and find places where authors used words other than "said" along with the person who did the speaking. Generate a list of these words. Encourage children to brainstorm other words as well: *screamed, yelled, called,* and the like. Keep this list for the children to use in Lesson 24 as they begin work on a cumulative story that incorporates descriptive words, dialogue, and speaker tags.

➤ Working with the class, have the children complete Reading/Writing Connection, page 47. They should select a speaker tag to complete each sentence.

If there is time, children can look for places where they used dialogue in their stories and see whether they want to change any of the speaker tags. Others may want to write in their journals.

Name

Lesson 23

Reading and Writing

"Let's make a house!" squeaked the mouse.

"Over there!" roared the bear.

"Next to the log," barked the dog.

"Near the thicket," chirped the cricket.

"By the tree," buzzed the bee.

"Under the twig," oinked the pig.

"I'll use my plow," mooed the cow.

"I'll use my rake," hissed the snake.

"I'll use my trowel," hooted the owl.

"I'll make it flat," purred the cat.

"I'll rest then!" clucked the hen.

roared
squeaked
purred
barked
hooted
clucked
mooed
chirped
hissed
buzzed
oinked

Speaker Tags

"The Wolf in Sheep's Clothing" R/WC 47

Reading/Writing Connection, page 47

3 GUIDED AND INDEPENDENT EXPLORATION

WORKSHOP

Remind the children that they may use this time to work on projects on their own or in small groups. Be sure that each child knows what projects he or she may choose and how to complete any independent work. Suggestions for teacher-guided, collaborative, and independent activities follow.

Learning Framework Card 11, Workshop, contains a complete discussion of establishing and conducting Workshop and suggestions for helping English Language Learners during Workshop.

Work with the Teacher

- To assess their progress, repeat today's Blending exercise with a small group of children. Then have them return to "The Wolf in Sheep's Clothing" and locate the following words from the blending lines: *jumped, dressed, raced, grabbed, wink, shepherd, clothing,* and *sheep.* As a hint, tell the children that one of the words *(clothing)* can be found only in the title of the selection. Each time a child finds a word, have him or her tell which word it is. Have the child then read aloud the sentence in which the word is located.
- Play Bingo with a small group of children. Include the following spellings on their Bingo cards and in the words you call out : *gn-* and *kn-; -ckle, -ngle, -rtle, -rgle,* and *-mble.* Words you might use include *know, knew, knot, knight, gnaw, gnash, gnarled, gnat, tackle, tickle, buckle, jingle, single, bangle, turtle, startle, gurgle, gargle, ramble, mumble, jumble, nimble.*
- Repeat today's dictation lesson for children who had difficulty during the lesson. If time permits, you might extend the lesson by adding the words *stronger* and *strongest* to line 2, and/or adding the following sentence: *The gnat stung the nurse on the knee.*
- If the children have not yet finished publishing their folk tale, continue at this time to help them recopy it onto fresh sheets of chart paper.

Collaborative/Independent Activities

- Encourage peer tutoring by pairing independent readers with less confident readers for partner reading. Have the children reread "The Lion and the Mouse" or "The Wolf in Sheep's Clothing," or provide them with a collection of fables to choose from. Instead of Aesop's fables, you may want to locate some fables from other parts of the world.
- The children who have been working on a folk tale can meet at this time to finish their illustrations and make a cover for their tale. When they finish, they should put the tale on display for their classmates to peruse.
- Children who began making posters during Seminar can continue their work at this time.
- Activity Sheet 93 focuses on *-le* words. Tell the children that they can complete the words in each box by filling in the correct vowels. Explain that sometimes more than one vowel will fit in a word, but the other words in the box will help determine which letter to use. Each of the vowels provided may only be used once, and there is only one right combination of letters in the words. The children may want to work in pairs to complete this activity sheet.

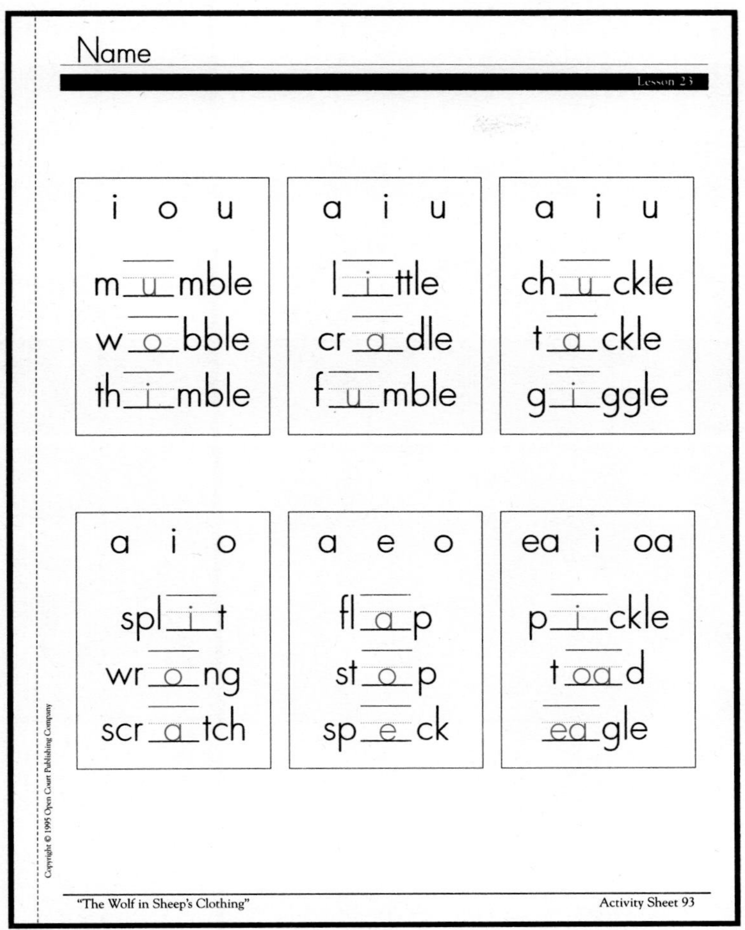
Name

Lesson 23

i o u	a i u	a i u
m_u_mble	l_i_ttle	ch_u_ckle
w_o_bble	cr_a_dle	t_a_ckle
th_i_mble	f_u_mble	g_i_ggle

a i o	a e o	ea i oa
spl_i_t	fl_a_p	p_i_ckle
wr_o_ng	st_o_p	t_oa_d
scr_a_tch	sp_e_ck	_ea_gle

"The Wolf in Sheep's Clothing" Activity Sheet 93

Activity Sheet 93

LESSON 24

Lesson Overview

Materials

- "The Wolf in Sheep's Clothing," pages 92–93
- Learning Framework Cards 3, 5
- Reading/Writing Connection, pages 48–49
- Activity Sheet 94

GETTING STARTED

Choose one or both of the following activities to focus the children's attention and to review some of the concepts they have been learning.

Team Words Game Have the children sit in teams and give each team a sheet of paper. Write the spelling *igh* on the chalkboard. The first member of each team should write a word using the *igh* spelling and pass the paper to the next team member to write a new word. Continue until each member has written a word. Have the teams compare their lists.

Find a Word Game Write words on the chalkboard that contain various vowel sounds and spellings. Use at least fifteen words, such as *coat, tail, moon, tuna, tree, team, staple, cape, mind, light, here, few, cute, nice, pile, robe.* Name a vowel Sound/Spelling Card and have a child find and read a word that contains that sound. The child should identify the spelling used in the word, then erase the word. Continue with other children.

1 READING

PHONICS

Review /j/ and /g/ Sounds Take down the Gopher and Jump Rope Sound/Spelling Cards and place them far apart. Write the following words on the board. Have the children read each word and point to Jump Rope or Gopher according to the sound the *g* makes in the word.

bridge	cage	gentle
giant	get	large
goat	gem	

➤ Reading/Writing Connection, page 48, reviews the /j/ and /g/ sounds. Have the children read the story and write the /j/ and /g/ words under the correct Sound/Spelling Card.

* **Blending** Have the children blend the following words and sentences. For reference and additional suggestions for blending, see **Learning Framework Card 3.**

Reading/Writing Connection, page 48

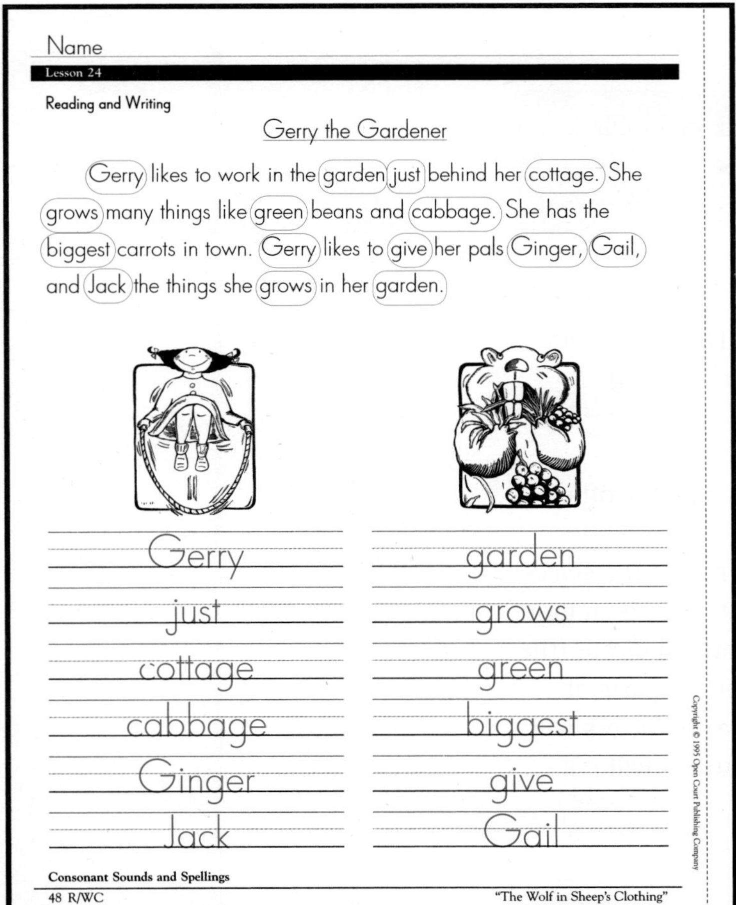

Name

Lesson 24

Reading and Writing

Gerry the Gardener

Gerry likes to work in the garden just behind her cottage. She grows many things like green beans and cabbage. She has the biggest carrots in town. Gerry likes to give her pals Ginger, Gail, and Jack the things she grows in her garden.

Gerry	garden
just	grows
cottage	green
cabbage	biggest
Ginger	give
Jack	Gail

Consonant Sounds and Spellings

48 R/WC "The Wolf in Sheep's Clothing"

Line 1:	**happy unhappy unhappiness happily**
Line 2:	**strike find shy tried frighten**
Line 3:	**here shore share hire cure**
Line 4:	**beagle bugle stable title total**
Line 5:	**broom shook balloon football**

Line 1 shows how a base word changes as prefixes and suffixes are added. Point out that to make *happy* into *unhappy*, you add the prefix *un*. Explain that this prefix means *not* and give other examples where it is used; for example, *lucky/unlucky*, *tie/untie*, *safe/unsafe*. To go from *unhappy* to *unhappiness*, you change the *y* to *i* and add *-ness*. Finally, to form *happily*, you change the *y* in *happy* to *i*, then add *-ly*.

Line 2 reviews the different long *i* spellings. Have the children circle each one, using Sound/Spelling Card 34, Long I, as a guide. The focus on long vowels continues in line 3, where each word contains a long vowel followed by a consonant and silent *e*, and in line 4, where long vowels appear in two-syllable words.

Line 5 reviews the two sounds for the *oo* spelling. If the children are unsure of a word, they should try both sounds as they blend the word.

Review the words by having the children fill in the blank in sentences such as the following:

She skipped _____ down the street. (*happily*)
The baby hid behind his father's back because he was _____. (*shy*)
Roberto blew a _____ to wake up his family. (*bugle*)

Encourage the children to give clues to each other.

✱ READING THE STUDENT ANTHOLOGY

"The Wolf in Sheep's Clothing"
pages 92–93

Activating Prior Knowledge

Ask the children to turn to page 92 in their readers. Then ask them what they remember about this fable from their previous reading.

Recommendations for Reading

- Call on individuals to read two or three sentences each as the other children follow along.
- To emphasize the use of dialogue, have the children reread the selection by taking the parts of the characters. Point out the words in quotation marks and ask the children what quotation marks indicate (the words a character speaks). Then accept volunteers for the parts of one or two narrators, the shepherd, and the wolf. The characters will read the lines within quotation marks, and the narrator(s) will read the other parts of the story.

Responding

- Ask the children what they liked about this story and why.
- Ask the children why this story is considered a fable. (Point out that the animal characters in a fable often act as people might.)
- Ask the children to comment on the kind of person the wolf might represent by asking something like, "In what ways did the wolf act or think like a wolf? In what ways did the wolf act or think like a person?"

Vocabulary Have the children discuss any interesting or unusual words from the selection. Ask them to use the words in oral sentences. They may want to add these to the Vocabulary Chart or their journals to use in their own writing.

➤ Reading/Writing Connection, page 49, reviews this selection. Have the children use the words in the box to complete the sentences.

TEACHING TIP

Have the children do some partner reading daily. Using previously read Phonics Minibooks and Step-by-Step Practice Stories for this purpose will help the children review and solidify their knowledge of the sounds and spellings they have learned. This is a good opportunity to read with children individually and to record their progress.

Reading/Writing Connection, page 49

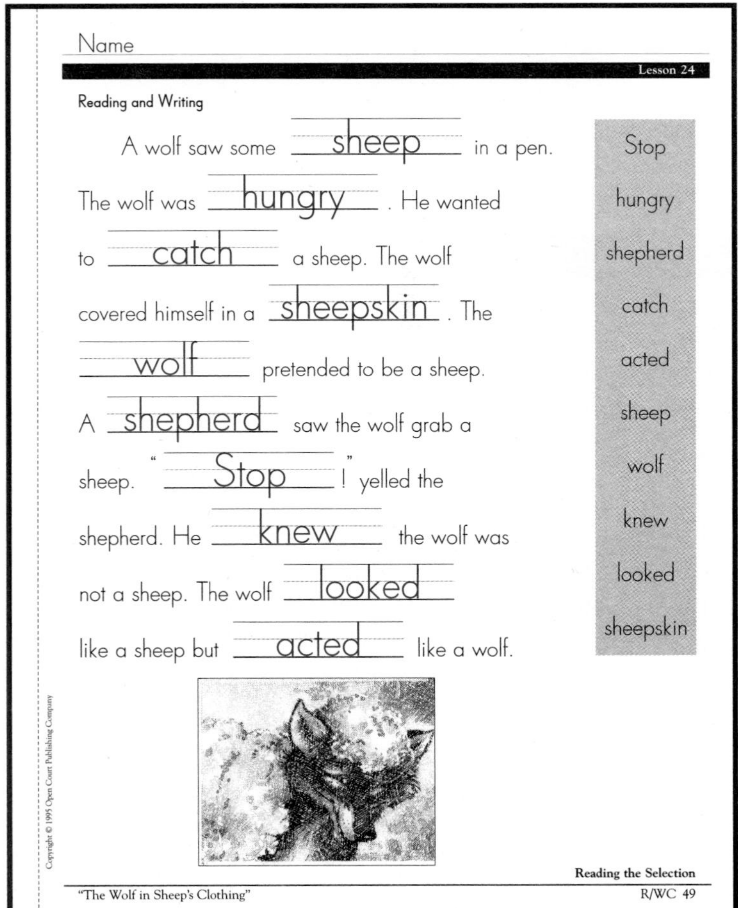

Name

Lesson 24

Reading and Writing

A wolf saw some sheep in a pen. The wolf was hungry. He wanted to catch a sheep. The wolf covered himself in a sheepskin. The wolf pretended to be a sheep. A shepherd saw the wolf grab a sheep. "Stop!" yelled the shepherd. He knew the wolf was not a sheep. The wolf looked like a sheep but acted like a wolf.

Stop
hungry
shepherd
catch
acted
sheep
wolf
knew
looked
sheepskin

Reading the Selection

"The Wolf in Sheep's Clothing" R/WC 49

✱ READING ALOUD

Since the anthology selection for the next day will be a folk tale, you may want to discuss some of the differences between folk tales and fables as you share one of the following folk tales with the children:

Once a Mouse by Marcia Brown
The Riddle of the Drum: A Tale from Tizapan, translated by Verna Aardema
The Two Foolish Cats by Yoshiko Uchida
Why the Sun and the Moon Live in the Sky: An African Folktale by Elphinstone Dayrell

See **Learning Framework Card 5** for suggestions for modeling as you read aloud.

2 WRITING

✱ DICTATION AND SPELLING

Word-Building Game Have the children use paper and pencil to play the Word-Building game. Use the following words:

zoo
too
tool
tube
tune
soon
spoon
spool

TEACHING TIP

Give children the vowel spellings if they ask.

INDEPENDENT AND COLLABORATIVE WRITING

Start with Seminar. Continue to have children share their describing sentences. Ask questions and make comments that lead students to add describing words to their sentences. Since you modeled these activities in Lesson 21, encourage the children now to ask the questions and make the comments to help each other.

Have children revise their sentences. If several children have described animals from the same story, they may want to work together to make a poster with their pictures and sentences on it. Have them make a title for the poster, for example, "The Special Animals in Anansi" and then paste their pictures with sentences on a large sheet. As an alternative, children may want to cut their pictures apart from their sentences and play a game—matching the picture to the sentence.

TEACHING TIP

Children do not have to redraw their pictures when they rewrite their sentences. Simply have them cut their sentence off the page, paste the picture to a clean sheet and then rewrite the revised sentence.

3 GUIDED AND INDEPENDENT EXPLORATION

WORKSHOP

Remind the children that they may use this time to work on projects on their own or in small groups. Be sure that each child knows what projects he or she may choose and how to complete any independent work. Suggestions for teacher-guided, collaborative, and independent activities follow.

Work with the Teacher

- Review long and short vowels. Say the word *bat.* Ask the children to tell you the name of the Sound/Spelling Card for the vowel and the spelling of the word, then have them write the word. Then say the word *kite.* Have the children point to the Sound/Spelling Card for long *i* and help them identify which spelling makes the long vowel sound in *kite.* Repeat with other words such as:

rope	rain	stop	bake
tree	pie	night	use
oats	sell	few	duck
toe	plant	chief	pit
cream	hay	cry	crow
oats	cue		

  As an extra challenge, say words that contain two vowel sounds and ask the children to point to both of the corresponding Sound/Spelling Cards. Example words include

rabbit	*rocket*	*stampede*
music	*pancake*	*berry*
daisy	*sunshine*	*peanut*
insect		

- Preread "The Three Billy Goats Gruff" or Phonics Minibook 17, *Princess Julia.*
- Review the words in Blending to provide additional support in blending.
- **Quick Change** Print *back* on the chalkboard. Blend it, then tell the children to print the word on paper. Have the children change the word as you give the following directions. Remind them to use the Sound/Spelling Cards to help them identify the spellings for the sounds. Ask individual children to model the changes at the chalkboard. After each change, have a child say the new word. Change:

  back to *pack*
  pack to *peck*
  peck to *pen*
  pen to *ten*
  ten to *tin*
  tin to *chin*

TEACHING TIP Note which children need support identifying the spelling for the long vowel sound. Together, you might generate lists of rhyming words to help the children become more familiar with a particular spelling pattern.

Collaborative/Independent Activities

- Children can continue revising their describing sentences.
- Partners may read to each other using classroom resources that may include a selection of fables.
- Distribute Activity Sheet 94. Explain to the children that they can find the answer to the question by coloring red the letter box above each long vowel word. The red letters spell the message.

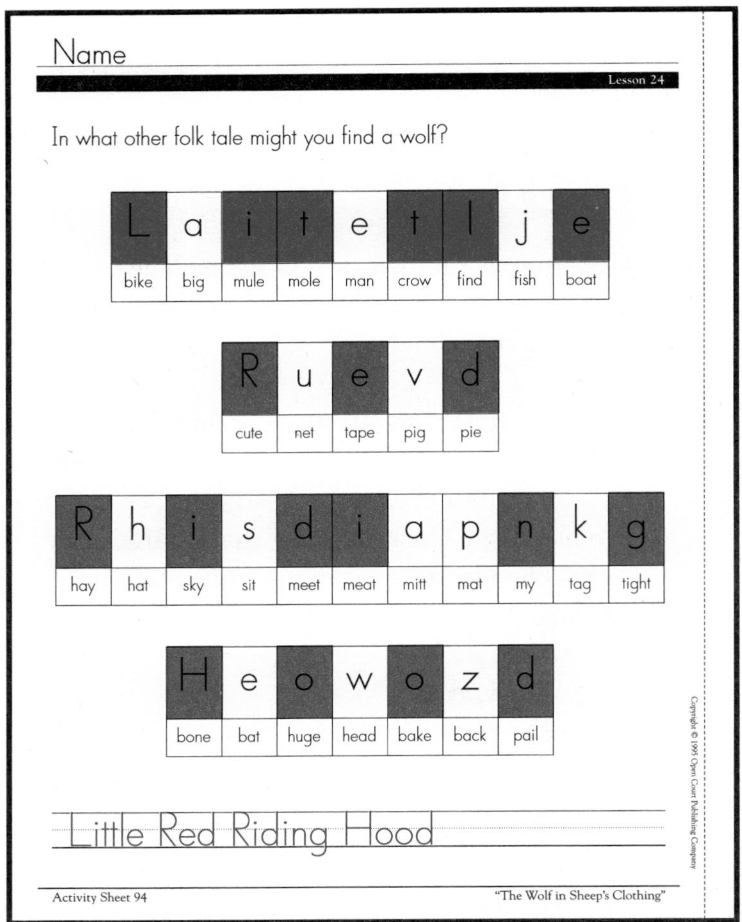

Name

Lesson 24

In what other folk tale might you find a wolf?

L	a	i	t	e	t	l	j	e
bike	big	mule	mole	man	crow	find	fish	boat

R	u	e	v	d
cute	net	tape	pig	pie

R	h	i	s	d	i	a	p	n	k	g
hay	hat	sky	sit	meet	meat	mitt	mat	my	tag	tight

H	e	o	w	o	z	d
bone	bat	huge	head	bake	back	pail

Little Red Riding Hood

Activity Sheet 94 "The Wolf in Sheep's Clothing"

Activity Sheet 94

LESSON 25

Lesson Overview

New Learning

- /r/ spelled *wr_*

Materials

- "The Three Billy Goats Gruff," pages 94–99
- Phonics Minibook 17, ***Princess Julia***
- Sound/Spelling Card 18, Robot
- Learning Framework Cards 3, 4, 5, 8
- Reading/Writing Connection, pages 50–51
- Activity Sheet 95

Prepare Ahead

- Wonder Word Flash Cards (see page 261)
- Scrambled Sentences Word Cards (see page 262)
- Flash Cards (see page 275)
- Fish for a Spelling Cards (see page 275)

GETTING STARTED

Choose one or more of the following activities to focus the children's attention and to review some of the concepts they have been learning.

Build a Story Game Collaborative storytelling helps children develop oral fluency and listening skills. In addition, it offers children a way to build their sense of story. Sit in a circle with the children. Put on a storyteller's cap and begin: "Once upon a time there was a beautiful, wooly sheep who lived in a lush, green . . ." Stop at that point and indicate the child on your left. Invite the child to tell another piece of the story, stopping when you say, "next." The story continues around the circle as the children build on one another's ideas.

Wonder Word Game Print the following words on cards: *knuckle, noodle, doorknob, sign, nasty, napkin, knee, knapsack, north, know, number, kneel, noon, gnat, knight, nice, knit, near, knock, gnaw, needle,* and *knot.* Say this verse as you pass a card around the circle.

TEACHING TIP

You might tape record the story and invite the children to listen to it in your classroom listening area.

The wonder word goes round and round.
To pass it quickly you are bound.
If you're the one to have it last,
Then you must read it rather fast.

The child who has the card when the verse ends reads the word. This child picks the next card from the top of the deck and continues the game. The game ends when all the children have read a card.

1 READING

REVIEW

Scrambled Sentences Game Set out, in mixed order, a group of word cards that could form a sentence:

drove the shepherd away. wolf The

Ask the children to help you rearrange the words to form a sentence. Remind the children that the capital letter on *The* and the period after *away* are clues to where to put these words. Have them read the completed sentence together. Then divide the class into small groups. Give each group a set of word cards to place in the correct order. The children can then read their sentences to the larger group.

Sentences:

found The an skin. sheep's wolf old
raced his hand. with He over big a stick in
what shepherd doing. The saw wolf the was
said yell me," the "Don't wolf. at
asked know?" do "How the you wolf.

TEACHING TIP

These sentences are from the story "The Wolf in Sheep's Clothing." You might choose sentences from other stories the children have read.

PHONICS

* **Introduce /r/ Spelled wr_** Review Sound/Spelling Card 18, Robot. Call the children's attention to the different spellings for /r/. Then tell the children that they will be learning the *wr_* spelling.

* **Blending** Have the children blend the following words and sentences. For reference and additional suggestions for blending, see **Learning Framework Card 3.**

Line 1:	**wrong wrote wrist wreck**
Line 2:	**wrench wreath wrinkle**
Line 3:	**right write ring wring rap wrap**
Line 4:	**royal broil spoil**
Line 5:	**troll saucer princess fairy**

Lines 1–3 focus on words that begin with the sound /r/ spelled *wr* and *r.* Point out the homophones *right* and *write* in Line 3. Ask the children which spelling means the opposite of *left* and which means *to print*. Have them use each word in a sentence. Repeat this procedure with the other homophones in the line.

Some children may be unfamiliar with the words *wrench* and *wring*. Children who are familiar with these words could explain them to the others.

After the children sound and blend words in line 4, ask them to circle or name the different spellings for /oi/.

Line 5 contains vocabulary from "The Three Billy Goats Gruff" and Phonics Minibook 17, which will be read in this lesson.

To review the words, point to them in random order and have volunteers read them.

➤ Reading/Writing Connection, page 50, provides practice with the *wr_* spelling.

Reading/Writing Connection, page 50

Name

Lesson 25

Sounds and Spellings

r

wr_

Writing Words and Sentences

wrist wrist wrap wrap

A robot wrestles wriggly snakes.

A robot wrestles wriggly snakes.

Dictation and Spelling

Consonant Sounds and Spellings

50 R/WC "The Three Billy Goats Gruff"

*** READING THE STUDENT ANTHOLOGY**

"The Three Billy Goats Gruff"
pages 94–99

About the Selection

Three billy goats long to taste the tall green grass across the river. How will they get past the mean, hungry troll that guards the bridge?

Link to the Unit Concept

Tell the children that "The Three Billy Goats Gruff" is a folk tale. Review what they already know about folk tales. After reading this selection, the children may point out how this folk tale is like others they have read, and they may describe some of the characteristics of folk tales they have noticed.

Activating Prior Knowledge

Have a volunteer read aloud the title of the selection on page 94. Ask whether anyone has heard this story. Ask the children what they already know about billy goats and trolls.

Setting Reading Goals and Expectations

- Have the children browse the selection, pointing out any words that might be difficult to read or understand. Encourage them to try to figure out these words as they read, using other words in the sentence as well as accompanying illustrations as clues.
- If children are having difficulty blending any of the words, remind them to check the Sound/Spelling Cards. If any words cannot be easily blended, pronounce the words for the children.

Recommendations for Reading

- Have the children read the selection aloud.
- Be sure to model reacting to the story with surprise or wonder when appropriate. Encourage the children to do the same.

Note: Partner reading of this selection is a good activity for Workshop.

About the Reading Strategies

In reading this selection, children will find the strategies for clarifying words and summing up useful. Refer to the posters, Clarifying Unfamiliar Words and Passages, and Checking Understanding. Explain that you will use these strategies as you read the selection together.

Think-Aloud Prompts for Use in Oral Reading Notice the think-aloud prompts with the page miniatures. These are merely suggestions. Continue to model using appropriate strategies while reading and to encourage children to use the strategies on their own. For a review of information about modeling and generating think-alouds, see **Learning Framework Card 8, Reading the Student Anthologies.**

STRATEGIC
R·E·A·D·I·N·G
PROMPTS
These prompts may be used as guides when working with reading strategies.

1 Ask the children what *meadow* means and how they can tell. Encourage them to use word clues as well as the illustration, if necessary.

2 Ask the children what *poker* means and how they can tell. Have the children sum up what has happened in the story so far.

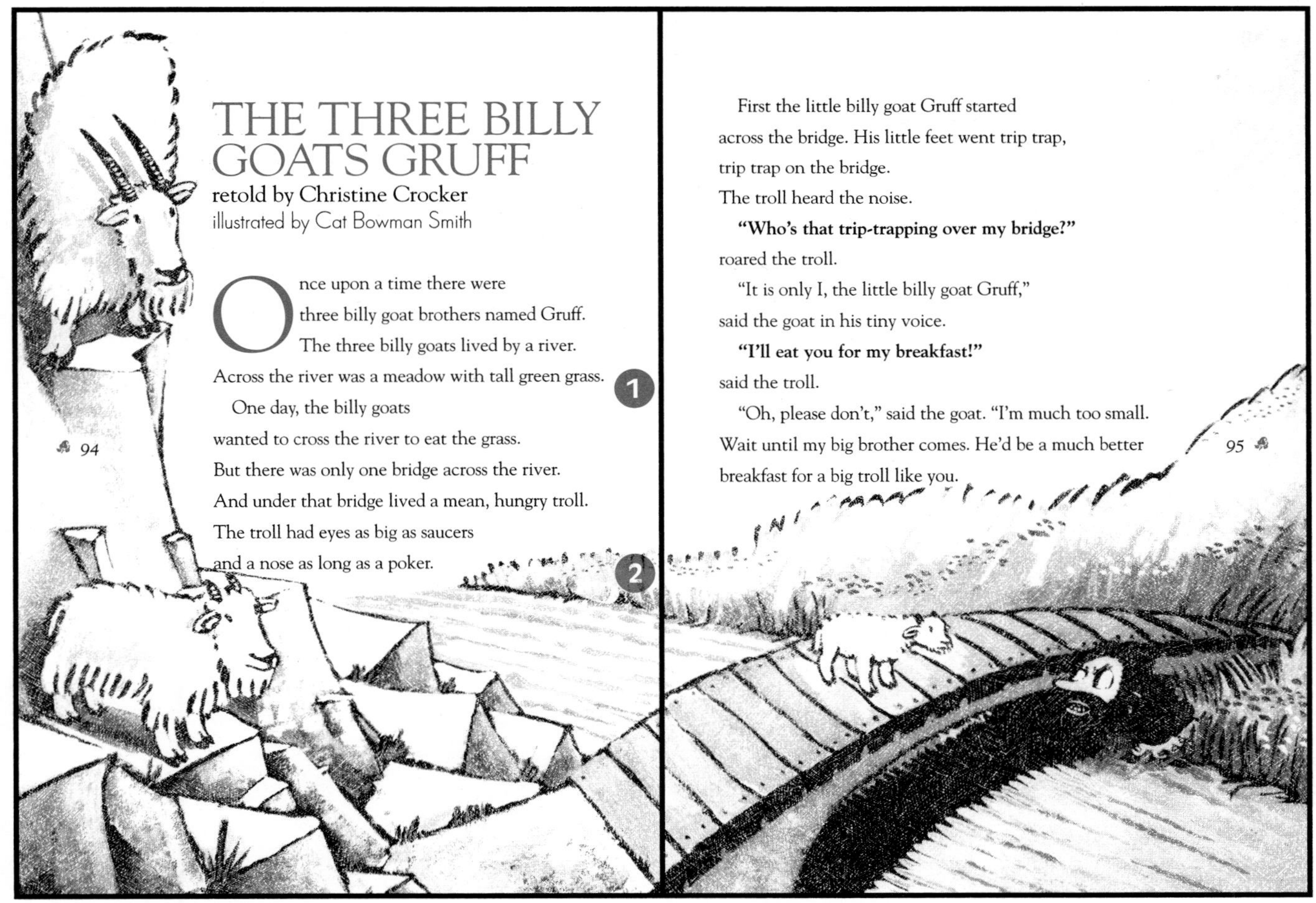

THE THREE BILLY GOATS GRUFF

retold by Christine Crocker

illustrated by Cat Bowman Smith

Once upon a time there were three billy goat brothers named Gruff. The three billy goats lived by a river. Across the river was a meadow with tall green grass. 1

One day, the billy goats wanted to cross the river to eat the grass. But there was only one bridge across the river. And under that bridge lived a mean, hungry troll. The troll had eyes as big as saucers and a nose as long as a poker. 2

94

First the little billy goat Gruff started across the bridge. His little feet went trip trap, trip trap on the bridge.

The troll heard the noise.

"Who's that trip-trapping over my bridge?" roared the troll.

"It is only I, the little billy goat Gruff," said the goat in his tiny voice.

"I'll eat you for my breakfast!" said the troll.

"Oh, please don't," said the goat. "I'm much too small. Wait until my big brother comes. He'd be a much better breakfast for a big troll like you.

95

96

"Very well," said the greedy troll.
So he let the little billy goat Gruff cross the bridge. ❸
Next, the middle-sized billy goat Gruff
started across the bridge. His middle-sized
feet went trip trap, trip trap.
"Who's that trip-trapping over my bridge?"
shouted the troll.

It's only I, the middle-sized billy goat Gruff,"
said the goat in his middle-sized voice.
"I'll eat you for my breakfast!" roared the troll.
And he jumped up on the bridge
"Oh, please don't," said the goat.
"I'm much too small. Wait for my big brother.
He'd be a much better meal for a big troll like you."
"Very well," said the greedy troll.
So he let the middle-sized billy goat Gruff cross the bridge. ❹

97

❸ Have the children sum up additional information in the story.

❹ Have the children sum up additional information in the story.

Soon the big billy goat Gruff started
across the bridge.
His big feet went trip trap, trip trap.
The bridge shook.
"Who's that trip-trapping over my bridge?"
shouted the troll.
"It is I, the big billy goat Gruff!"
said the goat in his big voice.
"I'll eat you for my breakfast!"
roared the troll.
"Oh no, you won't," said the goat. The big billy
goat Gruff ran at the troll and butted him into the river.
The troll was never heard of again.
99
Then the three billy goats Gruff went
into the meadow. They ate all the grass
5 they wanted and lived happily ever after.
And so—
Snip, snap, snout,
6 This tale's told out.

5 Have the children sum up additional information in the story.

6 Ask the children what this means and how they know what it means.

Responding

- Encourage discussion of anything that interested the children about this selection. To stimulate discussion, you might ask, "What did you think of [a character]?" or "What did you like best about this story?"
- Ask the children how they can tell that "The Three Billy Goats Gruff" is a folk tale. They may point out that the good characters win, the story begins and ends in a certain way, or that the story uses animal characters. Encourage them to comment on how this story is like, or different from, other folk tales they have heard or read.

TIP FOR ENGLISH LANGUAGE LEARNERS

Have English Language Learners practice using and producing language to communicate ideas. Pair English Language Learners with native English speakers. Have them discuss what they think is the most important idea of the folk tale. Informally monitor the conversations to assess the children's understanding of the selection.

* READING A PHONICS MINIBOOK

Princess Julia
Phonics Minibook 17

Getting Ready to Read

- Call on a volunteer to read aloud the title of the book.
- Encourage the children to browse the book, commenting on any words or illustrations that catch their eye.

Recommendations

- Call on volunteers to read the story aloud. Change readers at the end of each page.
- Reread the story at least twice, encouraging new volunteers to participate in each reading.

Printed in the United States of America

ISBN 0-8126-1287-6

10 9 8 7 6 5 4 3 2 1

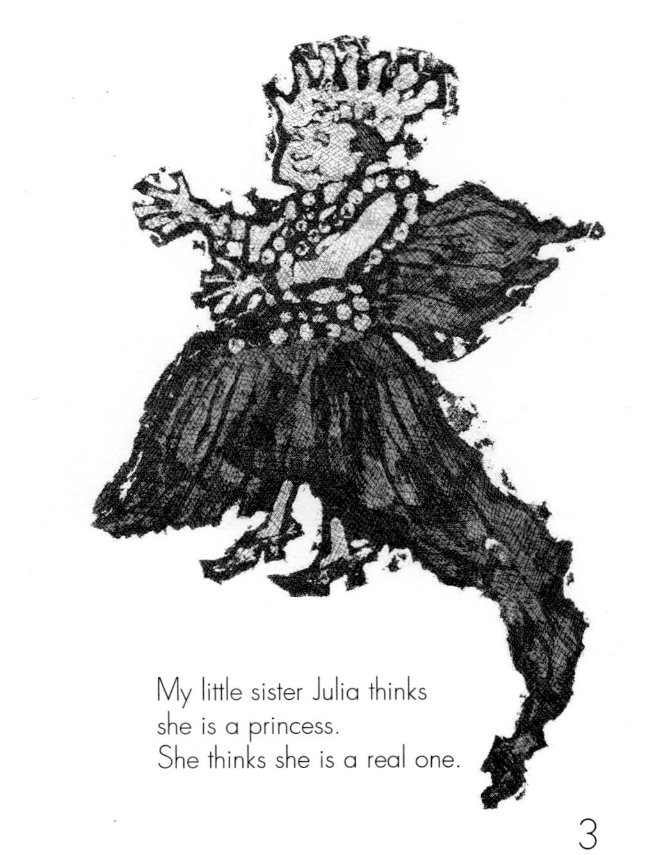

My little sister Julia thinks
she is a princess.
She thinks she is a real one.

Julia wears fancy gowns and shoes.
She wears a silly paper crown.
She even wears the crown to bed!
"I'm a princess! A real princess!" Julia says.

I tell Julia she is wrong.
Julia says that rude sisters
should bow and beg her royal pardon.

One night Dad read us a fairy tale.
It was The Princess and the Pea.
In the story, a queen tested a visitor.
The visitor said she was a real princess.
The queen put a pea in a bed.
The visitor tried to sleep on the bed.

6

The visitor could not sleep.
She felt something hard in the bed.
Only a real princess could have felt
a single pea in such a bed!

7

The story of the princess and the pea
gave me an idea.

8

The next night, I put a marble
under my sister's mattress.
She never felt a tickle.
She slept like a baby all night.

9

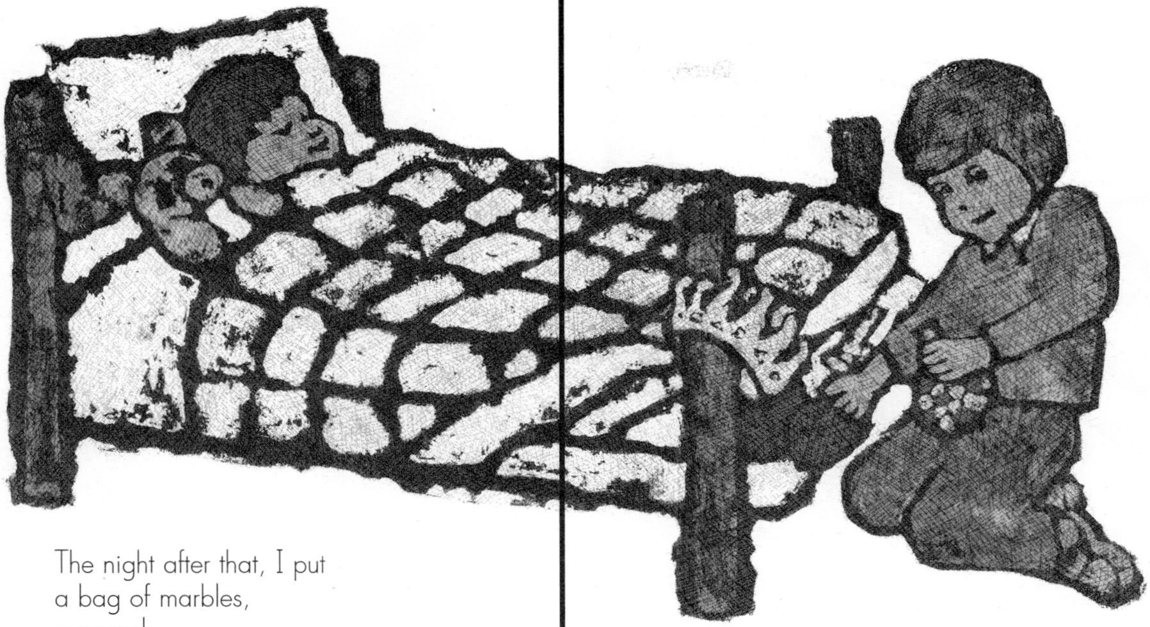

The night after that, I put
a bag of marbles,
a wrench,
and a toy truck
under Julia's mattress.
Julia never even wiggled.

10

11

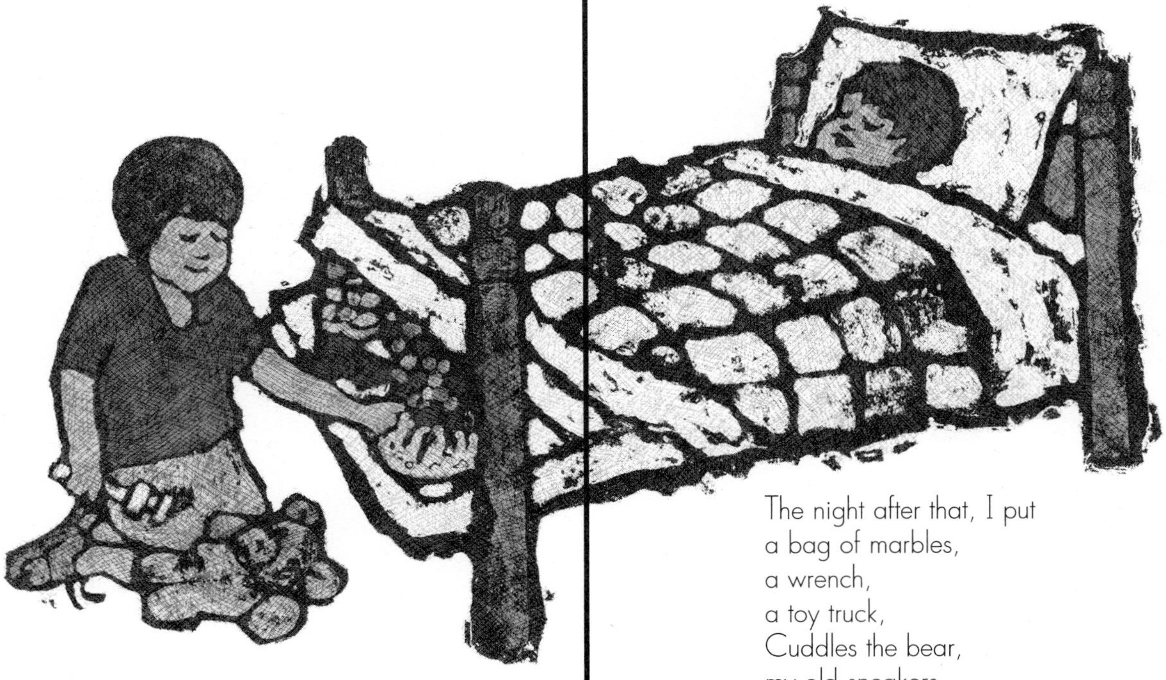

The night after that, I put
a bag of marbles,
a wrench,
a toy truck,
Cuddles the bear,
my old sneakers,
and Julia's own crown
under her mattress.
Julia never even missed Cuddles!

12

13

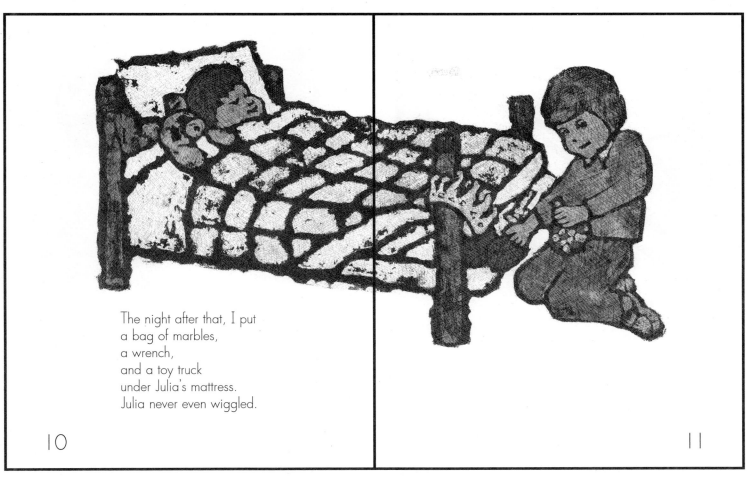

The next day, Julia looked for her crown.
I picked up her mattress.
"You see?" I said.
"You are not a real princess!
Remember The Princess and the Pea?
Look under your bed!
No real princess could sleep on all that!"

14

Julia put on her wrinkled crown.
"That was only a fairy tale," she said.
"A real princess can sleep
any place, any time,
any way she wants!
And I am a real princess!"

15

Then the real princess
ordered her royal sister
to take the marbles,
the wrench,
the toy truck,
Cuddles,
and the sneakers,
out from under her royal mattress.

16

Responding

- Have the children tell in their own words what happens in the story.
- Have the children point out any difficult words in the selection and explain how they figured them out.
- To make sure the children are focusing on the words in the story, have them point out the appropriate words in the text as they answer questions such as the following:

  After Julia says that she is a princess, what does her older sister tell her?

  After hearing the story *The Princess and the Pea*, what did the older sister put under Julia's mattress first?

  What were all the things that the older sister put under Julia's mattress?

  How did Julia's crown look after it was taken out from under her mattress?
- Before rereading, focus the children's attention on the *wr* sound and ask the children to point out words during reading that begin with this sound.
- Before rereading a second time, focus the children's attention on the *le* ending of some words and ask the children to point out words with this ending during reading.
- Ask what the children liked best about this story.

Have pairs of children reread this book.

➤ Reading/Writing Connection, page 51, may be completed at this time. Help the children read the paragraph and answer the questions.

TEACHING TIP

Set aside ten minutes for partner reading every day. During this time, you should read with individuals, recording their progress. Reading Assesment sheets for Phonics Minibooks are available in *Assessment Masters, Grade 1*.

* READING ALOUD

There are many versions of the story of the three billy goats. You might enjoy reading one of these other versions to the children.

See **Learning Framework Card 5** for suggestions for modeling as you read aloud.

2 WRITING

* DICTATION AND SPELLING

Have the children turn to page 50 of their Reading/Writing Connection book. Dictate the following words and sentence, using the suggestions for dictation that appear on **Learning Framework Card 4**.

Line 1: tickle jungle candle

Line 2: quick quilt squeeze

Sentence: The pig squeals loudly.

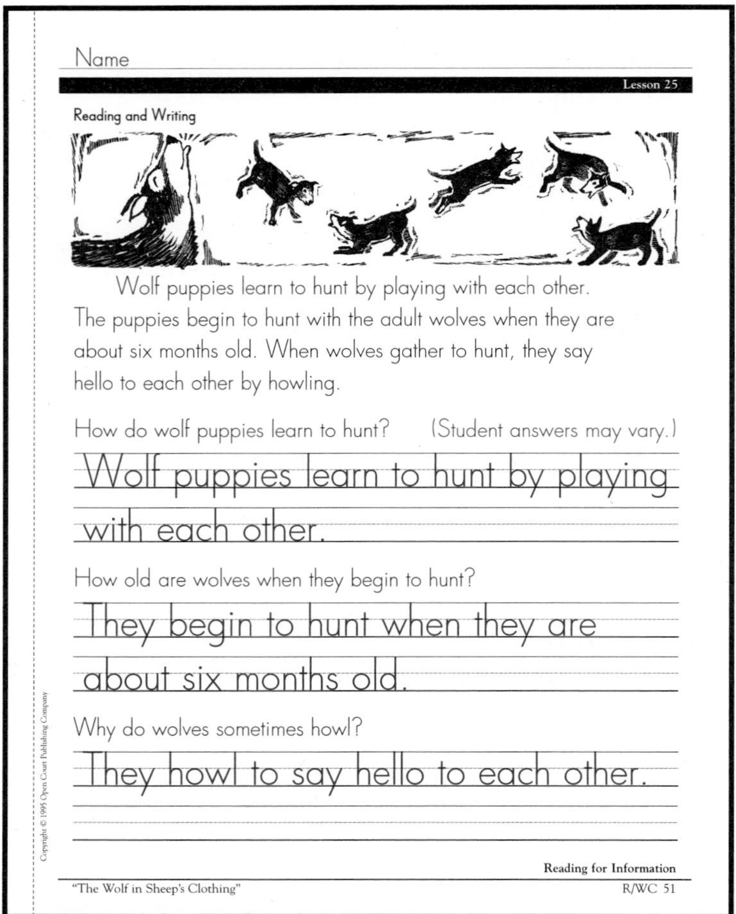

Name

Lesson 25

Reading and Writing

Wolf puppies learn to hunt by playing with each other. The puppies begin to hunt with the adult wolves when they are about six months old. When wolves gather to hunt, they say hello to each other by howling.

How do wolf puppies learn to hunt? (Student answers may vary.)

Wolf puppies learn to hunt by playing with each other.

How old are wolves when they begin to hunt?

They begin to hunt when they are about six months old.

Why do wolves sometimes howl?

They howl to say hello to each other.

Reading for Information

"The Wolf in Sheep's Clothing" R/WC 51

Reading/Writing Connection, page 51

Have the children proofread each line, following the guidelines on **Learning Framework Card 4.** Point out that *squeeze* contains *ee* followed by a consonant and silent *e.* Print other words on the chalkboard that follow this pattern, for example, *sneeze, breeze,* and *cheese.* Remind the children to use the Sound/Spelling Cards as they think about the spellings.

INDEPENDENT AND COLLABORATIVE WRITING

The children will begin writing their stories using animal characters. Review the key vocabulary and concepts on the chalkboard. Remind the children to review their own plans and ideas before beginning their stories. Some children may have written plans or drawn illustrations regarding what they intend to happen in their story. Encourage the children to use the words on the board that will help them tell their stories. Have them use the sounds they hear to write words they are not sure how to spell. Remind them that soon they will be able to share their stories with others.

TEACHING TIP

Remind the children to use the words from the Vocabulary Chart in their writing.

3 GUIDED AND INDEPENDENT EXPLORATION

WORKSHOP

Remind the children that they may use this time to work on projects of their own or in small groups. Be sure that each child knows what projects he or she may choose and how to complete any independent work. Suggestions for teacher-guided, collaborative, and independent activities follow.

Learning Framework Card 11, Workshop, contains a complete discussion of establishing and conducting Workshop and suggestions for helping English Language Learners during Workshop.

Work with the Teacher

- Form a small group of children who had difficulty during today's reading of "The Three Billy Goats Gruff." Reread the entire story with them so that they may follow along more easily during tomorrow's lesson.
- Assess children's reading progress by having individuals or pairs of children read Phonics Minibook 17 aloud to you.
- Prepare flash cards containing a variety of words beginning with *w, r,* and *wr-*. Use the cards to work with those children who need help in decoding /r/ spelled *wr_*. Words you might use include *rap, rain, rumble, rooster, roadway, rabbit, walk, winner, white, willow, week, whistle, warthog, wrap, wrench, wrong, write, wrist, wrestle.*

Collaborative/Independent Activities

- Partners may reread *Princess Julia,* Phonics Minibook 17. When they have reread the story once or twice they should go back through it, copy all the words they can find that begin with /r/, and underline the letter or letters that spell the /r/ sound.
- Prepare Fish for a Spelling cards containing the spellings *gn-, kn-, wr-, oy,* and *oi.* Mix these in with some of the vowel-spelling cards from previous games, place them all in a jar, and invite a small group of children to play.
- Pairs or groups of children may review compound words by playing the Compound Word Riddle Game. You may want to add new riddles to the game, with answers such as *wristwatch* and *toybox* that contain some of the new spellings the children have learned.
- Distribute Activity Sheet 95. Practice following directions. Have the children read aloud the first direction. Give them time to draw the circles. Then have them follow the remaining directions individually. When they have completed all of the directions, invite the children to compare pictures.

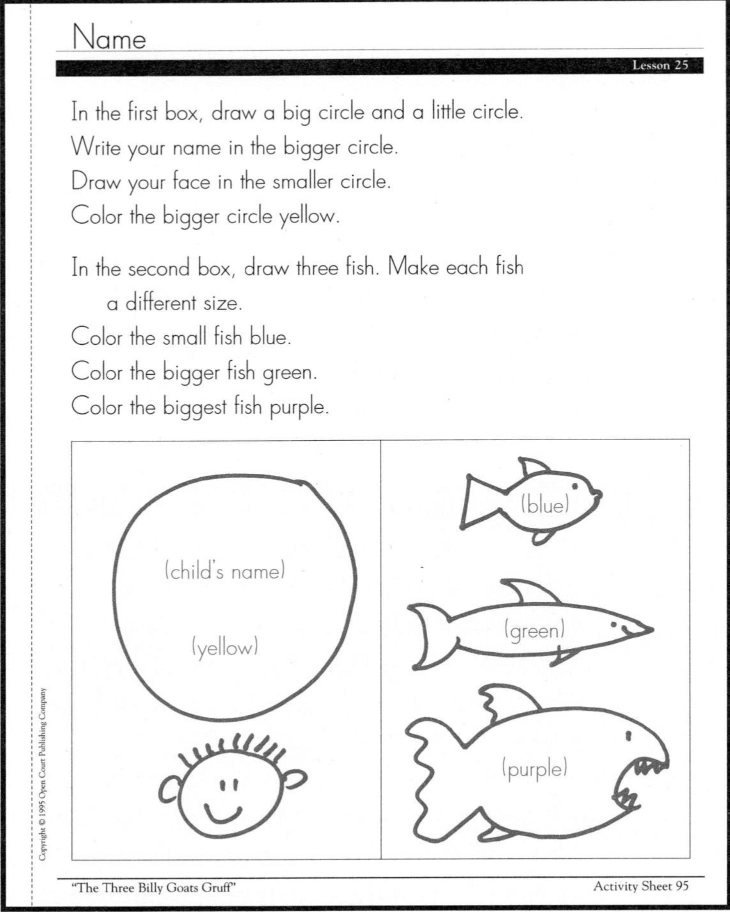

Name ______________________

Lesson 25

In the first box, draw a big circle and a little circle.
Write your name in the bigger circle.
Draw your face in the smaller circle.
Color the bigger circle yellow.

In the second box, draw three fish. Make each fish a different size.
Color the small fish blue.
Color the bigger fish green.
Color the biggest fish purple.

"The Three Billy Goats Gruff" Activity Sheet 95

Activity Sheet 95

LESSON 26

Lesson Overview

New Learning

- /f/ spelled *ph*

Materials

- "The Three Billy Goats Gruff," pages 94–99
- Learning Framework Cards 3, 5
- Reading/Writing Connection, pages 52–53
- Activity Sheet 96

Prepare Ahead

- Reading Relay Flash Cards (see page 277)

GETTING STARTED

Choose one or more of the following activities to focus the children's attention and to review some of the concepts they have been learning.

Reading Relay Form two teams of children and have the players on each team sit one behind the other. Make sufficient flash card words so that there is at least one card for each child. Words that review the /r/ sound spellings include *wrong, railroad, wrinkle, ribbon, wrist, rabbit, rumble, wreath, razor, wriggle, rocking, ragged.* To play the game, the first child on the team picks up a card, reads the word, then takes the card and goes to the end of the line. If a child reads the word incorrectly, the opposite team has an opportunity to say the word. The teams take turns choosing a card and blending and saying the word. The game ends when all the members on one team have successfully read a word.

Spelling Challenge Divide the class into three or four teams. Explain that you will write a spelling of a long vowel sound on the board and give the teams from thirty seconds to one minute to think of words that use that spelling. When time is up, call on each team to say and spell its words. Write them on the board and award one point for each correct word. The team with the most points is the winner. Remind the children to whisper so that those on other teams can't overhear their words.

1 READING

PHONICS

Review the Sound/Spelling Card 6, Fan. Point to the *ph* spelling and tell the children that this is another spelling for /f/.

* **Blending** Have the children blend the following words and sentences. For reference and additional suggestions for blending, see **Learning Framework Card 3.**

Line 1:	**photo phase graph telephone elephant**
Line 2:	**bridge ledge badge fudge**
Line 3:	**greedy shiny sleepy shady**
Line 4:	**poker toes stroke roar meadow**
Line 5:	**middle puddle marble wiggle**

Line 1 focuses on words in which /f/ is spelled *ph*. Point out that this spelling can occur at the beginning, middle, and end of a word.

Line 2 reviews words with the *dge* spelling. The children could suggest other words that end with *dge* by identifying rhyming words.

The words in line 3 all end with /ē/ spelled *y*.

Line 4 reviews different spellings for /ō/.

After the children sound and blend the words in line 5, ask what they notice. Some children may say that all the words end in *le,* while others may point out that three of the words have short vowel sounds and the same three words have a double consonant in the middle.

Some children may be familiar with words such as *phase, graph,* and *poker.* If so, ask children who know the words to use them in sentences.

Have the children use the words in sentences. Extend the sentences.

➤ Reading/Writing Connection, page 52, provides practice with the *ph* spelling. Help the children complete the page by reading and copying the words and the sentence.

* READING THE STUDENT ANTHOLOGY

"The Three Billy Goats Gruff"
pages 94–99

Activating Prior Knowledge

Review the story with the children by asking them to tell what they remember about it from yesterday.

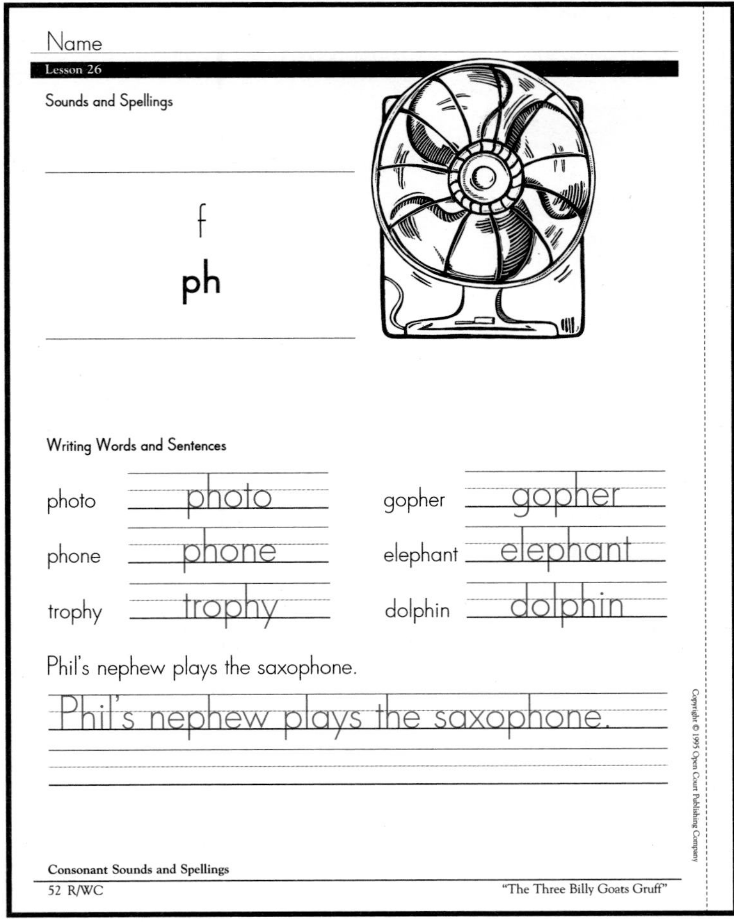

Name

Lesson 26

Sounds and Spellings

f

ph

Writing Words and Sentences

photo	photo	gopher	gopher
phone	phone	elephant	elephant
trophy	trophy	dolphin	dolphin

Phil's nephew plays the saxophone.

Phil's nephew plays the saxophone.

Copyright © 1995 Open Court Publishing Company

Consonant Sounds and Spellings

52 R/WC "The Three Billy Goats Gruff"

Reading/Writing Connection, page 52

Recommendations for Reading

Since this is the second lesson in which the children will read this selection, have the children read aloud in a readers' theater format. Select a different child to be the narrator of each page, while four groups of children play the three billy goats and the troll. By reading the selection aloud in this way, the children will be able to focus on who is saying what to whom in the story.

Responding

- Have the children sum up the entire story and discuss what they like best about it. Invite them to talk about what they think each character is like and why they think so. Allow the children to comment freely on the story.
- Discuss any ideas the children would like to add to the Concept Board.

Vocabulary Discuss any words and phrases the children found interesting or unusual. Have them use these words in oral sentences. Add the words to the Vocabulary Chart. Possible words include the following:

shook, tiny, trip trap

TEACHING TIP

Have the children do some partner reading daily. Using previously read Phonics Minibooks and Step-by-Step Practice Stories for this purpose will help the children review and solidify their knowledge of the sounds and spellings they have learned. This is a good opportunity to read with children individually and to record their progress.

➤ Reading/Writing Connection, page 53, reviews this selection. Have the children write sentences to answer the questions.

* READING ALOUD

Be sure to set aside time for reading aloud. Folk tales are very popular among young children because of their lively action and because the children can easily identify the good and bad characters. You may want to share with your class one or more of the following books:

The Cock, the Mouse, and the Little Red Hen by Lorinda Bryan Cauley
The Silver Cow: A Welsh Tale, retold by Susan Cooper
The Wolf and the Seven Kids, translated by Anne Rogers

After reading a folk tale, you may want to ask the children questions about whether the characters were kind or cruel, clever or foolish, brave or cowardly, and so on. Ask the children to tell how they know.

See **Learning Framework Card 5** for suggestions for reading aloud.

Reading/Writing Connection, page 53

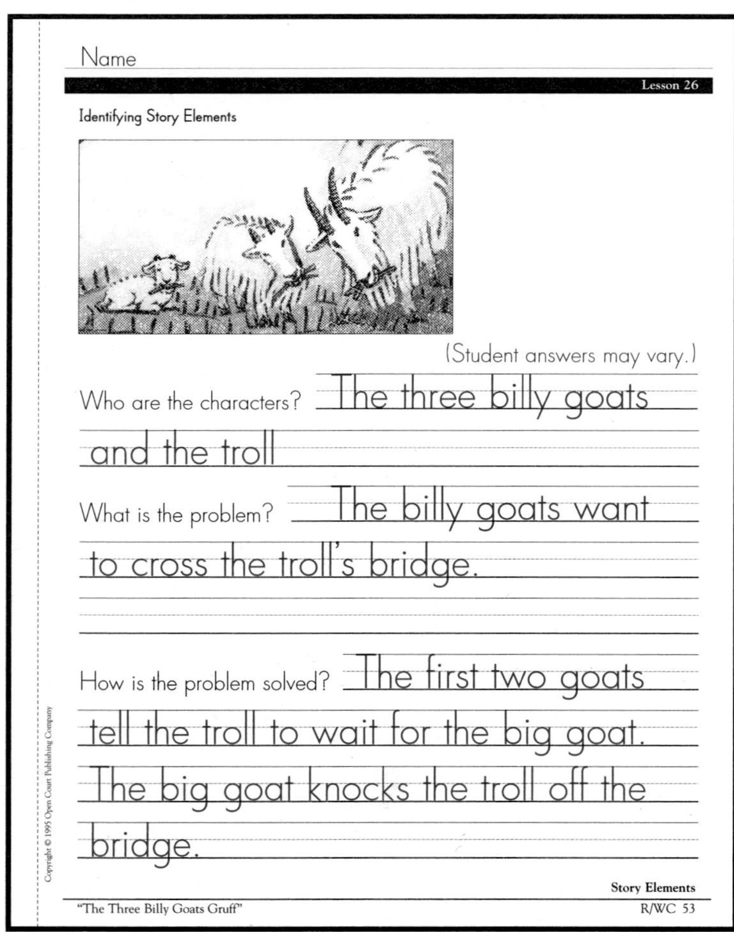

Name

Lesson 26

Identifying Story Elements

(Student answers may vary.)

Who are the characters? The three billy goats and the troll

What is the problem? The billy goats want to cross the troll's bridge.

How is the problem solved? The first two goats tell the troll to wait for the big goat. The big goat knocks the troll off the bridge.

Story Elements

"The Three Billy Goats Gruff" R/WC 53

2 WRITING

* DICTATION AND SPELLING

Word-Bulding Game Have the children use pencil and paper to build the following words.

rap (use in sentence)
wrap (use in sentence)
rope
wrote
write (use in sentence)
right (use in sentence)

Remind the children to ask if they are uncertain about which spelling to choose.

INDEPENDENT AND COLLABORATIVE WRITING

While children may find it difficult to actually write a folk tale or fable, the stories in this unit provide a good opportunity for children to respond to them in their journals. Children should feel free to write about their favorite stories, favorite characters, or favorite parts of stories.

3 GUIDED AND INDEPENDENT EXPLORATION

WORKSHOP

Remind the children that they may use this time to work on projects on their own or with small groups. Be sure that each child knows what projects he or she may choose and how to complete any independent work. Suggestions for teacher-guided, collaborative, and independent activities follow.

Work with the Teacher

- Reread Phonics Minibook 17, *Princess Julia,* with individuals or small groups of children.
- Play the Word-Building game with children for extra spelling practice. Repeat and build on today's game, or use any word list that will suit the children's needs.
- Have children practice reading words with /f/ spelled *ph.* You might write the following words on flashcards: *farm, fresh, fright, football, funny, fasten, flip, poker, puddle, airplane, potatoes, panhandle, photo, phase, Ralph, graph, Phillip, elephant, telephone.*
- Ask some of the more independent readers to read aloud to you from the books of their choice. Invite other children to listen in.

TEACHING TIP Encourage the children to read to each other. You, too, should choose children to read with. As you read with each child, note his or her progress.

Collaborative/Independent Activities

- Write the endings *-ckle, -ngle, -rtle, -rgle,* and *-mble* on the chalkboard. Have children copy the spellings onto scratch paper. Challenge them to list at least one pair of rhyming words beneath each spelling. When they are finished, they should exchange lists with a partner for proofreading. Tomorrow, they can use their lists to make new cards for the Go Fish! deck.
- Children who began new pieces during today's Independent Writing period may return to their journals to continue their work.
- Encourage the children to read independently. Remind them that they can always return to their small copies of the Big Books and reread old favorites. They may enjoy finding out how many of the words they can now read on their own.
- Distribute Activity Sheet 96, which reviews the /f/ sound in words spelled with *ph.* Have the children read the directions aloud and complete the first sentence by writing a word from the list. Then tell the children to complete the page independently.

Home/School Connection

Send home the take-home version of Phonics Minibook 16, *Mr. Lee,* and encourage the children to read it to their families.

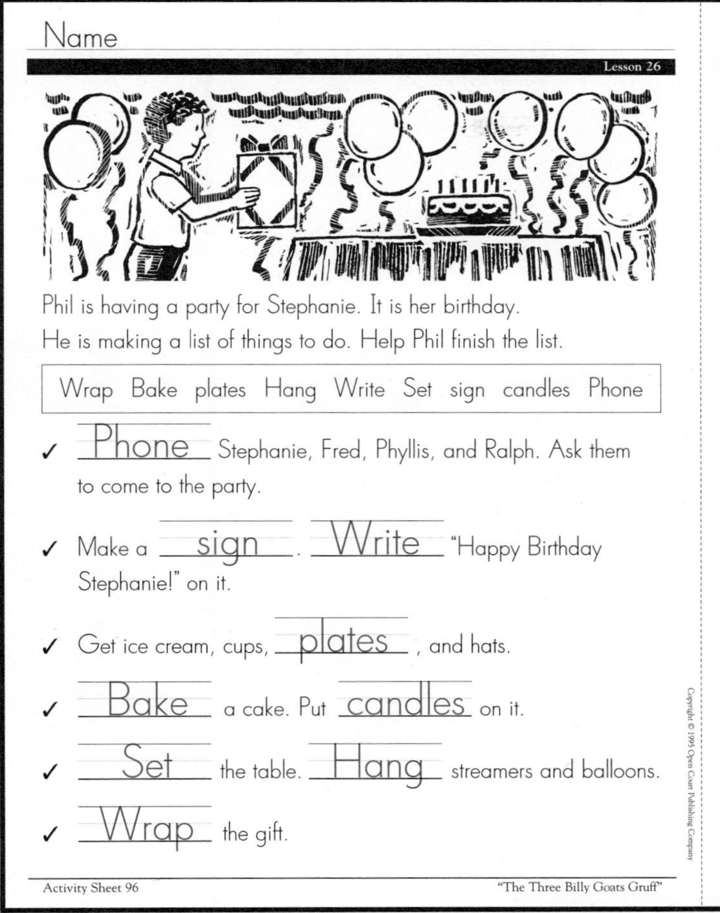

Name
Lesson 26
Phil is having a party for Stephanie. It is her birthday.
He is making a list of things to do. Help Phil finish the list.
Wrap Bake plates Hang Write Set sign candles Phone
✓ Phone Stephanie, Fred, Phyllis, and Ralph. Ask them to come to the party.
✓ Make a sign. Write "Happy Birthday Stephanie!" on it.
✓ Get ice cream, cups, plates, and hats.
✓ Bake a cake. Put candles on it.
✓ Set the table. Hang streamers and balloons.
✓ Wrap the gift.
Activity Sheet 96
"The Three Billy Goats Gruff"

Activity Sheet 96

LESSON 27

Lesson Overview

Materials

- Phonics Minibook 18, ***How the Rabbit Caught the Tiger: A Korean Folk Tale***
- Learning Framework Cards 3, 4, 5, 6
- Reading/Writing Connection, pages 54–55
- Activity Sheet 97

Prepare Ahead

- Bingo Game Cards (see page 293)

GETTING STARTED

Choose one or more of the following activities to focus the children's attention and to review some of the concepts they have been learning.

Add to the Pattern Game Review the Hawk and Hoot owl Sound/Spelling Cards, then write the spellings *aw, au, oo, ue*, and *u_e* on the chalkboard. Write the words *tube, moon, blue, tooth, tune, awful, dawn, because, naughty* on the board. Call on children to read a word and write it under the correct spelling. Read each completed list, then challenge the children to suggest other words for each spelling.

Sound/Spelling Card Review Have the children review the Sound/Spelling Cards by giving clues from the sound stories, for example, "I am an owl and this is the sound I make." Have the children give the name of the card and tell what spellings stand for the sound. Vary responses by calling on individuals or by naming different groups.

1 READING

PHONICS

* **Blending** Have the children blend the following words and sentences. For reference and additional suggestions for blending, see **Learning Framework Card 3.**

Line 1:	**staple spray strain shape**
Line 2:	**share scrap scrape**
Line 3:	**ruling waking writing phoning**
Line 4:	**cute rude huge tube**
Line 5:	**September October November December**

Line 1 focuses on various spellings for /ā/. Using Sound/Spelling Card 33, Long A, as a guide, have the children point to the spelling used in each word.

After the children sound and blend the words in line 2, point to *scrap* and *scrape* and ask the children what they notice (the words are the same except for the short vowel/long vowel sound). You may wish to give examples of other pairs of words that follow this pattern: *cap/cape, hop/hope, tub/tube, rip/ripe.*

Line 3 reviews words that drop the *e* before adding the *-ing* ending. Have the children identfy each base word and explain how the *-ing* word was formed.

Line 4 compares /o͞o/ and /ū/, both spelled *u_e*.

Line 5 focuses on months of the year. Ask the children if any of them were born in these months. Invite children who were born in other months to name their birth months. Print them on the chalkboard.

To review the words, play a clapping and tapping game. The number of times you clap refers to the line and the number of times you tap refers to the particular word in that line. For example, if you clap five times and tap four times, the children read and circle the fourth word in the fifth line—*December*. After you clap, give the children time to locate the line before you begin tapping. Alternatively, just give the line number and word position: For example, "Second line, first word ______."

➤ Reading/Writing Connection, page 54, reviews decoding and spelling. Have the children complete the top part of the page by circling the word that does not belong in each sentence. They should then write a correct word to put in the sentence.

✱ READING A PHONICS MINIBOOK

How the Rabbit Caught the Tiger: A Korean Folk Tale

Phonics Minibook 18

Getting Ready to Read

- Have the children turn to the first page of the selection, and invite them to read the story's title, *How the Rabbit Caught the Tiger: A Korean Folk Tale.*
- Point out that this story was first told in the country of Korea. Ask the children to tell anything they know about Korea. You might want to point to a world map and trace the distance between Korea and the United States. Explain that the story has been told and retold many times to people in many countries all over the world.

Name

Lesson 27

Reading and Writing

1. Squares, circles, and (snakes) are shapes. (Answers will vary.)

2. Birds, children, and (cats) can sing.

3. Tennis, (daisy,) and soccer are sports.

4. (Cars,) rulers, and girls have feet.

5. Sandals, (books,) and sneakers are shoes.

Dictation and Spelling

Decoding/Spelling

54 R/WC "The Three Billy Goats Gruff"

Reading/Writing Connection, page 54

- Allow the children to page through the book, commenting on what they see in the illustrations and what they think the story will tell them. Ask them if they notice anything about the words.

Recommendations

Follow the usual procedure for reading a Phonics Minibook:

- Call on a different child to read each page of the story aloud.
- If a child has difficulty with a word, help him or her to sound and blend it before going on.
- Reread the story at least twice, calling on different children to read.

For the complete procedure for reading Phonics Minibooks, see **Learning Framework Card 6.**

Printed in the United States of America

ISBN 0-8126-1288-4

10 9 8 7 6 5 4 3 2 1

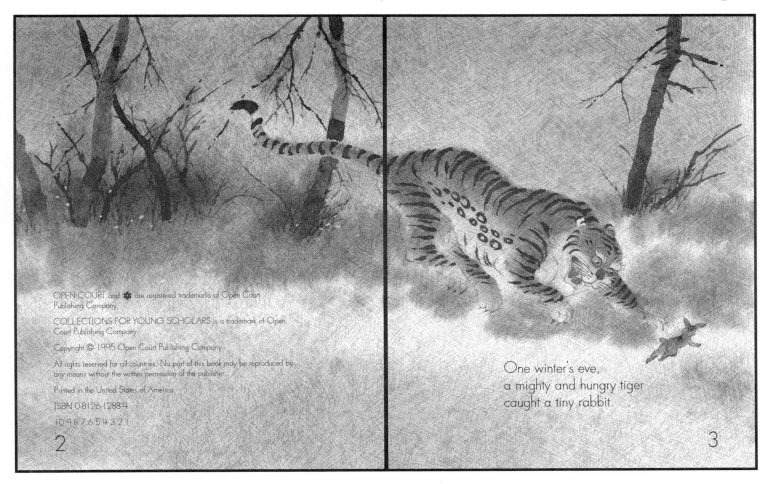

One winter's eve,
a mighty and hungry tiger
caught a tiny rabbit.

"Do not eat me!" cried the rabbit.
"I am too small to make a good meal.
If you let me go, I will show you
how to catch all the fish you can eat!"

The tiger was greedy.
His hunger was bigger than his brain.
"Show me now, or I will eat you!" he roared.
Then he let the rabbit go.

The rabbit led the tiger
down to the river.
"Put your tail in the water,"
said the rabbit.

6

"Now wait all night.
The fish will grab onto your tail.
Your tail will grow very heavy.
Then you can pull it out
and eat all the fish!"

7

"I'll stay close by," said the rabbit.
"I will let you know when
you have caught plenty of fish."
The rabbit climbed up the riverbank
and sat down to watch the tiger.

8

The tiger put his tail into the river.
He waited and waited.
It grew cold and dark.

9

"Is your tail getting heavy?"
called the rabbit.

"Oh, yes!" said the tiger.
"I must be catching lots of fish!
Should I pull my tail out now?

10

11

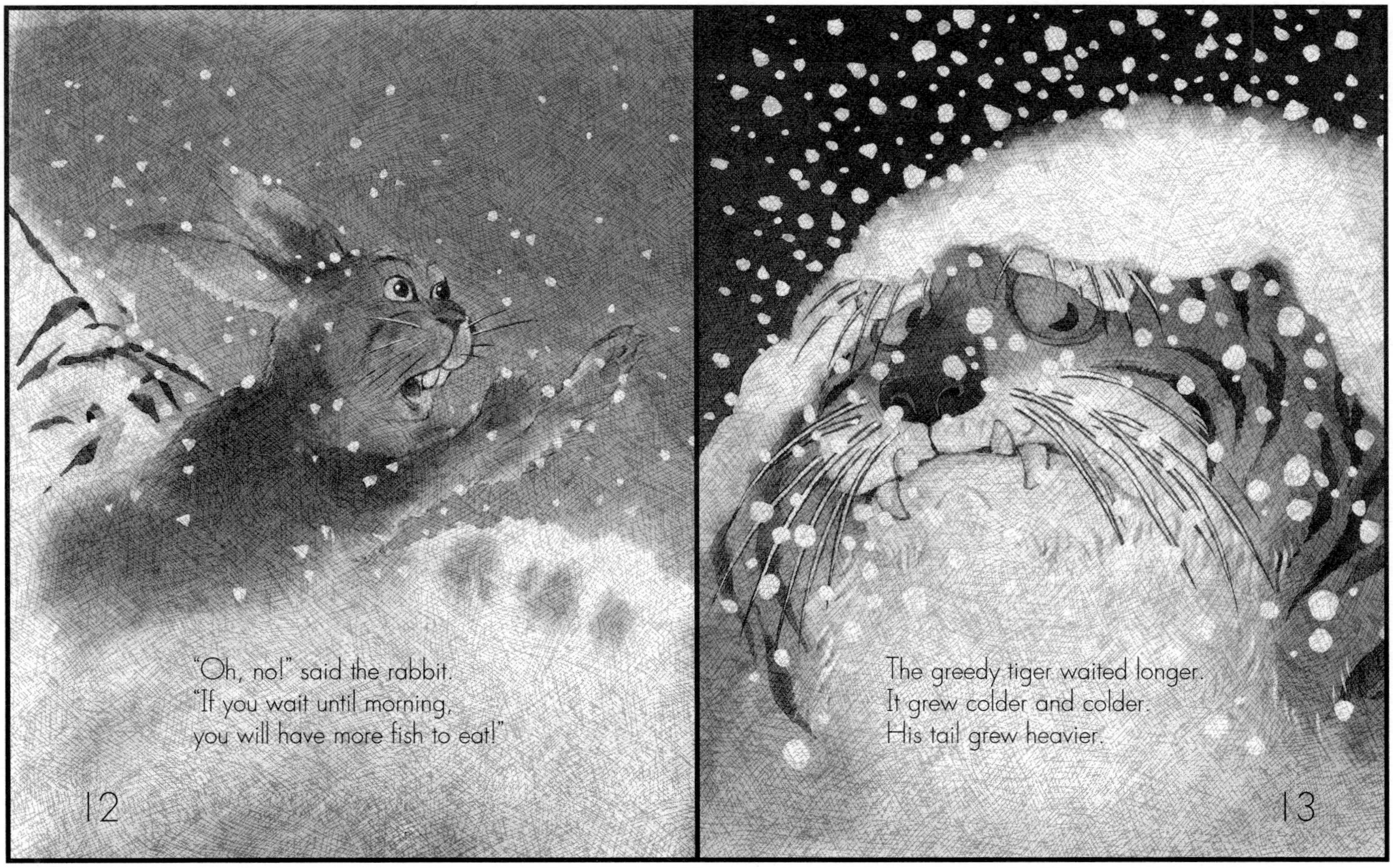

"Oh, no!" said the rabbit.
"If you wait until morning,
you will have more fish to eat!"

12

The greedy tiger waited longer.
It grew colder and colder.
His tail grew heavier.

13

Finally the sun came up.
The tiger's tail was very heavy.
"It is time!" called the tiger.
"I am pulling the fish out now!"

14

The tiger pulled and pulled,
but his tail did not come out of the river.
It was frozen in the ice!
"I'm going to get you, rabbit!"
roared the angry tiger.
But he could not budge at all.

15

The rabbit giggled and scampered away.
He had tricked the mighty tiger!

16

Responding

- Ask the children to talk about any hard words they came across in their reading, and how they figured out the words.
- To make sure the children are focusing on the words in the story rather than on the pictures, have them answer questions such as the following by pointing to and reading the words aloud.
  What was the tiger like?
  What was the rabbit afraid of?
  What does the rabbit show the tiger?
  What happened to the tiger?
  What did the rabbit do?

  Have children reread the book with a partner.

➤ Reading/Writing Connection, page 55, can be completed at this time. Help the children read the paragraph and write sentences to answer the questions.

TIP FOR ENGLISH LANGUAGE LEARNERS

Encourage English Language Learners to point out any word they don't know the meaning of. Discuss what the meaning of the word has to do with the selection and with their lives in general. Have the children draw a picture to illustrate the meaning of the word. Drawing pictures of words helps to make the words more meaningful to the children.

Reading/Writing Connection, page 55

Name

Lesson 27

Reading and Writing

A billy goat is a male goat. A billy has long horns and a beard. A female goat is called a nanny. She has smaller horns and a shorter beard. Billy goats use their horns for fighting. Many goats live on high peaks. They can go up and down steep rocks.

What is a male goat called? (Student answers may vary.)

A male goat is a billy goat.

Why don't nanny goats look like billy goats?

A nanny has smaller horns and a shorter beard.

Why can goats live on high peaks?

They can go up and down steep rocks.

Reading for Information

"The Three Billy Goats Gruff" R/WC 55

* READING ALOUD

Be sure to set aside time later in the day for reading aloud. In preparation for reading the selection "Little Green Riding Hood" in the next lesson, you may wish to read aloud the story of "Little Red Riding Hood." One traditional version that is popular with children is *Little Red Riding Hood,* retold and illustrated by award-winning author/illustrator Trina Schart Hyman. Hyman's simple telling of the story and richly detailed illustrations are sure to delight the children.

In addition, you may want to share one or more of the following books:

The Nose Tree, retold by Warwick Hutton
Two Greedy Bears by Mirra Ginsburg

After reading, remember to ask what the children found interesting about the story and why, and also to ask what they liked best about it. Discuss what new folk tale characters are introduced. They may want to add some of these ideas to the Concept Board. See **Learning Framework Card 5** for additional suggestions for reading aloud.

2 WRITING

* DICTATION AND SPELLING

Have the children turn to page 54 of their Reading/Writing Connection book. Dictate the following words and sentence, using the suggestions for dictation that appear on **Learning Framework Card 4.**

Line 1: wrap wrist wrinkle

Line 2: cube train slow

Sentence: I write a letter to my teacher.

Remind the children to use the Sound/Spelling Cards as they think about the sounds. The children should be encouraged to ask for help with any of the long vowel spellings. Help the children proofread each line. Point out the word *write* and write the word *right* beside it. Use each word in a sentence to help the children differentiate the meanings.

INDEPENDENT AND COLLABORATIVE WRITING

Have the children continue working on pieces they have started or encourage them to write in their journals. They may, instead, want to write about the Korean folk tale they read in their Phonics Minibook.

TEACHING TIP

Remind the children to use words from the Vocabulary Chart in their writing.

3 GUIDED AND INDEPENDENT EXPLORATION

WORKSHOP

Remind the children that they may use this time to work on projects on their own or in small groups. Be sure that each child knows what projects he or she may choose and how to complete any independent work. Suggestions for teacher-guided, collaborative, and independent activities follow.

Learning Framework Card 11, Workshop, contains a complete discussion of establishing and conducting Workshop and suggestions for helping English Language Learners during Workshop.

Work with the Teacher

- To assess their progress, reread *How the Rabbit Caught the Tiger,* Phonics Minibook 18, with individuals or small groups of children.
- Play Bingo with a small group of children. Be sure to incorporate the most recently learned sounds and spellings into the game. For word ideas, refer to recent Blending lessons.
- Review the Blending activity.
- Preteach "Little Green Riding Hood" in preparation for the next lesson. You may want to read a version of "Little Red Riding Hood" to prepare the children for the humor of the mixed-up version (see the Reading Aloud suggestions).
- Invite any children who have been responding to folk tales in their journals to share their responses with you individually or in small groups.

TEACHING TIP Encourage the children to read to each other. You, too, should choose children to read with. As you read with each child, note his or her progress.

Collaborative/Independent Activities

- Encourage pairs or groups of children to reread Phonics Minibook 18 and discuss how they can tell it is a folk tale. Challenge them to write down one thing that makes this tale similar to many other folk tales. (They might, for example, note that the characters are animals; that the story is about someone getting tricked; that the tiger is punished for being greedy; or that the little rabbit tricks the much bigger, stronger tiger.)
- Small groups of children might want to design posters for their favorite folk tales, fables, or other outside reading they have done (in Workshop or at home with their families) during the course of this unit. On the posters, they can print words, draw pictures, paste magazine cut-outs, and add anything else that they think will make other children want to read the stories.
- Distribute Activity Sheet 97 and tell the children to complete the page by reading the sentences in each box and deciding where each word choice belongs.

Name

Lesson 27

1. A turtle moves slower than a rabbit. | turtle rabbit

2. A bear is stronger than a frog. | frog bear

3. A stick is skinny. A pencil is skinnier. A hair is skinniest. | pencil hair

4. A squirrel is small. A gerbil is smaller. A ladybug is smallest. | ladybug gerbil

5. A desk is large. A car is larger. A house is largest. | house car

6. Birds are quiet. Bees are quieter. Fish are quietest. | Fish Bees

"The Three Billy Goats Gruff" Activity Sheet 97

Activity Sheet 97

LESSON 28

Lesson Overview

Outlaw Words

buy, eight

Materials

- "Little Green Riding Hood," pages 100–109
- Learning Framework Cards 3, 5
- Reading/Writing Connection, pages 56–57
- Activity Sheet 98

GETTING STARTED

Choose one or both of the following activities to focus the children's attention and to review some of the concepts they have been learning.

Spelling Challenge Divide the children into three or four teams. Explain that you will write a spelling of a vowel sound on the board and give the teams thirty seconds to a minute to think of words that contain the spelling and to write them on scratch paper. When time is up, call on each team to say and spell its words. Write the team's words on the chalkboard and award one point for each correct word. Remind each group to work quietly so that the other groups do not overhear their words.

Write a Word Game Have one child go to the chalkboard and call on a second child to name any vowel Sound/Spelling Card. The child at the board should write a word that contains the sound from the named card. Have the class read the word. The child who named a card then goes to the board and the child who wrote the word selects another child to name a card.

1 READING

PHONICS

Review Long Vowel Spellings To review long vowel sounds made by two vowels together, write the following spellings on the chalkboard: *ai, ay, ie, oa, oe, ue, ee, ea.*

Point to the spellings one at a time and ask the children what sound each makes.

Print some words on the chalkboard with vowel spellings missing. Have the children fill in the blanks with the appropriate spellings. In some cases more than one word may be made.

r __ n *(rain)*
h __ *(hay, hoe, hue)*
t __ *(tie, toe, tee)*
b __ t *(bait, boat, beet, beat)*
gr __ n *(grain, groan, green)*
s __ l *(sail, seal)*
f __ ld *(field)*

* **Blending** Have the children blend the following words and sentences. For reference and additional suggestions for blending, see **Learning Framework Card 3.**

Line 1: **sorry carry berry terrible**

Line 2: **few chew blew crew**

Line 3: **replied denied hurried married**

Line 4: **horse giraffe chimpanzee caterpillar**

Line 5: **newspaper doorway supermarket grandpa**

Sentence: **What's three times eight?**

Sentence: **I will buy some chewing gum.**

Words Help the children blend words in line 1, sounding the first vowel as a short vowel. Depending on the children's background, they may adjust their pronunciation once they recognize the words.

Line 2 reviews the /ū/ and /o͞o/ sounds spelled *ew.*

In Line 3, have the children identify each base word and explain how the past tense was formed. Some of the children may be unfamiliar with the words *replied* and *denied.* Discuss their meanings and invite children to use them in sentences.

Line 4 focuses on animal names.

The words in line 5 are compound words. Have the children give the two small words that make up each larger one.

As a review, say the words in random order and have the children find, say, and erase the words.

Sentences Introduce the outlaw words *eight* and *buy*, write each word on the board and read the word to the children. Have the children use each word in an oral sentence; then write the sentences on the board and have children read them.

➤ Reading/Writing Connection, page 56, provides practice reading and writing long vowel words. Have the children read the sentences and find the long vowel words. They should write the words in the correct column at the bottom of the page.

* READING THE STUDENT ANTHOLOGY

"Little Green Riding Hood"
pages 100–109

About the Selection

The tale of "Little Green Riding Hood" is presented as a game in which the storyteller—in this case, Grandpa—gives all the wrong details as he tells an old, familiar story to a young child. Each time Grandpa says something silly, the child is compelled to correct him. The child's frustration builds when the things Grandpa says become more and more absurd. Young readers will have a merry time predicting what the child

Reading/Writing Connection, page 56

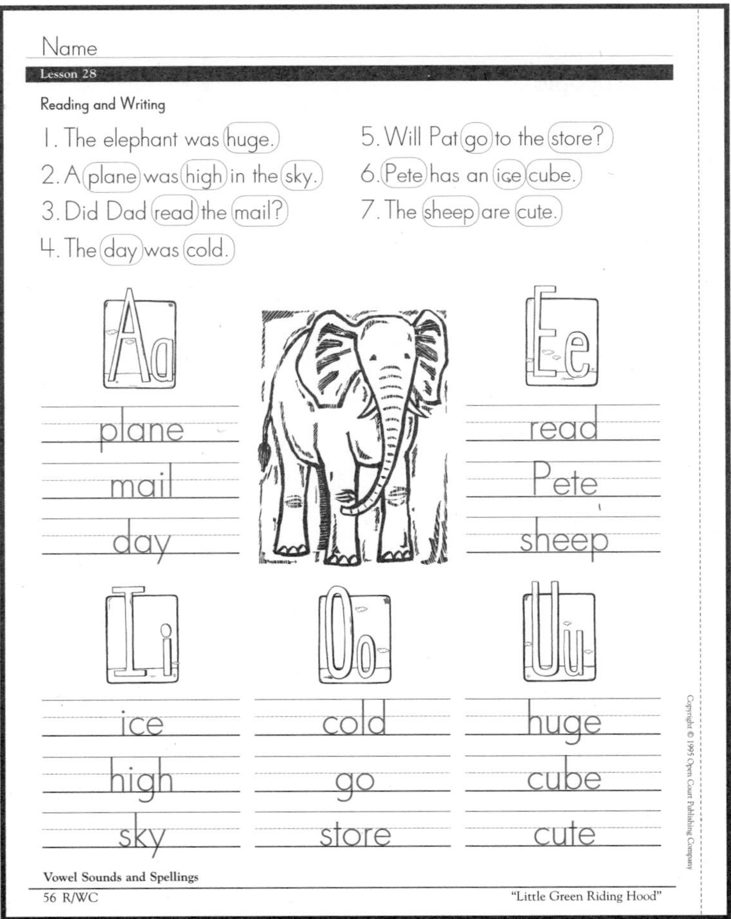
Name

Lesson 28

Reading and Writing

1. The elephant was huge.
2. A plane was high in the sky.
3. Did Dad read the mail?
4. The day was cold.
5. Will Pat go to the store?
6. Pete has an ice cube.
7. The sheep are cute.

Vowel Sounds and Spellings

56 R/WC "Little Green Riding Hood"

in the story will say to correct each of Grandpa's mistakes. The combination of Gianni Rodari's simple dialogue and Nadine Bernard Westcott's humorous illustrations make this story a treat for young readers. For this version, the original text has been adapted into a play.

Link to the Unit Concept

In "Little Green Riding Hood," author Gianni Rodari shows what happens when the details of a well-known folk tale are turned upside down. Because the traditional version of Red Riding Hood's adventures is so familiar to so many readers, Grandpa's new twists on the tale seem both absurd and hilarious.

Additionally, Rodari portrays an adult telling a story to a child. Not only does this image impart to children a positive message about the value of reading, it also conveys a sense of how folk tales were originally passed on from storyteller to audience and of how they may have changed as they passed from one generation to the next and traveled from one country to another.

After reading this story, the children may ask themselves what other traditional stories they have heard or read and how they might tell the stories to others.

About the Author

Gianni Rodari is a popular Italian author of children's books. His many books have been translated from Italian to English, Russian, and French.

About the Illustrator

Nadine Bernard Westcott began her career as a greeting-card designer. Through her work designing cards, Westcott discovered that people enjoyed her humorous illustrations even more than the rest of her work. She also realized that she enjoyed using her art to make people laugh. She decided that her next step would be to start illustrating children's books. Now, she says, "I draw every day, and although it can be demanding and frustrating, it is also a job with numerous rewards. It's fun to do, and if my artwork can encourage just one child to get involved with reading, it is truly worthwhile."

Activating Prior Knowledge

Ask a child to read the title of the selection. Then ask the class if anything about the title seems strange. If they say that it should be "Little *Red* Riding Hood," ask volunteers to tell what happens in that story.

Setting Reading Goals and Expectations

Have the children browse the selection and discuss anything unusual they notice about this story. They may point out that there seem to be two sets of pictures, at the top and at the bottom of the page. Discuss why they think this is so. In addition, children may notice that the word *Grandpa* or *Child* appears before each section of text. Point out that these words tell who is speaking and that this is the way a play is written.

Recommendations for Reading

- Have the children read the story aloud. For each page, assign one reader as Grandpa and one as the child. If children are having difficulty reading any of the words, remind them to check the Sound/Spelling Cards. If any words cannot be easily blended, pronounce the words for the children.
- Ask the the rest of the class to listen carefully to the story. Since most of the children are probably familiar with the traditional version of "Little Red Riding Hood," they will naturally be predicting what will happen next in the selection. Ask them to try to predict what the Child listening to the story will say and to share their predictions aloud. If necessary, prompt them by asking, "What do you think the Child will say next?"
- To allow time for the children to correct Grandpa's story, briefly delay each reading of the Child's part.
- Continue to express your responses to the story.
- When this first reading is complete, ask the children to sum up the entire story. Help them shorten their summary down to the main idea that the Grandpa kept telling the story wrong and the Child kept telling him how the story really goes.

102

Grandpa: Sorry! Red.
"Now, my child, go to Aunt Mary
and take her these potatoes."

Child: No! It doesn't go like that!
"Go to Grandma and take her
these cakes."

103

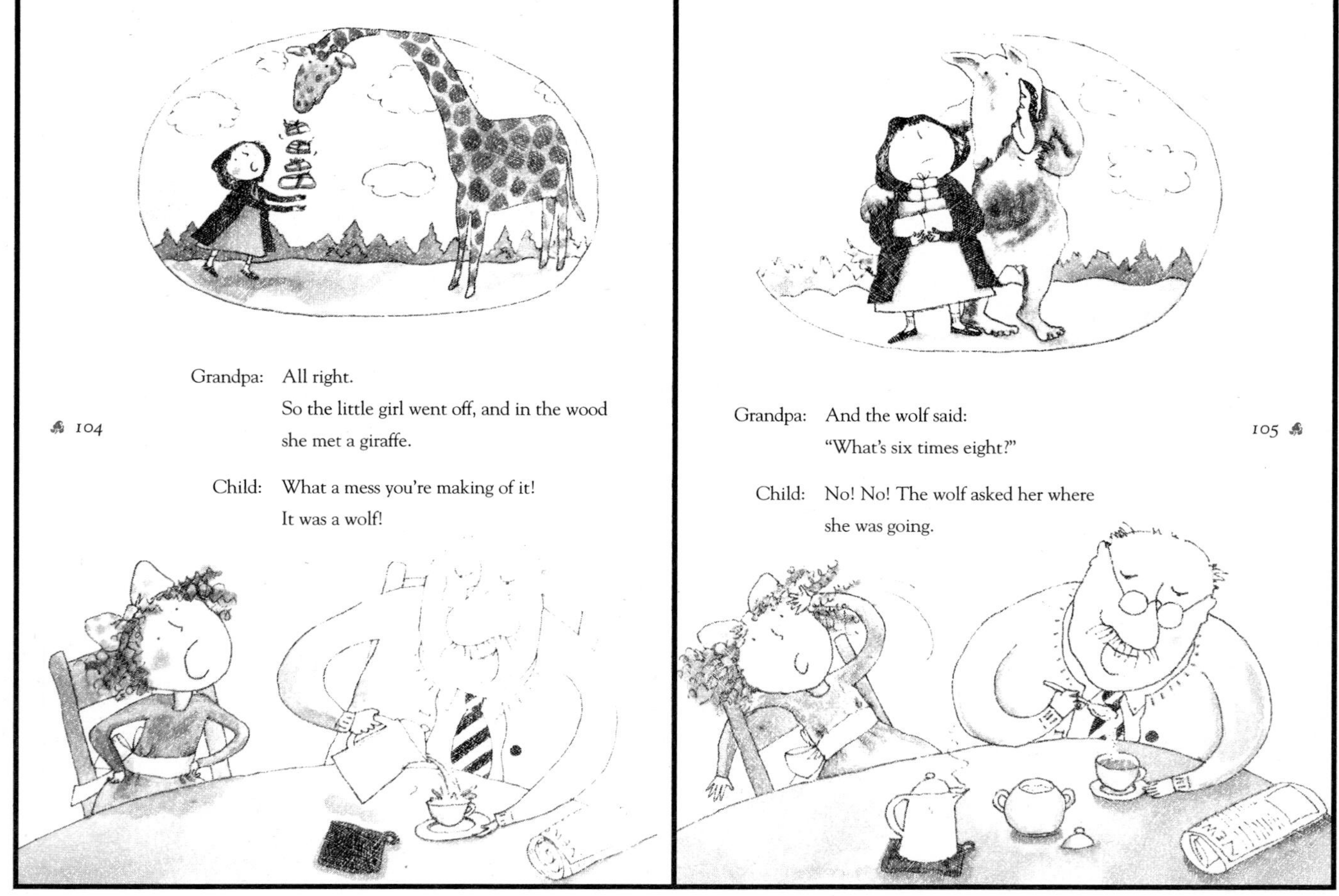

104

Grandpa: All right.
So the little girl went off, and in the wood
she met a giraffe.

Child: What a mess you're making of it!
It was a wolf!

Grandpa: And the wolf said:
"What's six times eight?"

Child: No! No! The wolf asked her where
she was going.

105

106

Grandpa: So he did. And Little Black Riding Hood replied—

Child: Red! Red!! Red!!!

Grandpa: She replied: "I'm going to the market to buy some tomatoes."

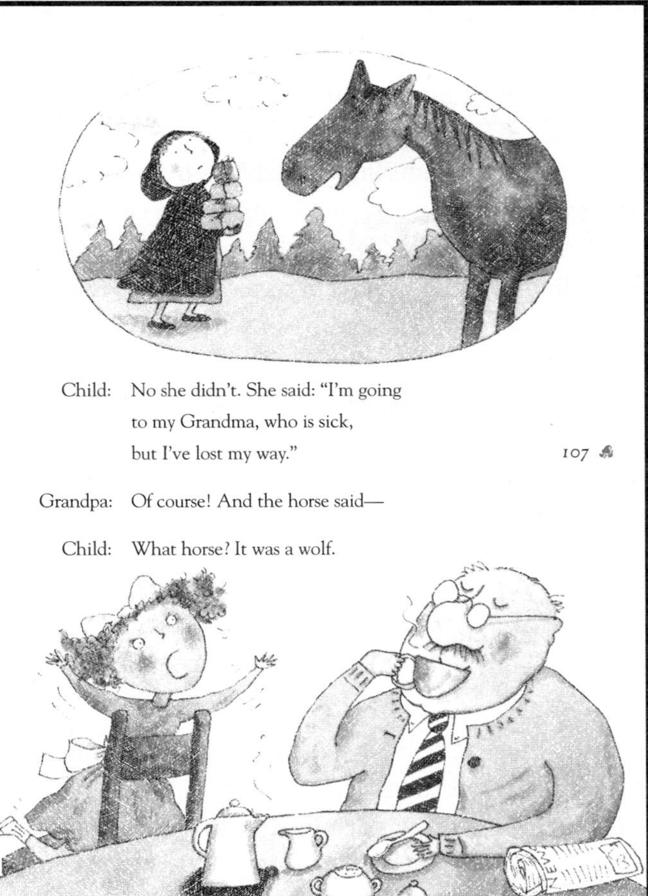

Child: No she didn't. She said: "I'm going to my Grandma, who is sick, but I've lost my way." 107

Grandpa: Of course! And the horse said—

Child: What horse? It was a wolf.

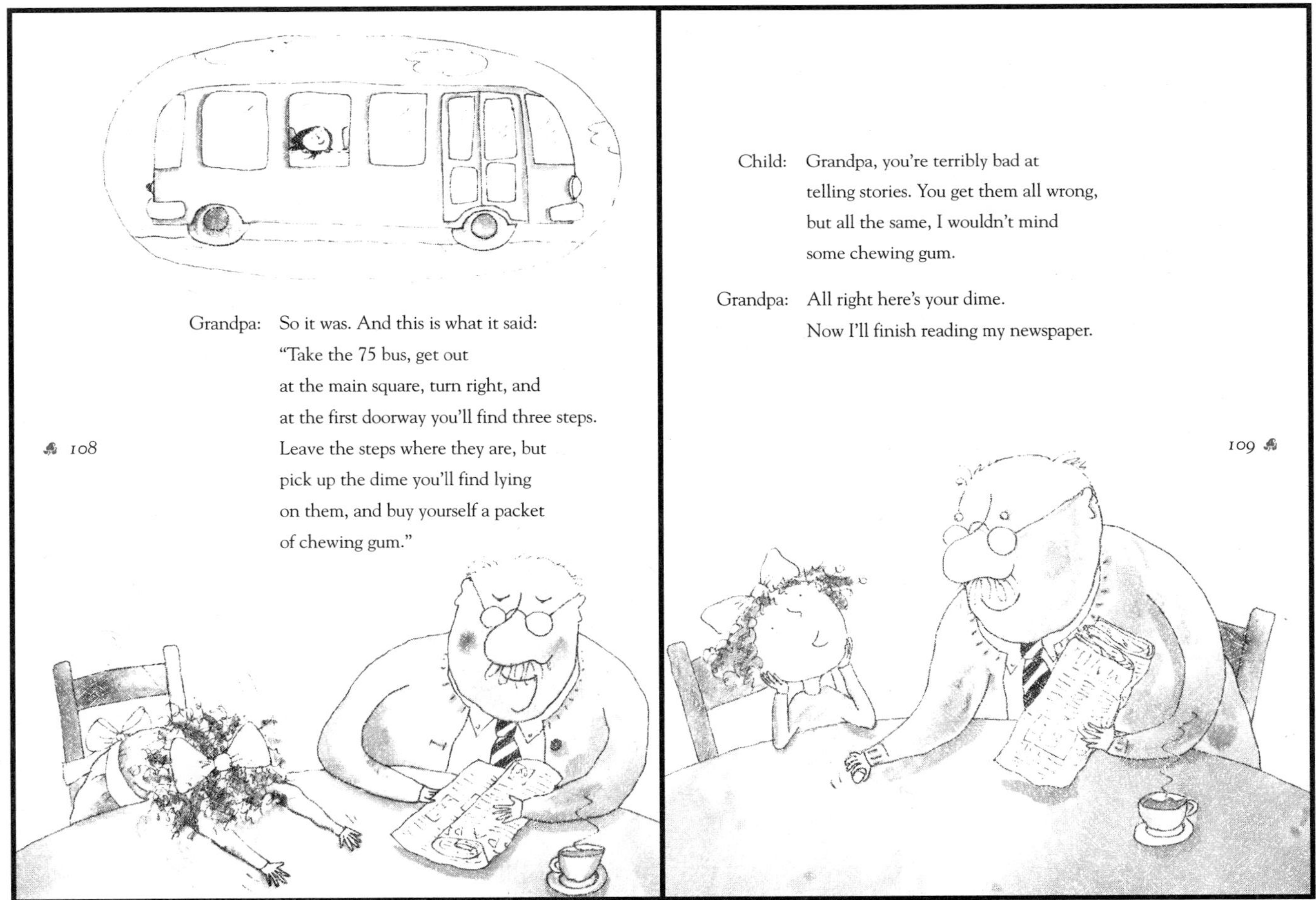

108

Grandpa: So it was. And this is what it said: "Take the 75 bus, get out at the main square, turn right, and at the first doorway you'll find three steps. Leave the steps where they are, but pick up the dime you'll find lying on them, and buy yourself a packet of chewing gum."

Child: Grandpa, you're terribly bad at telling stories. You get them all wrong, but all the same, I wouldn't mind some chewing gum.

Grandpa: All right here's your dime. Now I'll finish reading my newspaper. 109

Responding

- Ask the children what they thought was funniest about the story and what they liked best about it. They may want to read these parts to the class.
- Return to any wonderings the children raised during browsing and discuss how these were answered in the selection.

➤ Reading/Writing Connection, page 57, reviews this selection. Have the children use words from the box to complete the sentences.

TEACHING TIP

Have the children do some partner reading daily. Using previously read Phonics Minibooks and Step-by-Step Practice Stories for this purpose will help the children review and solidify their knowledge of the sounds and spellings they have learned. This is a good opportunity to read with children individually and to record their progress.

* READING ALOUD

Be sure to set aside time later in the day for reading aloud. A number of humorous folk tales have been retold to delight children of all ages. You may want to share one or more of the following books:

Chicken Little by Steven Kellogg
Old Lars, adapted by Erica Magnus
The Three Bears by Tomie dePaola

After reading, remember to ask questions such as, "What did you find funniest about the story? Why?"

See **Learning Framework Card 5** for suggestions for reading aloud.

Reading/Writing Connection, page 57

Name

Lesson 28

Reading and Writing

potatoes reading Red mixed
Yellow giraffe bad grandpa

The child wants to hear the story of Little Red Riding Hood. Her grandpa tries to tell the story. Grandpa gets the story all mixed up.

First, he calls the girl Little Yellow Riding Hood. Then he says that she has a sack of potatoes. Next he says that the little girl met a giraffe in the wood.

The child thinks her grandpa is bad at telling stories. Grandpa will finish reading his newspaper.

2 WRITING

* DICTATION AND SPELLING

Word-Building Game Have the children use pencil and paper to build the following words. Give sentences when you dictate the words *blue* and *blew* to help the children distinguish the meanings.

few
chew
clue
blue
flew
blew
glue

EXPLORING THE WRITER'S CRAFT

"Little Green Riding Hood" is based on a familiar folk tale that the author rewrote to make funny. You may want to share with the children other humorous adaptations of fairy tales. Two possible options are the following:

The True Story of the Three Little Pigs by Jon Scieszka
Goldilocks by Dom DeLuise

Have the children name some of the folk tales they already know. From this list, choose one story and talk about how it could be changed to make it silly or funny. For example, if you selected "Cinderella," you might have the children talk about what happened in the original version and then what could be changed. For example, Cinderella wants to go to the ball, but when she gets there, she realizes that the prince isn't all he's cracked up to be. He wants to marry her, but she decides she'd rather stay with her stepmother than marry the prince. Remind the children that they still should use folk or fairy-tale language like "Once upon a time." The story elements of **character, problem,** and **solution** can also be tied into this exercise. Cinderella is the character, and her problem is how to rid herself of the pesky prince.

Have the children work in pairs or groups to write their new version of a fairy tale. Suggest that they identify the story they want to change and then list all the changes they might make. Some children may prefer to continue responding to stories in their journals.

Conference with children to help them decide on humorous changes. Suggest to those children having trouble getting started that they identify the character(s), problem, and possible solutions.

During Seminar, have some students share their ideas for a humorous fairy tale.

3 GUIDED AND INDEPENDENT EXPLORATION

WORKSHOP

Remind the children that they may use this time to work on projects on their own or in small groups. Be sure that each child knows what projects he or she may choose and how to complete any independent work. Suggestions for teacher-guided, collaborative, and independent activities follow.

Work with the Teacher

- Repeat today's Blending exercise. Encourage children to read the words as whole words. Have each child use a different blending word in a sentence and then extend the sentence.
- Play the Word-Building game with children who need to work on their spelling. Make up a word list that focuses on the spellings with which the children have the greatest difficulty.
- Read Phonics Minibook 18 with children. This is a good opportunity to work with children who were absent when the class read it.

Collaborative/Independent Activities

- Children may enjoy making a mural to display their favorite words from the Vocabulary Chart. Have them write a sentence for each word. They may draw pictures or cut out magazine pictures to illustrate their words and sentences. When the mural is complete, display it in the classroom and allow time for the children to explain why they chose the words they did.
- The words for today's Blending exercise included some animal names. Invite children to write a sentence or two about one of the animals, using at least one other word from the exercise in each sentence. Now that they have learned about writing dialogue, you might suggest that the children make up sentences that they think the animals might say. Remind them to use capital letters and end punctuation. When they are finished writing, the children may illustrate their sentences.
- Invite the children to play Go Fish! or a memory game, using the rhyming-word card decks.
- Distribute Activity Sheet 98 and tell the children that two messages are hidden in this page. They should read the word under each box. If the word has a long vowel, color the letter box green. If the word has a short vowel, color the letter box orange. The green letters spell out one message and the orange letters spell out the other message. Children may want to work with a partner on this page.

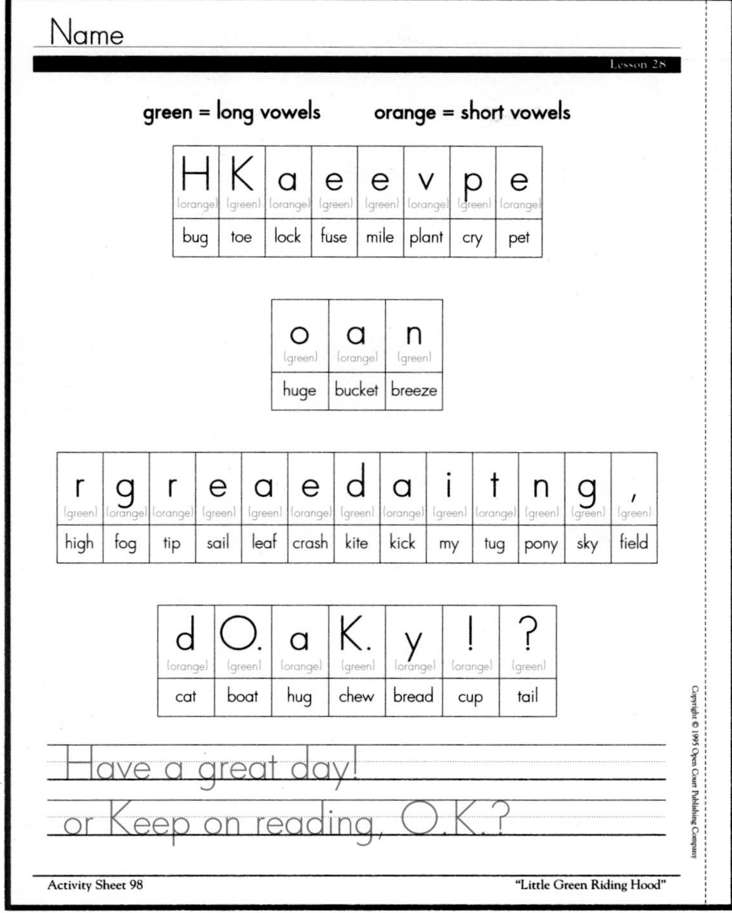

Name

Lesson 28

green = long vowels orange = short vowels

H	K	a	e	e	v	p	e
(orange)	(green)	(orange)	(green)	(green)	(orange)	(green)	(orange)
bug	toe	lock	fuse	mile	plant	cry	pet

o	a	n
(green)	(orange)	(green)
huge	bucket	breeze

r	g	r	e	a	e	d	a	i	t	n	g	,
(green)	(orange)	(orange)	(green)	(green)	(orange)	(green)	(orange)	(green)	(orange)	(green)	(green)	(green)
high	fog	tip	sail	leaf	crash	kite	kick	my	tug	pony	sky	field

d	O.	a	K.	y	!	?
(orange)	(green)	(orange)	(green)	(orange)	(orange)	(green)
cat	boat	hug	chew	bread	cup	tail

Have a great day!

or Keep on reading, O.K.?

Activity Sheet 98 "Little Green Riding Hood"

Activity Sheet 98

LESSON 29

Lesson Overview

Materials

- "Little Green Riding Hood," pages 100–109
- Learning Framework Cards 3, 4, 5
- Reading/Writing Connection, pages 58–59
- Activity Sheet 99

Prepare Ahead

- Scrambled Sentences Game (see page 310)

GETTING STARTED

Choose one or both of the following activities to focus the children's attention and to review some of the concepts they have been learning.

Who Comes First? Call on four children to come to the front of the classroom. Challenge the rest of the class to put the children in alphabetical order according to their first names. If two of the names begin with the same letter, tell the children to look at the next letter to determine who comes first. After you have worked as a whole class, have the children work in groups of four to six to put themselves in alphabetical order. Invite each group to explain the order they chose. You might also play the game by asking the children to put themselves in alphabetical order according to their last names.

Riddle Me This Variation Give the children a category of words, such as animals. Have the children think of words to give to the class as riddle-me clues. For example, a child may give these clues: Ball, Long A, and Robot for the word *bear.* Classmates should guess the word.

1 READING

PHONICS

* **Blending** Have the children blend the following words and sentences. For reference and additional suggestions for blending, see **Learning Framework Card 3.**

Line 1:	**potato cauliflower broccoli spinach**
Line 2:	**sandwich milkshake noodles macaroni**
Line 3:	**universe useful argue pew**
Line 4:	**mess moss miss mass**
Line 5:	**stick stock stuck stack**

Line 3 reviews various spellings for /ū/. Have the children circle or name each spelling, using Sound/Spelling Card 36, Long U, as a guide.

Lines 4 and 5 review short vowel spellings.

Review the words. Have one child name any word and a second child erase that word. Continue with other children.

➤ Reading/Writing Connection, page 58, provides reading practice. At the top of the page, have the children circle the word that does not belong in each sentence, and ask them to write a new word to replace it.

Reading/Writing Connection, page 58

Name

Lesson 29

Reading and Writing

1. Horses, chairs, and snakes have legs. (Answers
2. Robins, eagles, and lizards have feathers. will vary.)
3. Bread, tubas, and sandwiches are food.
4. Phones, alarm clocks, and pigs can ring.
5. Ropes, buckets, and sneakers can be tied.

Dictation and Spelling

Decoding and Spelling

58 R/WC "Little Green Riding Hood"

* READING THE STUDENT ANTHOLOGY

"Little Green Riding Hood"
pages 100–109

Activating Prior Knowledge

Review the story with the children by asking them what they remember about it.

Recommendations for Reading

- Since this is the second lesson in which the children will be reading this selection, have them read it aloud in a Readers' Theater format. Have different pairs of children read. One child will read the Grandpa part and one child will read the Child part, as before; however, let each pair read at least two pages. You may prefer to have groups of children read the different parts.
- Remind the children to read with expression. Have them say the words the way they think the characters in the story would say them.
- Discuss with the children any new ideas they might have about folk tales, particularly the realization that the tales may be told in many different ways. Add this information to the Concept Board.

Responding

Discuss with the children how this story is different from the traditional "Little Red Riding Hood."

Vocabulary Discuss any interesting or unusual words from the selection that the children might want to add to the Vocabulary Chart. Have them use the words in oral sentences. Possible words include the following:

chewing, sorry, terribly

Also, *asked* and *replied* are good words to add as speaker tags.

➤ Reading/Writing Connection, page 59, provides practice with revising. Have the children circle the mistakes in the paragraph and write it correctly.

* READING ALOUD

Be sure to set aside time later in the day for reading aloud. A number of unusual variations of traditional folk tales have been written. You may want to share one or more of the following books:

Stone Soup by Tony Ross
The Stinky Cheese Man and Other Fairly Stupid Tales by Jon Scieszka
What's in a Fox's Sack: An Old English Tale by Paul Galdone

After reading, ask questions such as, "Which part did you think was the funniest? What did you find most interesting? Why?" See **Learning Framework Card 5** for suggestions for reading aloud.

TEACHING TIP

Have the children do some partner reading daily. Using previously read Phonics Minibooks and Step-by-Step Practice Stories for this purpose will help the children review and solidify their knowledge of the sounds and spellings they have learned. This is a good opportunity to read with children individually and to record their progress.

TIP FOR ENGLISH LANGUAGE LEARNERS

Encourage English Language Learners to use new vocabulary in their speaking and writing. Praising their efforts in using new vocabulary is an effective method for improving vocabulary and increasing the children's comprehension of the text.

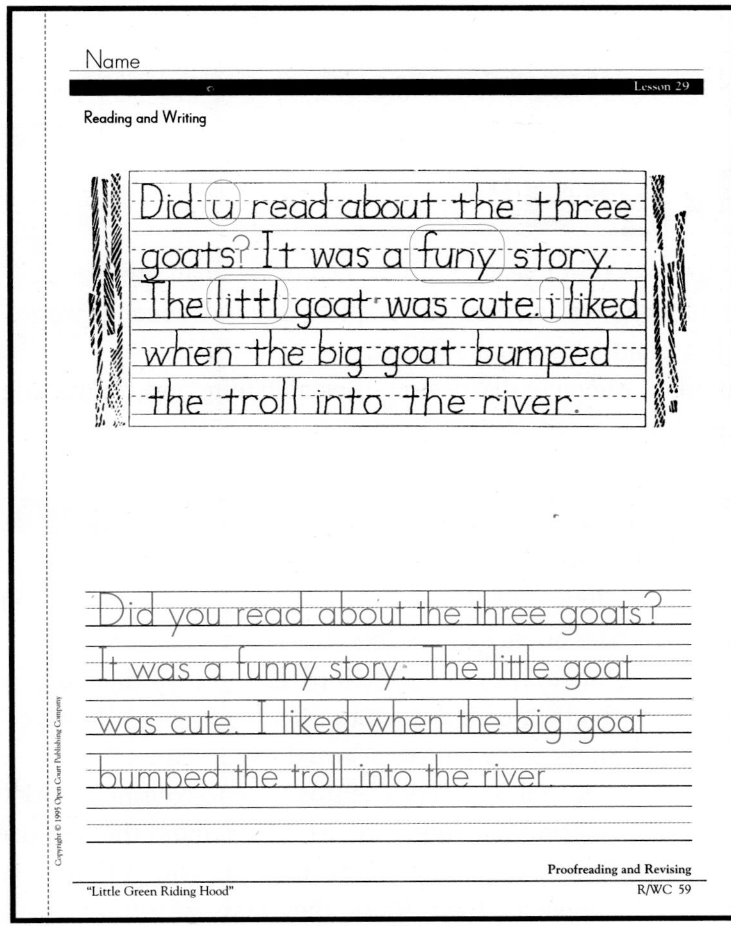
Name

Lesson 29

Reading and Writing

Did u read about the three goats? It was a funy story. The littl goat was cute. i liked when the big goat bumped the troll into the river.

Did you read about the three goats? It was a funny story. The little goat was cute. I liked when the big goat bumped the troll into the river.

Proofreading and Revising

"Little Green Riding Hood" R/WC 59

Reading/Writing Connection, page 59

2 WRITING

✱ DICTATION AND SPELLING

Have the children turn to page 58 of their Reading/Writing Connection book. Dictate the following words and sentences, using the suggestions for dictation that appear on **Learning Framework Card 4.**

Line 1: phone dolphin graph

Line 2: cook spoil broom

Sentence: I took a photo of the moon.

Remind the children to use the Sound/Spelling Cards and to ask for help with vowel spellings. Help the children proofread each line.

INDEPENDENT AND COLLABORATIVE WRITING

Have children continue working on their funny fairy tales. Remind them to use funny describing words or dialogue.

Conference with children and then have several share their work during Seminar. Suggest that children continue working on their stories in Workshop. Remind them to date their papers before putting them in their folders.

TEACHING TIP

Remind the children to use words from the Vocabulary Chart in their writing.

3 GUIDED AND INDEPENDENT EXPLORATION

WORKSHOP

Remind the children that they may use this time to work on projects on their own or in small groups. Be sure that each child knows what projects he or she may choose and how to complete any independent work. Suggestions for teacher-guided, collaborative, and independent activities follow.

Learning Framework Card 11, Workshop, contains a complete discussion of establishing and conducting Workshop and suggestions for helping English Language Learners during Workshop.

Work with the Teacher

- Repeat today's or any previous dictation lesson with those children who need extra help.
- Work with a small group of children who would benefit from spending some extra time on today's Blending exercise. Write the following sentences on the chalkboard:

  Popeye the Sailor likes to eat ______. *(spinach)*
  I want a peanut butter and jelly ______. *(sandwich)*
  I got a strawberry ______ at the ice cream shop. *(milkshake)*
  There are lots of stars in the ______. *(universe)*
  My sister and I like to ______. *(argue)*
  Clean your room—it's a ______. *(mess)*
  I roasted a hotdog on a ______. *(stick)*
  That poor pig got ______. *(stuck)*

  Have each child read a sentence, locate the word that belongs in the blank, come to the chalkboard and write the word in the blank, then read aloud the complete sentence.
- Listen to children reread "Little Green Riding Hood" in small groups. This is a good opportunity to assess the children's progress.

ASSESSMENT Give students the written test. See the Assessment Booklet for instructions.

Collaborative/Independent Activities

- Pairs of children can reread "Little Green Riding Hood," with one child reading Grandpa's part and the other reading the little girl's part. When they finish, they can switch parts and read the story again. Remind them to read the lines as they think the characters would say them.
- The children may use this time to continue working on their funny fairy tales. Remind them to use funny describing words and dialogue. If they have completed their drafts, they may want to exchange stories with a partner and comment on each other's stories.
- Small groups or pairs of children might want to play Scrambled Sentences. Distribute a Scrambled Sentence envelope to each pair or group. If two or more groups are participating in this activity, the group that finishes first may make up a new sentence, print each word on a blank note card, scramble the cards, and challenge another group to unscramble the new sentence.
- Activity Sheet 99 reviews long vowel sounds and spellings. Tell the children that they can complete the words in each box by filling in the correct vowels. Remind the children that sometimes more than one vowel may fit in a word, and that the other words in the box can help them determine which vowel to use. There is only one correct combination of letters in the words. The children may want to work in pairs to complete this activity sheet.

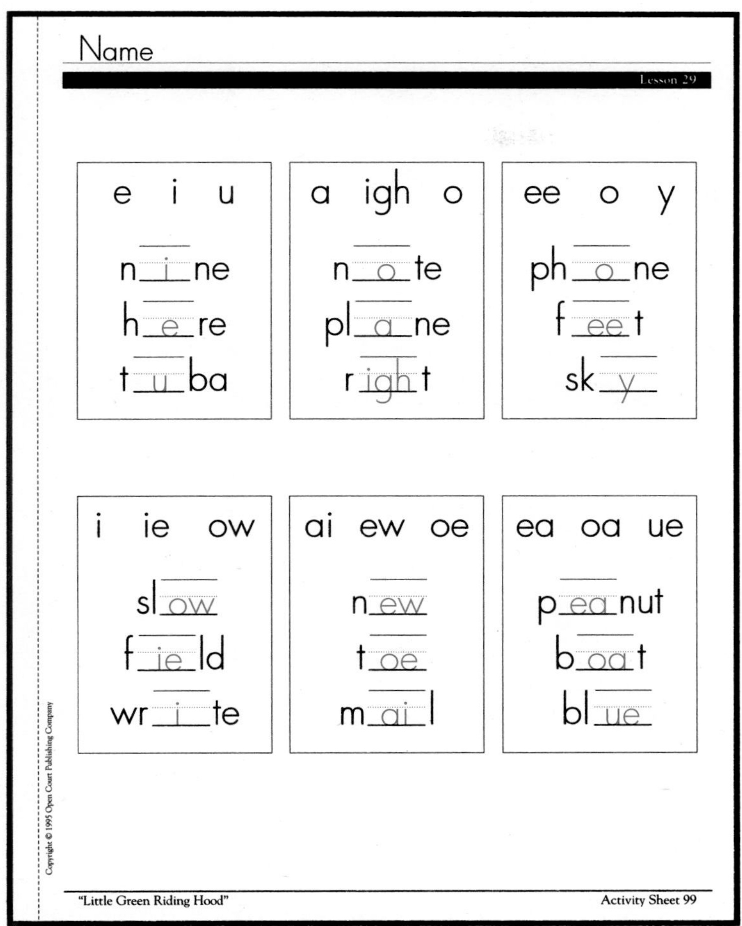

Name

Lesson 29

e i u	a igh o	ee o y
n_i_ne	n_o_te	ph_o_ne
h_e_re	pl_a_ne	f_ee_t
t_u_ba	r_igh_t	sk_y_

i ie ow	ai ew oe	ea oa ue
sl_ow_	n_ew_	p_ea_nut
f_ie_ld	t_oe_	b_oa_t
wr_i_te	m_ai_l	bl_ue_

"Little Green Riding Hood" Activity Sheet 99

Activity Sheet 99

LESSON 30

Lesson Overview

Materials

- Folk Tales Unit, pages 58–111
- Learning Framework Cards 3, 5
- Reading/Writing Connection, pages 60–61
- Activity Sheet 100

GETTING STARTED

Choose one or both of the following activities to focus the children's attention and to review some of the concepts they have been learning.

Long Vowel Spelling Review This activity will review some of the spellings of long vowel sounds the children have learned. Divide the class into two teams. Write the following words on each end of the chalkboard: *lightning, steam, toes, faint, useful, close, pride, sweetener, favorite, skewer*. (If you have more than twenty students, you will need additional words with long vowel sound spellings.) Tell the children that you will say a sound and that one child from each team should go to its list on the board, circle a word with that sound, and underline the letter or letters that spell that sound. For each sound that the children identify correctly, their team receives a point. At the end of the activity, point to the words one by one and have the children read them aloud in unison.

Sound/Spelling Card Review Name a Sound/Spelling Card and call on a child to say the sound of the card and to identify the spellings. That child then names another card and calls on a classmate to identify the sound and spellings. Continue with different children taking turns.

1 READING

PHONICS

* **Blending** Have the children blend the following words. For reference and additional suggestions for blending, see **Learning Framework Card 3.**

Line 1:	**gerbil germs package garbage**
Line 2:	**quickly swiftly suddenly surprisingly**
Line 3:	**thrifty threat throw thump**
Line 4:	**doctor dentist carpenter reporter**
Line 5:	**impossible dependable**

Line 1 reviews words that begin or end with the sound /j/ spelled *g.* Ask the children what they notice about the spellings for this sound, then invite them to suggest other words that follow the same pattern.

Line 2 reviews words with the *-ly* ending. Have the children use each word in a sentence.

The words in line 3 all begin with the sound /th/. Some of the children may be unfamiliar with the word *thrifty*. Invite children who are familiar with this word to use it in a sentence.

Line 4 introduces the children to the names of some occupations. Have the children tell what each person does.

The words in line 5 are formed by adding prefixes or suffixes. See if the children can think of the related words. For example, *possible* and *depend.*

Review the words by asking questions such as

- Which word means that you're careful with your money?
- Who would you call if you wanted to build a cabinet?
- What's the opposite of *possible?*
- What two words mean fast?
- What word names someone who takes care of your teeth?
- What is another word for trash?
- What word means a sound?

➤ Reading/Writing Connection, page 60, can be completed at this time. Have the children select a word from the box to complete each sentence.

* READING THE STUDENT ANTHOLOGY

Reread a favorite Folk Tales unit selection.

Link to the Unit Concept

In reading the Folk Tales unit, the children have encountered examples of different kinds of stories and have discussed the various

Name ______

Lesson 30

Reading and Writing

smile dress spilled spend money lay

A girl had a pail of milk to sell. She had the pail on her head. As she was walking along, she began to plan.

"The man will give me money for this milk. I will spend the money for a hen. The hen will lay eggs. Then I can sell the eggs."

"Soon I will have money for a fine new dress. Farmer Tom will smile at me. I will smile right back and nod my head, just like this."

When the girl nodded her head, the pail fell off. The milk spilled on the ground.

What did the girl learn? (Student answers will vary.)

Using Story Context

60 R/WC "Little Green Riding Hood"

Reading/Writing Connection, page 60

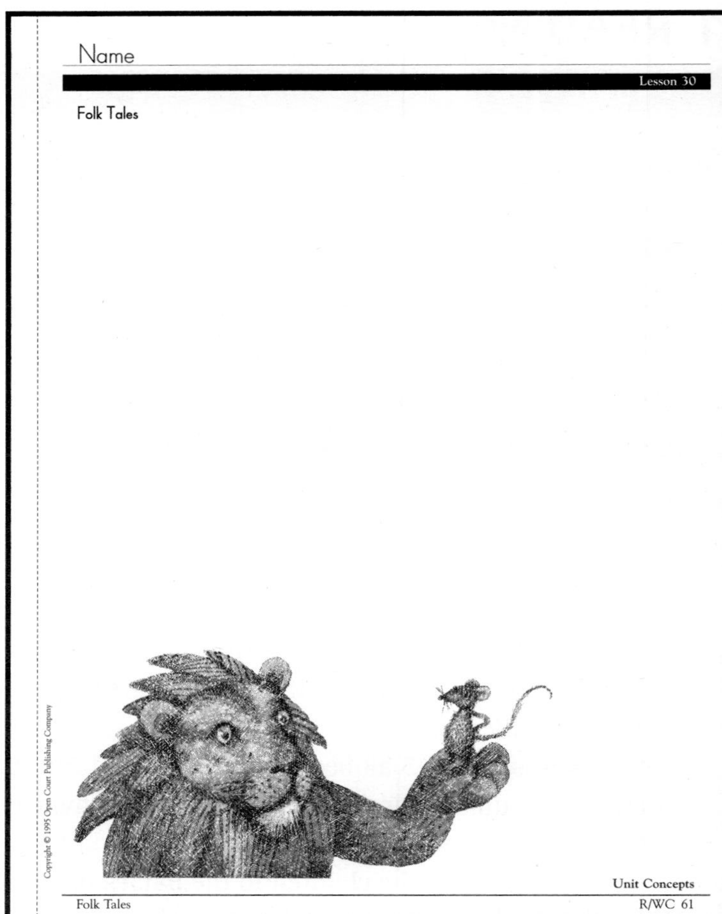
Name ______

Lesson 30

Folk Tales

Unit Concepts

Folk Tales R/WC 61

Reading/Writing Connection, page 61

characteristics of folk tales. Using the Concept Board, discuss what the children have learned in this unit. Review the questions and wonderings the children had posted on the board and discuss which of these have been answered or how they may have changed.

Recommendations for Reading

- Ask the children to select a story or a part of a story that they particularly enjoyed. Encourage them to tell what they have chosen, then have groups who may have chosen the same story or story part get together to reread their selection.

Responding

- Have children who have chosen the same story as their favorite tell the class why they chose as they did. You may want to point out that different aspects of the same story can appeal to different readers.

Unit Discussion

Have the children discuss the folk tales they have read in class and any that they may have heard or read at home. Discuss ways the stories are alike and different. Have the children tell about their favorite characters and how their problems were solved.

➤ Reading/Writing Connection, page 61, provides an opportunity for the children to draw or write about what they have learned through reading and discussion during this unit. First, have them refer back to page 31 to discuss what they drew or wrote about as they began the unit. Then have them draw or write about what they have since learned.

Celebrating the Unit

Celebrate the completion of the unit. You may want to have a story-telling time, or a "bedtime story" party in which the children can bring in a favorite stuffed animal or toy and gather around as you read or tell some favorite stories to them. Suggest that the children find some of the books listed in the bibliography at the end of the unit and share these stories with the class.

* READING ALOUD

Be sure to set aside time for reading aloud. There are many different versions of the folk tales included in the student anthology. The children might enjoy comparing another version of a folk tale with one they have read. You may want to share one or more of the following books:

The Gingerbread Boy by Paul Galdone
The Lion and the Rat by Jean de La Fontaine
The Three Billy Goats Gruff by Peter Christian Asbjornsen

Remember to ask questions such as, "How is this story like the one you have read?" "What does this make you wonder about?" "What does it remind you of?" See **Learning Framework Card 5** for suggestions for reading aloud.

2 WRITING

* DICTATION AND SPELLING

Word-Building Game Have the children take out paper and pencil for today's Word-Building activity. Tell them that, since this is the last lesson in this book, today's Word-Building game will be special. You will give them the first word to write, then you will ask them to suggest a word that they can make from that word. Start by writing the word *goat* on the chalkboard. Have a child read the word, then tell the children to write the word on their papers. Call on a child to suggest another word that can be made by changing any sound or spelling in this word, then have all the children write that word. Continue calling on children to suggest ways to change each new word. You may give suggestions, such as "change the vowel sound," or "change the beginning/ending sound."

INDEPENDENT AND COLLABORATIVE WRITING

Have the children revise and proofread their work. Remind them of the steps writers go through as they proofread and revise. If you have revision and proofreading suggestions on a wall chart in the room, refer the children to this chart.

During Seminar take time to share more of the children's funny tales. Some children may want to proofread their stories or recopy them for publishing during Workshop.

3 GUIDED AND INDEPENDENT EXPLORATION

WORKSHOP

Remind the children that they may use this time to work on projects on their own or in small groups. Be sure that each child knows what projects he or she may choose and how to complete any independent work. Suggestions for teacher-guided, collaborative, and independent activities follow.

Work with the Teacher

- Review dialogue with children who are having trouble identifying and punctuating dialogue.
- Play the Word-Building game with children. You might have the children form the words *stoop, stop, stock,* and *stuck,* in that order. Make up a sentence using one of the words from the game and dictate the sentence to the children.
- Ask independent readers to read aloud favorite folk tales that they have discovered on their own during this unit. Invite some of the other children to listen in.

TEACHING TIP Encourage the children to read to each other. You, too, should choose children to read with. As you read with each child, note his or her progress.

Collaborative/Independent Activities

- Invite pairs of children to select a favorite story from the Folk Tales unit and practice reading it together. Encourage peer tutoring by pairing confident readers with less fluent readers. You may want to arrange for these pairs to read their story to younger children.
- Children who have written funny fairy tales may want to proofread them at this time. If they are ready, they can begin recopying the stories for publishing.
- Children who have been responding to folk tales and fables in their journals may want to finish their work at this time.
- Activity Sheet 100 provides practice in reading and following directions. Tell the children to read the sentences and follow what the directions tell them to do.

Home/School Connection

Send home the take-home version of Phonics Minibook 17 and encourage the children to read it to their families.

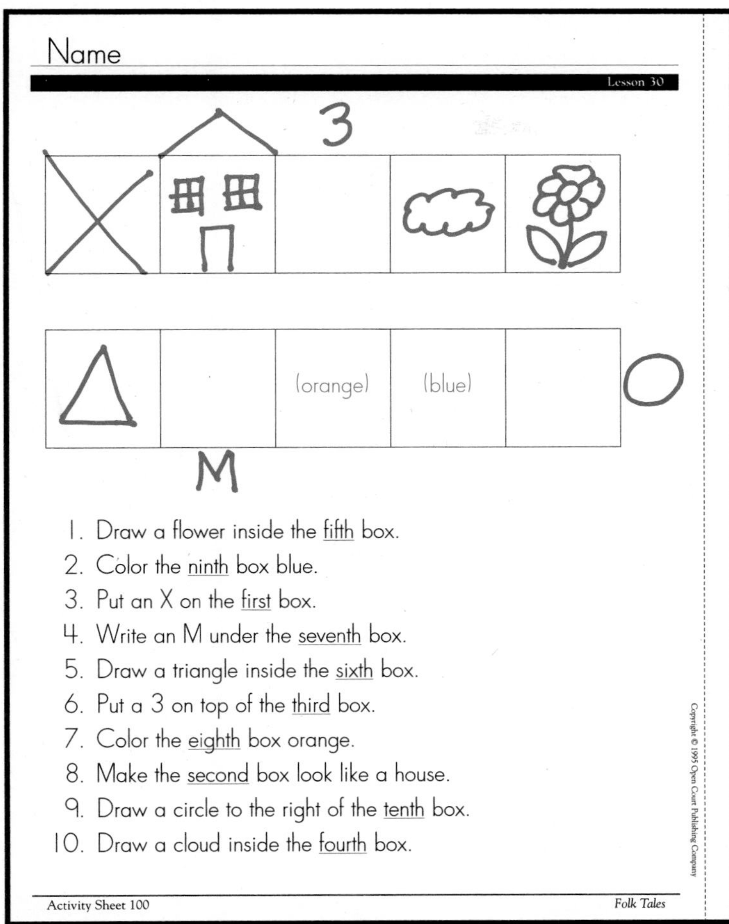

Name

Lesson 30

(orange) (blue)

1. Draw a flower inside the fifth box.
2. Color the ninth box blue.
3. Put an X on the first box.
4. Write an M under the seventh box.
5. Draw a triangle inside the sixth box.
6. Put a 3 on top of the third box.
7. Color the eighth box orange.
8. Make the second box look like a house.
9. Draw a circle to the right of the tenth box.
10. Draw a cloud inside the fourth box.

Activity Sheet 100 *Folk Tales*

Activity Sheet 100

Appendixes

Introduction of Sounds: Overview

Framework for Effective Teaching®
Thinking and Learning About Print, Parts A and B

LESSON	SOUNDS INTRODUCED	PRACTICE STORIES
1		
2		
3		
4		
5		
6		
7		
8		
9		A Table (SS 1)
10		The Egg (SS 2)
11	Monkey: /m/ spelled *m*	
12	Lamb: /a/ spelled *a*	The Cake (PM 1: *The Baby*)
13	Timer: /t/ spelled *t*	The Shirt (PM 1: *The Baby*)
14	Hound dog: /h/ spelled *h*	The Hat (SS 3)
15	Popcorn: /p/ spelled *p*	
16	Nose: /n/ spelled *n*	Pam and the Man (SS 4)
17	Camera: /k/ spelled *c*	
18	Dinosaur: /d/ spelled *d*	The Cat (SS 5)
19	Sausages: /s/ spelled *s*	On the Mat (PM 2: *Nan's Family*)
20	Pig: /i/ spelled *i*	The Tin Man (SS 6)
21		The Pans (PM 2: *Nan's Family*)
22	Ball: /b/ spelled *b*	Tim Spins (SS 7)
23	Robot: /r/ spelled *r*	Nat's Nap (PM 3: *Nat the Crab*) Nat's Trip (PM 3: *Nat the Crab*)
24	Fan: /f/ spelled *f*	Brad's Ram (SS 8)
25	Gopher: /g/ spelled *g*	The Sand Pits (SS 9)
26		Sinbad Acts Fast (PM 4: *Sinbad the Pig*) Sinbad and Anna (PM 4: *Sinbad the Pig*)
27	Frog: /o/ spelled *o*	The Cot (SS 10)
28	Exiting X: /ks/ spelled □ *x*	A Fox and His Box (SS 11)
29		Amanda's Sax (PM 5: *Panda Band*) Amanda's Band (PM 5: *Panda Band*)
30	Armadillo: /ar/ spelled *ar*	Grab a Star (SS 12)
31	Camera: /k/ spelled □ *ck*	My Trip (SS 13)
32	Tugboat /u/ spelled *u*	The Bug (SS 14)
33	Zipper: /z/ spelled *z*	Zip on the Run (SS 15)

LESSON	SOUNDS INTRODUCED	PRACTICE STORIES
34		Zack the One-Man Band (SS 16)
35	Lion: /l/ spelled *l*	PM 6: *In the Pond*
36	Hen: /e/ spelled *e*	Meg's Sled (SS 17)
37	/e/ spelled *ea*	Hen in a Pen (SS 18)
38	Yaks: /y/ spelled *y*	The Stand (SS 19)
39	Washer: /w/ spelled *w* Whales: /hw/ spelled *wh*	Wendell Gets a Pet (PM 7: *Wendell's Pets*)
40	Bird: /er/ spelled *er, ir, ur*	Wendell's Pets (PM 7: *Wendell's Pets*)
41		What Is It? (SS 20)
42	Shark: /sh/ spelled *sh*	Jen's Web (SS 21)
43	Thongs: /th/ spelled *th*	Seth's Bath (SS 22)
44	Chipmunk: /ch/ spelled *ch*	
45	Chipmunk: /ch/ spelled □*tch*	Patch Gets the Ball (SS 23)
46		The Trash Stash (SS 24)
47	Camera: /k/ spelled *k*	Can I Help You? (PM 8: *The Market*) The Lamp (PM 8: *The Market*)
48	/ā/ spelled *a, a e*	Gull and Crane (SS 25)
49	Jump rope: /j/ spelled *j,* □*dge*	Jane and Jake (SS 26)
50	Jump rope: /j/ spelled *ge, gi*	Magic Pages (SS 27)
51	/ī/ spelled *i, i e*	A Fine Parade (SS 28)
52	Sausages: /s/ spelled *ce, ci*	Spice Cake (SS 29)
53		PM 9: *The Spider Club*
54	/ō/ spelled *o, o e*	The Cold Troll (SS 30)
55	Zipper: /z/ spelled *s*	The Surprise (SS 31)
56	Vacuum: /v/ spelled *v*	
57	/ū/ spelled *u, u e*	Cupid the Mule (SS 32)
58	/ē/ spelled *e, e e*	Steve's Secret (SS 33)
59		The Step Problem (PM 10: *Eva Uses Her Head*) The Bug Problem (PM 10: *Eva Uses Her Head*)
60	/ē/spelled *ee, ea*	Dragons Don't Get Colds (SS 34)
61	Quacking ducks: /kw/ spelled *qu*	Queen Squid and Her Sea Pals (SS 35)
62	Long vowels + *r*	
63	/ē/ spelled *_y, ie*	The Fancy Party (SS 36)
64		PM 11: *Dog Dreams*
65	/ā/ spelled *ai , ay*	Sail Day (SS 37)
66	/ī/ spelled *igh*	The Opossum (SS 38)
67	/ī/ spelled *y, ie*	Why, Bly? (SS 39)
68	Gong: /ng/ spelled □*ng*	
69		Cranky Hank (SS 40)
70		PM 12: *Mail Train*

Framework for Effective Teaching®
Grade 1, Book 1

LESSON	SOUNDS INTRODUCED	PRACTICE STORIES
1	/ō/ spelled *_oe*	
2	/ō/ spelled *_ow*	
3	/ō/ spelled *oa*	PM 13: *The Snow Game*
4	/ū/ spelled *_ew, ue*	
5		
6	Cow: /ow/ spelled *ow*	
7	Cow: /ow/ spelled *ou*	PM 14: *The Everybody Club*
8		
9		
10		
11		
12		PM 15: *Superhero to the Rescue*
13	Hawk: /aw/ spelled *aw, au*	
14		
15	Hoot owl: /o͞o/ spelled *oo, ue, u e, u, ew*	
16	Brook: /oo/ spelled *oo*	
17	Nose: /n/ spelled *kn*	PM 16: *Mr. Lee*
18		
19	Coil: /oi/ spelled *oi, oy*	
20		
21		
22		
23		
24		
25	Robot: /r/ spelled *wr*	PM 17: *Princess Julia*
26	Fan: /f/ spelled *ph*	
27		PM 18: *How the Rabbit Caught the Tiger*
28		
29		
30		

NOTE: Phonics instruction is reviewed and consolidated in grade 1 *Framework for Effective Teaching*®, Book 2.

Scope and Sequence

STRATEGIES AND SKILLS	LEVEL					
	1	2	3	4	5	6
Print Awareness						
Capitalization	■					
Constancy of words	■					
End punctuation	■					
Follow left-to-right, top-to-bottom	■					
Letter recognition and formation	■					
Paragraph indention	■					
Relationship between illustrations and print	■					
Relationship between spoken and printed language	■					
Word boundaries in text	■					
READING STRATEGIES						
Setting Reading Goals and Expectations						
Activate prior knowledge.	■	■	■	■	■	■
Browse the text.	■	■	■	■	■	■
Consider why you are reading.	■	■	■	■	■	■
Decide what you expect from the text.	■	■	■	■	■	■
Responding to Text						
Make connections between what you are reading and what you already know.	■	■	■	■	■	■
Visualize, or picture, what is happening in the text.	■	■	■	■	■	■
Wonder freely as you read.	■	■	■	■	■	■
Predict what will happen next.	■	■	■	■	■	■
Think about how the text makes you feel.	■	■	■	■	■	■
Checking Understanding						
Interpret as you read.	■	■	■	■	■	■
Sum up to check your understanding as you read.	■	■	■	■	■	■
Ask questions to check your understanding as you read.		■	■	■	■	■
Clarifying Unfamiliar Words and Passages						
Apply decoding skills if there are unknown words.	■	■	■	■	■	■
Determine what is unclear.		■	■	■	■	■
Apply context clues if there are words whose meanings you don't know.	■	■	■	■	■	■

STRATEGIES AND SKILLS	LEVEL					
	1	2	3	4	5	6
READING STRATEGIES						
Clarifying Unfamiliar Words and Passages *continued*						
Check the dictionary.						
Reread the passage that didn't make sense to you.						
WRITING STRATEGIES						
Planning and Setting Writing Goals						
Use reading to improve your writing.						
Record interesting and important topics to write about.						
Note information you will need in order to write.						
Decide on the main goals of the writing.						
Revise your plans.						
Considering Readers						
Make your topic interesting.						
Decide what effect you want to have on your readers.						
Determine if readers will understand.						
Predict your readers' reactions, and then compare their reactions to what you expected.						
Summarize audience reactions.						
Revising Content						
Reread very carefully.						
Pinpoint parts of your writing that can be made clearer.						
Identify information confusing to readers.						
Reorganize ideas or information.						
Use a story frame or plot line.						
Consider your own reactions and ideas.						
CONVENTIONS/SKILLS						
Writer's Craft/Reading						
Causal indicators						
Characterization						
Choosing vivid verbs						
Dialogue						
Elaboration through comparisons and contrasts						
Elaboration through forming questions and conjectures						
Elaboration through giving opinions						
Elaboration through giving reasons or causes						

STRATEGIES AND SKILLS	LEVEL					
Writer's Craft/Reading *continued*	1	2	3	4	5	6
Elaboration through including lists and examples						
Elaboration through providing background						
Elaboration through providing descriptions						
Elaboration through providing explanations or definitions						
Elaboration by providing opposing viewpoints						
Elaboration through providing problems and solutions						
Elaboration through providing specific facts						
Exaggeration						
Figurative language						
Formal versus informal writing						
Foreshadowing						
Genre—adventure						
Genre—biography and autobiography						
Genre—expository text						
Genre—fable						
Genre—fairy tale						
Genre—fantasy						
Genre—folk tale						
Genre—historical fiction						
Genre—legend						
Genre—myth, tall tale						
Genre—play/drama						
Genre—poetry						
Genre—realistic fiction						
Genre—science fiction						
Humor						
Indicators of additional information						
Indicators of differing information						
Indicators of place and location						
Indicators of time and order						
Irony						
Persuasive writing						
Plot						
Point of view						
Process description						
Setting						
Staying on subject						
Strong topic sentences						

STRATEGIES AND SKILLS	LEVEL					
Writer's Craft/Reading *continued*	1	2	3	4	5	6
Suspense and surprise		■	■	■	■	
Using headings and captions	■	■	■	■	■	■
Using quotations in writing				■	■	■
Variety in writing		■	■	■	■	■
Writing good beginnings		■	■	■	■	■
Writing paragraphs		■	■	■	■	■
Writing personal experiences		■	■	■	■	■
Grammar, Mechanics, and Usage						
Capitalization	■	■	■	■	■	■
Clauses and phrases			■	■	■	■
Comparing with adjectives and adverbs	■	■	■	■	■	■
Complete and incomplete sentences	■	■	■	■	■	■
Compound sentences		■	■	■	■	■
Compound subject and predicate				■	■	■
End punctuation	■	■	■	■	■	■
Kinds of sentences	■	■	■			
Parts of a sentence		■	■	■	■	■
Parts of speech		■	■	■	■	■
Pronoun/antecedent agreement		■	■	■	■	■
Punctuating titles of works (books, movies etc.)				■	■	■
Subject/verb agreement		■	■	■	■	■
Using adjectives and adverbs		■	■	■	■	■
Using colons and semicolons				■	■	■
Using commas in dates, addresses, and parts of a letter		■	■	■	■	■
Using commas in introductory phrases			■	■		
Using commas in a series		■	■	■	■	■
Using dashes and ellipses			■	■	■	■
Using gerund phrases				■	■	■
Using negatives correctly			■	■	■	■
Using parentheses		■	■	■	■	■
Using possessive nouns	■	■	■	■	■	■
Using possessive pronouns		■	■	■	■	■
Using prepositions and prepositional phrases		■	■	■		
Using and punctuating dialogue	■	■	■	■	■	■
Using reflexive pronouns				■	■	■
Verb tense		■	■	■	■	■

STRATEGIES AND SKILLS	LEVEL					
	1	2	3	4	5	6
Phonics/Decoding						
Blending sounds into words		*	*			
Consonant clusters		*	*			
Consonant digraphs		*	*			
Consonant sounds and spellings		*	*			
Outlaw words		*	*			
Phonemic awareness		*	*			
Syllables		*	*			
Vowel diphthongs		*	*			
Vowels: long sounds and spellings		*	*			
Vowels: *r*-controlled		*	*			
Vowels: short sounds and spellings		*	*			
Spelling and Vocabulary						
Adding prefixes and suffixes						
Building vocabulary						
Compound words						
Frequently misspelled words						
Homophones						
Inflectional endings						
Long-vowel spelling patterns						
Regular and irregular plurals						
Short-vowel spelling patterns						
Spelling generalizations						
Synonyms and antonyms						
Unstressed vowel sounds (schwa)						
Using and punctuating contractions						
Study and Research						
Alphabetical order						
Choosing sources						
Comparing information across sources						
Formulating questions and conjectures						
Interviewing						
Making a bibliography						
Making and using a time line						
Note taking						
Observing and recording details						

* *Optional review at this level*

STRATEGIES AND SKILLS	LEVEL					
Study and Research *continued*	1	2	3	4	5	6
Organizing information in a chart		■	■	■	■	■
Outlining				■	■	■
Parts of a book	■	■	■	■	■	■
Using a dictionary or glossary	■	■	■	■	■	■
Using a thesaurus				■	■	■
Using an encyclopedia		■	■	■	■	■
Using and understanding diagrams				■	■	■
Using maps, globes, and atlases		■	■	■	■	■
Using primary sources				■	■	■
Using the card catalog (including electronic cc)		■	■	■	■	■
Using the *Reader's Guide*			■	■	■	■

Outlaw Words

a
after
again
am
an
and
anyone
are
as
ask
at
away
be
bear
beautiful
berry
best
big
break
build
built
busy
but
buy
can
clothes
come
could
cover
did
do
does
eight
enough
every
eyes
fast
first
five
for
four
friend
gave
get
give
gone
great
guess
had
has
have
he
heard
help
her
here
him
his
hurray
I
if
in
is
it
just
keep
laugh
laughter
like
little
lived
look
love
make
many
me
move
much
my
no
none
not
nothing
of
off
oh
on
once
one
out
pretty
pull
put
ran
ride
said
say
says
see
seven
she
shoe
should
show
so
some
somewhere
special
that
the
their
them
then
these
they
thing
this
three
through
to
today
too
trouble
two
under
up
us
walk
want
was
water
we
were
what
when
where
which
who
why
will
with
woman
would
yes
you
your

Acknowledgments

Grateful acknowledgment is given to the following publishers and copyright owners for permission granted to reprint selections from their publications. All possible care has been taken to trace ownership and secure permission for each selection included.

Carolrhoda Books, Inc.; Minneapolis, MN: *Jafta* by Hugh Lewin, illustrated by Lisa Kopper, text copyright © 1981 by Hugh Lewin, illustrations copyright © 1981 by Lisa Kopper.

Dutton Children's Books, a division of Penguin Books USA Inc.: *Matthew and Tilly* by Rebecca C. Jones, illustrated by Beth Peck, text copyright © 1991 by Rebecca C. Jones, illustrations copyright © 1991 by Beth Peck.

Edizioni E. Elle, Trieste, Italy: "Little Green Riding Hood" from *Telephone Tales* by Gianni Rodari, © Edizioni E. Elle.

HarperCollins Publishers: An excerpt entitled "A Game Called Piggle" from *Piggle* by Crosby Bonsall, copyright © 1973 by Crosby Bonsall. "The Big Team Relay Race" from *On Your Mark, Get Set, Go! The First All-Animal Olympics* by Leonard Kessler, copyright © 1972 by Leonard Kessler.

Holiday House: *Anansi and the Talking Melon* by Eric A. Kimmel, illustrated by Janet Stevens, text copyright © 1994 by Eric A. Kimmel, illustrations copyright © 1994 by Janet Stevens.

Index